RIGHTS CLAIMING IN SOUTH KOREA

Although rights-based claims are diversifying and opportunities and resources for claims-making have improved, obtaining rights protections and catalysing social change in South Korea remain challenging processes. This volume examines how different groups in South Korea have defined and articulated grievances and mobilized to remedy them. It explores developments in the institutional contexts within which rights claiming occurs and in the sources of support available for utilizing different claims-making channels. Drawing on scores of original interviews, readings of court rulings and statutes, primary archival and digital sources, and interpretive analysis of news media coverage in Korean, this volume illuminates rights in action. The chapters uncover conflicts over contending rights claims, expose disparities between theory and practice in the law, trace interconnections among rights-based movements, and map emerging trends in the use of rights language. Case studies examine the rights of women, workers, people with disabilities, migrants, and sexual minorities.

Celeste L. Arrington is Korea Foundation Associate Professor of Political Science and International Affairs at the George Washington University. She is the author of Accidental Activists: Victim Movements and Government Accountability in Japan and South Korea (Cornell, 2016) and articles in Comparative Political Studies, Law & Society Review, Journal of East Asian Studies and elsewhere.

Patricia Goedde is Professor at Sungkyunkwan University School of Law in South Korea, and a member of the Washington State Bar Association. She serves on the board of directors for the Korea Human Rights Foundation and is also a core faculty member of the SSK Human Rights Forum in Seoul.

T0381719

Rights Claiming in South Korea

Edited by

CELESTE L. ARRINGTON
George Washington University

PATRICIA GOEDDE
Sungkyunkwan University

CAMBRIDGE
UNIVERSITY PRESS

University Printing House, Cambridge CB2 8BS, United Kingdom

One Liberty Plaza, 20th Floor, New York, NY 10006, USA

477 Williamstown Road, Port Melbourne, VIC 3207, Australia

314-321, 3rd Floor, Plot 3, Splendor Forum, Jasola District Centre, New Delhi - 110025, India

103 Penang Road, #05-06/07, Visioncrest Commercial, Singapore 238467

Cambridge University Press is part of the University of Cambridge.

It furthers the University's mission by disseminating knowledge in the pursuit of
education, learning and research at the highest international levels of excellence.

www.cambridge.org
Information on this title: www.cambridge.org/9781108810340
DOI: 10.1017/9781108893947

First published 2021
First paperback edition 2022

A catalogue record for this publication is available from the British Library

ISBN 978-1-108-84133-7 Hardback
ISBN 978-1-108-81034-0 Paperback

This book is dedicated to our daughters

Contents

Contributors

Celeste L. Arrington is Korea Foundation Associate Professor of Political Science and International Affairs at the George Washington University. She specializes in comparative politics, with a regional focus on the Koreas and Japan. Her research and teaching focus on law and social change, legal professionals, social movements, the media, comparative policy processes, and qualitative methods. She is the author of *Accidental Activists: Victims Movements and Government Accountability in Japan and South Korea* (Cornell University Press, 2016) and has published in journals such as *Comparative Political Studies, Law & Society Review, Law & Policy, Journal of East Asian Studies*, and *Asian Survey*. Her current book project analyzes the growing prominence of litigation, lawyers, and rights language in Japanese and Korean politics through paired case studies related to disability rights and tobacco control. She earned her Ph.D. in political science from the University of California, Berkeley.

Erin Aeran Chung is the Charles D. Miller Associate Professor of East Asian Politics in the Department of Political Science at Johns Hopkins University. She previously served as the director of the East Asian Studies Program and the codirector of the Racism, Immigration, and Citizenship (RIC) Program at Hopkins. She specializes in East Asian political economy, international migration, and comparative racial politics. She is the author of *Immigration and Citizenship in Japan* (Cambridge, 2010, 2014; Japanese translation, Akashi Shoten, 2012) and *Immigrant Incorporation in East Asian Democracies* (Cambridge, 2020) and coeditor of the Cambridge Elements Politics and Society of East Asia series. Her research has been supported by grants from the Academy of Korean Studies, the Japan Foundation, the Japan Foundation Center for Global Partnership, the Social Science Research Council, and the American Council of Learned Societies.

Patricia Goedde is Professor at Sungkyunkwan University, School of Law. She received her Ph.D. and J.D. from the University of Washington, School of Law, and is a member of the Washington State Bar Association. Her research interests and publications are in the areas of transnational legal mobilization, public interest lawyering, human rights, refugee advocacy, clinical legal education, and North Korean legal issues. She is on the board of directors of the Korea Human Rights Foundation in addition to other human rights and public interest foundation committees.

Sheena Chestnut Greitens is Associate Professor at the Lyndon B. Johnson School of Public Affairs at the University of Texas at Austin. Her work focuses on authoritarianism and security in East Asia, particularly China and the Korean peninsula. Her first book, *Dictators and Their Secret Police* (Cambridge, 2016) won the Best Book Award from the International Studies Association and the Comparative Democratization section of the American Political Science Association.

Ju Hui Judy Han is a cultural geographer and Assistant Professor in Gender Studies at UCLA. Her comics and writings about (im)mobilities, religious politics, and queer activism have been published in *Scholar & Feminist Online*, *East Asia Forum*, *Geoforum*, *Critical Asian Studies*, *positions: asia critique*, and *Journal of Korean Studies* as well as in several edited books including *Territories of Poverty: Rethinking North and South* (2015) and *Ethnographies of U.S. Empire* (2018).

Sung Soo Hong is Associate Professor of Law at Sookmyung Women's University, Seoul, Korea. He received a Ph.D. degree at London School of Economics and has studied at the Human Rights Consortium University of London, Oxford Centre for Socio-Legal Studies and International Institute for the Sociology of Law. He has published many articles and books in Korea addressing human rights and law, and he has worked as a board member for academic associations such as the Korean Association of Human Rights Studies, Korean Association of Human Rights Law, and Korean Association of Legal Philosophy.

Soo-Young Hwang works on environmental rights with United Nations Environment Programme (UNEP). Prior to joining UNEP, she worked with the Office of the UN High Commissioner for Human Rights (OHCHR), the Ministry of Gender Equality and Family of Korea as well as the National Human Rights Commission of Korea (NHRCK). She received a Ph.D. in political science from the University of Hawai'i at Manoa. Her research interests includes states' compliance with international law and norms and the process of construction of rights. She plans to undertake research on how the human right to a healthy environment has evolved, especially over the last ten years.

Eunkyung Kim is Assistant Professor of Liberal Arts College at Hansung University and a member on the board of directors of the Korean Association of Women's History. Her research focuses on issues of gender, sexuality, family, and cultural history of cinema in South Korea. She is the author of *Cultural History of Korean Students: From Liberation to the 1960 April Revolution* (in Korean, Seohaemunjip, 2018). In recognition of her contribution to academic development with the book, she was awarded a commendation by South Korea's deputy prime minister and education minister in 2019. She is working on her second book, *Movie, a Modern Ecstatic State*.

Hun Joon Kim is Associate Professor at the Department of Political Science in Korea University. He has research interests in human rights, transitional justice, and international norms and institutions. He is the author of *The Massacres at Mt Halla: Sixty Years of Truth-Seeking in South Korea* (Cornell University Press, 2014) and a coeditor of *Transitional Justice in the Asia Pacific* (Cambridge University Press, 2014).

JaeWon Kim is Professor at Sungkyunkwan University, School of Law. His research and teaching focuses on the legal profession, comparative law and society, and disability law. As a regular contributor to *Korean Journal of Law & Society*, Professor Kim previously served as President of the Korean Association of Law and Society. He also is a Director of the Korean Disability Law Association. Kim's article, "Legal Profession and Legal Culture during Korea's Transition to Democracy and a Market Economy" appeared as a book chapter in *Raising the Bar* (William Alford, ed.) published by Harvard University Press in 2007. JaeWon Kim received his LL.M. and J.D. from the American University Washington College of Law and his J.S.D. from Cornell Law School, where he was honored as a Clarke Fellow. He is a member of the Pennsylvania State Bar and the District of Columbia Bar.

Jihye Kim is Associate Professor of Multicultural Studies at Gangneung-Wonju National University. Her academic research focuses on law and human rights, with particular interests in LGBTI, migrants, and children. She actively works with NGOs in advocating for minority rights and has published many articles in scholarly journals and books. Her recent publications include a book about being introspective about our own unintended discriminatory biases, *Seollyanghan chabyeoljuuija* (Changbi, 2019). She holds a Ph.D. in Social Welfare from Seoul National University and a J.D. from University of Washington School of Law.

Jisoo M. Kim is Korea Foundation Associate Professor of History, International Affairs, and East Asian Languages and Literatures and Director of the Institute for Korean Studies at George Washington University. She is also Editor-in-Chief of the *Journal of Korean Studies*. Her specialties are gender and the legal history of early modern Korea, and broader research interests include gender and sexuality, crime and justice, forensic medicine, literary representations of the law, history of emotions, vernacular, and gender writing. Her first book, *The Emotions of Justice: Gender, Status, and Legal Performance in Chosŏn Korea* (University of Washington Press, 2015), was awarded the 2017 James Palais Prize of the Association for Asian Studies. She is also the coeditor of *The Great East Asian War and the Birth of the Korean Nation* by JaHyun Kim Haboush (Columbia

University Press, 2016). She is currently working on a book project entitled *Sexual Desire, Gendered Subjects: Decriminalization of Adultery Law in Korean History.*

Yoonkyung Lee is a political sociologist specializing in labor politics, social movements, political representation, and the political economy of neoliberalism with a regional focus on East Asia. She earned her Ph.D. in political science from Duke University and was Associate Professor in Sociology and Asian and Asian-American Studies at SUNY-Binghamton before joining the Department of Sociology at the University of Toronto in 2016. She is also the Korea Foundation Endowed Chair of Korean Studies. Her publications include *Militants or Partisans: Labor Unions and Democratic Politics in Korea and Taiwan* (Stanford University Press, 2011) and numerous journal articles that appeared in *Globalizations, Studies in Comparative International Development, Asian Survey, Journal of Contemporary Asia, Critical Asian Studies, Global Asia, and Korea Observer.*

Sungyun Lim is Associate Professor of History at the University of Colorado Boulder. Her first book, *Rules of the House: Family Law and Domestic Disputes in Colonial Korea* (University of California Press, 2019), examines the emergence of the small patriarchal family as the legal unit of the family in Korea under the Japanese colonial rule through close examination of records of women's civil suits over rights of inheritance, adoption, and divorce. Her current project deals with the history of burial sites and lineage property disputes from the end of the Joseon dynasty through the Japanese colonial period.

Hannes B. Mosler holds the chair for Politics and Society of Korea at the University of Duisburg-Essen, where he is affiliated with the Institute of Political Science (IfP) and the Institute of East Asian Studies (IN-EAST). He received his Ph.D. from the Political Science Department at Seoul National University and was a lecturer and professor at the Institute of Korean Studies and the Graduate School of East Asian Studies at Freie Universität Berlin. His major research interests are the political system, political remembrance, constitutional law, and civic education in Korea and comparatively. His publications include (co)edited volumes such as *South Korea's Democracy Challenge* (Peter Lang, 2020) and *The Quality of Democracy in Korea: Three Decades After Democratization* (Palgrave Macmillan, 2018), as well as numerous journal articles.

Acknowledgments

This volume began as the George Washington Institute for Korean Studies (GWIKS) signature conference entitled "The Evolution of Rights in Korea," held in Washington, DC on April 20–21, 2018. We sincerely thank all the participants, who traveled from multiple continents to join the conference. In addition to lively discussions among the contributors to this volume, the papers all benefited immensely from the insightful comments of other conference participants, including Li Chen, Hae Yeon Choo, Eric Feldman, Steph Haggard, Aram Hur, Sida Liu, and Andrew Yeo. Hae Yeon Choo, Sida Liu, and Andrew Yeo kindly gave us excellent feedback on the final draft, too. We also appreciate Soo-Young Hwang and Eunkyung Kim's hard work, after joining later in the process. The conference and the book that resulted from it would not have been possible without the generous and sustained support from GWIKS, and especially its director Jisoo Kim. GWIKS program assistant Ann Yang and program coordinator Minhye Kim provided superb logistical and organizational support. We also thank the Sigur Center for Asian Studies and the Elliott School of International Affairs, both at the George Washington University. We appreciate the editorial assistance from Maddie Yingling, Trevor Haefner, and Sung Yeon Hong, and the outstanding indexing by John Grennan. Our deepest appreciation goes to Joe Ng, Finola O'Sullivan, and the CUP team for shepherding this volume through the publication process. While none of us could have foreseen that we would be finalizing this volume during a pandemic, we cannot express how grateful we are for the timely and excellent work that the contributors did under unprecedented and challenging circumstances. Finally, we thank our daughters and husbands from the bottom of our hearts.

This work was supported by the Core University Program for Korean Studies through the Ministry of Education of the Republic of Korea and Korean Studies Promotion Service of the Academy of Korean Studies (AKS-2016-OLU-2250009).

Note: This volume uses the Revised Romanization system for Korean transliterations of terms and names, except when there are preferred or commonly known spellings of names (e.g., Roh Moo-hyun or Lee Myung-bak). All translations of Korean are by the authors unless otherwise noted.

Abbreviations

ADA	Americans with Disabilities Act
AIDS	acquired immunodeficiency syndrome
APF	Asia-Pacific Forum of National Human Rights Institutions
APIL	Advocates for Public Interest Law
APRRN	Asia Pacific Refugee Rights Network
BKL	Bae, Kim & Lee LLC
CCEJ	Citizens' Coalition for Economic Justice
CCK	Christian Council of Korea
CEDAW	UN Committee on the Elimination of Discrimination against Women
CERD	UN Committee on the Elimination of Racial Discrimination
CESCR	UN Committee on Economic, Social and Cultural Rights
COVID-19	coronavirus disease 2019
CRC	UN Committee on the Rights of the Child
CRPD	2006 UN Convention on the Rights of Persons with Disabilities
DDA	Disability Discrimination Act
DPI	Disabled Peoples' International
DPRK	Democratic People's Republic of Korea
EPS	Employment Permit System
FKTU	Federation of Korean Trade Unions
HIV	human immunodeficiency virus
ICC	International Coordinating Committee of National Institutions for Promotion and Protection of Human Rights
IDAHO	International Day Against Homophobia
ILO	International Labor Organization
ITTP	Industrial and Technical Training System
JCMK	Joint Committee for Migrant Workers in Korea
JRTI	Judicial Research and Training Institute
KCIA	Korean Central Intelligence Agency

KCPA	Korea's Civil Procedure Act
KCTU	Korean Confederation of Trade Unions
KDAWU	Korea Differently Abled Women United
KFEM	Korea Federation for Environmental Movement
KFSB	Korean Federation of Small and Medium Businesses
KIS	Korea Immigration Service
KLPH	Korean Lawyers for Public Interest and Human Rights
KOCUN	Korea Center for UN Human Rights Policy
KODAF	Korea Differently Abled Federation
LGBTI	lesbian, gay, bisexual, transgender, and intersex
LOS	legal opportunity structure
MOEL	Ministry of Employment and Labor
NEIS	National Education Information System
NGOs	nongovernmental organizations
NHRCK	National Human Rights Commission of Korea
NHRI	National Human Rights Institution
NIMBY	Not in My Back Yard
NIS	National Intelligence Service
NPOs	nonprofit organizations
NSL	Korean National Security Law
NSPA	National Security Planning Agency
OHCHR	Office of the United Nations High Commissioner for Human Rights
OKA	Overseas Korean Act
PILnet	Global Network for Public Interest Law
PRC	People's Republic of China
PROK	Presbyterian Church in the Republic of Korea
PSPD	People's Solidarity for Participatory Democracy
QCF	Queer Culture Festival
QUV	Solidarity of University Queer Societies
RIDRIK	Research Institute for Disability Rights in Korea
ROK	Republic of Korea
SADD	Solidarity against Disability Discrimination
UN	United Nations
UPR	Universal Periodic Review
WPA	World Program of Action Concerning Disabled Persons

Introduction

Rights in Action

Patricia Goedde and Celeste L. Arrington

People in South Korea are increasingly asserting their rights. They make rights claims in public and via the courts, the National Human Rights Commission, legislative and bureaucratic processes, and international human rights mechanisms. In recent years, for example, people with disabilities have litigated for accessible public transit and welfare benefits; citizens have turned to the courts and truth commissions for exoneration and compensation for the Korean government's actions during the Korean War (1950–53) or authoritarian rule (1950s–87); sexual minorities have campaigned for comprehensive anti-discrimination legislation and constitutionally challenged the prohibition against gay marriage; victims of sexual harassment have sued private companies and demonstrated *en masse*; and refugee and migrant advocates have traveled to Geneva to report violations of treaty principles.

This book investigates how rights are enacted, constructed, and challenged in South Korea. Rather than focus on jurists and legal institutions, it adopts a broader conception of rights claiming, which we define as the diverse and changing ways in which people interpret and articulate grievances and engage in claims-making to remedy them. Although the concept of individuals' private rights did not appear until the late nineteenth century in Korea, the Joseon state (1392–1910) did provide legal channels for voicing and relieving *won*, or the sense of having been wronged, to help maintain the rigidly hierarchical social and moral order (see J. M. Kim 2015, chap. 1). Even women were able to bring claims through such petitioning channels, albeit in cases circumscribed by Korea's social hierarchy. Under Japanese colonial rule (1910–45), interesting contests occurred over Korean subjects' legal capacity to bring claims and the legal status of Korean customs. Although wives lacked legal capacity in nearly all contexts and took comparatively few legal actions, they had some rights that they leveraged in claims-making that simultaneously empowered them and solidified Japan's household registry system for controlling Korean subjects. The modern system of law on which rights claims would later be based was thus not just imposed from Japan but also developed through state–society interactions and jurisprudence in Korea (M. S.-H. Kim 2012). After liberation and the US

1

military occupation, the Republic of Korea created democratic institutions and a constitution that protected citizens' rights. Much rights claiming since then has appealed to the rule of law or for new laws to codify rights. However, these institutions also left room for those in power to circumscribe citizens' rights in the name of anti-communism, national security, capitalist economic development, and family values. As a result, claims-making often entailed contestation over how to interpret and implement rights protections.

From the petition drum of the Joseon period, which allowed subjects to directly appeal to the king regarding perceived injustices, to the Constitutional Court and the presidential Blue House's new online electronic petition system, the institutions and practices that shape rights claiming in Korea deserve fuller analysis. So do the historical experiences and social interactions that imbue rights concepts with distinctive meanings and overtones. We argue that the prism of rights offers a useful framework within which to analyze why and how people in Korea have sought to redress grievances or social inequalities, overcome marginalization, and catalyze social and political change or in some cases fail to do so. Recognizing the modern, Western pedigree of rights as a concept, we remain attentive to the need to examine the underlying logics of indigenous legal practices and institutions.

Since the twentieth century, the language of rights (*gwolli*) and human rights (*ingwon*) have become increasingly widely invoked in South Korean media, government agencies, schools, and households. For example, anti-government dissidents actively propagated human rights discourses in Korea in the 1970s. The lawyers who defended them called themselves human rights lawyers (*ingwon byeonhosa*) and greatly influenced the development of civil society after Korea's democratization in 1987 (Chang 2015; Goedde 2009). Among poor tenants who felt unjustly evicted by urban redevelopment projects in Seoul, calls for the right to subsistence (*saengjongwon*) morphed into the right to housing (*jugeogwon*) in the 1990s (Shin 2018). Discussions about decriminalizing adultery pitched arguments about rights to privacy (*gaein saenghwalgwolli*) and sexual freedom against arguments about protecting women's economic rights vis-à-vis adulterous husbands (K. Cho 2002). In the early 2000s, people with disabilities asserted a right to mobility (*idonggwon*) when protesting for reforms to make public transit accessible. Increasing numbers of migrant workers, marriage migrants, and North Korean refugees residing in Korea in the new millennium prompted discussions about which groups have access to which rights, leading to complex hierarchies among groups, as Erin Chung details in Chapter 13. Most recently, women's groups gained a boost from the Korean Constitutional Court's April 2019 ruling against the country's six-decade old abortion ban for limiting women's rights to self-determination (*jagigyeoljeonggwon*), health (*geonganggwon*), and life (*saengmyeonggwon*) (M. Kim 2019). This book's chapters analyze the proliferation of rights claiming in Korea from different perspectives and illustrate how rights claiming targets not just the state but also business and societal actors. While the chapters do not explicitly trace any overarching narrative of rights in Korea, they together demonstrate the overall expansion of rights over time and learning among rights claimants.

Usually, only as a last resort do such strategic assertions of rights entail time-consuming and costly litigation. Before that stage, rights can serve to define injurious experiences as an injustice or violation of some legal principle that is justiciable, imbue a person with legal capacity to make claims, spur mobilization based on shared feelings of injustice, and identify remedies by tapping into international principles and associated policy instruments (Felstiner, Abel, and Sarat 1981). They can also spur backlash, countermobilization, and rights retrenchment. Being cognizant of the discrepancies between ideals and reality – between law on the books and law in action – this book investigates what bases people in Korea use to make claims, what channels they employ, what rights mean to those deploying them and to bystanders, and how rights-based claiming affects their activities and interactions with other actors.

DEFINITIONS

Rights come in many different shapes and flavors, but are usually linked with concepts of human rights, social justice, and rule of law. They may be encoded in national statutes or international treaties like the Universal Declaration of Human Rights or the Convention on the Rights of Persons with Disabilities. Other times they take looser forms, such as when aggrieved parties make demands for some injustice to be rectified. Some scholars criticize efforts to study rights outside specific historical contexts or the economically dominant Global North, which developed notions of individual rights and promoted them via international organizations and NGOs. They emphasize cultural and historical differences and challenge the assumption that norm diffusion automatically or necessarily proceeds from advanced liberal democracies to more marginal polities (e.g., Alford 2007, chap. 7; Ishay 2008; Stammers 1999; Towns 2012). We agree that rights concepts do not necessarily mean the same thing across time and context, and rights sometimes emerge organically in localities. While being sensitive to the conceptual contours of rights as they emerge from our empirical cases in Korea, we reject a sharp contrast between rights claiming in Korea versus in other countries.

For the purposes of this volume, our position is that rights are not completely subjective but are grounded in similar baseline notions about human worth and dignity, state protections and legal restraints on state actions, and the utility of claiming some legal entitlement. We think therefore that there is value from employing the concept of rights. How different groups mobilize and flesh out this shared baseline conception of rights is the focus of our chapters' empirical analyses. We thus move beyond terminological debates about using Western concepts to instead examine rights in action in the context of South

Korea.[1] We investigate claims-making and clarify what the people who invoke rights language and contest rights in Korea understand rights to mean. To scholarship about "Western" rights conceptions, our volume adds evidence about how home-grown conceptions of justice and human dignity grew into rights discourses and about the productive feedback loops between local rights-based mobilization and transnational rights-promotion activities.

"Rights" as used in this book encompasses varied conceptions and subsets, including but not limited to constitutional rights, human rights, substantive and procedural rights; civil, political, social, economic, and cultural rights; citizens' rights; women's rights; and minority rights. In so doing, this book broadens the aperture compared to classic studies like William Shaw's edited volume *Human Rights in Korea* (1991), which focused on civil and political rights. Like Shaw's volume, however, we find that "there is no monolithic consensus in Korean society, or even within the Korean government, on human rights issues. There is no longer, if there ever was, a single Korean orientation or political culture considering the subject" (Shaw 1991, 5). Indeed, Chapters 4 and 9, for example, show that claims related to violence on Jeju Island in 1948 and workers' rights have shifted over time in interaction with counterclaiming and socioeconomic changes, respectively. There is thus a baseline conception of rights that then gets shaped, defined, and acted upon within particular temporal-spatial contexts. As Stuart Scheingold (2004) did in his classic work on "the politics of rights," this volume's contributors adopt a relational approach to claims-making and investigate *how* diverse groups use rights to frame and debate policy issues, sometimes even before the asserted rights are legally codified or protected by courts. Much as Chaihark Hahm and Sung Ho Kim (2015) emphasize the mutually constitutive relationship between "we the people" and their constitution in their analysis of democratic constitutional founding in Korea and Japan, we employ a bottom-up approach and trace how mobilizing the law and rights language constitutes rights and imbues them with meaning. The mechanisms and iterative processes of claims-making are ultimately how rights become legible.

This book's chapters thus analyze how rights conceptions are deployed and contested in discourses, institutional mechanisms, and other modes of claims-making in South Korea. Discussions of human rights and "rights talk" are ever more prevalent in scholarship about mobilization and the interactions between law and social change outside East Asia (Merry 2006; Risse, Ropp, and Sikkink 1999; Simmons 2009; Vanhala 2018). In addition, there is a burgeoning literature about legal mobilization in East Asia (e.g., Chua 2014, 2018; Diamant, Lubman, and O'Brien 2005; Feldman 2000; Sidel 2010; Steinhoff 2014; Stern 2013). By examining

---

[1]   For similar approaches to rights-based mobilization in Japan and China, see, respectively, Feldman (2000) and Woo and Gallagher (2011).

the strategies and channels that South Korean claimants use to articulate and assert their rights and the tensions or discrepancies in rights language, this volume contributes to this literature.

THIS VOLUME'S BOTTOM-UP AND INTERACTIONIST APPROACH

This volume probes the following questions through diverse case studies, approached via different disciplines and methods. Why and how have people in Korea claimed their rights through institutional mechanisms and extrajudicial tactics? To what extent have state or nonstate actors assisted or limited rights claiming? And what remains fundamentally challenging for groups asserting their rights? Spanning 150 years, the following chapters trace the social and political emergence and development of rights in Korea, analyzing how the experiences of Japanese colonial occupation, war and national division, authoritarian rule, democratization, and the complexification and diversification of contemporary Korea infused the concept of rights with distinctive meanings and institutional operation.

This volume is divided into four main parts: (1) historical cases, (2) existing and emergent institutional channels, (3) the experiences of marginalized Korean communities, and (4) the experiences of noncitizens who seek to become South Korean residents or citizens. Since covering all possible rights claims would require multiple volumes, this book foregrounds instead groups that have been overlooked in the extant scholarship, such as by focusing on the historical cases on women. We adopt an interactionist approach, exploring changes in the institutional contexts within which rights claims occur and in the sources of support available for utilizing different claims-making channels. The chapters analyze the rights narratives and claims-making of diverse groups, including women, victims of state violence, lawyers, workers, people with disabilities, sexual minorities, new citizens, and migrants.

We examine how different groups define and interpret rights and the effects that these processes have on their activities and interactions with other actors. In the process, we uncover tensions and selectivity – both intended and not – in certain rights discourses. The chapters highlight conflicts over contending rights claims, expose disparities between law on the books and law in practice, trace interconnections among some rights in that a violation of one is considered a violation of another, and map emerging trends in the use of rights language. The book's second part analyzes how real or perceived changes and continuities in the institutional context of rights claiming affect the likelihood of rights claiming and its efficacy. We also investigate the sources of support that claimants have in terms of civil society organizations, legal assistance, and funding (Epp 1998). While many of the chapters document how effective rights-based mobilization has been in terms of catalyzing social and legal change in Korea, some reveal the limits of law and legal institutions, including where the state fails to promote rights or remedy grievances.

The case studies in this book trace how people navigate deficiencies in the system or exploit alternative channels for grievance articulation. Finally, many of the chapters look beyond South Korea, to understand how groups engage with international rights discourses and mechanisms, including UN bodies and international treaties.

The subjects of rights, law, citizenship, and social change are fertile for analysis from diverse disciplinary angles in history, law, sociology, political science, geography, and gender studies. This collection offers unique breadth in its analysis of rights claiming in Korea by providing opportunities for cross-issue and cross-temporal comparisons of institutional and legal developments, patterns of mobilization, both domestic and international civil society activism, and linkages to global rights discourses. Drawing on scores of original interviews, systematic analysis of court rulings and statutes, close reading of primary sources in archives and online, and interpretive analysis of news media coverage in Korean, this volume illuminates rights in action. Some of our contributors bring not only their specific disciplinary training and insights but also their direct advocacy experiences in rights activism and claiming.

THE VOLUME'S CONTRIBUTIONS

Rights Claiming in South Korea makes several significant theoretical contributions, including to scholarly debates that have focused mostly on Western contexts to date. First, we elucidate how rights-based mobilization relates to other forms of political participation or exclusion. Through careful case studies, this book's chapters explain how diverse groups leverage rights as they seek to influence the media, attentive bystanders, and the government. The nuanced picture that emerges from our volume offers rich material for comparative analysis and challenges the common perception that Korea is a "Republic of Demonstrations" (S. Kim 2009). Rather than just protest, Korean rights claimants use diverse combinations of litigation, protest, lobbying, and media campaigns as part of a repertoire of tactics. However, this volume reveals the interrelationships across different tactics because, as one review article noted, the importance of legal versus other tactics varies even when rights language and lawyers are involved (Marshall and Hale 2014, 663). As summarized in our conclusion, the case studies demonstrate how activists obtain the synergies between legal tactics and other forms of activism. The volume thus advances scholarship about how societal actors do not just respond to perceived judicial receptivity to particular rights claims but also shape it.

Second, this volume adopts more of a bottom-up approach than existing work on law and courts in Korea and places rights claiming and judicial processes in their broader sociopolitical context (for a similar approach in the Chinese context, see Woo and Gallagher 2011). Studies of Korean legal reform usually focus on substantive legal content, case analysis, or politico-institutional developments without including claimants' voices (K. Cho 2010; Ginsburg 2004; Mayali and Yoo 2014).

Research about the "judicialization of politics" in Korea tends to emphasize the role of political and judicial elites and new institutions like the Korean Constitutional Court (e.g., Ginsburg 2003; Kim and Park 2012). It also often focuses on "mega-politics" questions, such as the president's impeachment or the disbanding of political parties (Hirschl 2004). In contrast, we analyze a variety of forms of rights claiming in diverse contexts, including the courts, National Human Rights Commission, civil society organizations, the streets, and international human rights bodies. Our interactionist and bottom-up approach reveals the fluid and plural meanings of rights and unintended or intended hierarchies that emerge from rights discourses, as elaborated in the Conclusion.

Meanwhile, in the existing research focused on social movement mobilization and civil society in Korea, rights talk is usually taken for granted rather than explicitly analyzed in terms of legal discourse, tactics, and outcomes for rights claiming. *South Korean Social Movements* edited by Gi-Wook Shin and Paul Chang (2011) partially remedies this gap by including topics on discursive shifts and institutional mechanisms such as the National Human Rights Commission of Korea and public interest lawyer groups. Importantly, it asks, in part, whether the institutionalization of social movements has helped to advance or co-opt causes. While prior scholarship on Korea offers excellent studies detailing how intertwined democracy and human rights became in challenging Korea's abusive authoritarian regimes (Chang 2015, chap. 6; H. Cho 2010), the lens of democratization or democratic consolidation is insufficient for capturing the range of rights discourses and mobilization our volume details. Indeed, democratization and rights are related but not synonymous, though channels for rights claiming proliferated in democratic Korea. Our volume thus builds upon Korean scholarship that addresses methods of legal advocacy and reform for civil, political, economic, and social rights since democratization (Minbyeon 1998; 2018; Park 2003; Yoon 2010, chaps. 12–13).

Finally, we document how infrastructures for legal mobilization – including advocacy organizations, funding, and lawyers – are becoming increasingly institutionalized in Korea. Charles Epp (1998) argued that advocacy groups, funding, and lawyers were necessary "support structures" for effective rights claiming. Sociolegal scholars have shown that subsets of the private bar in many countries have used their professional skills to curb state power and protect citizens' rights, but this "cause lawyering" literature has largely overlooked East Asia (e.g., Sarat and Scheingold 2001, 2006; also see Arrington 2014; Arrington and Moon 2020; Goedde 2009; Liu and Halliday 2011; Tam 2013). The cases in our book add substantial empirical evidence about the interactions between rights-based movements and lawyers in East Asia.

To date, most English-language studies of legal mobilization in Korea have been scattered across academic journals and edited volumes in diverse disciplines (e.g., Arrington 2014, 2019; K. Cho 2007; Goedde 2011; H. J. Kim 2012). Or they concentrate on activism related to North Korean human rights (Goedde 2010; Yeo and Chubb 2018). One notable exception is Hyunah Yang's *Law and Society in Korea*, which ours complements by bringing together scholars from more diverse disciplinary perspectives to examine a wider range of claims (Yang 2013). We now proceed to introduce the volume's chapters as a way of elucidating the genealogies of rights and rights claiming in Korea.

ORGANIZATION AND CONTENT: A GENEALOGY OF RIGHTS IN KOREA

Part I: Rights in Historical Perspective: Bringing Women Back In

Part I of this volume provides a panoramic treatment of how women's rights were articulated or transformed in the Joseon, Japanese colonial, and postliberation eras. In so doing, we highlight a group in Korean history – women – that has been relatively overlooked by scholars (but see J. M. Kim 2015; Kim and Pettid 2011; Lim 2019). We see how the legal capacity of women to bring claims to the state varied under the different governing structures of the time and as women went from being subjects of a kingdom, to colonial subjects, and finally to rights-bearing citizens in a democratizing nation.

However, the notion of rights must be deconstructed when applying it to Korean history. "Rights" and "legal consciousness" were not part of the indigenous vocabulary. Nonetheless, the acts of seeking to right a wrong or to remedy a grievance are universal behaviors. Strategically making rights-like claims has a long history in Korean society and arguably predates Korean use of the words rights (*gwolli*) and human rights (*ingwon*). Hahm Pyong-choong's (1986) influential assertion that Koreans were averse to resolving disputes legally has been refuted (Shaw 1981; Yang 1989). Alongside sophisticated legal codes and administrative protocols, the language of "law" and "(in)justice" was pervasive in the Joseon period, thus allowing petitioners a framework with which to address grievances. However, pursuit of legal claims occurred without invoking the Western concept and language of individual (natural) rights to be claimed vis-à-vis the government (Yang 2002, 191).

While acknowledging the distinctions between contemporary conceptions of rights and their precursors, chapters in Part I trace how claimants creatively leveraged the fact that Joseon-era and Japanese colonial authorities permitted and heard people's grievances, albeit primarily to maintain an orderly and strict social hierarchy. These state–society interactions colored the subsequent formation and implementation of legal codes in the postliberation period as Koreans constructed democratic institutions. Chapters in Part I highlight the understudied claims-making activities of women, even though they were not the most numerous claimants and mobilized the law within restricted confines delineated by family and inheritance laws and neo-Confucian traditions (for a sampling of typical cases during parts of the Joseon era, see Shaw 1981 and Kim and Kim 2014). As we discuss in the conclusion chapter, claims-making by Korean women in the nineteenth and early twentieth centuries reveals that legal mobilization can be both empowering and stymied by existing rights hierarchies and social orderings that privilege men above women and *yangban* (elites) over peasants. As such, the sociocultural context of Korea colored conceptions of rights and rights claiming across the decades.

Instead of retrofitting Western or modern concepts, Jisoo Kim in Chapter 1 begins with the puzzling prevalence in the Joseon period of hundreds of petitions from women, whom scholars usually characterize as silent outside the domestic sphere. Based on the neo-Confucian principle that the ruler's mandate depended on listening to his people's grievances, however, women used petitions to try to rectify infringements of the privileges they enjoyed within their status. Through an analysis of such petitions, the chapter shows that petitioning complicated gender dynamics in Joseon society. On the one hand, petitioning reinforced rigid hierarchies because women used narratives of domesticity. On the other hand, women also constructed a sense of legal identity and personhood through their petitioning. Challenging the mischaracterizations of Joseon women as having no legal capacity, this chapter parses the vernacular and narrative strategies of women who petitioned. While the discourse of (equal) rights (*gwolli*) only began appearing in official documents and public writings in the last two decades of the nineteenth century, Koreans' practices of engaging institutional mechanisms to make claims related to life, property, and inheritance were evident in the cases brought to the Joseon kings.

In Chapter 2, Sungyun Lim contests the postcolonial Korean narrative that wives had no legal capacity (*cheoui muneungnyeok*) during the colonial period. She argues that Korean women had some space in which to claim legal entitlements, especially when it came to separate property rights as introduced under the Japanese colonial legal system. Though heavily discriminatory against Koreans, the modern judicial structure opened more litigation channels to Koreans, explaining the rise of lawsuits among Koreans during the colonial period (M. S.-H. Kim 2016). Relying on civil court records, Lim relates how widowed household-heads were surprisingly successful in defending and developing their separate property rights during this period. The chapter shows how the colonial judicial system accommodated Korean women's ability to bring certain suits by granting them full legal capacity to do so, despite their being colonial subjects. The cases studied reveal contests between legal rights and Korean customs and how the Japanese colonial state's prerogatives, especially regarding the household registration system, influenced the outcomes of such contests and the lawsuits.

In Chapter 3, Eunkyung Kim carries the discussion of women's legal capacity forward into the postcolonial era, arguing that although women became equal rights-bearing subjects under the new Republic of Korea's democratic Constitution of 1948, they retained their unequal status in family law, which was codified in 1958. As lawmakers debated family law reforms in the context of postcoloniality and institutionalizing democracy in South Korea's first decade, patriarchal family traditions and aspirations for capitalist economic development justified gender discriminatory features in the new Civil Code. The new legal framework restricted women's rights in the private family sphere and undermined women's full rights as equal citizens relative to men in the family hierarchy. The author also recounts her experiences during the democratization demonstrations of the 1980s, wherein gender equality was similarly subjugated to more basic civil and political rights, ultimately deprioritizing women's rights. Korea's democratization efforts abortively began in the 1940s, resurged around 1960 and 1979–80, and were finally successful in 1987. This chapter provides a fascinating and understudied historical lens on the position of women's rights in this fitful process of democratization and enriches our understanding of more recent battles over the discrimination and sexual harassment of women in Korea.

Part II: Institutional Mechanisms for Rights Claiming and Support Structures for Claiming Rights

For rights claims to result in recognition and remedies, institutional mechanisms and support structures are needed. These include various state institutions, such as courts and commissions, as well as legal professionals to interpret and apply the laws that guarantee certain rights. Part II examines the legal and quasi-legal institutions and mechanisms that have arisen since the transition to democracy in 1987: the Constitutional Court, Truth Commissions, the National Human Rights Commission, the modern judiciary, the expanding professional bar, and public interest law groups. From the chapters in Part II, we can see the different channels open to rights claimants, to what extent these channels have been used to defend and develop different rights, the role of various institutional actors in creating legal opportunities through structural reforms, and how the institutional context is influenced by domestic politics or international norms. This part addresses broader concerns, such as whether litigation has become more accessible to the public or if rights claiming has had a democratizing effect on judicial procedures. At the same time, the chapters in this part also investigate the National Human Rights Commission's lack of enforcement power, constraints on judicial activism, limited budgets and political will for truth commissions, the precedential impact of negative court decisions, and remaining challenges of public interest lawyering.

Chapter 4 serves as a bridge between the historical section and the book's contemporary analyses. In it, Hun Joon Kim follows the variations in rights claims stemming from the postliberation and Korean War events on Jeju Island (commonly known as the 4.3 or April 3 events), when communist revolts were violently suppressed, leading to the massacre of more than 30,000 people by state forces. Kim uses social movement theory to show how victims and opponents shifted their framing of rights claims over the ensuing seventy years of activism and counter-activism, essentially expanding rights claims on a range of bases – individual, collective, general, special, constitutional, and human rights. Beyond constitutional and human rights treaty provisions, rights were sometimes particularized, such as with the right to know the truth and the right to justice and retribution. The chapter indicates that rights claims diversify when there are strong counterclaims and a liberalizing political opportunity structure.

Chapter 5 by Soo-Young Hwang analyzes another case of cross-temporal shifts in rights-related discourse, focusing on the relationship between human rights and national development. Hwang contends that South Korea established the National Human Rights Commission of Korea (NHRCK) in 2001 as a means of gaining international legitimacy. The subsequent consolidation of the NHRCK helped the state to realize its desired identity: that of a *seonjinguk* (advanced country). But the priorities within this desired identity have shifted over time, sometimes to include the advancement of people's rights. This chapter traces the rise and fall of the NHRCK during the critical period of 2001–12, explaining how and why the state decided to comply with the global human rights norms by establishing a national human rights institution, and how the NHRCK became a key stakeholder in promoting rights domestically under progressive presidents. Hwang's analysis highlights the state's powerful role in fostering or frustrating rights claiming options, as happened when the presidency returned to the conservatives in 2008.

Hannes Mosler, in Chapter 6, sheds light on the Constitutional Court's accessibility and analyzes how citizens have been making use of the constitutional appeal system to claim their rights. While there existed a constitutional review system since the founding of the Republic in 1948, it was only after transition to formal democracy that infringement of fundamental rights could be appealed to the Constitutional Court, which was established in 1988. This new court has received considerable scholarly attention as the vanguard of increased judicial activism in the democratic era (Ginsburg 2003; Kim and Park 2012). Justine Guichard (2016) also contends that the Court was assigned the task of "redefining the contours of enmity" or tackling challenging issues related to national security. But the focus has been on judicial behavior, the institution, and major political issues. Adopting a more participative approach, Mosler uses caseload statistics to show how citizens have been making use of the constitutional appeal system for claiming their rights since the late 1980s. He then discusses cases related to gender equality, sexual autonomy, and freedom of conscience to uncover conceptual shifts in constitutional rights over time in terms of citizens' perceptions of the rule of law and fundamental rights, which are mutually constitutive with the Court's decisions.

Chapter 7 turns to the judiciary itself. Celeste Arrington asks: To what extent and how has civil litigation become an institutional mechanism for rights claiming in South Korea in the democratic era? She uses the concept of legal opportunity structures to foreground the rules, procedures, and statutes related to access to the courts, adjudication, and judicial remedies. They influence the likelihood that individuals and groups will use civil litigation to try to enforce rights. This chapter traces the breakdown of barriers to entry, civil procedural changes, and potentially improved remedies in the past two decades. It suggests that rights claimants, activist lawyers, partisan politics, and international factors may be driving some of the changes in the structure of legal opportunities. The chapter shows how citizens – with help from lawyers – are recognizing and using legal opportunities, and sometimes even forging new opportunities, in pursuit of rights.

In Chapter 8, Patricia Goedde focuses on the role of public interest lawyers in the rights claiming process. She provides a brief history of the rise of human rights lawyering and explains how Korean public interest law organizations have mobilized professionally and institutionally in the past decade to complement social movements. This chapter identifies patterns in the institutional development and sustainability of the major public interest law entities that have emerged since the early 2000s, including nonprofit public interest law groups, those affiliated with private law firms, and the cause-specific network of lawyers found across public interest law organizations. These case studies shed light on a densely networked and vital component of rights claiming in Korea that is often taken for granted or overlooked. The dynamics of rights advocacy mechanisms in Korea that emerge elucidate how nonprofit public interest law organizations operate, collaborate, and generate more public interest lawyers.

Part III: Mobilizing Rights for the Marginalized

Part III centers on how various vulnerable groups (i.e., workers, people with disabilities, sexual and racial minorities) perceive injustice, claim rights and remedies, talk about rights, leverage domestic and transnational mechanisms, and resort to other institutional and extra-institutional tactics – and to what effect. Despite being Korean citizens with the presumption of constitutional rights, these claimants demand to be recognized as full human beings. Perceptions of being less than fully human are consistent among marginalized groups, accompanied by degrees of exploitation, charity, stigma, and invisibility. How do state and nonstate actors assist or obstruct their rights claiming? Are there intersections, alliances, collisions, or shifts in rights and the claims-making process? Since overcoming marginalization entails not just litigation and pushing for legal reform but also deploying contentious tactics such as sit-in protests, marches, and media campaigns, this part demonstrates the interactions among diverse tactics.

In Chapter 9, Yoonkyung Lee traces the changing notion of labor rights. She investigates how structural conditions in the labor market generate workers' primary grievances, how these grievances enlighten workers' rights consciousness, and how workers' interactions with employers and state institutions, which revolve around labor laws, shaped the core claims of labor rights in the 1980s and the 2000s, respectively. While workers demanded humane treatment and the right to form autonomous labor unions in the 1980s, labor rights in present-day Korea center on workers' status recognition and the right to secure employment. Also, the methods through which workers press for their rights have shifted from union-based collective action to symbolic and extreme forms of protest in recent years.

JaeWon Kim, in Chapter 10, discusses a different paradigm shift with respect to rights: the campaign for the recognition of people with disabilities. Long viewed as recipients of charity or medical treatment, people with disabilities began to advocate for legislation based on equal treatment and rights in the 1980s. While disability rights activists achieved important gains prior to 2007, the chapter argues that the Disability Discrimination Act of that year was a key turning point because it accelerated shifts in societal perceptions and government policies toward a rights-based model of disabilities. Rights-based mobilization in the streets, at the NHRCK, and in front of the National Assembly by scores of disability groups contributed to this new legislation. It also coincided with advocacy for mobility rights (*idonggwon*) and reforms to education and employment policies for people with disabilities. The chapter analyzes how the policy changes and paradigm shift were reinforced by increasingly assertive rights claiming in the courts and the National Human Rights Commission.

The two remaining chapters in this section are about shifts in rights recognition that have yet to occur for sexual minorities in Korea. In Chapter 11, Judy Han contends that while LGBTI politics have gained visibility in Korea, resistance to fully recognizing their rights has come not just from Christian conservative groups but also from progressive and feminist groups that attempt to silence and defer sexual minorities' demands for equality. Such explicit and implicit prioritization of which rights to recognize and defend echoes earlier democratization proponents' subjugation of women's rights for the sake of broader civil and political rights. The "politics of postponement" describes the immediate and indefinite denial of rights to sexual minorities. The chapter elucidates countermobilization dynamics in Korea.

This theme also manifests in Chapter 12, where Jihye Kim and Sung Soo Hong challenge narratives about the continual failure of Korean society to enact a general anti-discrimination law. While exhorted by international human rights bodies to provide comprehensive legal protection to racial and sexual minorities, anti-discrimination bills have failed to pass mainly due to powerful conservative Protestant groups' opposition. Despite this, the authors argue that the dialogue between international and local communities has had a critical effect in bringing issues of nondiscrimination and equal rights to the fore. Strong opposition against comprehensive anti-discrimination legislation has paradoxically exposed Korean society's prevalent but hidden intolerance of diversity and prompted the growth of identity politics, shaping the nondiscrimination movement and increasing the visibility of minorities in the public sphere. Through transnational processes involving local and global civil society, minorities have begun to gain the "right to have rights."

Part IV: Shaping Rights for New Citizens and Noncitizens

While the previous parts reviewed the implications of rights claiming for Korean citizens, Part IV investigates the rights of new citizens or noncitizens who reside or wish to reside in South Korea. Part III's evidence of hierarchies of rights compels us to examine whose rights matter in an increasingly less homogeneous society. That varying degrees of rights are granted based on an ethno-national hierarchy contradicts the basic premise of rights based on equality enshrined in international human rights norms, though not necessarily in countries' respective constitutional norms or national immigration policies. This part focuses on those who seek citizenship or residential status in South Korea; what rights are accorded to them; whether they can leverage these rights successfully in claims-making; and to what extent the state regulates their status as rights-bearing citizens. How do rights arise within the tension between Korea's long-standing ethno-nationalism and its emergent discourse of multiculturalism? How do the processes of becoming a rights-bearing citizen compare for ethnic Koreans, partially ethnic Koreans, and non-Koreans?

To answer these questions, Erin Chung in Chapter 13 exposes how rights are relative to one's status as a citizen or noncitizen, with gradations in between. Migrants are located on various rungs of an immigration hierarchy and accorded specific rights in relation to their visa status. Here, Chung elaborates the distinctions also made in Chapter 4 between specific rights and general rights. Chung contends that, in countries where noncitizens range from migrant laborers with almost no rights to native-born foreign residents who are generations removed from their immigrant ancestry, visa categories are critical determinants of a migrant's eligibility for state-sponsored rights and services. This chapter examines how the growth of multiple visa categories created to accommodate labor shortages within South Korea's restrictive immigration regime has led to the development of noncitizen hierarchies that have become the basis for how migrants relate to the state, mobilize themselves, and voice their collective interests.

In Chapter 14, Sheena Chestnut Greitens focuses on the rights of a subset of migrants: North Koreans who defect or resettle in South Korea. The fact that North Koreans are generally considered to have "automatic citizenship" in the South under both constitutional and communitarian conceptions of citizenship aligns largely with the previous chapter's assessment that ethnic Koreans are at the top of the migrant hierarchy. But it is only partly accurate. Focusing on the security screening process that occurs immediately after North Korean migrants arrive on South Korean soil, this chapter shows that claiming citizenship rights requires considerable agency from North Koreans, whose rights are circumscribed and contingent on the South Korean state's priorities and recognition of their identity in the screening process. The chapter elucidates the rights claiming experiences of North Koreans in a context of in-betweenness and maximal state control, as well as gaps between legally recognized rights and their instantiation in state practice.

CONCLUSION

In sum, *Rights Claiming in South Korea* presents interdisciplinary analyses of why and how communities and individuals in Korea have mobilized the law and rights language to express grievances and claim entitlements. This volume explores the varieties of discursive rights frames that claimants and activists deploy. It introduces the primary institutional mechanisms and professional resources for rights claiming, including the leveraging of international human rights norms and networks. By scrutinizing the gaps and interactions between rights on the books and rights in practice, we can gain a more comprehensive and nuanced understanding of rights discourses and claims-making options in Korea. In the Conclusion chapter, we deduce that the meanings of rights are fluid and plural as applied in Korea, and that some rights discourses implicitly or explicitly privilege certain people over others. Our volume also highlights the value of an interactive and dynamic analytical approach to rights claiming that unpacks "the *process* of mobilizing the law" (Arrington 2019, 333). The Conclusion synthesizes and elaborates these three core findings from our empirical cases and contemplates challenges for the future of rights claiming in South Korea.

REFERENCES

Alford, William P., ed. 2007. *Raising the Bar: The Emerging Legal Profession in East Asia.* Cambridge: Harvard University Press.

Arrington, Celeste L. 2014. "Leprosy, Legal Mobilization, and the Public Sphere in Japan and South Korea." *Law & Society Review* 48 (3): 563–93.

2019. "Hiding in Plain Sight: Pseudonymity and Participation in Legal Mobilization." *Comparative Political Studies* 52 (2): 310–41.

Arrington, Celeste L., and Yong-il Moon. 2020. "Cause Lawyering and Movement Tactics: Disability Rights Movements in South Korea and Japan." *Law & Policy* 42 (1): 5–30.

Chang, Paul. 2015. *Protest Dialectics: State Repression and South Korea's Democracy Movement, 1970–1979.* Stanford: Stanford University Press.

Cho, Hyo-Je. 2010. "Two Concepts of Human Rights in Contemporary Korea." *Development and Society* 39 (2): 301–27.

Cho, Kuk. 2002. "The Crime of Adultery in Korea: Inadequate Means for Maintaining Morality and Protecting Women." *Journal of Korean Law* 2: 81–100.

2007. "Transitional Justice in Korea: Legally Coping with Past Wrongs after Democratization." *Pacific Rim Law & Policy Journal* 16: 579–612.

Cho, Kuk, ed. 2010. *Litigation in Korea.* Cheltenham: Edward Elgar Publishing.

Chua, Lynette J. 2014. *Mobilizing Gay Singapore: Rights and Resistance in an Authoritarian State.* Philadelphia: Temple University Press.

2018. *The Politics of Love in Myanmar: LGBT Mobilization and Human Rights as a Way of Life.* Stanford: Stanford University Press.

Diamant, Neil Jeffrey, Stanley B. Lubman, and Kevin J. O'Brien. 2005. *Engaging the Law in China: State, Society, and Possibilities for Justice*. Stanford: Stanford University Press.

Epp, Charles R. 1998. *The Rights Revolution: Lawyers, Activists, and Supreme Courts in Comparative Perspective*. Chicago: University of Chicago Press.

Feldman, Eric A. 2000. *The Ritual of Rights in Japan: Law, Society, and Health Policy*. Cambridge: Cambridge University Press.

Felstiner, William L. F., Richard L. Abel, and Abel Sarat. 1981. "The Emergence and Transformation of Disputes: Naming, Blaming, and Claiming." *Law & Society Review* 15 (3/4): 631–54.

Ginsburg, Tom. 2003. *Judicial Review in New Democracies: Constitutional Courts in Asian Cases*. Cambridge: Cambridge University Press.

Ginsburg, Tom, ed. 2004. *Legal Reform in Korea*. New York: Routledge.

Goedde, Patricia. 2009. "From Dissidents to Institution-Builders: The Transformation of Public Interest Lawyers in South Korea." *East Asia Law Review* 4: 63–90.

     2010. "Legal Mobilization for Human Rights Protection in North Korea: Furthering Discourse or Discord?" *Human Rights Quarterly* 32 (3): 530–74.

     2011. "Lawyers for a Democratic Society (Minbyeon): The Evolution of Its Legal Mobilization Process since 1988." In *South Korean Social Movements: From Democracy to Civil Society*, edited by Gi-Wook Shin and Paul Y. Chang, 224–44. London: Routledge.

Guichard, Justine. 2016. *Regime Transition and the Judicial Politics of Enmity: Democratic Inclusion and Exclusion in South Korean Constitutional Justice*. New York: Palgrave.

Hahm, Chaihark, and Sung Ho Kim. 2015. *Making We the People: Democratic Constitutional Founding in Postwar Japan and South Korea*. Comparative Constitutional Law and Policy. New York: Cambridge University Press.

Hahm, Pyong-choon. 1986. *Korean Jurisprudence, Politics, and Culture*. Seoul: Yonsei University Press.

Hirschl, Ran. 2004. *Towards Juristocracy: The Origins and Consequences of the New Constitutionalism*. Cambridge: Harvard University Press.

Ishay, Micheline R. 2008. *The History of Human Rights: From Ancient Times to the Globalization Era*. Berkeley: University of California Press.

Kim, Hun Joon. 2012. "Local, National, and International Determinants of Truth Commissions: The South Korean Experience." *Human Rights Quarterly* 34 (3): 726–50.

Kim, Jisoo M. 2015. *The Emotions of Justice: Gender, Status, and Legal Performance in Chosŏn Korea*. Seattle: University of Washington Press.

Kim, Jongcheol, and Jonghyun Park. 2012. "Causes and Conditions of Sustainable Judicialization of Politics in Korea." In *The Judicialization of Politics in Asia*, edited by Björn Dressel, 37–55. Oxon: Routledge.

Kim, Marie Seong-Hak. 2012. *Law and Custom in Korea: Comparative Legal History*. Cambridge: Cambridge University Press.

     2016. "Can There Be Good Colonial Law? Korean Law and Jurisprudence under Japanese Rule Revisited." In *The Spirit of Korean Law: Korean Legal History in Context*, edited by Marie Seong-Hak Kim, 129–54. Leiden: Brill.

Kim, Min Joo. 2019. "South Korea Court Strikes Down Six-Decade-Old Abortion Ban." *Washington Post*, April 11, 2019. www.washingtonpost.com/world/south-korea-court-strikes-down-six-decade-old-abortion-ban/2019/04/11/0200f028-5c43-11e9-842d-7d3ed7eb3957_story.html?noredirect=on&utm_term=.1bb58c88a2a6.

Kim, Sunhyuk. 2009. "Civic Engagement and Democracy in South Korea." *Korea Observer* 40 (1): 1–26.

Kim, Sunjoo, and Jungwon Kim (compiled and translated). 2014. *Wrongful Deaths: Selected Inquest Records from Nineteenth-Century Korea.* Seattle: University of Washington Press.

Kim, Youngmin, and Michael J. Pettid, eds. 2011. *Women and Confucianism in Chosŏn Korea: New Perspectives.* Albany: State University of New York Press.

Lim, Sungyun. 2019. *Rules of the House.* Berkeley: University of California Press.

Liu, Sida, and Terence C. Halliday. 2011. "Political Liberalism and Political Embeddedness: Understanding Politics in the Work of Chinese Criminal Defense Lawyers." *Law & Society Review* 45 (4): 831–66.

Marshall, Anna-Maria, and Daniel Crocker Hale. 2014. "Cause Lawyering." *Annual Review of Law and Social Science* 10: 301–20.

Mayali, Laurent, and John S. Yoo, eds. 2014. *Current Issues in Korean Law.* Berkeley: Robbins Collection. www.law.berkeley.edu/files/koreanlaw.pdf.

Merry, Sally Engle. 2006. *Human Rights and Gender Violence: Translating International Law into Local Justice.* Chicago: University of Chicago Press.

Minbyeon. 1998. *Minbyeon baekso* [Minbyeon white paper]. Seoul: Minbyeon.

2018. *Hangukeui gongik ingwon sosong (2)* [Korea's public interest/human rights litigation, Vol. 2]. Seoul: Beopmunsa.

Park, Won-soon. 2003. *Yeoksaga ideureul mujoero harira* [History shall acquit them]. Seoul: Durae.

Risse, Thomas, Stephen C. Ropp, and Kathryn Sikkink, eds. 1999. *The Power of Human Rights: International Norms and Domestic Change.* New York: Cambridge University Press.

Sarat, Austin, and Stuart A. Scheingold, eds. 2001. *Cause Lawyering and the State in a Global Era.* Oxford: Oxford University Press.

2006. *Cause Lawyers and Social Movements.* Stanford: Stanford University Press.

Scheingold, Stuart A. 2004. *The Politics of Rights: Lawyers, Public Policy, and Social Change.* 2nd ed. Ann Arbor: University of Michigan Press.

Shaw, William. 1981. *Legal Norms in a Confucian State.* Berkeley: Institute of East Asian Studies, University of California.

Shaw, William, ed. 1991. *Human Rights in Korea: Historical and Policy Perspectives.* Cambridge: Harvard University Asia Center.

Shin, Gi-Wook, and Paul Chang, eds. 2011. *South Korean Social Movements.* London: Routledge.

Shin, Hyun Bang. 2018. "Urban Movements and the Genealogy of Urban Rights Discourses: The Case of Urban Protesters against Redevelopment and Displacement in Seoul, South Korea." *Annals of the American Association of Geographers* 108 (2): 356–69.

Sidel, Mark. 2010. *Law and Society in Vietnam: The Transition from Socialism in Comparative Perspective.* Cambridge: Cambridge University Press.

Simmons, Beth A. 2009. *Mobilizing for Human Rights: International Law in Domestic Politics.* Cambridge: Cambridge University Press.

Stammers, Neil. 1999. "Social Movements and the Social Construction of Human Rights." *Human Rights Quarterly* 21 (4): 980–1008.

Steinhoff, Patricia G., ed. 2014. *Going to Court to Change Japan.* Ann Arbor: University of Michigan, Center for Japanese Studies.

Stern, Rachel E. 2013. *Environmental Litigation in China: A Study in Political Ambivalence.* Cambridge: Cambridge University Press.

Tam, Waikeung. 2013. *Legal Mobilization under Authoritarianism: The Case of Post-Colonial Hong Kong.* New York: Cambridge University Press.

Towns, Ann E. 2012. "Norms and Social Hierarchies: Understanding International Policy Diffusion 'From Below'." *International Organization* 66 (2): 179–209.

Vanhala, Lisa. 2018. "Is Legal Mobilization for the Birds? Legal Opportunity Structures and Environmental Nongovernmental Organizations in the United Kingdom, France, Finland, and Italy." *Comparative Political Studies* 51 (3): 380–412.

Woo, Margaret Y. K., and Mary E. Gallagher, eds. 2011. *Chinese Justice: Civil Dispute Resolution in Contemporary China*. Cambridge: Cambridge University Press.

Yang, Hyunah, ed. 2013. *Law and Society in Korea*. Cheltenham: Edward Elgar Publishing.

Yang, Kun. 1989. "Law and Society Studies in Korea: Beyond the Hahm Theses." *Law & Society Review* 23 (5): 891–901.

   2002. "Hangugui beobmunhwawa beobui jibae" [Korean legal culture and rule of law]. *Beob cheolhak yeongu* 5(1): 184–202.

Yeo, Andrew, and Danielle Chubb, eds. 2018. *North Korean Human Rights: Activists and Networks*. Cambridge: Cambridge University Press.

Yoon, Dae-kyu. 2010. *Law and Democracy in South Korea: Democratic Development since 1987*. Seoul: Kyungnam University Press.

PART I

Rights in Historical Perspective

Legal Disputes, Women's Legal Voice, and Petitioning Rights in Late Joseon Korea

Jisoo M. Kim[1]

In the second month of 1786, Sodok, a female slave and the wife of Pak Chadol, presented a written petition to King Jeongjo (r. 1776–1800). She stated in her petition that her husband, who was a slave of the Board of Taxation (*Hojo*), died in 1776, and thereafter she had been unfairly levied a tax of her husband's. She thus pleaded to be relieved from the tax burden. Jeongjo considered her grievance legitimate and ordered that her request be granted (*Ilseongnok*, Jeongjo, 1786/2/26).[2]

This short anecdote is just one among a multitude of petitions preserved in historical legal records. While these petitions predate the first usage of the term "rights" (*gwolli*) in Korea by centuries, they nonetheless constitute claims-making in that claimants appealed to commonly accepted norms when seeking to remedy grievances. Interestingly, women, who had limited legal capacity during the Joseon dynasty (1392–1910), filed hundreds of petitions. I argue that women's narrative and linguistic practices in claims-making demonstrate how female subjects appropriated the "discourse of domesticity" and the Confucian rhetoric of female virtue to seek their interests. This argument is based on nearly 600 records of women's petitions from the Joseon dynasty, including at both local and capital levels, and most petitions are from the eighteenth and nineteenth centuries.[3] Compared to extant

---

[1] I would like to thank the *Journal of Asian Studies* for giving its permission to reprint my article, "Women's Legal Voice: Language, Power, and Gender Performativity in Late Joseon Korea," *The Journal of Asian Studies*, 74(3) (August 2015): 667–86. It has been slightly modified to fit into this volume.

[2] All references to lunar calendar dates in the text and notes appear as year/month/day (e.g., 1786/2/26).

[3] Local-level petitions are located in the *Gomunseo* (Old documents) and *Gomunseo jipseong* compiled by the Kyujanggak Archive of Seoul National University and the Academy of Korean Studies, respectively. Unlike petitions submitted to local courts, most of the petitions presented to the king are recorded in official documents such as the *Sillok* (Veritable records), *Ilseongnok* (Records of daily reflections), *Seungjeongwon ilgi* (Daily record of the Royal Secretariat), *Bibyeonsa deungnok* (Records of the Border Defense Command), and *Simnirok* (Records of *simni* [hearings]). Many of the records in these different sources overlap. For example, a number of women's petitions recorded in the *Simnirok* can be traced in the *Sillok* as well as in the *Ilseongnok*. In Han Sang-gwon's research on petitions of the late Joseon, there are detailed statistics based on the *Ilseongnok*'s records during the reign of Jeongjo. Although he provides raw numbers of women's petitions, he does not analyze them, as men's petitions are the focus of his study. For statistics on women's petitions, see S. G. Han (1996, 110–11 and 120–21).

men's petitions from the late Joseon period, the number of women's petitions is relatively small. For example, Han Sang-gwon's (1996, iii) meticulous study identifies 4,427 total petitions submitted to King Jeongjo between 1776 and 1800. Among these, Han documents 108 petitions from elite women and 310 petitions from commoner women, or about 10 percent of the total. Yet these 418 women's petitions do not include those from lowborn women, those submitted to county and provincial courts, or those from periods beyond Jeongjo's reign. Therefore, to complement Han's research, highlight women's voices, and analyze petitions from other regions and time periods, I identified an additional 151 women's petitions that were submitted to county and provincial courts between the mid-seventeenth and the nineteenth centuries. Hence, approximately 25 percent of the 600 petitions I examine are from county and provincial levels; these petitions exist in original form and are rich in anecdotes. Even though women's petitions were fewer in number compared to men's and limited to individual or family grievances, this does not mean that their petitioning activity was less significant when considering the procedures these women went through in petitioning the state. Indeed, women's acts of petitioning alongside their male counterparts greatly influenced the legal culture of the late Joseon period. Sungyun Lim (Chapter 2) and Eunkyung Kim (Chapter 3) similarly demonstrate the value of analyzing women's claims-making, even within the institutional and social constraints placed on women.

Contrary to the common perception that women of the Joseon were silent subjects outside their domestic boundary, their petitioning activity shows that women, irrespective of their status, had the same legal capacity as their male counterparts to appeal grievances. Subordinate agents could make complaints against powerful subjects when the privileges they were allowed to enjoy within their status had been infringed upon. Conversely, while the petitioning practice reinforced the social hierarchy by requiring subjects to execute duties within their status boundary, it concurrently allowed them to seek protection of their position enjoyed within that boundary. As the short opening anecdote shows, even female slaves were recognized as legal subjects and authorized to voice grievances and seek justice. By "legal subjects," I mean those who had the capacity to engage in legal actions, such as filing petitions or suits, entering into contracts, buying or selling, borrowing or lending, and making bequests. Among different kinds of legal activities women engaged in, the primary focus of this chapter is on the practice of women's petitioning.[4]

It is unclear when the appeals system was first institutionalized in Korean history. The extant sources show that people addressed their grievances to the

---

[4]   In *Gomunseo*, it is possible to find a variety of legal sources, such as petitions, contracts, wills, property documents, and officially endorsed documents (*iban*).

state using the appeals system during the Goryeo dynasty (918–1392).[5] But it was not until the Joseon dynasty that the legal channel was established to voice concerns directly to the sovereign. This legal channel was instituted by installing the "petition drum" (*sinmungo*) during Taejong's reign (r. 1400–18) in 1401 based on a neo-Confucian vision that the monarch's mandate relied on listening to his people regardless of one's gender or status.

When petitioning to redress a grievance, petitioners initially turned to county magistrates for rectification. If the grievance was not redressed at the county level, they then appealed to the provincial office. If it still was not redressed, then appellants went to the capital and appealed to the Office of the Inspector General (*Saheonbu*). If the grievance was not fully redressed after all these judicial remedies were exhausted, then petitioners appealed directly to the king as a last resort by beating the petition drum installed in front of the State Tribunal (Gyeongguk daejeon 1978, 473–74).

By no means did this moral and legal mandate and the petitioning processes instantiate rights, as discussed in later chapters in this volume. Yet the drum, installed in front of the State Tribunal (*Uigeumbu*), did provide subjects with an opportunity to redress grievances that had not been rectified in lower courts. With the advent of the petition drum, it was possible for even the voices of the lowest subjects, such as female slaves, to reach the apex of power in a rigidly hierarchical social structure.[6] The underlying meaning of every subject having the legal capacity to petition is that petitioning enabled even the most subordinate agents, such as female slaves, to claim a direct relationship with the authorities, one that provided an opportunity for communication between the ruler and those ruled.

There is no doubt that women's legal position in the Joseon was inferior to men's, especially when taking into consideration women's inability to take the civil service examination, unequal share of inheritances in the latter part of the dynasty, and lack of position in ritual heirship. However, one needs to pay special attention to the state's recognition of women as legal subjects and the power of the legal capacity they exercised when entering courts to file complaints against their family members, relatives, neighbors, and even magistrates. In such a highly stratified and gender-segregated society as the Joseon, it is striking to find that the hierarchies were

---

5 On the transition from the Goryeo to the Joseon dynasty, see Duncan (2000) and Deuchler (1992, 29–87).

6 During the Joseon, the small group of governing aristocrats at the top of the society was known as *yangban*. This group enjoyed most of the socioeconomic privileges. Due to class instability in the late Joseon, *yangban* no longer immediately signified the ruling class, whereas *sadaebu* (scholar-officials), who had reputable lineage and held official positions in the government, did denote the ruling group. There was another small group known as the "middle people" (*jungin*) that consisted mostly of technical specialists and functionaries. Commoners, most of whom were peasants, were called *yangin* or *sangmin* and made up the majority of the population and carried most of the burden of taxation, military service, and corvée labor. Lastly, the lowborn, or *cheonmin*, were mostly slaves but also included those with debased occupations, such as butchers, tanners, shamans, and female entertainers.

neutralized to a certain degree as people of different genders and statuses all interacted in courts as legal subjects.

Based on the recognition of women as legal subjects, it is of course naïve to assume that discrimination did not exist in the realm of law. Inequalities in Confucian law were evident when subjects became the objects of punishment, as punishment was unequally determined based upon one's status, rank, privilege, gender, and age. Also, Confucian law prohibited sons, wives, and slaves to file complaints against fathers, husbands, and masters, respectively. Nevertheless, what I mean by neutralizing gender or status hierarchies here is that every person was recognized as a legal subject when he or she appealed to redress a grievance through petitioning.

The juridical domain was often a site of contestation between privileged and underprivileged, *yangban* (aristocrat) versus commoner, affluent commoner versus destitute commoner, ex-owner versus manumitted slave, widow versus male relative, and public official versus private individual. The legal space was one of the few social sites where women, regardless of status, were empowered to publicly challenge men, even of higher status.[7] In a highly stratified and gender-segregated society such as the Joseon, the puzzling question is how it was possible for the state to recognize every subject regardless of gender or status as an independent legal subject. Since I have limited space here and have discussed this question elsewhere in depth, this chapter introduces women's petitions as claims-making and analyzes their voice as legal agents in the late Joseon.[8] Previous studies have examined the establishment of the petition drum and its practice but have not questioned *how* people of different genders and statuses were empowered to utilize the system (U. G. Han 1956, 357–408; S. G. Han 1996; G. S. Kim 2005).

---

[7]   Despite the proximity of China and Korea, Joseon women shared more similarities with those in the Middle East in terms of their recognition as legal subjects prior to the introduction of a modern Western legal system at the turn of the twentieth century. Islamic law made little distinction between women and men when it came to their legal capacity, and women in Islamic cultures were authorized to engage in legal transactions without depending on men's guardianship. While a husband had the right to control his wife's sexuality, women had the right to manage or dispose of all kinds of property that they acquired, even after marriage (Tucker 2008, 187–99). Women in the Middle East were also empowered to petition in person to seek royal justice (Zarinfraf-Shahr 1997). In the case of China, a woman had to employ a proxy filer, who had to be a coresident male relative. In 1873, the Qing state further restricted women's participation in legal activity by requiring that an adult son file the litigation, unless she had no male relatives. Mark Allee (1994, 148–74) suggests that requiring women to employ proxy filers may have been an artifact of cultural norms that secluded women. Meanwhile, in many jurisdictions of Europe until the 1800s, single women and widows often had the right to own property, draft wills, and appear in court on their own behalf, but married women were restricted in their legal role and prevented from obtaining legal independence (e.g., Blaine 2002, 58; Kuehn 1991, 212–37; Orchard 2002, 12–13). Yet studies show that women were able to exercise power and gain economic independence by appropriating loopholes in law codes.

[8]   The discussion of the state's recognition of every subject regardless of gender or status as legal subjects and the two petition cases used for this article appear in chapters 2 and 3 of my book, *The Emotions of Justice: Gender, Status, and Legal Performance in Joseon Korea* (2015).

By focusing on women's grievances addressed to the state during the Joseon, this chapter unpacks the exercise of petitioning rights and analyzes the narratives women used to seek their interests. Before proceeding, it is worth explaining how this chapter engages with the volume's usage of "rights" or *gwolli*. The term *gwolli* combines two Chinese characters 權 and 利. William Martin and Chinese translators first invented this neologism to translate the English word "rights," which appeared in *Elements of International Law* in 1864 (Liu 1999, 148). It was introduced in Japan the following year by Mitsukuri Rinshō (Feldman 2000, 18). In Korea, the term *gwolli* was first used in official documents such as the *Veritable Records of King Gojong* (r. 1863–1907) in 1883 (*Gojong sillok*, 1883/6/22) and began to appear more commonly in other public writings about a decade later in the 1890s.

It is beyond the scope of this chapter to precisely excavate the initial usage of the term *gwolli* in Korean history. Also, the chapter avoids the hollow debate about whether the Western notion of "rights" existed in Korean legal tradition before the nineteenth century. It is pointless to investigate the modern notion of rights that has its etymological, epistemological, and ideological roots in the Western tradition in an early modern Korean context. We need to avoid the risk of distortion by imposing Western concepts onto Korean legal and cultural formations.

The lack of a word "rights" before the nineteenth century in Korea does not mean the concept was absent. Although people in the Joseon did not use the same language of rights associated with freedom and equality as in the contemporary Korean cases discussed in other chapters, they sought legal justice by going to court to protect what they were legally entitled to, such as life and property. As mentioned earlier, every subject regardless of gender or status was conferred with the capacity to engage in legal activities such as filing petitions or suits, entering into contracts, buying or selling, borrowing or lending, and making bequests.

Based on legal sources such as petitions, contracts, land deeds, wills, lawsuit documents, and criminal records, scholars have shown how people actively went to court to redress grievances and sought the state's protection. It is not that the lack of a Korean term equivalent to the English word "rights" implied the lack of such a concept, but rather it was expressed in different languages according to its own cultural features. For example, when people exercised their petitioning right, they would claim that they were seeking legal protection to "relieve *won*" or rectify injustice. The feeling of injustice is what motivated people to go to court to exercise their rights. The state's recognition of one's embodiment of *won* made it possible to confer the right to petition to every subject regardless of gender or status. Although the society was based on a hereditary status system that was hierarchical and discriminated subjects according to one's social status, the judicial system protected people within their status boundaries while strictly preventing them from defying social order. In other words, the legal system functioned as a safety valve but simultaneously functioned to reinforce the state's legitimacy and enforced subjects to comply with social norms (J. S. Kim, 2015, 1–13).

The aim of this chapter is to demonstrate how female subjects exercised their petitioning rights and what narrative strategies these women utilized to actively seek their interests. By closely reading women's petitions, I show how women used the narrative of pity to make their case. In the following, I first outline my method of narrative analysis. I then describe the Joseon dynasty's neo-Confucian system of rule and then delve into several case studies that illustrate how women exercised legal rights to address their grievances and shaped their narrative to claim their interests.

1.1 THE LINGUISTIC PRACTICES OF CLAIMS-MAKING

My focus is to analyze women's linguistic practices manifested in petitions to show how their patterns of behavior shaped, molded, and formed gendered legal practice. By examining women's petitions addressed to the state, I show how their linguistic practices, regardless of their different social statuses, converged to meet the demands of the linguistic market in the realm of law. In doing so, I demonstrate how both elite and non-elite women utilized legal narratives based on Confucian language that adhered to the official representation of gender distinctions. Although women were conferred with the same legal capacity as men, their concerns were limited to personal and domestic affairs, unlike men, who also appealed on collective griev-ances such as tax and corruption. The practice of petitioning was performed in a culturally restricted setting that was regulated by legal codes and bound within preexisting norms. By carrying gender norms to the legal space, the gender hierarchy was reinforced through women's narrative strategy as they appropriated the "dis-course of domesticity." However, women as legal agents were also re-gendering legal identity by constructing a sense of personhood via their petitioning activity. Through articulating their gendered narratives, women struggled to defend not only them-selves and their own sense of morality but also their entire family.[9]

Borrowing Judith Butler's (2007) usage of gender performativity, I demonstrate how female petitioners possessed a keen gender consciousness, and how they constructed their identity through a particular vocabulary of gender behavior. Performativity of gender, according to Butler (1999, 163–80), is a *stylized repetition of acts*, imitation, or miming of hegemonic gender and very often the repetition of oppressive gender norms. Engaging with Butler's reflections on how a woman must negotiate a position for her identity in relation to established prescriptive norms, I consider how women's gender identity was deeply related to their linguistic usage of Confucian rhetoric in their representations of grievance. Through their repetition

---

[9] Susan Hirsch, in her study of Swahili Kenya, eloquently shows how women worked within the confines of Islamic law while they utilized the social conventions of female speech and behaviors to shape rules in their favor. In court, women represented themselves as obedient and persevering wives using the conventional gendered speech but simultaneously spoke of husbands' shortcomings (Hirsch 1998). I was inspired by Hirsch's book when formulating ideas related to women's legal activities in the Joseon.

of petitioning acts, women performed gendered legal identity by appropriating Confucian language of female virtue and a narrative of pity. In her examination of late Joseon-era criminal records and female suicide, Jungwon Kim (2007, 2014) similarly claims that women negotiated their positions based on their socioeconomic status in their legal testimonies. My examination of petitions corroborates this claim and finds that the kind of grievances women addressed differed based on their socioeconomic status. My study further shows how women sought to win the favor of ruling authorities and advance their interests by using a narrative strategy that relied on Confucian rhetoric about female virtue and appropriated women's weaker position in the society to achieve their ends.

1.2 THE CONFUCIANIZATION OF LANGUAGE IN LEGAL SPACE

Conventional wisdom about the Confucianization of Korea suggests that numerous societal changes occurred through a gradual process and only became evident by the mid-seventeenth century (Choe 1966; Deuchler 1992; Haboush 1991; Peterson 1996). The changes brought adverse effects on women, especially the elite, as they were deprived of ritual, economic, and social privileges. Although one cannot deny the negative effects Confucianization had on women, it must be emphasized that women were not deprived of legal capacity even as they lost other privileges toward the late Joseon. Examining their exercise of that legal capacity reveals just how Confucianization affected women.

When the Joseon dynasty was established in 1392 and adopted neo-Confucianism as its state ideology, the society underwent drastic changes as the state envisioned a normative Confucian society by implementing the Confucian model of patriarchy and patrilineality. This Confucianization of society was a process of change accomplished through a dynamic interaction between Confucian norms and Korean indigenous practices (Deuchler 1992; Haboush 1991). Although certain elements of Confucianism were in place before the Joseon, it was with the advent of this dynasty that neo-Confucianism was adopted as official ideology and was accompanied by a reorganization of the indigenous family structure. For example, during the Goryeo dynasty, sons and daughters were treated as equal members of the family, whether married or unmarried, and received equal shares of inheritances. The marriage practice was uxorilocal, and women remained active in their natal homes. Remarriage was not a problem, and women divorced when necessary. The society was bilateral, which allowed daughters' children to succeed the family line.

In the Joseon, these practices shifted according to the Confucian patriarchal and patrilineal systems. As ancestral rites were introduced, the ritual duties were given to sons only[10]; daughters were no longer treated as equal members of the family and

---

[10] In the early years of the Joseon, daughters shared ritual duties and continued to receive equal shares of inheritance with sons. However, these practices gradually changed as the society Confucianized by the mid-seventeenth century (Deuchler 1992).

thus received lesser shares of inheritances (Deuchler 1992; Peterson 1996); the marriage practice shifted to virilocal, and women left their natal homes to serve their husbands' families; remarriage became socially stigmatized, and restrictions on remarriage were imposed on elite women; clear demarcations were drawn between legal wife and concubine, creating hierarchy and tension between them; and the society shifted from bilateral to patrilineal, such that only through sons could the family line be succeeded.

However, as recent studies on women of the Joseon have demonstrated, exploring the lives of non-elite women reveals that these women led much more diverse lives compared to elite women. Their lives show a much more complex picture according to their socioeconomic situations, and they were less bound by official representations of gender norms (Jeong 2001; G. S. Kim 2005; J. Kim 2007; J. M. Kim 2010b; Kim and Pettid 2011). These recent studies are significant in that they use a variety of sources to examine the lives of non-elite women, who had been mostly invisible throughout Korean history. The results of these recent studies raise critical questions about the late Joseon society: To what extent were the lower strata Confucianized? If sexual and marriage practices of non-elites were not greatly influenced by the Confucianization process, then what aspects of Confucianization were reflected in the lives of non-elites, who were the majority of the population? In order to answer these questions, it is necessary to break down the Confucianization process into various components and explore its multilayered manifestations in the context of a gendered and stratified society.

As far as women's linguistic practices in petitions are concerned, however, they were Confucianized in the sense that female subjects relied on the rhetoric of Confucian virtue regardless of their different social status backgrounds. For example, as women's concerns revolved around domestic affairs, it is very common to find women's narratives emphasizing their marital fidelity and filial piety.[11] Even though non-elite women had different lives than elites in many ways, the petitions indicate that they also knew how to use the Confucian language when engaging in dialogue with neo-Confucian bureaucrats. According to Pierre Bourdieu (1994, 45–46), a unified linguistic market dominated by an official language is created in the process of state formation, and this state language becomes the theoretical norm that defines linguistic practices. The political process of unification is then determined by a set of speaking subjects who are led to adopt the official language, which then reinforces the authority by integrating the subjects into a single linguistic community. When the linguistic practice in the juridical domain of the Joseon is taken into consideration, one can see that legal subjects adopted the official Confucian language, and the state succeeded in creating a "single linguistic community." This not only enhanced the power of the state but also empowered female subjects as they demanded that

---

[11]   For a discussion of elite women's petitioning activity during the late Joseon, see J. M. Kim (2009, 2010a).

the state listen and redress the grievances of weaker subjects to manifest its supposed benevolence of Confucian governance.

1.3 WOMEN'S CHOICE OF LANGUAGE

In petitioning both local authorities and the king, women submitted written petitions in two different languages: classical Chinese and vernacular Korean. This was one of the primary differences between women's and men's petitions. Since the invention of the Korean script (*Eonmun*) in 1446, the Joseon dynasty had maintained a diglossic culture in the literary space. While classical Chinese dominated the writings of the public realm, women mostly used vernacular Korean in the private realm. Men also used vernacular Korean when exchanging letters with female members of their family. Because classical Chinese was perceived as men's language and was also difficult to learn, women were educated with vernacular Korean, which was much easier to acquire. Although the two representative volumes of Joseon legal codes, the *Gyeongguk daejeon* (Administrative Great Code) and the *Sok daejeon* (Continuation of the Great Code), do not explicitly stipulate the written language for petitions, it was taken for granted that petitions should be submitted in classical Chinese, as were all other public documents.

Although the state conferred the legal capacity to petition to all subjects, women, as well as men of the lower social strata, who were mostly illiterate in classical Chinese, were unable to draft petitions themselves. Thus, it was necessary for them to rely on scriveners or male family members who were versed in classical Chinese.[12] Despite this limitation that women faced, what is intriguing is that they actively appropriated their knowledge and submitted petitions in vernacular Korean instead, thereby challenging the public literary space. This public literary space had also been challenged by dowager queens who wrote royal instructions in the vernacular Korean script (see Haboush 2002). However, writing royal instructions at court was limited to women of the royal family, whereas drafting petitions applied to women of all social statuses, including aristocrats, commoners, and the lowborn.

The earliest Korean script petition I found was submitted in 1509, during the reign of King Jungjong, by a daughter of the royal clan whose name was Cheolbi. She appealed to be exempted from being demoted to a private slave. The court officials argued that her crime (unspecified in the record) was unpardonable, and they further criticized her for writing the petition in the Korean script, which digressed from the proper form (*Jungjong sillok* 1509/4/16, and 1509/9/11). Nevertheless, the king granted her immunity from being sent as a slave to the house of a meritorious subject (*Jungjong sillok* 1510/12/12). Later, during the Gwanghae-gun period (r. 1608–23), government officials first discussed seriously whether Korean

---

[12] For details on scriveners, see Pak (1996, 337).

script petitions should be accepted.[13] Although the state made no effort to codify this matter, it eventually acknowledged such petitions because rejecting them countered the state's intention of redressing grievances.[14]

Among the 151 petitions that I found had been submitted to county and provincial courts during the late Joseon, 25 were drafted in vernacular Korean and the rest in classical Chinese. Of the twenty-five vernacular Korean petitions, eleven were presented by elite *yangban* women and fourteen by commoner women. For an example of a vernacular Korean petition concerning a land dispute submitted by a commoner woman, see Figure 1.1. Although the numbers show that women used classical Chinese in petitions more often than vernacular Korean, what is vital about the petitions written in the Korean script is that they were officially recognized by local governments, despite the fact that such petitions did not follow formal written language.

Although the state continued to take issue with women's vernacular petitions when presented to the king, the petitions submitted to county and provincial levels show that women succeeded in receiving official red seals even with the language they employed in the domestic sphere. Kim Gyeong-suk (2005, 97) suggests that female petitioners must have relied on scriveners or male kin even when they drafted the petitions in vernacular Korean, and thus their role was limited. When viewed this way, it is not only female petitioners whose role was limited, but also illiterate non-elite men. Yet it is conceivable that illiterate female and male petitioners shaped their own narratives, even if they did not write the petitions themselves. Whoever wrote the petitions could not have put pen to paper without the stories told by the petitioners. At the same time, scriveners may have employed narrative skills to better articulate grievances when producing written petitions.[15] Unfortunately, we have no access to original stories told by female petitioners to scriveners. It is difficult to assess to what extent the stories presented in petitions followed the petitioners' original stories. Most likely, however, the role of drafters was not to invent new stories but to effectively package the grievances of petitioners to win favor.[16]

When taking into consideration that even men relied on professional male scriveners, there is not much point in discussing whether it was women's voices in their written petitions. From a gender perspective, what is more noteworthy in the

[13] The two versions of the *Gwanghae-gun ilgi* both record the discussion of whether the Korean script petition submitted by Madam Kim, wife of Yi Hongno (1560–1610), should be accepted. See *Gwanghae-gun ilgi*, 1610/5/5, 1610/5/10, and 1610/5/16. Also cited in Haboush (2002, 250).

[14] For example, Madam Yi, wife of the private scholar (*yuhak*) Jo Jinseong, submitted a Korean script petition, but the state did not question its written language (*Ilseongnok*, Jeongjo, 1787/4/4).

[15] Unfortunately, the role of scriveners is almost invisible from the extant sources. However, it is possible to find scant writings about them in literary works. For the role of scriveners in the Joseon, see Pak (1974, 257) and S. G. Han (2008, 284–89).

[16] For the significant role of scriveners and the crafting of plaints in late imperial China, see Macauley (1998) and Karasawa (2007).

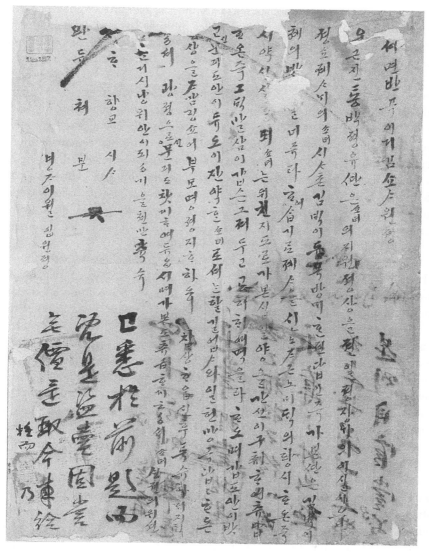

FIGURE 1.1 A commoner woman Kim's vernacular petition (land dispute). *Gomunseo* 194167. Courtesy of Kyujanggak Archives, Seoul National University.

context of Confucian society is the multilayered process of storytelling in petitioning and how the process eventually generated gendered legal narrative. In other words, instead of focusing on whether women ipso facto wrote their petitions, it is more fruitful to discuss the gendered narrative that was produced as a result of multiple actors involved in the storytelling. If petitioners told their grievances, then it was the scriveners' task to "craft" those stories to amplify the narrative of grievance.[17] The process of producing written petitions entailed multiple layers of storytelling, which ultimately generated a bifurcated, gendered legal narrative that conformed to the conventional norms.

In addition to these multiple layers of storytelling, what is noteworthy is their participation in the process of drafting the petitions and the fact that it was female subjects rather than their male counterparts who decided to petition in the Korean script, which was unacceptable in the public realm. If women relied entirely on men's assistance, it hardly would have been likely for vernacular Korean petitions to appear in court. Therefore, I contend that it was a woman's choice to draft a petition in the language she was versed in when seeking her own interests. This was a way of identifying herself and representing femaleness through the very performance of public writing. By capitalizing on the capacity to petition, women challenged the literary space that was dominated by classical Chinese and extended the usage of vernacular Korean to the legally sanctioned public realm.

In addition, it was not uncommon for women to strategically use both languages when they submitted several petitions. For example, Madam Cho, who was involved in a property dispute, submitted four petitions in total; the first petition, submitted in the ninth month of 1816, was written in classical Chinese, but the other three petitions, submitted in the following month, were all drafted in vernacular Korean.[18] When petitions written in classical Chinese and vernacular Korean are compared, there is not much difference in the content, which makes it difficult to discern the petitioner's intention behind using the two different languages. The petitions do not provide even a hint concerning the language issue. However, it is not far-fetched to assume that it was female subjects themselves who made the language choice.

As early as 1509, women began to utilize vernacular Korean to communicate with authorities at the capital level. However, Korean script petitions, although not entirely rejected, continued to be criticized when presented to the king. In stark contrast, Korean script petitions from the later Joseon show that they were officially recognized at county and provincial courts. This point is vital because it reflects how women, as legal agents, actively capitalized on their legal capacity to petition. The fact that it is rare to find men's Korean script petitions prior to the late nineteenth century further substantiates how it was women who successfully introduced vernacular Korean to the petitioning process. It was possible, at least at the local level, to observe Korea's diglossic culture in the public literary sphere, previously dominated by classical Chinese, through the performance of women's legal writing.

---

[17] For a discussion of reading "fictional" elements in pardon letters in sixteenth-century France, see Davis (1987).

[18] Hong Eun-jin (1998) first introduced Madam Cho's vernacular Korean script petition in her article.

1.3.1 *Tension between Madam Yi and Secondary Son*

Madam Yi's vernacular Korean petition shows that she actually drafted the petition herself. In the will she left for her children, she emphasized that she was writing in vernacular Korean with her own handwriting to show that she was the person drafting the will. Similarly, she had also drafted the petition, which shared the contents of the will, in vernacular Korean.[19] Madam Yi submitted the petition in the language she was accustomed to based on her own discretion. Madam Yi's petition, which was drafted in the mid-1650s, was about a legal dispute with Seogu, who was the son of her stepson Seungji's concubine.[20] She filed a complaint to punish him for attempting to usurp the lineal heir's position of the family, along with other crimes he had committed. Madam Yi was the second wife of Hwang Yeoil (1560–1608), who was a high-ranking scholar-official during the reign of King Seonjo (r. 1567–1608). Hwang had a son named Seungji with his first wife and then had four sons with Madam Yi, in the order of Jungmin, Jungheon, Jungsun, and Jungwon. Seungji, who was the lineal heir, failed to produce a son with his primary wife and thus needed to adopt a son in order to maintain the patriline. Hwang, before his death, had ordered Seungji to adopt one of his half-brothers' sons. Following this wish, Seungji decided to adopt Seongnae, Jungheon's son. However, Seungji's untimely death led his concubine's son Seogu to covet Seongnae's position and conspire to replace him with Jungmin's son. Seogu claimed that it was illegitimate to adopt Jungheon's son while Jungmin's son, who was the eldest in the line, was alive.

Madam Yi regarded Seogu's action as a challenge and petitioned the king in order to report his attempt to go against his father's will in selecting the heir of the family.[21] After reviewing Madam Yi's petition, the state banished Seogu to Baengnyeong Island for three years. Madam Yi, still concerned that he would continue to cause trouble, decided to write a will to confirm Seongnae's position as lineal heir. On the twentieth day of the third month in 1651, she drafted a will stating that if Seogu and Jungmin fabricated the document of family succession and attempted to displace Seongnae, then other family members should take her testimony as evidence to report to the government, asking to punish them. She ended the will by stating that she had drafted it herself in vernacular Korean to show her determination to maintain family order.[22]

On the eighth day of the first month in 1656, Madam Yi drafted a petition to submit to the magistrate of her county. Unlike other petition documents in the records, this petition lacks an official's written judgment, which implies that it was

---

[19] Madam Yi's petition and will can be found in Kim Yong-gyeong (2001). The aim of the journal, *Munheon gwa haeseok* [Sources and Interpretation], is to introduce newly excavated sources intact with scholarly analysis. Madam Yi's original petition and will are both introduced in this journal.

[20] For a discussion of secondary sons and their inferior status in the Joseon, see Deuchler (1988/1989).

[21] The petition sent to the king no longer exists but is mentioned in Madam Yi's will, as is the petition written in 1656.

[22] The will was first introduced in Yi (1982). It was reintroduced in Y. G. Kim (2001, 79–82).

either never submitted to the county office or is a copy of the version that had been submitted. Whatever the case, Madam Yi wrote the petition in vernacular Korean and intended to have Seogu punished for a second time. She addressed how Seogu had continued to misbehave even after his release from Baengnyeong Island. Seogu stole Madam Yi's family document and bribed powerful officials in the central bureaucracy to gain their support. Moreover, he tore up the letter she sent to him asking him to return the document he stole. In her petition, she stated:

> I am extremely afraid to report to Your Honor, who is in such a high position. I am old and sick, but I write this petition without any shame or fear because my rage has soared up to the sky. . . . When he [Seogu] read my note, he tore it into pieces and humiliated me in every possible way and never showed up. How on earth can he be so insolent and vicious! . . . I first pitied him because he was, in one way or another, one of my family members. Because I pitied him, I am humiliated by him today. . . . Please consider the following six crimes he committed and punish him strictly based on the laws: the crime of humiliating the legitimate grandmother of the family, the crime of betraying the master-slave relationship, the crime of attempting to succeed his father's lineage by following the father's bloodline instead of his mother's, the crime of stealing the family document and selling it, the crime of not participating in the ancestral rituals for his father, and the crime of abandoning his mother. Please consider each of these six points and apply all the existing laws to make him realize the importance of state law (*gukbeop*). By doing so, please protect this aged and weak widow. I end here as I am afraid to write any further. (Y. G. Kim 2001, 82–87)[23]

Although Madam Yi's grievance stemmed from Seogu's attempt to deprive Seongnae of his rightful position, the tone of her petition resonates more of her rage provoked by humiliation or frustration. Madam Yi was determined to punish Seogu for disrespecting the senior member of the household and challenging her authority. It was possible for Madam Yi to make a complaint against Seogu because he was a son of a concubine. She also described her relationship with Seogu as master–slave: Seogu's mother was previously Madam Yi's slave. Madam Yi allowed Seungji to take her slave as a concubine when he had asked for permission. According to the matrilfilial succession law (*jongmobeop*), the status of offspring was defined by the mother's status. If Seogu's mother bore him without having gained commoner status, then in principle his status would have been slave. Because his master was the grandmother and senior member of the family, it was possible for him to live a life that distinguished him from ordinary slaves.

In her vernacular Korean petition, Madam Yi opened and ended her statement by relying on a narrative of pity, which is very common in women's petitions, emphasizing her age and illness. As a widow and senior member of her household, she appealed to the magistrate regarding how Seogu, a secondary son, had dared

---

[23] All the translation of original sources in this article is mine.

challenge her authority and thereby dishonored her. When writing her petition, she utilized the narrative of pity by underlining her position as a feeble widow but simultaneously claimed her authority as head of the household. While relying on the narrative of pity, she urged the magistrate to punish Seogu, stating that the laws should be applied appropriately to restore her honor and protect her interests. In women's petitions of the Joseon, it is not difficult to find instances where female subjects rely on the narrative of pity, emphasizing their subordinate position as women but concurrently use strong statements to seek their interests.

1.3.2 *Rights Claiming on Behalf of Family Members*

The next case, which is about a gravesite dispute and written in classical Chinese, shows how a non-elite woman similarly used a narrative of pity to achieve her ends. Gravesites were an issue about which women of different statuses commonly petitioned, along with issues of property.[24] A gravesite dispute, known as *sansong* in Korean, was about the usage of a mountainside or gravesite. Along with suits involving land and slaves, this was considered one of the three major types of lawsuits in the late Joseon period. Unlike land and slave litigation, gravesite disputes were rarely witnessed in the earlier part of the dynasty. However, they gradually increased as the society Confucianized toward the later Joseon and became the most frequently filed type of lawsuit, especially in the eighteenth and nineteenth centuries.

Scholars who have examined this issue have claimed that it reflected broader socioeconomic problems of the late Joseon period and was not merely about land used for graves. One of the reasons people increasingly engaged in this type of dispute was that the state lacked the ability to devise an appropriate policy regarding the usage of mountains according to its changing practices. Although mountains were treated as public property, subjects devised various means to possess them. For instance, people demarcated the boundary surrounding an ancestor's gravesite and inhibited woodsmen or others from trespassing to gather firewood or cut trees. As the gravesite zone passed down three or four generations, it gradually came to be possessed by private individuals. By the end of the Joseon, contracts show that different zones of mountains were bought and sold like any other private property. Because the state neither punished nor officially approved the possession of mountain areas by private individuals, the number of gravesite disputes continually increased and became one of the major social phenomena in the late Joseon (Jeon 1996, 1998; S. G. Kim 1993).

In addition to understanding the gravesite dispute as a conflict over possession, one can also see it as a conflict stemming from the consolidation of the neo-Confucian patrilineal system. Although this type of dispute was initially considered to be a conflict only among elite aristocrats, it gradually spread to even the lowborn

---

[24] For a discussion of elite women's property dispute, see Jisoo M. Kim (2013).

by the late eighteenth century (G. S. Kim 2002). The most common type of gravesite dispute occurred when someone furtively buried a body in another's ancestor's gravesite in order to dispossess them of their site. The following case, that of commoner woman Jeong, manifests such a dispute and also reflects the typical strategy defenders used when they were sued. Defenders purposefully delayed exhuming a body day after day in order to displace the gravesite zone through the presence of the body.

In the third month of the year *sinhae*, a commoner woman with the surname Jeong, wife of Kim Manbok and resident of Gongju County of Chungcheong Province, submitted a petition written in classical Chinese to the magistrate of Geumsan County of Jeolla Province, concerning a gravesite dispute.[25] Prior to this petition, she had initially appealed to the predecessor of the current magistrate in a complaint against Yi Sunbong, who had stealthily dug up the front segment of her father-in-law's gravesite and buried his own relative's body there. The first magistrate issued an order to exhume the body and bury it elsewhere. However, Yi deliberately delayed carrying out the order by providing endless excuses. Jeong's husband was aggrieved by the situation and ultimately became ill. Jeong used the narrative of pity when addressing her grievance, stating:

> Under such circumstances, how could I sustain my life to tragically live alone? I planned to grab a hoe and go to Yi Sunbong's gravesite to dig up the body and kill myself afterward. My husband will then recover from this and my mother-in-law will also be able to preserve her life. This is my wish. I bow and implore Your Honor to redress my grievance. I beg a thousand and ten thousand times and hope Your Honor will settle this case. (*Gomunseo* 16:200–201)

The magistrate gave an order to investigate Yi's crime and to bring a drawing of the two gravesites. The magistrate commanded that if Yi's trespassing of the burial site was deliberate, he should be arrested. Although the petition does not provide further information, it seems Yi was directed to exhume the body according to Jeong's ensuing petition.

In the eleventh month of that same year, Jeong appealed again because Yi had failed to follow the order. She traveled to Geumsan and sojourned there for about twenty days waiting to directly petition the magistrate, who was out of town. When he returned, she pleaded to him once again about her situation. After reviewing the petition, the magistrate commanded that Yi be punished with beating, and this time he specifically stipulated a date by which to exhume the body (*Gomunseo* 18:438–39).

---

[25] The date of the petition is unknown except that it was submitted in the year *sinhae*, which could be 1731, 1791, or 1851, depending on the sixty-year cycle in which the year fell. The private documents, including petitions, in the *Gomunseo* (Old documents) volumes compiled by the Kyujanggak Archive of Seoul National University and the Academy of Korean Studies are mostly from the late Joseon period.

Despite the magistrate's command, Yi continued to shirk his duty to exhume the body. Jeong had no choice but to visit Geumsan for the third time in the eighth month of the year *eulmyo*.[26] However, the magistrate was suddenly reassigned to a post in Daegu and was replaced by a new one. Jeong reiterated to the new magistrate what had been previously addressed and entreated that her grievance be redressed. She stated:

> I feel that even if I use my ten fingers to dig the ground, this [conflict] will end only when the body has been moved. I bow and plead to Your Honor to examine the documents of this case in detail and sympathize with my grievance. Please urge [Yi] to exhume [the body] by a designated date so that my husband and I, whose lives are about to cease, can sustain our lives. I beg a thousand and ten thousand times with my tears of blood and hope that Your Honor will settle this case. (*Gomunseo* 18:439–40)

The magistrate ordered that Yi be arrested and interrogated as to why he was not exhuming the body even though he had lost the litigation. He commanded Yi to exhume it by the tenth day of the tenth month (*Gomunseo* 18:439–40). As Yi failed to execute this new order, Jeong desperately petitioned the magistrate again in the same month. She stated that when her husband heard of the magistrate's command, there was hope for him to recover. However, his joy lasted only momentarily, as Yi again neglected the order. The magistrate, like his predecessors, commanded that Yi be vigorously pressed and arrested (*Gomunseo* 18:440–41).

In Jeong's case, Yi had continuously put off digging up the body by appropriating a loophole in the law. In principle, only the person who had buried the body was permitted to exhume it, and those who arbitrarily dug without authorization were exiled. Even the county office was not allowed to order compulsory exhumation unless the case was considered particularly extreme (G. S. Kim 2002, 75–83). Thus, if Yi risked being punished to protect the gravesite zone, it was difficult to arbitrate the case since Jeong would have been punished for exhuming the body.

The outcome of Jeong's case remains unknown, besides the fact that Yi was ordered to move the body. Nevertheless, the significance of Jeong's petitions lies in the usage of a narrative of pity as her petitioning strategy and effort to appeal several times to the county office, which was far away from her residence, in order to reclaim the gravesite of her father-in-law, even though her husband was alive and technically should have done the petitioning.

Because marriage did not affect women's right to petition, wives often represented husbands when the husbands themselves were incapable of appearing at court. As we have seen in Jeong's case, when women did appear to petition on family concerns as wives, their narratives were constructed to show that they appealed for the sake of their husbands' well-being, which would ultimately aid the entire family. Such a narrative complemented women in representing female virtues and made it

---

[26] The year *eulmyo* could refer to 1735, 1795, or 1855.

seem as though they were complying with gender norms without defying patriarchal authority.

As shown in cases analyzed in this chapter, women utilized a narrative of pity and evoked the female gender when addressing grievances to convey that the degree of grievance or the sense of being wronged was felt much greater by widows, wives, and mothers than by male subjects. However, this does not necessarily mean that such a narrative only implied female weakness. For instance, Jeong stressed her pain as a wife by elaborating on how she was undergoing hardships due to her husband's illness and how it was beyond her capacity as a woman to resolve the conflict. However, she concurrently characterized herself as a strong agent who was ready to assume a patriarchal role for the sake of the family. She conveyed her firm determination by stating that she even planned to grab a hoe and exhume the body, then kill herself afterward. Because her husband failed to psychologically overcome his grief, Jeong undertook responsibility on the part of the entire family and confronted Yi herself. While her husband was incapacitated by the dispute, she traveled at least five times to Geumsan to reclaim the gravesite of her father-in-law, which reflects the vulnerability of the husband's authority. By using a narrative that intricately entwined both femininity and masculinity, Jeong was gendering herself but simultaneously reaffirming the gender hierarchy. Conversely, she was redefining norms of womanhood by representing both femininity and masculinity through her exercise of the domestic patriarch's legal role.

In both the mid and late Joseon, the narrative used in women's petitions relied on the Confucian language that was expected by the state when entering the legal realm, but concurrently their narratives were constructed in a way that best suited their interests depending on their position within the household. Although women's lived experiences varied according to their different social statuses, linguistic practices converged across status boundaries through the Confucian language of female virtue. Being able to use such language did not necessarily mean every female subject lived according to the prescribed norms. However, by using the conventional form of speech, women voiced their concerns to seek their interests and did not remain silent.

1.4 CONCLUSION

In the juridical domain of the Joseon, gender and status hierarchies remained neutral in terms of a subject's legal capacity; this means that even female slaves were allowed to bring suits against male aristocrats. Since the state upheld neo-Confucianism as its sole ideology and reorganized society according to patriarchal, patrilineal, primogeniture, and gender systems that conflicted with some indigenous practices, the juridical domain was used as a space to contest and negotiate grievances generated by the new systems. At the level of official representation, the state clearly attempted to impose a uniform vision of gender order based on Confucian norms. However, the state's creation of new policies to enforce gender order was fraught with contradictions. Although the state forced female subjects to internalize Confucian gender norms, it was also the state that provided leeway for women to voice their concerns stemming from the same Confucian gender system. Furthermore, women exercised legal agency through the use of vernacular Korean, which eventually penetrated the literary space dominated by classical Chinese in the public realm.

By carrying Confucian gender ethics enforced in the domestic sphere to the legal sphere, cultural conventions about gender norms and hierarchy were reinforced through women's linguistic practices despite the fact that women and men were equally recognized as legal subjects. What female subjects gained from addressing personal grievances was a sense of personhood constructed around the Confucian patriarchal system. Petitioning to redress grievances at times reinforced the gender hierarchy but at other times enabled women to challenge domestic patriarchy and manifest a powerful form of female agency. For those who were wronged, petitioning was a means of self-assertion and self-construction. Their agency was represented through the performance of petitioning when women were legally violated as moral individuals.

By capitalizing on the rights to petition, legal subjects engaged in dialogue with the authorities, which enabled them to make a profound assertion of personhood by employing various narrative strategies to defend their own sense of morality. Women expressed their grievances and underlined their weakness through narratives of pity, vulnerability, and subordination within society but at the same time boldly demanded that the state had a mandate to redress their grievance. Conversely, while cultural conventions about gender norms were reinforced in the judicial domain through their discourse of domesticity, women as legal subjects exercised agency by actively appropriating the petition system and using vernacular Korean and narratives of Confucian female virtue to advance their interests.

REFERENCES

Primary Sources

Gojong sillok [Veritable records of King Gojong]. http://sillok.history.go.kr/id/wza_12006022_004.

Gomunseo [Old documents]. Compiled by Kyujanggak Institute of Seoul National University. Vols. 16–26.

Gomunseo jipseong [Compilation volume of *Old documents*]. Compiled by Academy of Korean Studies. 80 vols.

Gwanghaegun-ilgi [Daily records of King Gwanghae-gun]. In *Joseon wangjo sillok* [Veritable records of the kings of the Joseon dynasty]. 48 vols. Reprint, Seoul: Guksa pyeonchan wiwonhoe, 1970.

Gyeongguk daejeon [Administrative Great Code]. 1978. Translated by Beopjecheo. Seoul: Iljisa.

Ilseongnok [Records of daily reflections]. 1992. Edited by Kyujanggak Institute of Seoul National University. Seoul: Kyujanggak Institute of Seoul National University.

Jungjong sillok [Veritable records of King Jungjong]. In *Joseon wangjo sillok* [Veritable records of the kings of the Joseon dynasty]. 48 vols. Reprint, Seoul: Guksa pyeonchan wiwonhoe, 1970.

Seungjeongwon ilgi [Daily record of the Royal Secretariat]. 1961–. Seoul: Guksa pyeonchan wiwonhoe.

Simnirok [Records of *simni* (hearings)]. 1998–. Translated by Minjok munhwa chujinhoe. 6 vols. Seoul: Minjok munhwa chujinhoe.

Sok daejeon [Continuation of the Great Code]. 1965. Seoul: Beopjecheo.

Secondary Sources

Allee, Mark. 1994. *Law and Local Society in Late Imperial China: Northern Taiwan in the Nineteenth Century*. Stanford: Stanford University Press.

Blaine, Marcia Schmidt. 2002. "Women and the New Hampshire Provincial Government." In *Petitions in Social History*, edited by Lex Heerma van Voss, 57–77. Cambridge: Cambridge University Press.

Bourdieu, Pierre. 1994. *Language and Symbolic Power*. Cambridge: Harvard University Press.

Butler, Judith. 1999. *Gender Trouble: Feminism and the Subversion of Identity*. New York: Routledge.

——— 2007. "Performative Acts and Gender Constitution: An Essay in Phenomenology and Feminist Theory." In *The Performance Studies Reader*, edited by Henry Bial, 187–99. New York: Routledge.

Choe, Jae-seok. 1966. *Hanguk gajok yeongu* [A study of the Korean family]. Seoul: Minjung seogwan.

Davis, Natalie Zemon. 1987. *Fiction in the Archives: Pardon Tales and Their Tellers in Sixteenth-Century France*. Stanford: Stanford University Press.

Deuchler, Martina. 1988/1989. "Heaven Does Not Discriminate: A Study of Secondary Sons in Joseon Korea." *Journal of Korean Studies* 6: 121–64.

——— 1992. *The Confucian Transformation of Korea: A Study of Society and Ideology*. Cambridge, MA: Council on East Asian Studies, Harvard University, distributed by Harvard University Press.

Duncan, John. 2000. *The Origins of the Joseon Dynasty*. Seattle: University of Washington Press.

Feldman, Eric A. 2000. *The Ritual of Rights in Japan: Law, Society, and Health Policy*. New York: Cambridge University Press.

Haboush, JaHyun Kim. 1991. "The Confucianization of Korean Society." In *The East Asian Region: Confucian Heritage and Its Modern Adaptation*, edited by Gilbert Rozman, 84–110. Princeton: Princeton University Press.

——— 2002. "Gender and Politics of Language in Joseon Korea." In *Rethinking Confucianism: Past and Present in China, Japan, Korea, and Vietnam*, edited by Benjamin A. Elman, John B. Duncan, and Herman Ooms, 220–57. UCLA Asia Pacific Monograph Series. Los Angeles: UCLA Asia Institute.

Han, Sang-gwon. 1996. *Joseon hugi sahoewa sowon jedo: sangeon/gyeokjaeng yeongu* [Late Joseon society and the petition system: A study of written and verbal petitions to the king]. Seoul: Iljogak.

——— 2008. "Joseon sidae sosonggwa oejibu: 1560 nyeon gyeongjubu gyeolsong iban bunseok" [Litigation and scriveners during the Joseon: An analysis of Gyeongju County's legal case in 1560]. *Yeoksawa hyeonsil* 69: 255–92.

Han, U-geun. 1956. "Sinmungo eui seolchi wa geu silchejeok hyoneung e daehayeo" [The establishment of the petition drum and its effectiveness]. In the Publication Committee of Dugye Yi Byeongdo baksa hwangap ginyeom nonchong, [Festschrift in commemoration of the sixtieth birthday of Dr. Dugye Yi Byeongdo], 357–408. Seoul: Iljogak.

Hirsch, Susan. 1998. *Pronouncing and Persevering: Gender and the Discourses of Disputing in an African Islamic Court.* Chicago: University of Chicago Press.

Hong, Eun-jin. 1998. "Gurye munhwa Yussigaui hangeul soji e daehayeo" [Vernacular Korean petition of Gurye Yu clan]. *Gomunseo yeongu* 13: 111–43.

Jeon, Gyeong-mok. 1996. "Joseon hugi sansong yeongu: 18, 19 segi gomunseo jungsimeuro" [A study of gravesite lawsuits in the late Joseon based on old eighteenth- and nineteenth-century documents]. Ph.D. diss., University of North Jeolla.

———. 1998. "Joseon hugi sansongui han sarye" [A case study of late Joseon gravesite disputes]. *Gomunseo yeongu* 14: 69–98.

Jeong, Ji-yeong. 2001. "Joseon hugiui yeoseong hoju yeongu" [A study of women householders in the late Joseon]. Ph.D. diss., Sogang University.

Karasawa, Yasuhiko. 2007. "Between Oral and Written Cultures: Buddhist Monks in Qing Legal Plaints." In *Writing and Law in Late Imperial China: Crime, Conflict, and Judgment,* edited by Robert E. Hegel and Katherine Carlitz, 64–80. Seattle: University of Washington Press.

Kim, Gyeong-suk. 2002. "Joseon hugi sansonggwa sahoe galdeung yeongu" [A study of gravesite lawsuits in the late Joseon and social conflicts]. Ph.D. diss., Seoul National University.

———. 2005. "Joseon hugi yoseong-ui jeongso hwaldong" [Women's petitioning activity in the Late Joseon]. *Hanguk munhwa* 36 (December):89–123.

Kim, Jisoo M. 2009. "Individual Petitions: Petitions by Women in the Joseon." In *Epistolary Korea: Letters in the Communicative Space of the Joseon, 1392–1910,* edited by JaHyun Kim Haboush, 68–76. New York: Columbia University Press.

———. 2010a. "Crossing the Boundary of Inner Quarters: Elite Women's Petitioning Activity in Late Joseon Korea." In *Korean Studies Forum,* edited by Hyuk-Rae Kim, 4: 221–43. Seoul: Yonsei University Press.

———. 2010b. "Voices Heard: Women's Right to Petition in Late Joseon Korea." Ph.D. diss., Columbia University.

———. 2013. "Law and Emotion: Tension between Filiality and Fidelity in a Property Dispute of Early Joseon Korea." *Dongbang hakji* 162: 203–39.

———. 2015. *The Emotions of Justice: Gender, Status, and Legal Performance in Joseon Korea.* Seattle: University of Washington Press.

Kim, Jungwon. 2007. "Negotiating Virtue and the Lives of Women in Late Joseon Korea." Ph.D. diss., Harvard University.

———. 2014. "'You Must Avenge on My Behalf': Widow Chastity and Honour in Nineteenth-Century Korea." *Gender and History* 26(1):128–46.

Kim, Seon-gyeong. 1993. "Joseon hugi sansonggwa sanrim soyugwon-ui siltae" [Gravesite lawsuits in the late Joseon and the ownership of mountains and forests]. *Dongbang hakji* 77–79: 497–535.

Kim, Yeong-min, and Michael J. Pettid, eds. 2011. *Women and Confucianism in Joseon Korea: New Perspectives.* Albany: SUNY Press.

Kim, Yong-gyeong. 2001. "Byeonghae Hwangssiga Wansan Yi ssiui yueon mit soji" [Will and petition of Madam Yi from the Byeonghae Hwang]. *Munheon-gwa haeseok* 14: 76–77.

Kuehn, Thomas. 1991. *Law, Family, and Women: Toward a Legal Anthropology of Renaissance Italy*. Chicago: University of Chicago Press.

Liu, Lydia H. 1999. *Tokens of Exchange*. Durham: Duke University Press.

Macauley, Melissa. 1998. *Social Power and Legal Culture: Litigation Masters in Late Imperial China*. Stanford: Stanford University Press.

Orchard, Christopher. 2002. "The Rhetoric of Corporeality and the Political Subject: Containing the Dissenting Female Body in Civil War England." In *Women as Sites of Culture: Women's Roles in Cultural Formation from the Renaissance to the Twentieth Century*, edited by Susan Shifrin, 9–24. Burlington: Ashgate.

Pak, Byeong-ho. 1974. *Hanguk beopjesa go* [Thoughts on Korean legal history]. Seoul: Beommunsa.

———. 1996. *Geunse-ui beopgwa beopsasang* [Early modern law and legal thought]. Seoul: Jinwon.

Peterson, Mark A. 1996. *Korean Adoption and Inheritance: Case Studies in the Creation of a Classic Confucian Society*. Ithaca: Cornell University Press.

Tucker, Judith E. 2008. *Women, Family, and Gender in Islamic Law*. New York: Cambridge University Press.

Yi, Jeong-ok. 1982. "Wansan Yi ssi yueon go" [A study of Wansan Madam Yi's will]. *Munhak gwa eoneo* 3: 165–67.

Zarinfraf-Shahr, Fariba. 1997. "Ottoman Women and the Tradition of Seeking Justice in the Eighteenth Century." In *Women in the Ottoman Empire*, edited by Madeline C. Zilfi, 253–63. New York: Brill.

2

Defying Claims of Incompetence

Women's Lawsuits over Separate Property Rights in Colonial Korea

Sungyun Lim

2.1 INTRODUCTION

Although the Western notion of "rights" was not introduced to Korea until the nineteenth century, Koreans historically enjoyed various legal rights over life and property, as Jisoo Kim discussed in Chapter 1. By the period of Japanese colonial rule (1910–45), Koreans had also gained the Western legal concept of exclusive and individual rights, in principle, through Japanese laws, which had been modeled after Western laws in the nineteenth century (Itō 1966; Nakamura 1963). Yet in practice, legal rights in colonial Korea were defined by a hybrid colonial legal system that operated under the overall framework of the Japanese legal system but used Korean customs as the legal source for family matters (M. Kim 2012; S. Yi 2012). This hybrid legal system has long been considered especially detrimental for women whose legal rights were curtailed by the principle of "wives' legal incompetence" (K: *cheoui muneungnyeok*; J: *tsuma no munōryoku*) and the household system (*ie seido*) from Japan, combined with existing patriarchal customs in Korea.[1] However, the hybrid system also resulted in diverse and colliding claims about different customary rights in colonial courts. Active rights claiming by Korean women served to clarify rights, sometimes in women's favor.

The kind of rights that saw the most contention was property rights because enforcing the Western legal concept of property ownership involved depriving some Koreans of important customary rights.[2] By property rights I mean rights of

---

[1] The "household system" is the translation of *"ie seido,"* which is more commonly translated as the (Japanese) family system. I chose the new translation to reflect the fact that the family system implemented in colonial Korea was different from the Japanese original (as the Korean version also utilized Korean custom), as well as the fact that it functioned in Korea to break larger traditional lineages into smaller (patriarchal) households. The system – or the modified version of it – was maintained in postcolonial South Korea and was most commonly referred to as *"hojuje,"* that is, the household-head system, to emphasize the patriarchal power given to the household head in this system. The system was abolished in 2005, with the abolition of the household registry (*hojeok*). For more information, see T. Yi (1992) and Yang (2011).

[2] Land rights were among the most hotly debated issues at the time of colonization and later in academia. At issue was how exclusive land rights were and how much liberty an individual owner

exclusive ownership as well as rights to inherit and bequeath without the permission of anyone (such as the husband or the household head). The process of delineating property rights was messy and prolonged. Lawsuits over various customary rights pertaining to land ownership continued during the colonial period, well beyond 1918, when the colonial land survey was completed.

One type of property rights stands out as being the subject of active claims-making by women during the colonial period: separate property (K: *teugyu jaesan*; J: *tokuyū zaisan*). This term describes property designated separate from family property and owned by family members other than the household head. There were two instances when a woman held property rights in the colonial period: when she became the household head and when she owned separate property. As will be clear later, property rights among family members continued to be clarified throughout the colonial period.

To investigate how women struggled to defend and define their rights despite legal and societal constraints on their legal capacity, this chapter focuses on women's lawsuits over separate property rights. Ironically, Japanese colonial institutions and laws provided legal bases for women's claims-making regarding separate property rights and helped women win many of these cases. Women litigants' opponents claimed that Korean customs categorically denied property rights to women. Yet, faced with such competing claims about Korean women's rights, the Japanese judges of the High Court of colonial Korea (*Chōsen Kōtō Hōin*) often sided with the women claiming rights over separate property, albeit to advance the Japanese authorities' own objectives of implementing the household system in Korea. Thus, I argue that the colonial household system, which strengthened the rights of household heads over family property, inadvertently also resulted in the protection of separate property rights, many of which were held by women.

The household system and the strengthening of the household head's rights (*hojugwon*) are usually considered to have had negative effects on the rights of women (Bae 1988, 254–59; S. Kim 2000, 45–47; Yang 2011, 386–401). But I show further that these institutional changes had the opposite effect in the case of separate property rights. In fact, these changes led to the clarification of separate property rights. Civil case records concerning separate property rights illuminate how the Korean custom of exclusive male inheritance clashed with the colonial household system based on the principle of patrilineal inheritance. Depending on the nature of the property, women's claims to separate property were more easily secured in the colonial legal system. Women's rights over property that was clearly not part of the family property were strengthened, while claims over property with unclear owner-ship were weakened. Women's rights over separate property were thus bolstered in the colonial period, as they became more clearly delineated against the rights of the

had over the property that he or she owned versus the state or various customary stakeholders in village communities. For an overview of such debates, see S. Jo (2003, 9–27) and Choe (2019, 29).

household head, which were also strengthened during this period. Rights claiming by women in colonial courts was crucial in developing these rights.

Emphasizing wives' legal incompetence, as postcolonial Korean thinkers (see Chapter 3) and more recent scholars have, therefore, obfuscates the diverse legal activities of women in the colonial period. Analyzing cases related to separate property claims, many of which involved women, helps us to discern a subtle but significant transformation in the inheritance regime under Japanese colonial rule, from that of the traditional lineage-based system that excluded all women from inheritance to a new household-based one under the colonial legal system that allowed a limited number of women a share in the household property. Because of their marginal position in the patrilineage family, women's involvement in the separate property cases provides a unique window into the process of transition toward the household system and reveals the incremental impact of legal assimilation of the Japanese empire on Korean society.

This chapter analyzes a number of separate property cases to show how women's rights to separate property were defined by colonial courts. The arguments of litigants and the decisions of the judges will show that, due to the strengthening of the household system, women's rights over separate property were protected in colonial courts. Repeated decisions by colonial judges acknowledged women's rights over separate property and helped to undermine counterclaims that Korean custom categorically denied such rights to women. The last case, though, shows that these gains were precarious, because once a piece of property was declared part of family property, the court denied women any rights over it, even when it was quite clear that the property was accumulated by the woman. Before analyzing the cases, I will give a brief overview of the legal system in colonial Korea. I will then turn to the issue of women's legal incompetence during the colonial period, as it predominates in the previous understandings of women's legal rights during the colonial period.

2.2 RIGHTS AND KOREAN CUSTOMS IN THE COLONIAL LEGAL SYSTEM

After Japan took Korea as its protectorate in 1905 and took control over its legal affairs in 1909, the Japanese began to modernize the Korean legal system after the Western style, as Japan itself had done during its own reforms following the Meiji Restoration (1868). These efforts included establishing division between civil and judicial administration, establishing tertiary levels of courts, and writing new modern laws in Korea (B. Kim 1979). On civil matters, following the full annexation of Korea in 1910, Japan extended its own Civil Code to Korea, with the exception of the family law, which it replaced with Korean customs. These decisions were formalized with the Civil Ordinances on Civil Matters in Korea (*Minjirei*, 1912).

In order to use Korean customs as a legal source, the Japanese collected information about Korean customs through surveys and published the results in the *Kanshū Chōsa Hōkokusho* (Customs Survey Report, 1912). This was in no way complete, however, and many of the details of specific cases had to be hammered out through additional surveys, inquiries to the Korean advisory committee of the Central Council (*Chūsūin*), and at the courts (Atkins 2010, 69–70). A particularly important forum for clarifying competing claims was the High Court, whose decisions were distributed widely throughout the colony for reference (M. Kim 2012).

The use of Korean custom in the courts played an important role in shaping how rights were claimed in the courts during the colonial period. Because the Japanese colonial state used Korean custom as the legal source to adjudicate Korean family matters, civil disputes frequently centered around different claims to authentic Korean custom. As we see later, Korean litigants often claimed polar opposites to be Korean custom, and it was up to the Japanese judges to decide which side was claiming the correct custom. In their decision, the judges would choose one of the customs presented in the courts and declare it as the correct one; Marie Seong-hak Kim (2007, 1086, 1090; 2012, 175) calls this the "bureaucratic invention of customs." Scholars have debated about how true to authentic customs or distorting such judgments were. Some have argued that the Japanese malignantly distorted Korean customs, while others have argued that what appears to be colonial distortion is merely reflecting changing customs on the ground (G.-S. Jeong 2001, 186–87; 2009; S. Yi 2003). Rather than debate the authenticity of the Korean customs recognized by Japanese colonial courts, others have focused on the ways in which certain patriarchal customs were solidified under the colonial rule in the name of Korean customs (Hong and Yang 2008; Yang 1998). Scholars have also exposed the varying quality of the customs surveys, as well as the fact that customs on some matters were diverse, not quite having reached a national consensus.

There was also the fact that the colonial civil courts were operating within the larger colonial legal system that was based on the Japanese household system. In addition to accurately discerning authentic family customs, Japanese judges had to consider the new household system, the governing administrative framework for the entire colony as well as the empire at large. Accordingly, they had to discard customs that did not fit in with the household system, such as the customary authority of lineage elders that superseded the rights of the household head. Rather than an accurate reflection of existing customs, the overall principle of the household head's rights over the integral unit of the household influenced judicial interpretations of family customs – which to keep and which to discard. Thus, the framework of the household and the associated privileges of the household head became a crucial factor for defining women's property rights in colonial Korea.

2.3 THE NOTION OF COLONIAL DECLINE OF WOMEN'S LEGAL STATUS

Women's rights were certainly unequal to men's during the colonial period. The household system installed by the Japanese colonial government privileged the household head's authority over the household, thus compromising individual family members' rights. As women only rarely became household heads, their rights were curtailed against their male counterparts. In addition to their limited access to household head position, further restrictions on women were as follows: women could not divide a house on their own or inherit the household headship permanently, and they had lower priority in terms of property inheritance than brothers born out of wedlock. A wife did not have equal rights in divorce because she could not sue for divorce on the grounds of the husband's extramarital affairs, unless the husband was criminally charged for it, while the husband could.[3] Wives also had less than equal parental rights: upon divorce, the wife would lose parental rights over children, which the husband always kept (J. Kim 1973).

Among the many inequities, wives' legal incompetence (K: *cheoui muneung-nyeok*; J: *tsuma no munōryoku*) has prevailed in common understandings of women's legal status in the colonial period. Article 14 of the Japanese Civil Code, which defined wives as lacking in full legal capacity, was extended to Korea in 1922, following the revision of the Ordinances on Civil Matters in Colonial Korea (Ha 2018, 149–50). The article declared that the wife did not have full legal capacity and must obtain her husband's permission on important legal transactions.[4] After Korea regained independence following the end of World War II, this article was one of the earliest Japanese laws to be abolished, and the restoration of a wife's legal capacity was celebrated as a decisive moment in the history of women's legal rights (E. Kim 2016; T. Yi 1992, 122–29).

As Eunkyung Kim shows (Chapter 3), the abolition of wives' legal incompetence was an important moment when Korean women were enfranchised with full membership in the newly born nation-state of South Korea. Yet, in celebrating this reform, the significance of restoring wives' legal capacity was exaggerated, and the ill-effects of wives' legal incompetence were magnified by some. In her discussion of how Japanese colonial rule had diminished Korean women's legal status, for example, historian Jang Byeong-in claims that "with the onset of the Japanese colonial rule, [Korean] *women lost status as a legal subject*. In other words, the Japanese severely restricted the capacity of married women, *denying the validity of all their legal acts* by claiming that it was according to 'Korean custom' [emphasis mine]" (Jang 2003, 224). This statement could be read as though women lost *all* legal capacity under Japanese colonial rule, which was simply not true. Jang's

---

[3] This inequality in divorce laws (as was with other restrictions laid out here) was also in effect in Japan, but Japanese divorce laws were reformed before those in Korea. For example, the first Supreme Court (Daishinin) decision that affirmed a wife's right to a divorce on the account of her husband's concubinage appeared in 1918, while such right was denied to wives in Korea until 1938. Such delays in colonial Korea were blamed on Korean customs, which the Japanese considered as always falling behind compared to those in Japan. For discussion of changes in divorce case decisions, see Lim (2016, 76–77). For discussion of Japanese divorce law, see Fuess (2004).

[4] Kim Ju-su (1973) claims that even in common commercial transactions like buying and selling things, women did not have full legal capacity. He also claims that a wife could not exercise property rights over her own property. Both were not entirely true.

interpretation of Article 14 of the Japanese Civil Code as complete erasure of a wife's legal capacity seems to have left a strong mark on Korean women's history and led many historians astray. First, women, even married women, did not entirely lose the right to litigate under Japanese rule. While waging lawsuits was one of the important legal transactions that required a husband's permission according to Article 14, Article 17 put restrictions on husbands' ability to deny permission and allowed wives full legal capacity when their interests collided with their husbands', such as when they were suing for divorce. For this reason, legal scholar Jeong Gwang-hyeon (1936) considered the extension of Articles 14 and 17 to colonial Korea as an *improvement* in women's legal status compared to what was in place in the 1910s. It is also important to remember that Article 14 applied to only married women and not to all women. Widows, for example, who did not have husbands from whom to get permission had full legal capacity and were quite active at the colonial courts (Lim 2019).

The problem with the narrative of rights retrenchment in the colonial period followed by a postcolonial reclamation of women's legal capacity is that it obfuscates the presence and efforts of those women who actively participated in the colonial courts to claim their rights. That is, in the celebration of postcolonial progress in women's legal rights, colonial-era restrictions on women's legal capacity were exaggerated. What is produced through such a narrative is the image of Korean women as passive victims who had to wait for postcolonial lawmakers and reformers to have full legal rights handed over to them. The pitfalls of such a narrative are presented by Lisa Yoneyama, who analyzes a similar narrative that emerged in postwar Japan. According to Yoneyama, the Cold War abruptly changed American depictions of Japanese women from warriors to victims, and such narratives were used to justify the Cold War image of Americans as liberators of women (2016, 86–90). A similar dynamic seems to have existed in South Korea, where postcolonial progress in women's legal rights was hailed without acknowledging that some women had actively litigated in colonial courts and defended and developed their rights through such claiming.[5]

Shifting evaluations about women's status in certain periods is indicative of how susceptible to manipulation our perceptions of historical facts are, especially those concerning women and women's status. Instead of the Japanese colonial government, it used to be the Joseon dynasty that was blamed for women's low status and legal rights (Bae 1988, 38–44; Y. Jeong 1964; J. Kim 1981).[6] In the late nineteenth century, when the Western concept of "women's rights (*yeogwon*)" first entered

---

[5] Dorothy Ko (2005, 10) shares a similar problem about how women in bound feet had been viewed as passive victims in China.

[6] One may question the use of "rights" to discuss a period when the term did not yet exist in Korean. I am merely relaying the language used by scholars. All the authors, Jeong, Bae, and Kim Chu-su, cited here use the word rights (*gwolli*) to refer to the range of actions that women had the legitimate capacity to engage in. All claim that the legal status of women, that is, the extent to which women enjoyed equal (legal) rights (compared to their male counterparts) was lower in Joseon dynasty than in periods after.

Korea, many reform-minded intellectuals thought that women utterly lacked rights in Korea and used the term to push various reform agendas (S. Yi 2014). The term was usually used in the context of demands for gender equality, mostly in social customs rather than legal rights, strictly speaking. Among the things criticized were gender segregation (*naeoebeop*), marriage customs (early marriage and a ban on widow remarriage), and the lack of education for women (Choi 2009, 22; S. Yi 2014, 197–201). Reform-minded people during the colonial period campaigned to improve Korean women's status and continued to demand the expansion of women's rights in Korean society. "Expand women's rights" was a common phrase that appeared frequently in newspapers by the 1920s and the 1930s, although these later usages had more specifically legal meanings (Donga Ilbo 1927, 1933a, 1933b; Lim 2019, 55–64).

Similarly, the plight of women was highlighted to serve reformers' purposes in China, in what Dorothy Ko described as a "new global episteme" (2005, 23–24). Under the emerging hegemony of the Western imperialist powers in the nineteenth century, Chinese people took the perspective of Westerners – what Ko calls an "offshore vantage point" (2005, 31) – and reevaluated their own customary practices in a negative light, especially those concerning women. It goes without saying that Westerners, who passed judgment on the allegedly less equal status of women in Asia, often did not practice gender equality themselves in social or legal matters. Hyaeweol Choi has described how female American missionaries in Korea, who were eager to "save" Korean women from grave gender inequities, were themselves being subject to gender inequality (Choi 2009).

Revisionist historians have since taken a more complex view of gender relations during the Joseon dynasty and proposed some correctives to the grim perceptions of women's status in the period. For example, historian Bak Yong-ok argues that women during the Joseon dynasty enjoyed a rather powerful status, especially as mothers in the elite class (1975, 14–31). Legal historian Bak Byeong-ho contends that Korea had never restricted wives' legal capacity before Japanese rule, when Korean women lost legal capacity for the first time (1987, 182). Jang Byeong-in (2003) also asserts that women's legal status declined in the colonial period, rather than during the Joseon dynasty. Jang notes that Joseon-era women enjoyed inheritance rights equal to those of men, which were done away with under the Japanese colonial state through its distorted interpretations of Korean customs.[7] In addition, Jisoo Kim

For example, "It would have been utterly meaningless to discuss the legal position of women in Korea even as recently as sixty years ago, for in those days women were not vested with any rights at all. The Confucian ideals that dominated political thinking in the feudalistic Yi dynasty demanded absolute obedience from women . . . . In the 1920s, during the Japanese colonial period when monogamy was made the law of the land, Korean women began to be granted certain limited rights and were also permitted to sue for divorce" (J. Kim 1981, 19).

7 What Jang (2003, 2013–14) has called "equal inheritance rights" of daughters in the Joseon dynasty is exaggerated. While it is true that even property held by men was often divided among all progeny, her

(Chapter 1) shows that women had significant legal standing during the Joseon dynasty, including the right to make public legal appeals (J. M. Kim 2015).

A more complex understanding of women's legal status and rights in the Joseon dynasty is worthwhile, but it may also rely on a misunderstanding of women's conditions in the colonial period. It is important not to exaggerate the effect of wives' legal incapacity and ignore women's diverse legal activities under colonial rule. As I have shown elsewhere, many women litigated in colonial civil courts. Around 30 percent of all cases related to family customs dealt with widows' rights, and among the 156 cases that concerned Korean family custom, women were the litigating party in 93 (Lim 2019, 10). The high number of such cases in colonial courts does not mean that the legal status of women under the Japanese colonial state was particularly high or that the colonial authorities were particularly interested in expanding women's rights, although they were promoted as part of the colonial ideology (Atkins 2010, 97–98). The parameters of women's rights were delineated through these lawsuits, and as a result a significant number of customary rights that women held in Korean society were reaffirmed in the colonial courts, albeit modified to fit the new legal framework based on the Japanese-style household system.

Instead of hastily concluding that certain provisions were critically restrictive to women, further exploration of *how* these constraints were defined and articulated in practice is crucial for fully understanding the changes that the restoration of legal capacity brought to Korean women in the postcolonial years. As I show further, women had the capacity to wage lawsuits during the colonial period despite regulations concerning a wife's legal incompetence. This was true all the way into the late colonial period. Marking the 1922 extension of Article 14 of the Japanese Civil Code as a decisive moment when Korean women completely lost legal capacity is therefore erroneous.[8]

Separate property cases are ideal for examining how women's legal capacity was claimed, resisted, and eventually retained in the colonial legal system in this period. Women in colonial Korea managed to claim rights over separate property against opposing claims. Interestingly, these opposing claims tried to deny women such rights not on the grounds of Japanese Civil Code but on the grounds of Korean customs, arguing that women customarily lacked any such legal capacity in Korea. As Jisoo Kim has shown in Chapter 1 and elsewhere, this was not true, as women during the Joseon period had robust legal capacity and actively participated in legal processes, such as petitioning. Instead of linear progress or regression in women's rights, therefore, women's legal capacity was shaped in a much more complex way in the transition from Joseon to the Japanese colonial period. Women and their active

examples make it clear that the property received by daughters was not equal in amount to those that the sons received.

8 One article that treats civil case records on women's separate property rights in the colonial period stops its analysis immediately before 1922, strengthening this chronological framework (W. Kim 2005).

rights claiming in colonial courts were much more pivotal in the shaping of their rights than has thus far been suggested.

2.4 DID WOMEN HAVE ANY PROPERTY RIGHTS IN KOREA? A 1916 CASE

The term "separate property" refers to a family member's property that was not a part of family property owned by the household head. Separate property was most commonly held by women, but also by men who were not head of the household. The concept, if not the legal term itself, had a long history in East Asia. Such distinction between family property and the property that was brought in by marrying-in women did exist in Korea's past, although as recent works show, such rights of the natal families were increasingly threatened since the eighteenth century when the patrilineal family system was strengthened and marriage customs gradually transitioned from uxorilocal to virilocal, meaning that married couples transitioned from living with the wife's family to the husband's family (Deuchler 1995).[9] The increasing threat to the rights of the natal families on such properties led many families to bequeath less property (such as land and slaves) to their daughters and resort to movable property in a bride's dowry upon marriage (Mun 2004, 159–74).

Because the concept of separate property was defined against the concept of family property, which was supposed to be transmitted along the patrilineal line, the concept of separate property was also more clearly defined as the family property concept strengthened under the Japanese colonial legal system. Separate property followed a distinctly different law of disposal. Unlike family property, separate property was distributed equally among descendants and could even be transmitted across household boundaries. In other words, women had more freedom in designating recipients as well as inheriting the property herself, if the property was considered not part of the family property. The distinct laws of inheritance for separate property were affirmed and reaffirmed through multiple lawsuits in colonial civil courts against different claims of Korean litigants, who tried to deny the validity of such customs. Therefore, in an ironic outcome, under the colonial legal system where the patrilineal succession principle of property was strengthened, in some cases concerning separate property, women found more room to maneuver in claiming their rights.

In 1916, a woman named Yi Jong-ok was involved in a lawsuit at the High Court of colonial Korea with her stepfather over a piece of land that her deceased mother had owned. Yi's mother had married the defendant, Go Hak-nyun, three years earlier and had died after only a year of her marriage. Upon her death, she left her property to Yi, her daughter from a previous marriage. Go, the husband, did not approve and brought the matter to court, arguing that "it was Korean custom for the wife to be absolutely obedient to the husband. A wife's capacity for legal action is extremely

[9] Bak Byeong-ho (1981, 5) has called uxorilocal marriage "matrilocal."

limited and must wait for the husband's permission for everything." He argued that his wife should have requested his permission before she engaged in such an "important legal action," and since she had not received permission, he had the right to cancel the transaction. The local court and the appeals court both sided with Go.[10]

In her appeal to the High Court, Yi, the daughter, refuted Go's account of Korean custom, stating that Korean custom as she knew it was totally different from what Go was claiming:

> Custom is not consistent in Korea. The power relations between a married couple are different depending on whether they are upper class, middle class, or lower class, or if they are in a second marriage (K: *jaehon*, J: *zaikon*), or a later marriage (K: *huhon*; J: *gokon*). Between a remarried couple, even more if the remarriage is in old age, the power of the husband is especially weak. .... And in this case, the old wife does not need the husband's permission to dispose of her property.

Did some women in Korea have full legal capacity to own and dispose of property at will as Yi Jong-ok claimed?

Yi won the case in the High Court, but the High Court ignored her claim about special customary rights of "older wives." Moreover, the judges acknowledged the overall principle of a wife's incompetence, quoting almost verbatim from the *Kanshū Chōsa Hōkokusho* (The Customs Survey Report) when noting that "according to Korean custom, the wife must receive the husband's permission in important legal actions, and if she acts without permission, the husband may cancel the action."[11] Yet, the judges still gave the property to the daughter, Yi, stating that when bequeathing her own property on her death bed, a wife did not need to obtain her husband's permission. The elaborate reasoning of the High Court behind this decision was worded thus:

> Bequest usually occurs immediately before death, and usually there is no time for her to receive permission from the husband. Moreover, marriage is dissolved at death, and inheritance takes effect at the time of death. So, by the time the bequest takes effect, the marriage is already dissolved. Therefore, the wife is free to bequest her property when she dies. The husband cannot cancel the bequest that the wife made with the reason that he did not give permission. (443)

Bypassing the daughter's claim to diverse customs altogether, this very convoluted statement achieved many things at once: While the High Court managed to uphold the dead wife's wishes about how to dispose of her property, it did so while acknowledging the general principle of wives' incompetence in legal actions in Korea. Yet it also opened up a space for women to have certain rights over property

---

[10]   *Kōtō hōin hanketsuroku* (*Hanketsuroku* from here on), vol. 3, 439–43.

[11]   *Hanketsuroku*, vol. 3, 440; *Kanshū Chōsa Hōkokusho*, 16–17.

by denying the claim that Korean custom categorically denied women the right to make any legal decisions about the property they owned.

Go was not alone in claiming that wives did not have full legal capacity in Korea. Japanese jurists likewise acknowledged the extreme limitation of a wife's legal capacity as Korean custom. According to *Kanshū Chōsa Hōkokusho*, wives in Korea customarily "must absolutely submit to their husbands" and seek their husbands' permission in a variety of matters such as a "contract that requires bodily restriction, lawsuits, and other important legal transactions." The *Hōkokusho* further claims that wives could not carry out even trivial matters on their own.[12] The report was criticized for many inaccuracies (and even distortions) but was generated from both textual and interview evidence, meaning that at least some interviewees for the report (most of them local notables) claimed such legal incompetence for women as Korean custom.[13]

Claims categorically denying women's legal capacity, which emerged consistently in courts throughout the colonial period, were regularly challenged by opposing parties – many of whom were women – and consistently denied by Japanese colonial judges as a legitimate Korean custom.[14] In some cases, the litigants presented claims about women's property rights from the other end of the spectrum. In one case from 1913, a plaintiff went so far as to argue that a wife naturally had co-ownership over the family property and therefore did not have to hand over the family property to the adopted heir when she was widowed.[15] This very liberal claim about a wife's customary rights, however, was not accepted by the High Court. This case was not over separate property rights but nonetheless illustrates that there were competing ideas about women's legal capacity over property among Koreans. While operating under the general principle that women lacked full legal capacity, colonial judges often chose to tamp down claims that denied all property rights to women.

Eventually, the concept of separate property rights came to be fully acknowledged in Korea. In 1917, a widow waged two High Court cases to reclaim her property from her deceased husband's son, who claimed the property on the grounds that women in Korea had no rights to own property. The High Court judges delivered a decision that first acknowledged the possibility of "separate property" rights in Korea; they granted the property to the widow, stating that there was no custom in Korea that denied women separate property rights.[16] In 1933, the High Court issued an agreement that officially clarified the flow of inheritance concerning separate property: unlike family property, which followed patrilineal inheritance principles, separate

[12] *Kanshū Chōsa Hōkokusho*, 16–17.
[13] In some of the original customs report documents, the occupation of interviewees is usually listed as "Confucian scholar" and they are invariably male (Ariga 1913; Lim 2019, 35–36; Terazawa 1924).
[14] *Hanketsuroku*, vol. 1, 440–42, vol. 3, 733–48, and vol. 4, 102–07. For a detailed discussion of these cases, see Lim (2019, 1–2, 90–92).
[15] *Hanketsuroku*, vol. 2, 220–23.
[16] *Hanketsuroku*, vol. 4, 102–07. For a more detailed discussion of this case, see Lim (2019, 90–92).

property would be divided equally among progeny.[17] In other words, although prior scholars argue that the extension of the Japanese Civil Code's Article 14 to Korea eliminated wives' legal capacity, in practice it had limited effect. In fact, despite the extension of Article 14, Korean women's rights over separate property were more clearly delineated in the colonial legal system against more extreme positions that denied all legal rights to Korean women.

2.5 THE COLONIAL HOUSEHOLD SYSTEM AND SEPARATE PROPERTY RIGHTS

The Korean litigants whom we encounter in the civil cases from the colonial period appear to have adhered to a male-only inheritance regime in which male members of the agnatic (i.e., related by the paternal side) and patrilineal kin group shared exclusive access to property. Under this regime, the women of the family were excluded from inheritance. On the other hand, the inheritance regime that the Japanese judges were implementing was one in which a similar patrilineal succession principle governed the transmission of family property, but the principle of partible inheritance governed other kinds of property. In other words, family property was preserved into the hands of the heir along patrilineal lines, but other kinds of property were to be dispersed equally among all progeny, including daughters. Both inheritance regimes were patrilineal, but the boundary of the family as property sharing members were different. The boundary of the family that the colonial state was interested in maintaining coincided with the household in the family registry rather than the larger agnatic patrilineal kin group, which the Korean inheritance regime respected as the extent of the family. It seems that the two different family inheritance regimes clashed in colonial courts and were thrown into relief by disputes over women's legal capacity over separate property. Since the critical difference between the Korean and the Japanese inheritance regimes lay specifically in women's rights to separate property, conflicts over separate property rights emerged only when women entered the mix.

Cases of women's separate property rights demonstrate the utility of being mindful of women's position in the family when examining their rights under the patriarchal family system. Cho Haejoang (1998) notes that in a patriarchal family system, women's status and power is determined by their relationship and distance to the male patriarch. This is the reason the power of the mother of the male heir, due to her proximity to the future patriarch, is particularly strong in patriarchal society. Examining the transformation of the inheritance system in China, Kathryn Bernhardt similarly considers the different inheritance rights that women held depending on their familial status. Bernhardt argues that the changes in inheritance customs from the Song dynasty to the Qing dynasty can best be detected by focusing

---

[17] *Hanketsuroku*, vol. 20, 440–41.

on the different familial categories of women and how their rights were differently distributed. Although the Chinese inheritance system seems to have remained stagnant, Bernhardt shows that it shifted from partible inheritance that included daughters to primogeniture, where daughters were excluded from inheritance. Also, as the intra-agnatic inheritance principle became stronger during the Ming dynasty, widows lost significant rights in designating adopted heirs. In this way, while the overall rule of inheritance remained male dominated, women's inheritance rights were rearranged and shifted depending on their position in the family (Bernhardt 1999, 3–4). Previous scholarship on Korean property rights also notes the importance of diverse familial positions that women held. In her examination of the Joseon dynasty's transition in inheritance customs, Jo Eun (2004) shows that while a daughter's right to inherit from her natal family declined, mothers' rights were strengthened.

The exact contours of women's property rights are only discernible when one examines how women's rights are configured according to their familial status, or their position vis-à-vis the household head. Women's property rights differed depending on whether she was a daughter, wife, or widow and whether her spouse was the household head or a family member of the household. This is because the stance on property rights and inheritance during the colonial period, and well into the postcolonial period until the household head system was in effect, was defined against the rights of the household head rather than based on one's gender. Marni Anderson argues that gender became more significant than familial status (household head or not) in determining the political rights of women in the Meiji period (Anderson 2010). While it is true that gender affected how many rights women enjoyed, the household system still privileged the household head and its influence was crucial on how rights were distributed among household members in colonial Korea. With their lower priority standing in succession to household headship, women indeed had less access to the property rights accompanying that position. Property or inheritance rights given to women are best understood through how their property rights were arranged relative to the rights of the household head. It is therefore useful to consider the multiple categories of women to complicate the gender-binary framework that has been dominant in studying women's property rights. This is not to say that gender is irrelevant, but that it is not a sufficient factor to capture all socio-legal dynamics concerning property rights.

In the following cases, the women in question had their property rights challenged on the grounds of their gender, but their rights were eventually determined not by the gender of the owner but by the status of the property itself vis-à-vis the family property. If the property was not considered part of the family property (*gasan*), then the women's separate property rights were acknowledged, and the property was free to be distributed equally among her descendants. If it was considered family property, then it had to be inherited by the heir of the household head, as strictly defined by Korean lineal laws. In the first case, the widow was granted the property because it was considered separate property once owned by her husband. In the second case, addressed in Section 2.6, the property was considered part of the family property, engineered as such by a male relative, and therefore restricted in how it could be passed down.

In the first case, which is from 1929, the household head and his daughter-in-law each claimed a piece of property.[18] The daughter-in-law, Madam Kim (Kim-ssi), had the misfortune of losing her husband in 1923 and then her son in 1925.[19] The problem was that the two died in such close succession and the woman did not have time to register her husband's property to her name before her father-in-law claimed it. Upon their deaths, her father-in-law, Gang Gi-hyeong, claimed the land and registered it under his name. In response, Madam Kim sued him to reclaim the land. The father-in-law argued that "according to Korean custom," as the household head he had the right to inherit the property from any family member who died without having married, that is, his grandson. The widow Kim, on the other hand, argued that "according to Korean custom," when a married family member (her husband) died without an heir, it was his wife who inherited property; when an unmarried family member (her son) died, it was his father, then his mother, who inherits. Only if the person was lacking both could the household head claim the land.

The High Court judges ultimately sided with the widow and decided that the widow held the rights to the property that was once owned by her husband and then, theoretically albeit briefly and unofficially, her son. The status of the property as the separate property of a family member enabled the widow to claim the property ahead of the household head, her father-in-law. Therefore, the concept of separate property enabled the widow to resist the authority and claim of her father-in-law to protect her right to the property that her husband once owned.

As is shown here, separate property rights allowed limited yet significant rights, and a woman was able to act against the interests of the male authority figure of the family. As separate property was defined against the concept of family property, rights over separate property were more clearly delineated as the concept of family property became stronger. Perhaps ironically then, during the colonial period as the patriarchal power of the household head and his rights over family property were strengthened in laws, the parameters of the separate property also became more clearly defined. As a result, we see a more definite protection of the separate property rights of women once the property was defined as separate property.

---

[18] *Hanketsuroku*, vol. 16, 189–94.

[19] "Kim-ssi" means "married woman with natal surname of Kim." Korean women who were married were officially called by their natal surnames. "Ssi" connotes that she was considered of *yangban* status (although the status carried no legal meaning in colonial Korea). Commoner women who were married were called "sosa" or "joi," as in "Kim-sosa." These were practices left over from the Joseon dynasty. See similar usage during Joseon dynasty in Chapter 1. Later, this practice of referring to women by their natal surnames phased out as increasing number of women were registered with their given names.

It is important to note that any clarification or strengthening of separate property rights from which some women benefited is not to be confused with the expansion of their rights over all property, let alone as expansion of women's rights more generally. In fact, colonial inheritance law was designed, first and foremost, to promote the implementation of the household system by upholding the patrilineal succession line. As the last case discussed in this chapter demonstrates, the laws of separate property could be a double-edged sword: once a piece of property was deemed part of family property, women's rights to access said property were easily denied.

2.6 THE PITFALLS OF SEPARATE PROPERTY

Since the colonial family system was not designed to protect women's property rights, women were just as vulnerable to the principle of the household system under the colonial legal system, depending on how the property at hand was defined. In the following case from 1931, the disputed property ended up being defined as family property and was eventually enveloped as part of the agnatic inheritance.[20] The case involved a woman named Bak Chun-ok who died in 1929. She left behind a piece of land of unspecified area, over which two men were contending: one was Bak Jang-hyeok, Chun-ok's maternal grandson, and the other, along with four others who appear to be his creditors, was Bak Hong-in, the posthumous adopted heir of Chun-ok's father. Chun-ok was a concubine to a man named Kim Sun-eung who died in 1922, with whom she had one daughter. Since she did not have a son, she brought in one of her daughter's sons, Jang-hyeok, to make him an heir to her property and have him carry out ancestral rites for her, following a Joseon dynasty custom in which the maternal grandson inherits rites (*oeson bongsa*). According to Jang-hyeok, she gave him the contested piece of land in 1928 but did not register it under his name.

Bak Hong-in argued that, as the posthumous adopted heir of the Bak family, he had the right to inherit all of Chun-ok's property after she died without an heir. Hong-in further argued that Jang-hyeok was not a proper adoptee since he was not agnatic kin to Chun-ok.[21] In protest, Jang-hyeok argued that the land was Chun-ok's separate property and not the family's, and therefore it was not to be given to the heir as part of the family property. As separate property, it should be distributed to her descendants, that is, her daughter and Jang-hyeok's mother, Hyang-nam. Since Hyang-nam was deceased, her share should be given to Jang-hyeok, the plaintiff himself. Jang-hyeok also pointed out that Hong-in had been adopted too late; Chun-ok's father had passed away in 1877 without a male heir, making Chun-ok the female household head for fifty years. Only after Chun-ok's death was Hong-in adopted

---

[20] *Hanketsuroku*, vol. 18, 24–30.
[21] Only adoption of agnatic kin of the husband was acknowledged as the proper Korean adoption custom under the colonial legal system. *Oeson bongsa* was not acknowledged. See D. Kim (1968, 268–344); Jeong (2009); Lim (2019, 62–63).

posthumously to succeed Chun-ok's father's position. Jang-hyeok thus was insinuating that the true intention of Hong-in's adoption was monetary.

It is significant to note that as the female household head, Chun-ok's property could be considered both family property and separate property. Even though she had been in the position of the household head for over fifty years, as a woman she was considered a temporary holder of that position according to Korean custom as defined under the Japanese colonial legal system. In principle, she would not have been even a temporary holder of the household head position if the household was considered as headed by Chun-ok's father. Although Japanese family law acknowledged daughters' rights to inherit household headship, Korean customary law did not, even after the Civil Ordinances was severely assimilated to the Japanese Civil Code in 1940 (Lim 2019, 73–75). In this sense, Korean customary law more severely restricted women's inheritance rights than Japanese family law did. Also worth noting is that this was a very exceptional case: If there was no adoptee, she would have been considered the single female head of her own household and not a temporary successor to her father since a daughter's succession to the household head position was not acknowledged in colonial Korea. In a similar case from 1915, the High Court judges ruled that a former concubine heading her own household was free to leave her property to her maternal nephew and not to her partner's grandson, his heir.[22] In contrast, in this Bak family case, the family council was very quick to act and insert Hong-in as the posthumous adoptee of a person long deceased. The adoption then redefined Chun-ok as an unmarried daughter of a deceased household head whose succession had been merely postponed for over fifty years. After the adoption of an heir redefined the family structure, Chun-ok was deemed an irrelevant entity in relation to inheritance. The High Court judges were unwilling to annul an adoption that was already properly registered; instead, they found a suitable compromise that made sense within the rules of the household system. In the end, this case eventually came down to the fact that as a concubine-mother, the deceased Chun-ok had never shared a family registry with her daughter, Jong-nam, which, the judges claimed, meant that she could not bequeath property to the daughter, let alone her son, Jang-hyeok. In the end, the judges noted, it was the relationship in the registry that was the basis for the inheritance of separate property, and not blood relations.

As we see in this case, separate property rights for women were significant but limited and precarious. Ultimately, the widow's property went to the posthumous adoptee of her long-deceased father, who had probably not contributed anything to the accumulated property. In this case, between the two adoptions (of the maternal grandson and the posthumously adopted heir) with shaky validity, the judges chose to enforce the registry boundary as the deciding factor rather than test the validity and legitimacy of each adoption. In the name of enforcing registry boundaries, the

---

[22] *Hanketsuroku*, vol. 2, 132–34. I have analyzed this case at length elsewhere. See Lim (2019, 46).

judges restored the widow's status as the daughter of her long-deceased father, who was never registered on her family registry, as he was deceased long before the colonial registration system began. It seems that rather than acknowledge the widow's status as a grandmother because she was a concubine-mother, the court decided to reinstate her as her father's daughter. Ironically, as the only living progeny of this reclaimed family, she had no status to claim the property as her own separate property.

2.7 CONCLUSION

The three examples discussed earlier, of civil cases over women's separate property from the colonial period show that women actively asserted and defended their rights in colonial courts, and that many of these women often had their separate property rights acknowledged in colonial civil courts. However, these victories did not translate into an expansion of women's rights in Korea, as the strengthened separate property rights only happened because Japan's introduction of the household registry system strengthened household heads' rights.

Nonetheless, disputes over separate property can tell us several things. They show that, although limited, women in colonial Korea had rights to their property apart from household heads; in some cases, upon their deaths they were able to transmit this property free from the rules of patrilineal succession or the rules of agnatic inheritance. Once the property was considered separate property, the colonial courts were open to acknowledging such rights. Although most colonial and postcolonial analyses of women's property rights focused on a daughter's inheritance rights or lack thereof, these cases on separate property provide an alternative and potentially fruitful site for examining where and how women's property rights challenged male-only inheritance practices by leveraging gaps in the inheritance regime that prioritized patrilineal succession of family property.

Persistent disputes over women's separate rights reveal the longevity of claims to Korean custom that entirely denied such rights to women, even after the colonial courts repeatedly acknowledged these rights. One could argue that colonial courts' acknowledgment of separate property rights for women under the Japanese Civil Code was a distortion of Korean custom. Indeed, Korean litigants again and again argued thus. Whatever the case, we find a significant number of women benefiting from the colonial judges' decisions to acknowledge this category of property rights for Korean women. If it is true that Korean custom acknowledged only the practice of male-only agnatic inheritance, we can conclude that women certainly gained ground rather than lost via this exceptional category of property rights under the colonial court system. While the modernization of laws led to the formalization and, in turn, often the strengthening of gender inequality during the colonial period, this does not mean that women's legal rights were categorically diminished under the colonial legal system. Instead, women made the most of the limited rights allotted to them, actively protecting and struggling to expand them.

REFERENCES

Primary Sources

Ariga, Keitarō. 1913. "Kosekini kansuru jikō: chūwa-gun [Cases concerning household registers: Junghwa county]," manuscript. East Asian Rare Collection. C. V. Starr East Asian Library, University of California, Berkeley.

Chōsen Kōtō Hōin Shokika. 1913–43. *Chōsen kōtō hōin hanketsuroku* [Legal decision of the High Court of Colonial Korea]. 30 vols. Keijō (Seoul): Daeseong.

Customs Survey Report. 1912. *Kanshū chōsa hōkokusho* [Customs Survey Report]. Keijō (Seoul).

Donga Ilbo. 1927. "Boneundaero deunneundaero saenggak naneundaero [As I see, as I hear, as I think]." January 22, 1927. 2.

   1933a. "Yeogwon sinjangui hoetbul – gajogi dareun ttaldo eomeoni yusan sangsok [Torchlight of women's rights expansion – daughter in a different family registry can also inherit mother's estate]." December 9, 1933. 2.

   1933b. "Yeogwoneul sinjang hara [Expand women's rights]." December 10, 1933. 1.

Terazawa, Tokuzaburō. 1924. "Kanshū chōsa: kōkaido chihō [Customs survey: Hwanghaedo region]," manuscript. East Asian Rare Collection. C. V. Starr East Asian Library, University of California, Berkeley.

Secondary Sources

Anderson, Marnie S. 2010. *A Place in Public: Women's Rights in Meiji Japan*. Cambridge: Harvard University Asia Center.

Atkins, E. Taylor. 2010. *Primitive Selves: Koreana in the Japanese Colonial Gaze, 1910–1945*. Berkeley: University of California Press.

Bae, Gyeong-suk. 1988. *Hanguk yeoseong sabeopsa* [Judicial history of women in Korea]. Incheon: Inha Daehakgyo Chulpanbu.

Bak, Byeong-ho. 1987. "Uri beop uri sasang (7)" [Our laws, our thoughts]. *Gosigye* 21(6): 181–82.

   1981. "Family Law." In *Modernization and Its Impact upon Korean Law*, edited by Byeong-ho Pak, Chu-su Kim, Kweon-seop Cheong, Hyeong-bae Kim, and Tae-jun Kweon, 1–17. Berkeley: Center for Korean Studies, Institute of East Asian Studies, University of California Press.

Bak, Yong-ok. 1975. *Hanguk geundae yeoseongsa* [Modern women's history in Korea]. Seoul: Jeongeumsa.

Bernhardt, Kathryn. 1999. *Women and Property in China, 960–1949*. Stanford: Stanford University Press.

Cho, Haejoang. 1998. "Male Dominance and Mother Power: The Two Sides of Confucian Patriarchy in Korea." In *Confucianism and the Family*, edited by Walter H. Slote and George A. De Vos, 187–207. Albany: State University of New York Press.

Choe, Won-gyu. 2019. *Hanmal iljechogi gugyuji josawa tojijosa saeop* [State-owned land and land survey project in Daehan empire and early Japanese colonial period]. Seoul: Hyean.

Choi, Hyaeweol. 2009. *Gender and Mission Encounters in Korea: New Women, Old Ways.* Seoul-California Series in Korean Studies, vol. I. Berkeley: University of California Press.

Deuchler, Martina. 1995. *The Confucian Transformation of Korea: A Study of Society and Ideology.* Cambridge: Harvard University Asia Center.

Fuess, Harald. 2004. *Divorce in Japan: Family, Gender, and the State, 1600–2000.* Stanford: Stanford University Press.

Ha, Min-gyeong. 2018. "Cheoui haengwi neungnyeok injeonggwa anae ganggan injeong pangyeoreul tonghae bon yeoseongingwonui byeonhwa" [Transformation of women's rights through acknowledgment of wives' (legal) capacity to act and decision to recognize wife rape]. *Beopsahak yeongu* 57: 145–70.

Hong, Yang-heui [Hong, Yang-hee], and Hyeon-a Yang [Hyun-ah Yang]. 2008. "Singminji sabeop gwallyoui gajok 'gwanseup' insikgwa jendeo jilseo: gwanseup josa bogoseoui hojugwone daehan insigeul jungsimeuro" [The colonial judicial officials' perception of family custom and gender hierarchy: On perception of household-head rights in the Customs-survey report]. *Sahoewa yeoksa* (September): 161–95.

Itō, Masami. 1966. *Gaikokuhō to nihonhō* [Foreign laws and Japanese laws]. Tokyo: Iwanami Shoten.

Jang, Byeong-in. 2003. "Joseon sidaewa ilje sidae yeoseongui beopjeok jiwi bigyo" [Comparison of women's legal status in the Joseon dynasty and the Japanese colonial period]. *Yeoksa wa damnon* 36: 201–34.

Jeong, Geung-sik. 2009. "Singminjigi sangsok gwanseupbeopui tadangseonge daehan jaegeomto" [Re-examination of the legitimacy of the customary law of inheritance from the colonial period]. *Seoul daehakgyo beophak* 50(1):287–320.

——— 2001. *Hanguk geundaebeopsa go* [Study of the modern legal history of Korea]. Seoul: Bagyeongsa.

Jeong, Gwang-hyeon. 1936. "Joseon yeoseonggwa beomnyul (7)" [Joseon dynasty women and law]. *Donga ilbo*, April 12, 1936.

Jeong, Yo-seop. 1964. "Ijo sidaee isseoseo yeoseongui sahoejeok wichi" [Women's social status during the Yi dynasty]. *Asea Yeoseong Yeongu* 3: 39–84.

Jo, Eun. 2004. "Gabujangjeok jilseohwawa buingwonui yakhwa" [Establishment of patriarchal order and the weakening of wife rights]. In *Joseon jeongi gabujangjewa yeoseong* [Patriarchal domination and women in early Joseon], edited by Hong-gi Choe, Ju-heui Kim, Tae-hyeon Kim, Taek-rim Yun, Hyeong-suk Yun, Bae-yong Yi, Eun Jo, and Heui-seon Jo, 227–59. Seoul: Akanet.

Jo, Seok-geun. 2003. *Hanguk geundae tojijedoui hyeongseong* [The shaping of modern land system in Korea]. Seoul: Haenam.

Kim, Byeong-hwa. 1979. *Hanguk sabeopsa* [Judicial history of Korea]. 3 vols. Seoul: Iljogak.

Kim, Du-heon. 1968. *Hanguk gajok jedo yeongu* [A study of Korean family system]. Seoul: Seoul Daehakkyo Chulpanbu.

Kim, Eun-kyeong [Kim, Eunkyung]. 2016. "Talsingminji gajokbeopeseo minjujueui uije wa yeoseongui gungminhwa- 'cheoui haengwi neungnyeok' eul jungsimeuro" [The postcolonial family law and the making of women into national subjects – focusing on the "wife's legal incompetence"]. *Sarim* 57: 269–94.

Kim, Jisoo M. 2015. *The Emotions of Justice: Gender, Status, and Legal Performance in Joseon Korea.* Seattle: University of Washington Press.

Kim, Ju-su [Kim, Chu-su]. 1981. "The Legal Position of Korean Women." In *Modernization and Its Impact upon Korean Law*, edited by Pyeong-ho Pak, Ju-su Kim, Kweon-seop Cheong, Hyeong-bae Kim, and Tae-jun Kweon, 19–38. Berkeley: Center for Korean Studies, Institute of East Asian Studies, University of California, Berkeley.

1973. "Hanguk yeoseongui beopjeok jiwi" [Legal status of Korean women]. *Saegajeong* (January): 30–34.

Kim, Marie Seong-hak. 2012. *Law and Custom in Korea: Comparative Legal History*. Cambridge: Cambridge University Press.

———. 2007. "Law and Custom under the Joseon Dynasty and Colonial Korea: A Comparative Perspective." *Journal of Asian Studies* 66(4): 1067–97.

Kim, Sang-yong. 2000. "Dasi hojuje pyejireul malhanda" [Stating again the (argument for) abolishing household head system]. In *Hojuje gwallyeon toron jaryojip: Hojujedo mueosi munjeinga*, edited by Beopmubu yeoseong jeongchaek damdanggwansil, 23–75. Gwacheon: Beopmubu.

Kim, Won-tae. 2005. "Ilje gangjeom chogi cheoui teugyujaesane gwanhan gwanseupbeop: Joseon godeungbeobwon pangyeorui bunseogeul jungsimeuro" [Customary laws on wife's separate property rights in the early Japanese colonial period – focusing on the legal decisions from the High Court of Colonial Korea]. *Beopsahak yeongu* 31 (April): 197–236.

Ko, Dorothy. 2005. *Cinderella's Sisters: A Revisionist History of Footbinding*. Berkeley: University of California Press.

Lim, Sungyun. 2019. *Rules of the House: Family Law and Domestic Disputes in Colonial Korea*. Berkeley: University of California Press.

———. 2016. "Affection and Assimilation: Concubinage and the Ideal of Conjugal Love in Colonial Korea, 1922–1938." *Gender and History* 28(2): 461–79.

Mun, Suk-ja. 2004. *Joseon sidae jaesan sangsokgwa gajok* [Property inheritance and family in the Joseon dynasty]. Seoul: Gyeongin munhwasa.

Nakamura, Kikuō. 1963. *Kindai nihon no hōteki keisei- jōyaku kaisei to hōten hensan* [The legal construction of modern Japan; treaty revisions and law compilations]. Tokyo: Yushindo.

Yang, Hyeon-a [Yang, Hyun-ah]. 2011. *Hanguk gajokbeop ilki: jeontong, singminjiseong, jendeoui gyocharoeseo* [Reading Korean family law: in the intersection of tradition, coloniality, and gender]. Paju: Changbi.

———. 1998. "Hanguk gajokbeobeul tonghae bon singminjijeok geundaeseonggwa yugyojeok jeontong damnon" [Colonial modernity and discourses of Confucian tradition examined through Korean family law]. *Hanguk sahoehakhoe hugi sahoehak daehoe balpyomun yoyakjip* (December): 342–51.

Yi, Seung-il. 2012. *Joseon chongdokbu beopje jeongchaek* [Legal Policy of the Korean government-general]. Seoul: Yeoksa bipyeongsa.

———. 2003. "Joseon chongdokbuui beopje jeongchaege daehan yeongu: joseon minsaryeong je-11-jo 'gwanseup'ui seongmunhwareul jungsimeuro" [A study on the legislative policy of the Korean government-general: Focusing on codification of Article 11 of the Korean Civil Ordinances]. Ph.D. diss., Hanyang University, Seoul.

Yi, Suk-in. 2014. "Geundae chogi yeogwonui yuipgwa yugyoui jaeguseong" [Inflow of women's rights concept in the early modern period and the reconstruction of Confucianism]. *Gughak yeongu* 24: 187–218.

Yi, Tae-yeong. 1992. *Gajokbeop gaejeong undong 37-nyeonsa* [Thirty-seven years of family law reform movement]. Hanguk gajeong beomnyul sangdamso chulpanbu.

Yoneyama, Lisa. 2016. *Cold War Ruins: Transpacific Critique of American Justice and Japanese War Crimes*. Durham: Duke University Press.

3

"Equal" Second-Class Citizens

Postcolonial Democracy and Women's Rights in Postliberation South Korea

Eunkyung Kim

3.1 INTRODUCTION

The spread of sexual assault and harassment accusations in South Korea's #MeToo movement in 2018 offered opportunities for many to reflect on the position of women's rights in Korean democracy. The movement was jump-started in January 2018 by a prosecutor, Seo Ji-hyun, when she disclosed on national evening news that she had been sexually harassed by her superior. He was eventually convicted (JTBC January 29, 2018; Y. Jang 2019). Then, in March 2018, the chief secretary to Ahn Hee-jung, who was the governor of South Chungcheong Province at the time and an aspiring presidential candidate, divulged that she had been a victim of sexual power abuse (JTBC March 5, 2018).[1] Around the same time, accusations emerged against a Seoul mayoral candidate, Chung Bong-joo (Seo 2018). Similar allegations rocked the entertainment industry, literature world, higher education, and sports. Substantial street protests throughout the year sought to raise awareness of gender discrimination and sexual violence in Korea and asserted women's "right to live safely" (Han 2018; Hasunuma and Shin 2019, 97–111). The incidents involving the governor and mayoral candidate especially shocked Korean society because both were prominent progressive politicians who had been part of the student movement resisting the dictatorial government in the 1980s. These episodes suggested that gender inequality remained entrenched even among progressive sectors of South Korean society.

As a former participant in the pro-democracy movement in Korea, I was not especially surprised by these revelations. They reminded me of the discriminatory attitudes that I had experienced back in college in the 1980s, when sexist remarks and sexual comments, which today would be considered sexual harassment, among

---

I would like to thank the journal *Asian Women* for giving permission to reprint my article (2020), "Postcolonial Democracy and Women's Rights in Post-Liberation South Korea." *Asian Women* 36 (3): 71–89. It has been slightly modified to fit into this volume.

[1] On September 9, 2019, the Supreme Court reaffirmed the original sentence of three years and six months in prison. *Yonhap News*, September 9, 2019.

fellow activists were common. These cases never came to light because political reform took precedence over women's rights. We, male and female students, all considered gender inequality and sexual misconduct as "secondary" or "less important" problems compared to the "revolutionary cause" of democracy. Progressive women's movement groups were no different. In March 1985, the Korean Women's Congress commemorating the 85th International Women's Day chose their theme to be "The Women's Movement Together with the Nation, Democracy, and the People (*minjung*)," instead of a women-specific agenda.[2] The #MeToo incidents discussed earlier demonstrate how the rights of the socially weak (in this case, women) exist in a precarious fashion within complex webs of power dynamics and other rights-related agendas, and such an understanding has led many to rethink the gendered nature of rights in South Korean society. The first step toward the goal of consolidating women's rights is to reexamine the male-centered history of democracy that only paid attention to abstract concepts of equality and civil rights, ignoring gender differences in the process.

The #MeToo movement has inspired many to look back on the very foundation of the democratization process in South Korea. The sexual violence cases by male elites in progressive groups shattered the long-held belief that democratization in Korea was led by leaders who fully embodied the democratic spirit. Many felt betrayed by these male perpetrators and their supporters (Hong 2018). But in the history of democratization, there have been many such cases where democracy was promoted by not-so-democratic leadership. For example, it was the US occupation government that led the process of postwar reforms for democratization and the expansion of women's rights in Japan. In the newly established Republic of Korea, the "democratic reform of family law" was initiated by a politician who had been a Japanese collaborator and was a supporter of Syngman Rhee's increasingly authoritarian government.[3] Such cases challenge previous attitudes that put democracy on a pedestal, believing that democracy in and of itself would dispel inequality and promote liberty for all. While democracy may seem incompatible with gender inequality, feminist studies have contended that the former was established on the basis of the latter and reproduced systemic discrimination. As Carole Pateman argues, modern democracy was institutionalized by "consent and contract" with built-in discrimination against minority groups, including women (2001, 16–37;

---

[2] See *Minjuhwa undong ginyeom saeopoe*, Open Archives.

[3] According to General MacArthur's memoir, he presented the following directives to the Japanese Prime Minister Shidehara Kijūrō about the reforms concerning women's issues, urging him for hasty implementation of reform measures in Japan. "The emancipation of the women of Japan through their enfranchisement – that, being members of the body politic, they may bring to Japan a new concept of government directly subservient to the well-being of the home." See MacArthur 1964, 336. Ueno has pointed out the limits of such postwar reforms under the US occupation, as they did not dispel "the rule of husbands" and gender inequality. Yoneyama has argued that the US rendered Japanese women victims of male militarism and patriarchy to produce and disseminate the narrative "Cold War gender justice" and promote American democracy (Ueno 2009, 98–99; Yoneyama 2016, 81–107).

2018, 119–46, 323–46). Inspired by Carole Pateman's theory of "sexual contract," Christine Keating has argued that the institutionalization of democracy in postcolonial India was founded on racial and sexual discrimination. She focused on the ambivalent aspects of postcolonial reforms in India. On the one hand, the reforms had a liberalizing effect, by lifting restrictions on women's participation in the public sphere and by explicitly stating gender equality rights in statutes. On the other hand, they reaffirmed women's legal subjugation in property ownership, inheritance, marriage, and divorce (2011, 1–12). This analysis of the Indian case is illuminating for understanding the relationship between democracy and the principle of gender equality in postcolonial Korea.

Building on such scholarship, this chapter returns to the founding decade of Korean democracy from 1948 to 1958 to investigate the roots of women's unequal rights. I argue that postcolonial democracy in South Korea established women's rights but also institutionalized gender discrimination, especially in the 1958 Civil Code. In particular, this chapter demonstrates that South Korean family law, which was believed to have been based on a liberal democratic foundation, did not provide equal rights to women. Yang Hyun-ah, a prominent scholar of Korean family law, has attributed gender inequality in the family law to the colonial remnant that remained after 1945 in the form of the household head system (*hojuje*) (Yang 2011).[4] However, I argue that the process of democratization equally contributed to the gender inequality written into the family law portions of the 1958 Civil Code. In other words, postcoloniality and the ideal of democracy in the family law were intertwined in ways that had interesting implications for women's rights. Postcolonial democracy released women from colonial constraints such as wives' legal incompetence (see Chapter 2) but continued to limit the scope of their liberty by curtailing their rights in the private sphere. This ambivalence reflected the contested position of women's rights in the democratic project of establishing the Republic of Korea.

To understand this divergence in rights recognition, this chapter explores the following three questions: First, who were the subjects of rights in the 1948 Constitution and the 1958 Civil Code? Second, what perceptions and strategies did male lawmakers have on issues of gender and women's rights in the family law? Third, how were women's rights defined in the new family law, and what relationship did they have to Korea's broader postcolonial democracy? Answering these

---

[4] As detailed by Lim (Chapter 2), the household head system was a patriarchal family system, transplanted from the Japanese household system created during Japan's own nation-state building after the 1868 Meiji Restoration. Japanese colonial rulers of Korea considered Joseon's family system as premodern and old-fashioned because it was based on patriarchal kinship groups around the head of the family. Japanese reforms, which were considered as modernizing, shrank Joseon's extended family groupings to be led by a household head. Under the new structure, household heads became sole inheritors of family property and ancestral rites and had strong powers to control family members. When the household head died, the first son became the next household head, and the younger son became the household head of his own family when he got married (Hong 2005, 188–95).

questions, I demonstrate that through historical processes women formally gained equal rights but were actually subject to institutional discrimination.

3.2 WOMEN'S RIGHTS FROM THE 1948 CONSTITUTION TOWARD THE 1958 CIVIL CODE

On August 15, 1945, Korea was released from Japanese colonial rule, but this did not mean the nation was fully independent. The victors of World War II had divided the Korean peninsula at the 38th Parallel, which hardened as the border because the leaders of both Koreas and their patrons failed to reach a compromise. On August 15, 1948, the southern part of Korea established its own government, the Republic of Korea, and a committee was then created to draft a constitution and new laws (Hahm and Kim 2015). The first section of Article 1 of the 1948 Constitution (*Daehanminguk heonbeop*) declared that "The sovereignty of the Republic of Korea shall reside in the people, and all state authority shall emanate from the people." Koreans, who used to be the imperial subjects of the Japanese empire, now became "national subjects" with sovereign rights. Article 8 specified the protection of equal rights among all citizens, stating "All citizens shall be equal before the law, and there shall be no discrimination in political, economic, social or cultural life on account of sex, religion or social status."

However, full equal rights between men and women were already challenged in the process of creating a constitution. Yu Jin-o, who participated in drafting the 1948 Constitution, interpreted "the people" to be all individuals whose liberty and equality were guaranteed by the Constitution (Gukhoe samucheo 1948, 12). According to Yu's interpretation, the Constitution guaranteed democracy and protected the rights of all individuals without discrimination. Yu especially praised the progressive achievement of the new Constitution in promoting gender equality. "Considering that even countries with advanced democracy like France and Belgium only granted women's voting rights after World War II," Yu noted, "our constitution [that provides not only women's voting rights but also abolishes all discriminatory treatment of women as unconstitutional] is groundbreaking" (Yu 1953, 65–66). However, in his analysis of equality in Article 8, Yu added, "but gender equality means equality between the sexes before the law; it does not abolish the distinction between men and women based on biological differences, or all rules that are needed to protect family life."

He thus implied that biological differences could be a basis for discrimination between the sexes, and that the adoption of full equality could be postponed in order to protect the family. This impoverished sense of equal rights was echoed in a statement from another constitutional committee member, Gwon Seung-ryeol, during a session of the National Assembly in 1948. While he acknowledged that the gender equality clause in the Constitution meant equality of all national subjects before the law, he also emphasized that everyone had different rights depending on one's position as a national subject or a family member. When questioned whether the existence of concubinage contradicted Article 8's equality clause in the Constitution, Gwon answered that the gender equality guaranteed in the Constitution was only about legal equality between national subjects; equality between family members, such as with the practice of concubinage, was beyond the parameters of the Constitution.[5] Gwon assured National Assembly members that family matters like concubinage issues could be addressed later when writing the Civil Code (Gukhoe samucheo 1948, 13–14).

Both Yu and Gwon seemed to advocate for the basic principle of equality in the Constitution while also opening the possibility of applying different principles to women's rights via the family law. Their bifurcated understanding of "equality" strategically utilized the ideology of separate spheres, which justified gender discrimination based on physiological differences between women and men (Heo 1996; Pateman 2001, 16–37; 2018, 189–222). By granting different rights to men and women in the public and private spheres, Yu and Gwon paved the road for legal discrimination based on biological differences. In other words, while "the people" in the Constitution of 1948 seemed like a gender-impartial term on the surface, in practice, the concept left room for discrimination based on sexual difference.

Contestation over women's rights continued as Korea's first Civil Code was crafted over the next decade. The new Civil Code had to meet two goals: on the one hand, it had to realize the ideals of freedom and equality as basic principles of democracy; on the other hand, it had to build a modern family as the foundation of the modern nation-state and the family order that would contribute to the rebuilding of the nation.[6] In line with the first goal, the 1958 Civil Code declared that "All persons shall be subjects of rights and duties throughout their lives (Article 3)." This statement declared that the natural person is the rights bearer, and it fundamentally revised the rights bearer concept of the old Japanese Civil Code. The second goal, however, was more contested when it came to reformulating women's legal status

---

[5] A wife had various rights guaranteed by the Civil Code, but a concubine, who could not register in the husband's family registry, did not have any legal rights as a family member. No matter how long a concubine cohabited with the husband, she could not claim any rights to his property when he died or went missing. If the husband was killed in action during the war, she could not receive a survivor's pension. Also, even when a concubine registered her children on the husband's family registry and cohabited with them, she was not legally regarded as part of the family and could not exercise parental rights over said children.

[6] Given the fact that South Korea was in conflict with North Korea, the need for a new Civil Code was even more urgent. The Household Registration Law, which was a sub-set of the Civil Code, was the basis of South Korea's identification system and was used to keep track of the whereabouts of the citizenry. The following statement by Min Mun-gi, the Head of the Supreme Court Administration Legal Affairs, shows this well: "Family registry (*hojeok*) is official document that proves the status of the nationals, and all nationals have to have a family registry. Therefore, all personal status becomes clear by looking up the family registry at their original address (*bonjeok*) . . . distinguishing a proper national from a non-national is only possible through family registry" (Min 1953).

from what it had been under Japanese colonial rule, especially that of married women.

In colonial Korea, married women had been rendered legally incompetent, with some exceptions (see Chapter 2). In other words, a married woman could not purchase, lease, or transfer her own property, and could not take legal action without her husband's permission. Also, she had no right to bind herself by a labor contract. Even after Korea's independence, married women did not formally become legally independent because the US Military Government maintained laws from the colonial period, with minor exceptions (US Military Government Ordinance No. 21, November 2, 1945; Hanguk beopje yeonguhoe pyeon 1971, 139). Due to these transitional provisions, despite widespread eagerness to shed the legal yoke of Japanese colonial rule, the process of securing equal rights for women, especially married women, was complicated.

During the transitional period, however, women's rights in Korea's nascent democracy did see some progress. For example, just before the establishment of the Republic of Korea, the Supreme Court under the US Military Government recognized the legal capacity of married women without formally abolishing any existing restrictions on women's status in Korea. In 1947, a woman named Jeong Bo-nam demanded that her tenant, Yi Jeong-ja, give up her residence. When Yi rejected her claim, Jeong filed a lawsuit to request the delivery of real property in the Jeonju District Court and won. In response to her defeat, the defendant, Yi, appealed to the Supreme Court, citing Article 14 of the Japanese Civil Code (maintained under the US Military Government) that the original court had not considered the legal incompetence of the litigant; Jeong had filed the lawsuit without her husband's permission. Yet, the Supreme Court turned down Yi's appeal, noting that a married woman's legal incompetence was "absolutely inconceivable when the establishment of a new democratic nation is just around the corner." The judges explained their reasoning:

> This country was liberated from Japanese colonial rule on August 15, 1945, and it should be our aim to build a nation based on democracy, and to establish our entire system including legislation, politics, economy and culture according to democratic ideals. Accordingly, all people shall be equal, and the existing discriminatory system based on sexual differences is already starting to change following current moves to adopt democratic values in our society. Since women acquired equality in civil rights (*gonggwon*) such as rights of suffrage, electoral eligibility, and appointment to public office, so shall be the same in private rights (*sagwon*). Article 14 of the Civil Code (Japanese Civil Code), which had denied equality between men and women and contained extreme discrimination, is not appropriate for our current circumstances, so it is proper to make an adjustment. Thus, this court will not allow any claims that limit married woman's legal capacity.[7]

---

[7]   Supreme Court, *4280Minsang88 Gaongmyeongdo*, September 2, 1947; cited in Pak (1975, 529).

This ruling, first of all, declared that gender discrimination was incompatible with democratic values. Second, the ruling argued that as women gained equal civil rights with the general election of May 10, 1948, women should also be given equal private rights. However, the distinction between civil rights (*gonggwon*) and private rights (*sagwon*) was not clearly articulated at the time. "Civil rights" usually referred to the political rights of a citizen to elect and to be elected and "private rights" to rights in civil matters, such as rights of an individual and between family members. The Supreme Court ruling alone did not erase these distinctions. Nevertheless, the ruling clearly considered married women's legal incompetence a symbol of the old colonial legal system, which denied equality of the sexes. The ruling highlights how democratic values were significant elements in building the new polity and changing society, and that the judges felt that gender inequality was an inappropriate principle of the old governance that had obstructed the process of modernization.

Yet married women's legal capacity was contested from the beginning of the new republic. In early 1949, members of the Law Code Compilation Committee, the committee that was convened to prepare and review the new Civil Code following the promulgation of the new Constitution in September 15, 1948, agreed on the principle that married women were no longer legally incompetent but at the same time postponed clarifying the parameters of women's legal capacity until the Civil Code was finalized (Daehanminguk jeongbu gongbo cheo 1948, 1; C. Yang 1994, 307). Married women's legal incompetence disappeared with the 1958 Civil Code, which granted full legal capacity to married women in Article 3. With this change, married women officially became bearers of full rights. However, if one traces the debates over defining women's rights in the decade-long process of crafting the Civil Code, it becomes clear that the legislators, who were mostly male, only agreed to abolish married women's legal incompetence because they believed that other provisions in the Civil Code could sufficiently limit female spouses' legal capacity when needed.

In November 1949, the Compilation Committee produced an outline, which included provisions that "(1) A wife shall not need the consent of her husband to perform any juristic acts and procedures concerning her separate property; (2) A wife shall need her husband's consent when she makes a contract that will lead to physical bondage of her person." The annotated comments added further ambiguity and revealed the contested status of women's rights, noting that "the provision on married women's legal incompetence deserves criticism since it is anachronistic and incompatible with modern life and its social and economic necessities, but [some limitations on married women's rights] may be necessary to maintain a harmonious marriage" (Jang and Jang 1949, 13).

In the final draft of the Civil Code, the lawmakers expunged the provision of married women's legal incompetence, making women full rights-bearers. However, as detailed in Section 3.3, the provision's deletion did not end gender discrimination. Rather, it was a minimal gesture to acknowledge women's rights in order to facilitate democratic capitalist nation-building (E. Kim 2016). Granting women some legal rights and capacities in the 1958 Civil Code stands in tension with the detailed clauses that opened the possibility of limiting women's rights in certain cases. The discrepancy between the ostensible acceptance of gender equality and these exception clauses that permit gender discrimination produced a legal basis for justifying discriminatory practices. Accordingly, rights in the new Civil Code were also gendered.

3.3 INFLUENTIAL LAWMAKERS' CONCEPTIONS OF RIGHTS UNDER FAMILY LAW

The main architects of the 1958 Civil Code were the Law Code Compilation Committee and the National Assembly. Those who played major roles in the process were Kim Byeong-ro, the chairperson of the Compilation Committee, and Jang Gyeong-geun, the head of Civil Law Draft Review Division in the Legislative and Judiciary Committee. Women's voices were largely ignored in the Civil Code drafting process. In fact, the Committee members and the members of the National Assembly who participated in codification were all male. Only one female National Assembly member, Kim Cheol-an, reviewed the draft but seemed indifferent to the issue of women's rights. After the first draft of the Civil Code was released, a women's group led by the first female lawyer, Yi Tae-yeong, sent a "Declaration of Humanity Signed by 15 Million Women" to the National Assembly. They objected to the draft Civil Code and demanded a new one that guaranteed gender equality befitting the spirit of equality written into the Constitution, but their protest was set aside (Yi 1992, 395–404). In contrast, Kim and Jang not only designed the initial draft of the Civil Code but also greatly influenced the voting process in the National Assembly. While Kim utilized nationalistic rhetoric emphasizing national identity, Jang emphasized the gradual reform of customs in order to progress toward a "civilized society." Yet their arguments also overlapped in the sense that both advocated separating (and thus compromising) gender equality in the family sphere from political and social equality for women.

First, Kim's argument framed both family and women as the bastion of traditional values. Kim grew up studying Chinese classics and upholding Confucius values, but eventually became a legal expert educated in Tokyo, Japan. He was also a prominent nationalist and had been a lawyer during the colonial period, representing independence fighters in courts of law. This national leader maintained his conservative attitude while codifying family law in the 1950s. For example, Kim stated:

> Family law regarding succession should not imitate the laws of other countries. . . .
> The family law must be legislated according to our own national characteristics and

historical and cultural traditions. . . . All people of our country descended from Dangun. The blood of Dangun has flowed down to posterity through paternal succession of blood, great-grandfather to grandfather, and to father. . . . Man is made of the spirit of his fathers. (Gukhoe samucheo 1957, 7, 10)[8]

For Kim, the "national characteristics and historical and cultural traditions" were important elements to consider in the legislation process. Without mentioning any principles of the Constitution, he focused on bequeathed traditions. His ideas about equality revealed his conception of women's rights:

Many people seem to misunderstand the concept of gender equality in the Constitution. Gender equality means granting equal opportunities without discrimination between men and women in politics, social status, and culture, things like that. Confused people apply gender equality to old ethics of the family, kinship, or social and moral culture, which is useless to us. Nothing can be done if we seek equality in the relations between parents and children, and husbands and wives. Do you know how harmful this idea has become? Look at the immoral cases that are tainting the pages of newspapers and emerging at the court floors due to the loss of moral principles. (Gukhoe samucheo 1957, 11)

The first official draft (*jeongbuan*) designed by Kim thus emphasized preserving patrilineage and obscurely defined tradition. His emphasis on tradition was welcomed by conservatives such as the Confucian Association (*yurim*) and its supporters. Kim's arguments were as follows: (1) Korea possessed superior morality and culture compared to Western countries, despite their rapid development of science and technology, because Korea maintained its own traditional family system; (2) family law must be based on Korean morals and traditions, not Western legal principles, since the family is the fundamental basis of the nation-state; (3) equality of the sexes in political and social rights may be acceptable but extending equal rights to all family members will ruin Korean cultural tradition and morality (Gukhoe samucheo 1957, 11).

Kim Byeong-ro considered the democratic principles of the Constitution as something foreign and Western. Gender equality or women's rights, likewise, were foreign concepts that threatened the patrilineal consanguinity that was the essence of national tradition. Ironically, his zeal for national tradition led to his embracing of colonial legacy. The family system he embraced as Korean tradition was no different from the family system transplanted by the Japanese during the colonial period. In a similar vein, Partha Chatterjee has found that nationalists who were exposed to colonial rules tended to develop an exaggerated pride of cultural traditions in order to mitigate a sense of inferiority (1986, 131–71; 1990, 233–53). Yang Hyun-ah (2011, 248–49) analyzed the nationalist discourses of the male elites like Kim Byeong-ro

---

[8] Dangun is a legendary founding father of Old Joseon (*Gojoseon*).

and revealed how the colonial household-head system ended up being accepted as national tradition in the postliberation era.

However, Kim's position was a product of more than a simple reaction to the experience of colonialism. Instead, what was more important was Korea's postwar conditions as well as democratic and capitalist nation-building objectives. The inferiority complex of male elites produced by their experience of colonialism was exacerbated by the wrenching subsequent experiences of liberation, US occupation, and the Korean War. After the US occupation and the Korean War, many male nationalists perceived the rapid spread of American culture and western ideas as threats to society's traditional values.[9] From their point of view, Korean women having relationships with Americans – as lovers, wives, or prostitutes – and mixed-race children particularly threatened the homogeneity of the Korean nation and its paternal blood lines. They tried to resist Americanization by strengthening traditional values. In this context, Kim criticized women who permed their hair or went dancing as blindly following American culture and emphasized Korean tradition when he explained the legislative intent of the first official draft of the Civil Code in a plenary session of the National Assembly (Gukhoe samucheo 1957, 9).[10]

One might consider Kim's embracing of the household head system – an apparent colonial remnant – as ironic. However, the household head system in the 1958 Civil Code was not simply retained from the colonial period but rather was a reconceived amalgam influenced by the complex postcolonial context of American occupation and the division between the two Koreas. First of all, the new *hojuje* under the 1958 Civil Code massively shrank the authority of the household head to make it more "democratic." But retaining the *hojuje* was clearly a choice made by lawmakers faced with the particular postcolonial conditions of South Korea. The lawmakers believed that there was utility in retaining a "national tradition" like *hojuje* to bolster the family as a way to build a national identity to confront hegemonic American culture. In more practical terms, the *hojuje*-based family registration system was

---

9   For example, the philosopher and son of an independence movement activist, Sin Il-cheol criticized the rapidly spreading American culture in the 1950s and lamented, "Our capital, Seoul, is filled with the scent of butter and American scents. ... To us who slurp *doenjang*-soup in ramshackle straw-thatched houses, 'Americanism' is a tragedy." He also expressed anxiety about changing customs and values by noting that "our old life of frugality is being killed by American culture as an old and evil Confucian custom" (Sin 1957, 49–51).

10 "Madam Freedom," the novel serialized in *Seoul Sinmun* by Jeong Bi-seok in 1954 and its film version distributed in 1956, was very popular but also subject to much controversy. The story was about a wife of a college professor, who enjoys freedom dancing and dating other men. She eventually gets caught by the husband and returns home after a tearful contrition. With the popularity of the movie, women who wore Western clothes and enjoyed dancing were called "madam freedom," and were criticized for emulating Western culture and being sexually promiscuous. Western clothes and dancing became the symbols of "madam freedoms," who were liberated from patriarchal control. Kim Byeong-ro's critical remark about dancing and perms was related to this social situation.

useful as a population-tracking method under the anti-communist regime (Y. Kim 2007, 296–315; Min 1953).

Alongside Kim Byeong-ro, it was Jang Gyeong-geun, a judge during both the colonial and American Military Government periods, who had a major influence over the final draft of the new Civil Code and its implications for women's rights. Jang had visited the United States to study its judicial system for four months in 1947 and advocated that Korea learn from the American system with its "democratic spirit and its practice" (Jang 1948a, 20–28). His stance is ironic considering the fact that he later became a leading supporter of President Syngman Rhee's increasingly repressive rule, for example by dissolving the Special Investigation Committee for Anti-State Activities in 1949 as Vice Minister of Interior, and was later charged for interfering in the 1960 election after the April 19 protests that ended Rhee's rule. Jang was an interesting figure who could be seen as embodying the tensions inherent in postcolonial democracy; his attitude and conduct were not necessarily democratic, but he nevertheless mapped out a democratic and liberal future for the nation. From the beginning, he claimed that Korea's Civil Code must be modernized by eliminating old-fashioned feudalistic elements. In his private draft of the Civil Code, he argued that

> [w]hile codifying the family and inheritance law, it is imperative for us to consider maintaining beautiful customs only if they are not harmful, rejecting outmoded conventions, and promoting the national development and fortune through this legislation. The development of our nation depends not on the collective and communal group of the family but on the growth of each individual, which is compatible with the ideals of individualism, liberalism, and democracy. (Jang 1948b, 14)

Jang espoused a "gradual advancement theory," advocating for the modernization of family structures based on capitalism and liberal democracy and a balance between tradition and reform. Jang argued that families must accept a transition from ritual communities of ancestor worship to economic communities centered on the nuclear family in order to achieve a capitalistic system. He emphasized many times that the nuclear family was the core unit of a capitalistic society because it could adjust to the market more flexibly (Minuiwon 1957, 101). This was not his idea alone; his ideas were similar to lawmakers and legal scholars from the colonial period like the Japanese judge, Nomura Chōtarō (Lim 2019, 68–73). Such similarities show the colonial continuity of the so-called democratic reforms of the new Civil Code.[11] Jang may have been tainted by the colonial legacy, but he was also progressive in that he embraced the core principles of the Constitution: "individualism, liberalism, and democracy." Through his arguments, Jang emphasized the importance of building a democratic republic.

---

[11] I thank Sungyun Lim for pointing out the colonial continuity of Jang Gyeong-geun's reform ideas.

Jang's belief that Korean family law should promote a "gradual advance" toward individualism led him to promote a more egalitarian family system that could also accommodate women's rights within the family. He believed that the center of the family structure should be a horizontal and egalitarian spousal relation, not a vertical relationship that stressed the rights of the household head. Jang thus tried to steer family law toward undermining the household head's authority and weakening the line of patrilineal succession. He argued that in order to promote individualism, the new family law should protect the individual from the oppression of the household head or parents. He also argued that "[i]t is the growth of the individual that leads to the development of society and the state." Women could be this individual. Since "democracy is based on individualism" he noted, "there cannot be discrimination based on sex" (Minuiwon 1957, 101).

Why did Jang Gyeong-geun emphasize democracy and try to protect women's rights while supporting increasingly despotic rule by Rhee? We can find the answer in his commitment to national development. He saw the colonial period as feudal and the postcolonial period as modern, and he believed that democracy and individualism were two hallmarks of a modern civilized nation. In order to become a modern democratic society, from his perspective, it was necessary to undermine the patriarchal rights of the household head and improve the subordinate status of women. To him, the expansion of women's rights and democracy were signs of progress toward "civilized society."

At the same time, Jang thought that Korean cultural traditions could still be useful in promoting a sense of national unity. This led him to exhibit a duality of being both a "traditionalist" and a "modernist" on family law and women's rights issues. In explaining the purpose of the Civil Code to the Legislation and Judiciary Committee at the 1957 public hearing, he stated that "it is our obvious legislating principle that, on the basis of the spirit of our Constitution – the ideology of democracy, liberalism, and individualism – we need to lead our country towards progress, beyond current customs." Yet he also revealed a somewhat contradictory attitude toward gender equality by stating that "the complete application of gender equality might cause the destruction of the traditional family system" (Minuiwon 1957, 101). This shows that Jang was not too different from Kim in his belief in the need to protect the traditional patrilineal family system. Jang seems to have been less interested in the actual expansion of women's rights than in abolishing "the symbol of feudalism" (i.e., the low status of women that does not befit democratic citizens) that prevented Korea from developing into a "civilized country." For him, women's rights and gender equality were not immutable principles of democracy, but something that could be compromised any time. Such attitudes of male lawmakers demonstrate the peculiarity of postcolonial democracy: they were not fully free of coloniality and they treated the Constitution's equality clause as secondary to what they considered more important – national development. This is how women in postcolonial Korea were made into "equal" second-class citizens.

3.4 WOMEN'S RIGHTS IN FAMILY LAW: RIGHTS AMID PATRIARCHAL SUBMISSION

Korea's Civil Code was promulgated on February 22, 1958, and went into effect on January 1, 1960.[12] The code was the product of compromises between the constitutional principles of equality and liberty and those lawmakers who feared that these principles could undermine Korean traditional values. As a result, full protection of women's rights and equal status between men and women were postponed. Still, the status of women in Korea undeniably improved with the new family law, relative to the colonial period, through the significant reduction of the rights of the household head. Women's subordination was a symptom of backwardness and did not befit Korea's new national identity as a democratic republic. Accordingly, Korean women obtained a new status and rights as nationals of the new nation (*gungmin*).[13]

Some compromises regarding women's rights are to be expected, considering the cultural anxieties expressed by male lawmakers like Kim Byeong-ro. Most of the compromises regarding women's rights in the family law stemmed from the maintenance of the household head system, that is, the family structure that was organized under the authority of the household head.[14] Even though the new Civil Code diminished the rights of the household head as detailed later, the remaining rights were still significant. Because the household head controlled entrance into the family registry, women's rights could easily be compromised. For instance, if a woman remarried and sought to have her children added to her new husband's family registry, she would have to obtain consent from the household heads of both families, her ex-husband's and current husband's. In contrast, a male spouse would not need the consent of the household head – his father or grandfather – or his wife if he wanted to add his offspring to the family registry, including those born out of wedlock. Such laws highlighted the disparities between the rights of men and women.

The mere existence of the household registry (*hojeok*) with its patriarchal assumptions had problematic ramifications on women's rights. The family registry played a major role in determining who constituted a family. According to the new Civil

---

[12] The Family Law describes the fourth and fifth parts of the Civil Code of 1958, which is subdivided as follows: I. General Provisions, II. Real Rights, III. Claims, IV. Relatives, and V. Inheritance.

[13] After the Republic of Korea's establishment, the political subjects referenced in the Constitution, official documents, and school textbooks were "national subjects" (*gungmin*). In one sense, the term was an inherited concept from the colonial period that connoted (Japanese) imperial subjects. At the same time, it was also an ideological and political construct devised to contrast with the concept of the DPRK's notion of "people" (*inmin*) (Park 2009, 97–121). The male lawmakers who wrote the ROK's Civil Code considered women's rights as a minimal qualification to be considered a proper nation, rather than as a matter of guaranteeing universal rights to members of a democratic society.

[14] Japan abolished its old family system with a new Civil Code promulgated on December 22, 1947. This feat is attributed to the "Democratizing Project" of the GHQ in Japan. GHQ/SCAP contended that the old family system had facilitated fascism. On the ironic and contrasting fates of the household head system in postcolonial Korea and postwar Japan, see E. Kim (2017).

Code, a family consisted of "the spouse of the household head, his kin and spouses of them, and anyone who was added to a family register according to the Civil Code" (Article 779). In other words, a family in the Civil Code was defined not by affinity – by marriage or other relations – but by who was registered in the family registry. Only a male spouse could record his offspring born outside wedlock on the family register (Article 782, Sec. 1). In contrast, if a female spouse had children out of wedlock or from a previous marriage, she had to receive permission from both the household head and her husband in order to have her children added to the family register (Article 784, Sec. 1). In addition, the definition and extent of parental authority also undermined women's equal rights. The father had parental authority over minor children, and only in the absence of a father could a mother obtain parental rights over her children. If she remarried, she lost her rights (Article 909). Thus, the Code infringed on women's equal rights and hindered their freedom of remarriage.

The family law of 1958 failed to fully remove the yoke of the patriarchal family system, but it nonetheless provided significant improvements in women's rights, as shown later. While these improvements did not measure up to perfect gender equality, they were important. More than the extent of improvement in rights, what is notable is the area where the expansion of rights was allowed for women. As I will show later, the rights that were given to women were focused on those areas that enabled them to function as independent, liberal subjects in economic activity. In other words, women under the new Civil Code were made into full rights-bearing subjects for the new liberal capitalistic system more than anything else (E. Kim 2018).

The most notable change in the new Civil Code was the explicit protection of the wife's separate property rights. It acknowledged a wife's separate property rights by stating that "[p]roperty that was owned separately by either spouse before marriage or acquired during the duration of marriage by either spouse in their own name is considered separate property" (Article 830, Sec. 1). There was an unequal provision to this law, because the second clause of that law stated that "property the ownership of which is unclear is assumed to be owned by the husband" (Article 830, Sec. 2). But the first clause codified separate property rights of the wife, thereby supporting the principle of private property in the spirit of the modern Civil Code.

Women's rights saw improvement in other areas due to the curtailing of the rights of the household head. Adult women over the age of twenty-three obtained the right to marry (Article 808, Sec. 1). Divorce could be obtained by mutual consent between the husband and the wife (Article 834). The Civil Code also stipulated that admissible reasons for divorce should be equal between husband and wife (Article 840); whereas only the "wife's adultery" was grounds for divorce in the colonial period, the phrase was changed to "a spouse's adultery" in the new Civil Code (Bae 1988, 106–07).

Another economically meaningful area where the new Civil Code expanded women's rights was in the inheritance rights of the wife. The wife now had the right to inherit the household headship, in the absence of a biological or adopted son as the lineal descendent of a predecessor. Women during the colonial period were granted only a temporary headship before an adopted son was designated. Wives were also the last in line for inheritance during the colonial period, behind even the grandmother and mother of the deceased. Changes in married women's right to inherit property also expanded women's property rights. During the colonial period, a female spouse could not inherit any property if there were lineal descendants. In contrast, the new Civil Code designated the wife's share for inheritance even when she had lineal descendants, stating that "[i]f there were either a lineal ascendant or a linear descendant, the female spouse of the deceased becomes a co-heir. ... If there exists no inheritor, the spouse becomes the sole heir(ess)" (Article 1003). With these expansions in the inheritance rights of wives, married women were no longer ghosts without rights. There was a drawback, however: the share of inheritance for the wife was half that of the male lineal descendants and the same as those of the male lineal ascendants. Moreover, an unmarried daughter's share was half that of a son's, and daughters who were married were only entitled to a quarter of their brother's share.

In sum, women's rights saw meaningful expansion in the new Civil Code of 1958, but these improvements had limitations. These compromises were due to various anxieties among male lawmakers in the immediate postcolonial period. The particular postcolonial conditions created by the US occupation led them to adhere more strongly to what they perceived as Korean tradition and the last bulwark against the dangerous invasion of American culture and the breakdown of "beautiful customs." Yet, despite these anxieties, they allowed improvements in significant areas of women's rights. The reason for this was the lawmakers' commitment to national improvement and development, particularly for the new liberal capitalist nation that they were building. Therefore, women's rights were improved in precisely those areas that guaranteed individual economic rights.

3.5 CONCLUSION: THE LEGACY OF POSTCOLONIAL DEMOCRACY AND WOMEN'S CIVIL RIGHTS

By analyzing family law codification, this chapter argued that the process of institutionalizing democracy in South Korea entailed legal bases for both expanding and curtailing women's rights. Under the hasty beginning of the Cold War, with division, war, and the occupation by the US Military Government, South Korea began the institutionalization of democracy before it could complete the process of decolonization. In the historical context of postcoloniality and the establishment of a democratic republic, women's rights became a symbol of democracy; the new Civil Code that remade them into full legal subjects made them a crucial component of the new model of national sovereign citizenship. Yet women were also treated as repositories of "national tradition" in the legislative discussions that led to the promulgation of the new Civil Code, and their rights were consequently compromised. This duality demonstrated key tensions in the conceptualization of equal rights in postcolonial democracy.

The duality of women's rights has not been fully explored in previous scholarship. One surmises it was because the legislators who led the process of writing the new Civil Code did not fully embrace the democratic ideals of equal rights for all. Also, the fact that the preservation of the household head system squarely contradicted the principle of equality made it difficult for many to fully appreciate how certain provisions in the new Civil Code nonetheless improved women's rights. In spite of its compromised character in terms of gender equality and the colonial vestiges that legislators maintained, the 1958 Civil Code was an important part of the institutionalization of democracy in Korea, especially in the ways in which it diminished household head rights and made women full rights-bearers and part of the new model of national citizenship. Male lawmakers, in order to make women into national subjects, had to democratize the family law, however minimally. As was the case in Japan during the postwar "democratization" process, in Korea the "democratization" of the family law failed to dismantle the patriarchal order. Thus, women's rights shrank to wives' and daughters' rights within the domestic sphere, and the abolition of the household head system and other family law reform issues became core goals of the South Korean feminist movement. It is quite telling how it was only after the 2005 abolition of the household head system that issues of feminist movement in South Korea diversified (Choi 2005). Citizenship refers not only to political and legal rights but also to economic, social, and cultural rights of inclusion. It is not limited to the rights conferred by the state from above but includes rights that people can achieve through dynamic processes of demanding from below (M. Jang 2001). Recent gender conflict and the social debates provoked by the #MeToo movement can be considered part of this ongoing process of reconceptualizing women's citizenship and rights in Korea.

As feminist anthropologist Haejoang Cho stated recently in an interview, "gender disputes nowadays are arguably a much more serious social problem than even the conflict between South and North Korea" (Yang 2018). Recent public confrontations between men and women in South Korea accelerated violent reactions online and offline at the same time. In 2018, for example, a large demonstration by women at Hyehwa station protested unfair investigations of "hidden camera incident." Only "biologically female" persons were allowed at the demonstration, and radical slogans emerged protesting male power and demanding an end to misogyny. The situation escalated when a member of the young feminist group, Womad (a neologism combining women and nomad), outed and defamed a host of hidden camera footage on their website. In protest, male netizens congregated at the same metro station to support a man who had been given a prison sentence for sexual harassment and claimed the decision as unjust. The counterprotest's location made it clear that their intention was to challenge the feminists (Kim and Kim 2018; Newsis 2018). In this context, many women in South Korea feel they can no longer keep silent. They are rising up not only against sexual harassment and assault but also against long-standing legal discrimination in everyday life. Women's resentment in this post-#MeToo era may not be alleviated unless we tackle remaining legal and cultural roots of limits on women's rights. This chapter examined an earlier iteration of similar rights disparities and tensions in the context of postcolonial democracy – a democracy that nominally created "equal" people, but ultimately also institutionalized gender inequality.

REFERENCES

Primary Sources

Daehanminguk jeongbu gongbo cheo. 1948. "Gungmu hoeuiui gyeoljeongeul eodeo jejeonghan beopjeon pyeonchan wiwonhoe jikjereul ie gongpo" [Reorganization plan by the law code compilation committee promulgated by cabinet decision]. *Gwanbo* 4: 17–18.

Gukhoe samucheo. 1948. *Gukhoe sokgirok* [The stenographic records of the National Assembly]. 1 (18).

1957. *Gukhoe sokgirok* [The stenographic records of the National Assembly]. 26 (30).

Hanguk Beopje Yeonguhoe Pyeon. 1971. *Migunjeong beomnyeong chongnam (Gungmunpan)* [Military law and ordinance of US Military Government (Korean version)]. Seoul: Hanguk beopje yeonguhoe.

Jang, Gyeong-geun. 1948a. "Miguk sabeop jedo" [American judicial system]. *Beopjeong* 3 (1): 20–28.

1948b. "Chinjoksangsokbeop ipbeop bangchim mit yogang saan" [A private draft of the policy and principle of the Civil Code]. *Beopjeong* 3 (9): 13–17.

Jang, Gyeong-geun, and Seung-du Jang. 1949. "Minbeop chinjoksangsok pyeon yogang haeseol (2)" [Relatives and inheritance of the Civil Code (2)]. *Beopjeong* 4 (11): 13–19.

Minuiwon. 1957. *Minbeop ansimui jaryojip* [Source documents for reviewing the Civil Code draft]. Seoul: Minuiwon.

Min, Mun-gi. 1953. "Hojeok jeongbiui jeeon" [Opinion on reforming the family registry]. Dong-a Ilbo, January 16, 1953.

Sin, Il-cheol. 1957. "Saenghwal inyeomui jaebalgyeon: uri naraui amerikanijeum" [Rediscovery of life ideology: Americanism in our country]. *Saebyeok* 4 (1): 49–52.

Yu, Jin-o. 1953. *Singo heonbeop haeui* [Companion to the Constitution]. Seoul: Tamgudang.

Secondary Sources

Bae, Gyeong-suk. 1988. *Hanguk yeoseong sabeopsa* [The legal history of Korean women]. Incheon: Inha University Press.

Chatterjee, Partha. 1986. *Nationalist Thought and the Colonial World: A Derivative Discourse.* Minneapolis: University of Minnesota Press.

1990. "The Nationalist Resolution of the Women's Question." In *Recasting Women: Essays in Indian Colonial History*, edited by Kumkum Sangari and Sudesh Vaid. New Brunswick: Rutgers University Press, 233–53.

Choi, Eun-a. 2005. "Hojuje pyeji ihu, 'gajog'eul ditgo 'gaein' euro" [After the abolition of the household head system, beyond the "family" to the "individual"]. Ingwon undong sarangbang. www.sarangbang.or.kr/writing/53258.

Hahm, Chaihark, and Sung Ho Kim. 2015. *Making We the People: Democratic Constitutional Founding in Postwar Japan and South Korea*. Cambridge: Cambridge University Press.

Han, So-bum. 2018. "Seongpongnyeok kkeutjangnaeja" [Let us end sexual violence]. *Hankook Ilbo*, August 19, 2018. www.hankookilbo.com/News/Read/201808191607711243.

Hasunuma, Linda, and Ki-young Shin. 2019. "#MeToo in Japan and South Korea: #WeToo, #WithYou." *Journal of Women, Politics, & Policy* 40 (1): 97–111.

Heo, Ra-geum. 1996. "Seogu jeongchi sasangeseoui gongsa gaenyeomgwa gabujangjeokseong chabyeolseong" [The conceptual distinction of "public" and "private" in patriarchal western political thought]. *Yeoseonghang nonjip* 13: 333–57.

Hong, Sung-eun. 2018. "Dojeohi an sseul su eopneun geul #metoo: eummoronul naeseuneun ideurege mutgo sipda" [#MeToo blog: what I would like to ask those who believe the conspiracy theories]. *HUFFPOST*, March 7, 2018." www.huffingtonpost.kr/entry/story_kr_5a9f406ce4b0d4f5b66b577f?utm_id=naver.

Hong, Yang-hui. 2005. "Singminji sigi hojeokjedowa gajokjedoui byeonyong" [Transformation of family system through hojeok (family register) system in Korea by Japanese colonialism]. *Sahakyeongu* 79: 167–205.

Jang, Mi-kyoung. 2001. "Simingwon (citizenship) gaenyeomui uimi hwakjanggwa byeonhwa: jayujuuijeok simingwon gaenyeomeul neomeoseo" [The enlargement and change of the concept of citizenship: beyond the concept of liberal citizenship]. *Hankuksahoehak* 35 (6): 59–77.

Jang, Ye-ji. 2019. "Seongchuhaeng insabobok An Tae-geun, 2 simseodo jingyeok 2nyeon" [An Tae-geun, who retaliated with personnel decisions for exposing sexual harassment sentenced to two years in prison at the appeals court]. *Hankyoreh*, July 18, 2019. www .hani.co.kr/arti/society/society_general/902342.html.

JTBC. 2018. "*Geomchal nae seongpokhaengdo isseotjiman bimillie deopyeo*" [Sexual violence in the Prosecutors Office was concealed]. *JTBC News*, January 29, 2018. http://news .jtbc.joins.com/article/article.aspx?news_id=NB11582419.

⸻ 2018. "*Inteobyu: 'Ahn Hee-jung seongpongneok' pongno, Kim Ji-eun 'dareun pihaeja inneun geot ara*'" [Interview: "Ahn Hee-jung's sexual violence" revelations, Kim Ji-eun said, "I know that there are other victims"]. *JTBC News*, March 5, 2018. http://news .jtbc.joins.com/article/article.aspx?news_id=NB11598736.

Keating, Christine. 2011. *Decolonizing Democracy: Transforming the Social Contract in India*. University Park: Penn State University Press.

Kim, Eun-kyung. 2016. "Tal singmingi gajok beopeseo minjujuui uijewa yeoseongui gungmin hwa: 'cheoui haengwi neungnyeog'eul jungsimeuro" [The democratic issues of family law and nationalization of women in postcolonial Korea – focused on "the capable person system of wives"]. *Sarim* 57: 269–94.

⸻ 2017. "Poseuteu singmin/jegugui aireoniwa neisyeonui jagi byeonju: jeyicha segye daejeonhu hanil gajokbeop jejeonggwa yeoseongui wichi" [Irony of post-colony/empire and self-variation of nation: family law establishment of Korea and Japan after World War II]. *Hanguk geunhyeondaesa yeongu* 82: 253–79.

2018. "Hangukgwa ilbonui gajo beopeseo cheoui jiwiwa yeoseongui 'gwolli' (1945–1960)" [Position of wives and women's "right" in the new civil codes of South Korea and Japan (1945–1960)]. *Yeoseong gwa yeoksa* 29: 339–73.

Kim, Heon-ju, and Jeong-hwa Kim. 2018. "Yeoseong ingwon oechimgwa hamkkye jaraneun namseong hyomo" [Misandry that grows with the slogan for women's rights]. *Seoul Sinmun*, July 9, 2018. www.seoul.co.kr/news/newsView.php?id=20180709010020 &wlog_tag3=naver.

Kim, Yeong-mi. 2007. "Haebang ihu jumindeungnokjedoui byeoncheongwa geu seonggyeok: hanguk jumindeungnokjeungui yeoksajeok yeonwon" [Changes in the resident registration system and the characteristics thereof: historical origins of the resident registration card]. *Hankuksa Yeongu* 136: 287–323.

Lim, Sungyun. 2019. *Rules of the House: Family Law and Domestic Disputes in Colonial Korea*. Berkeley: University of California Press.

MacArthur, Douglas. 1964. *Reminiscences*. New York: McGraw-Hill.

Minjuhwa undong ginyeom saeopoe, Open Archives, https://archives.kdemo.or.kr/isad/view/ 00700365.

Newsis. 2018. "Oneureun yeoseong, 27-ilen namseong . . . hyehwayeok siwi seongdaegyeolrui jangeuro" [Today the women, on the 27th men – Hyehwa station demonstration becomes the stage for sexual competition]. *Newsis*, October 6, 2018. https://newsis.com /view/?id=NISX20181005_0000435600&cID=10201&pID=10200.

Pak, Byeong-ho. 1975. *Pallye gyojae: chinjok sangsokbeop* [Precedents textbook: family and inheritance law]. Seoul: Beommunsa.

Park, Myoung-kyu. 2009. *Gungmin, inmin, simin: gaenyeomsaro bon hangugui jeongchijuche* [Nation, people, citizen: Korean political subjects in the History of concepts]. Seoul: Sohwa.

Pateman, Carole. 2001 [1988]. *Namgwa yeo, eunpyeondoen seongjeong gyeyak* [The sexual contract]. Trans. Lee Chwunghwun. Seoul: Ihwu.

2018 [1990]. *Yeojadeurui mujilseo* [The disorder of women: democracy, feminism and political theory]. Trans. Lee Pyeonghwa and Lee Seongmin. Seoul: Doseochulpan b.

Seo, Eo-ri. 2018. "Dandok: 'Naneun Jeong Bong-joo jeon uiwonege seongchuhaeng danghaetda' hyeonjik gija pongno" [News reporter exposes, "former congressman Chung Bong-joo sexually harassed me"]. *Pressian*, March 7, 2018. www.pressian.com/news/ article/?no=188158.

Ueno, Chizuko. 2009 [1994]. *Geundae gajokui seongnipgwa jongeon* [Kindai Kazoku no Seiritsu to Shūen] [The establishment and end of the modern family]. Translated by Imijimunhwa yeonguso. Seoul: Dangdae.

Yang, Chang-su. 1994. "Jaryo: Beopjeon pyeonchan wiwon chonghoe uisarok (cho)" [The draft record of the Law Code Compilation Committee]. *Beophak* 35 (2): 298–323.

Yang, Hyun-ah. 2011. *Hanguk gajokbeop ikgi: jeontong, singminjiseong, jendeoui gyocharo eseo* [Reading the Korean Family Law: tradition, coloniality, and gender]. Seoul: Changbi.

Yang, Seong-hui. 2018. "Yang Seonghuiui jikgyeok inteobyu, Cho Hanhyejeong [Haejoang Cho] yeonse dae myeongye gyosu: 'namjaneun gukga, yeojaneun gajeong' ibunbeop kkaeya seongpyeongdeung ganeung" [Yang Seong-hui interview of Cho-Han Haejoang Yonsei University professor emerita: gender equality only possible by shattering the binary of "men for the state, women for the homes"]. *Joongang Ilbo*, December 28, 2018. https://news.joins.com/article/23243748.

Yi, Tae-yeong. 1992. *Hanguk gajokbeop gaejeong undong 37-nyeonsa* [37 years history of the family law reform movement in Korea]. Seoul: Hanguk gajeong beomnyul sangdamso.

Yoneyama, Lisa. 2016. *Cold War Ruins: Transpacific Critique of American Justice and Japanese War Crimes*. Durham: Duke University Press.

Yonhap News. 2019. "Top Court Reaffirms Ex-Governor Guilty of Sexual Abuse." *Yonhap News*, September 9, 2019. https://en.yna.co.kr/view/AEN20190909001900315?section=search.

PART II

Institutional Mechanisms for Rights Claiming

4

A Clash of Claims

The Diversity and Effectiveness of Rights Claims around the Jeju 4.3 Events

Hun Joon Kim

4.1 INTRODUCTION

Korea provides an excellent case to study transitional justice since its history has been marked by multiple transitions: Japanese colonialism (1910–45), the US military occupation (1945–48), the Korean War (1950–53), the dictatorship of Rhee Syngman (1948–60), a short-lived democracy of the Second Republic (1960–61), a military coup and subsequent dictatorship by Park Chung-hee (1961–79), the assassination of Park and the brief moment of the Seoul Spring (1979), another coup by Chun Doo-hwan and Roh Tae-woo and the authoritarian rule under Chun (1980–88), and finally, democratization in 1987. Since democratization, victims of past state abuse and their relatives have pursued rights claims via criminal prosecutions, truth commissions, and reparations applications, with truth commissions being the most frequently used.

This chapter's purpose is to understand the complexity of transitional justice and rights claiming processes in South Korea by focusing on claims related to the Jeju 4.3 events, which were "a series of armed communist uprisings and counter-insurgency actions that occurred between 1947 and 1954 in the region of Mt. Halla on Jeju Island" (Jeju Commission 2003, 19). Koreans call them the Jeju 4.3 events because the uprisings began in earnest on April 3, 1948. The counterinsurgency strategy was extremely brutal, involving mass killings, arrests, detentions, torture, and forced relocations, which resulted in an estimated 30,000 deaths (H. J. Kim 2014). After decades-long advocacy by citizens, the National Committee for the Investigation of the Truth about the Jeju 4.3 Events (the Jeju Commission) was finally created in 2000. As of December 2018, the government has identified 15,483 victims and 61,030 family members (Ministry of the Interior and Safety 2018).

This chapter asks three questions: First, how have rights claims by victims and opponents unfolded over seventy years of activism and counter-activism in South Korea? Second, why have we witnessed the diversification of rights claims either by victims or by opponents at certain points of time? Third, why is a certain rights claim – or a certain framing of rights claim – more effective than others in achieving purported goals of activism or counter-activism in the Jeju case?

The Jeju 4.3 events are an ideal case to explore the diversity and effectiveness of rights claims due to the long history of advocacy. Victims and opponents raised their voices since the massacres, and their claims and the effectiveness of those claims changed considerably depending on varying political contexts. The lengthy time span provides an opportunity to study changes in rights claims by both victims and opponents. In addition, the Jeju Commission is still functional as of October 2019, offering us the chance to analyze rights claiming by victims and opponents after the state acknowledged its past atrocities. Moreover, since conservatives retook the presidency in 2008, this chapter leverages changes in the political environment to explore how rights claiming and the Commission's work changed under a less supportive administration. It traces how clashes of rights claims intensified between victims and opponents around the Commission and its follow-up activities.

The answers to the questions posed earlier are based on field research conducted in January and November 2017 and October 2018. I explored local archives and interviewed local activists, scholars, politicians, and victims via semi-structured interviews and subsequent email or phone interviews. I collected and analyzed documents from Jeju National University's Jeju Archives, the Jeju 4.3 Peace Foundation's 4.3 Archives, and from individuals and local organizations such as former special investigator Kim Jong-min and the Provincial Solidarity for 4.3.

To understand the history of rights claiming processes surrounding the Jeju 4.3 events, this chapter consists of three sections. The first section provides definitions of rights and rights claiming and introduces aspects of social movement theory as applied to this chapter. The second section is an exploration of the changes of rights claims made by victims and opponents, divided into four distinct periods according to the nature and dynamics of rights claims and counterclaims. In this section, both the changes of rights claims and the clash between rights claims are explored. The third section analyzes the different rights claims made by victims and opponents in terms of opportunity structures and rights framing. Here, I found that rights claims diversify when the counterclaims are strong and the opportunity structure opens up. In addition, frame resonance is a key factor in determining the effectiveness of rights claims. The conclusion ends with implications for changes under different administrations.

4.2 DEFINITIONS AND THEORETICAL FRAMEWORKS

Rights provide "the rational basis for a justified demand" (Shue 1996, 13) and can be divided into two types: special rights and general rights. Special rights arise out of "special transactions between individuals or out of some special relationship in which they stand to each other" (Hart 1955, 183). General rights are rights that individuals have "simply because they constitute a particular kind of moral being" (Reus-Smit 2013, 37). By its nature, the former is particularistic, while the latter is universalistic, within the boundary of what contemporaries thought was a moral human existence. Rights can be further divided into two additional categories: individual rights and collective rights. Individual rights are the rights of sole persons, while collective rights are the rights of groups. This two-by-two categorization of rights is useful to understand different types of rights claims made in social movement processes and their effectiveness in achieving desired goals in the movements.

A rights claim is "more than a reminder or an appeal; it also involves a powerful *demand* for action [emphasis original]" (Reus-Smit 2013, 36). It is important to understand the contexts under which these rights claims are made, and the goals that these claims attempt to achieve. Social movement theory provides a useful conceptual framework to capture this process, especially to understand what accounts for the changes in rights claims and what affects their effectiveness (see Chapter 7). Three sets of factors have been emphasized in social movement theory: the forms of organization (mobilizing structures); the structure of political opportunity and constraints confronting the movement (opportunities structure); and the collective process of interpretation, attribution, and social construction that mediates between agents and opportunity structure (framing process) (McAdam, McCarthy, and Zald 1996, 2). In this chapter, I adopt Benford and Snow's understanding of victims/activists and opponents as agents who are engaging in "the production and maintenance of meaning for constituents, antagonists, and bystanders or observers" (2000, 613). This is the framing process that can be defined – again following Benford and Snow – as "an active, processual phenomenon that implies agency and contention at the level of reality construction" (2000, 614).

Frames can vary in terms of the degree of resonance. As Keck and Sikkink note, frame resonance is particularly important because it concerns "the relationship between a movement organization's interpretive work and its ability to influence broader public understanding" (Keck and Sikkink 1998, 17). Supporters and opponents of collective action always "seek ways to bring issues to the public agenda by framing them in innovative ways and by seeking a hospitable venue" (ibid.). Thus, the resonance of the frame is closely associated with the political opportunity structure. Frames that are consistent with the prevailing political discourse or culture at the time will have an enormous power to draw attention from politicians and the public. Meanwhile, two factors affect the effectiveness of frames used in social movements (Benford and Snow 2000, 618–22). First, frames can be exclusive and rigid, or inclusive and flexible. Second, frames can vary in their interpretive scope, ranging from those limited to a specific issue or group to those covering a set of similar problems. These two factors are related to the contents of rights claims. Claims for special and individual rights tend to be relatively exclusive/rigid and narrow in their interpretive scope, while claims for general rights tend to be inclusive and broad in their scope.

Like the framing process, rights claims are active, contentious, and involve agency. Here, ideas, meaning, and culture become important. Within this context, according to McAdam, McCarthy, and Zald, occur "the conscious strategic efforts by groups of people to fashion shared understandings of the world and of themselves that legitimate and motivate collective action" (1996, 6). Similarly, rights claiming is a process of cultivating shared interpretations of the problem and promoting collective action to solve them (Smith 2002, 510). In the following section, we see how the victims of Jeju 4.3 and their opponents organized for rights claiming and framed their respective rights claims in relation to opportunity structures over the last seventy years.

4.3 A CLASH OF CLAIMS

The path to the establishment of the Jeju Commission was a long and arduous one. In this section, I trace the changes of claims by victims and activists and counterclaims by opponents, which translate into four distinct periods: first, the period between the occurrence of the massacre and the end of the Roh Tae-woo regime (1947–92); second, the period of the first civilian administration under President Kim Young-sam (1993–97); third, the period between the inauguration of President Kim Dae-jung and the enactment of the Special Law for Investigation of the Jeju 4.3 Events and Restoration of the Honor of Victims (1998–99)[1]; and fourth, the period between the creation of the Jeju Commission and the end of the Park Geun-hye administration (2000–17). In each period, three aspects were examined: first, who the claimants were; second, what their claims were and how they were framed; and third, what tactics or strategies were used in claims-making.

4.3.1 *From 1947 to 1992*

Although the civilian death toll was unprecedented, the massacres were systematically hidden from the public, and calls for truth and justice were completely suppressed under anti-communist military and authoritarian regimes until 1992. Sometimes, political opportunities opened up for the victims, such as during the one-year period between the April 19 Student Revolution in 1960 and the May 16 military coup in 1961, or the short period known as the Seoul Spring after the assassination of President Park in 1979. A few courageous individuals made sporadic attempts to question, remember, and seek redress for this unjustifiable state violence (H. J. Kim 2014). With the 1987 democratic transition, the forgotten massacres slowly

---

[1] *Jeju 4.3 sageon jinsang gyumyeong mit huisaengja myeongyehoeboge gwanhan teukbyeolbeop*, Act No. 6177 (2000).

regained local attention in Jeju through the efforts of university students, progressive journalists, and activists. Their efforts reached a climax in April 1992 with the excavation of Darangsi Cave and the discovery of the skeletal remains of eleven civilians, which provided concrete and indisputable evidence of indiscriminate killings. During the preceding dark decades, however, only individuals, usually either a university student or a journalist, would raise this difficult and unresolved history (H. J. Kim 2014). In most cases, it was not the victims themselves who were active but rather those who sympathized with them or who were inspired by a sense of justice, truth, and historical awareness.

Immediately after the toppling of President Rhee Syngman's dictatorship by a student-led demonstration in 1960 – known as the April 19 Revolution – Jeju victims raised their voices. The public, including the victims, believed that "a new era had finally come" to act upon the massacres.[2] In May 1960, the National Assembly set up a special committee to investigate innocent civilian deaths (*yangmin haksal sageon jinsang josa teukbyeol wiwonhoe*). Seven victims testified in front of the committee, and the most common claim made by victims was that those who were killed were not communists at all and had no connection to communism. Jang Gap-sun, for example, argued strongly that "there were no communists at all" among the seventy civilians killed in his village (Jeju Commission 2002b, 163). Similarly, Ko Sun-hwa consistently emphasized that those killed were "innocent civilians," and Shin Du-bang also stressed that residents were not "reds" (*ppalgaengi*) (Jeju Commission 2002b, 166, 169). The victims' claims were defensive in nature, suggesting that their family members who were killed were not communists. Since the focus was on denying the false accusation of being communists, victims did not claim any further rights at the hearings.

A few years later, however, some victims became more vocal about their rights, and often their claims resulted in concrete actions. For example, in 1964, under Yang Bong-cheon's leadership, a small number of victims in the village of Uigui set up a common burial ground and erected a stone monument, which echoed the aforementioned victims' claim of innocence. The stone monument was inscribed with the words "A Monument to the Illustrious Memory of the Righteous" (*hyeonui hapjangmyo*). While victims again claimed that those murdered were innocent, they went one step further and claimed that they were also righteous. Yang's strong belief in the innocence of the victims, including his father and brothers, made it possible for him to claim their righteousness.[3] A claim of righteousness is more tightly linked to the rights claims than a claim of innocence. Since the victims were righteous, bereaved family members had a right to know the truth (*jinsang gyumyeong*), find and punish the perpetrators, and recover the honor of those victims (*myeongye*

---

[2] Interview, Lee Mun-gyo, former chairperson of the Jeju 4.3 Peace Foundation (April 22, 2006).

[3] Interview, Yang Bong-cheon, president of the Hyunui Victims Association (October 19, 2005).

hoebok). However, the Uigui case was an exception, and most victims remained silent during this period.

Often, it was not the victims themselves but students and activists who spoke out on behalf of victims. For example, in May 1960, seven students at Jeju National University organized a group to investigate the massacres (4.3 *jinsang gyumyeong dongjihoe*). The students released a statement in a local newspaper, claiming, "the time has come for us to appease the souls of the millions murdered by barbaric guns and swords by testifying to *their innocence*" (*mujoe*) [emphasis added] (Jeju Commission 2002a, 316). Here, students echoed the victims' claim that those killed were not communists but innocent civilians. Unlike the victims, however, students further insisted that "the truth must be revealed" and "historical and legal punishments" (*yeoksajeok, beopjeok simpan*) needed to be imposed on the perpetrators (Jeju Commission 2002a, 317). Inspired by the students' activism, journalist Shin Du-bang, who himself had been a victim of arbitrary detention and torture, started to investigate the massacres. He also repeated the victims' claims of innocence by pointing out that "ten members of one household, from a sixty-seven-year-old senior to a ten-day-old child" were killed at the same time (Jeju Commission 2002a, 340). Like the students, he did not stop there but asserted that the truth had to be found and the perpetrators had to be held responsible in courts (Jeju Commission 2002a, 341). Both students and journalists strongly believed that since the victims were innocent, bereaved families and their contemporaries had the right to know the truth and bring about justice. These claims of a right to truth and justice, however, were limited since they were the claims not of the victims themselves but of their sympathizers.

The state and opponents reacted to these claims by arguing that the Jeju 4.3 events were a communist rebellion (*gongsan pokdong*) and the victims were communists or at least pro-communist. This frame resonated strongly with President Rhee Syngman's anti-communist policy after the end of the Korean War. Communism was the main enemy of the state, and deterring internal and external communist threats was the highest policy priority. Rhee further pursued a "defeating communism" (*myeolgong*) policy, which was an upgraded version of "anti-communism" (Shin 2006). The National Security Law was enacted in 1948 and provided a legal justification to punish anyone with pro-communist sympathies (Robinson 2007, 122). A link between the victims' claim and communism can be clearly seen when the police chief, in an interview with a local newspaper, warned the public that communists could "take advantage of" claims to bring up the past wrongdoings of the state (Jeju Commission 2002a, 315). Here he warned that there was a very thin line between the victims' claims and communist instigation.

This logic continued even after the fall of Rhee in 1960. For example, in the National Assembly investigation in 1960, commissioner Choi Cheon responded to victims by stressing that not all of them were innocent because "Jeju was under strong communist influence at the time" (Jeju Commission 2002b, 167). He also questioned victims' claims that they were all innocent, since "some residents in mountainous areas secretly colluded with communist guerillas" (ibid.). He further justified harsh counterinsurgency operations by indicating that he also believed that "if [the situation in Jeju had not been] controlled, a huge rebellion would have started from Jeju" (ibid.). The same claims continued under the Park Chung-hee regime after the 1961 coup. Any claims accusing the military or police of past wrongdoing were regarded as communist acts benefiting the enemy (Park 1994). Furthermore, Park enacted the draconian Anti-Communism Law, which punished any challenge to the regime as an act of communism (ibid.). A strong emphasis on anti-communism in politics made it a social taboo, and it became almost impossible to claim any rights for communists and their sympathizers (Seo 1999, 713). Under these circumstances, the public – voluntarily or involuntarily – accepted and followed the state's interpretation of the Jeju 4.3 events, which denied victims the right to know or seek justice.

In this political context, opponents' claims overwhelmed victims' claims. Since the Jeju 4.3 events were so strongly associated with communism, victims censored themselves and restrained their voices and action.[4] The victims' claims of innocence and the counterclaims of anti-communism continued after democratization. Although the victims killed by the military and police outnumbered the victims of communist insurgents, the first association for victims was created by the bereaved families of anti-communist victims (*bangong yujok*). The association was named the Anti-Communist Association for the Civilian Victims' Families of the Jeju Island 4.3 Events (*Jejudo 4.3 sageon minganin huisaengja bangong yujokoe*), demonstrating the victims' innocent and anti-communist stance. The victims of state violence refrained from joining the association or joined but "simply kept silent and followed the anti-communist leadership."[5] This shows that victims themselves internalized the orthodox anti-communist claims of the state in the constrained political opportunity structure.

4.3.2 *From 1993 to 1997*

This all changed with the first civilian administration of President Kim Young-sam in 1993. Jeju 4.3-related advocacy became public and collective, although it was still at the local level. The Jeju Provincial Council created the first official body designed to specifically address the Jeju 4.3 events, the Provincial Special Committee on 4.3. Mediating different demands from students, activists, and victims, this committee made three critical achievements: the initiation of the first official investigation on the massacres; organization of the first united memorial service; and the launch of

---

[4] Interview, Kim Jong-min, *Jemin Ilbo* reporter and former investigator of the Jeju Commission (October 19, 2017).
[5] Interview, Lee Jung-heung, victim's son (April 2, 2006).

a province-wide petition movement to enact a special law to investigate the massacres.

With cooperation from the civilian government, civil society organizations emerged in Jeju to focus on labor, human rights, unification, the environment, farmers, students, women, social justice, culture, and political reform. Every organization in Jeju knew the importance of the Jeju 4.3 events and, individually and collectively, acted upon this cause. Different understandings of the Jeju 4.3 events and new interpretations of the massacres gradually emerged. Previously, an official and anti-communist understanding of the Jeju 4.3 events was expressed in terms like *pokdong* (riots) or *ballan* (rebellion). Under the democratic and civilian government, new frames emerged, such as *minjung hangjaeng* (popular uprising), *minjuhwa undong* (democratic movement), *tongil undong* (unification movement), or *banmi tujaeng* (anti-US struggles). Among the various frames, *hanjaeng* (uprising) was the most common frame, and students adhered to this interpretation (Ko 1989).

According to this view, although local communists initiated the armed uprising in April 1948, the conditions for the uprising were ripe even among the local public for almost a year (Yang 2008). Clear evidence of this is the unprecedented province-wide strike in March 1947 against the unjustifiable police shooting of civilians. From this point of view, the 1948 uprising was understood as an inevitable and last-resort response to the oppression and misrule of the US Military Government and the incompetent Korean government. Under this frame, those murdered were not just passive and innocent victims but also active and conscious participants in a glorious uprising. Since it happened at a critical time when the US Military Government was in power – another foreign authority after the surrender of Japan – and Syngman Rhee was pursuing a separate UN-monitored election in the southern part of the peninsula, students maintained that the victims must be remembered and honored as (anti-imperialist) freedom fighters or national-unification fighters.

Students demanded that the real truth of this uprising be revealed and the honor of participants restored. These claims were nevertheless somewhat different from the previous claims about the right to know and restore the victims' honor. Previously, these rights were demanded mainly because those killed were innocent, and the truth to be revealed was the innocent death of local victims. Under the new frame, the truth to be revealed is now the nature and process of the popular uprising. A new claim demanded these rights on the grounds that the participants in the uprising were patriots and heroes who fought for the nation. Hence, the intensity of rights claims was much stronger in the latter case than in the former. These claims were represented in the titles of the annual memorial services that students organized starting in 1988. Unlike victims and activists who just wanted to appease (*uiryeong*) the innocent souls, students wanted to cherish (*chumo*) the memory of participants in the uprising (H. J. Kim 2014, 91).

This new claim, however, directly clashed with the state, which still contended that the Jeju 4.3 events were a communist riot. Despite the end of the global Cold

War and the arrival of the civilian regime, the state's counterclaim was still effective at the national level. The national debate around the revision of the official history textbook represented this clash. In 1994, one member of the textbook revision committee, Seo Jung-seok, proposed to change "the Jeju 4.3 riot" to "the Jeju 4.3 uprising" (Choi 1994). Right-wing politicians, journalists, and intellectuals severely attacked Seo, and a leader of the ruling party openly criticized him, arguing that the Jeju 4.3 events were undoubtedly an attempt to "communize the state" (Donga Ilbo 1994). Faced with such backlash, the committee dropped any consideration of revisiting the Jeju 4.3 events and instead decided to add a line about civilian mass killings as a consequence of "riots" and collateral damage of counterinsurgency operations.

Similarly, anti-communism was still an effective frame in Jeju among victims. Although the association dropped "anti-communist" from its name in 1990, anti-communist victims were still a mainstream part of the victims' association. Any challenge to their leadership was implicitly perceived as communist-driven.[6] However, there was one interesting change after the inauguration of Kim Young-sam's civilian government. In addition to the anti-communism frame, local opponents started to use terms like *chiyu* (healing) or *hwahae* (reconciliation). However, "healing" usually meant personal and individualized healing without any collective action, and "reconciliation" was a code word for not digging up the past atrocities (G. Kim 1993).

Some activists were more moderate and wanted to focus on the massacres and victims rather than the nature of the uprising. Referring to the Jeju 4.3 events as *hangjaeng* entailed too many ideological controversies. For them, "4.3 *sageon*" (the 4.3 events) or just "4.3" (*sa-sam*) was enough to make claims without invoking contentious and endless debates between communism and anti-communism.[7] At the same time, many activists were not satisfied with the previous defensive posture of claiming that the victims were simply innocent civilians. Like students and journalists in the 1960s, activists made further rights claims. Their logic was that, since the victims were innocent, activists were entitled to the right to know the truth, the right to recover the victims' defamed honor, the right to recover lost properties, and the right to properly bury their ancestors. Activists, however, differed from the students and journalists of the 1960s in that they placed more emphasis on the perpetrators – the state. In other words, they stressed that innocent victims were killed because of the abuse of state power. Often, an expression like *gyeoljahaeji* ("one has to solve one's own problems") was used to push the state to address the massacres.[8]

Victims and activists first pressed the Jeju Provincial Council to satisfy their right to know the truth. A special committee was established and conducted the

---

[6] Interview, Lee Jung-heung (April 2, 2006).
[7] Interview, Yang Jo-hun (October 17, 2017).
[8] Ibid.

investigation. The committee published a report, announcing a list of 14,125 victims
and revealing that 84 percent of victims were killed by state agents and 11.1 percent by
insurgents (Jeju Provincial Council 1997). The report was a critical first step that
facilitated subsequent rights claims. First, albeit at the local level, it was an official
document that bolstered the credibility of victims' and activists' claims (see
Arrington 2019, 22). Second, the total number of victims was revealed through
empirical research. Third, the report vividly demonstrated that most victims were
killed by state agents, not by the insurgents. The fact-based report bolstered activists'
conviction about the innocent deaths and their momentum to push the state
further.[9]

Nevertheless, the committee had its limitations since it was a provincial institution, not a national one. Other unresolved issues, such as restoring the victims'
honor, had to be resolved by the central government. In 1993, victims and activists
started to use their constitutional rights to appeal to the National Assembly for
a special law to redress other rights claims. The right to petition was a citizen's
right guaranteed in the constitution, and victims of other massacres nationwide –
victims of the Geochang massacres and the Korean War victims, for example – had
submitted petitions to urge lawmakers to act on their behalf. Activists and local
lawmakers saw the petition as the most effective way to bring the local issue into
national politics. However, various attempts at such a petition ended in failure,
mainly because of a lack of interest and understanding of the Jeju 4.3 events at the
national level. Lawmakers in Seoul either had a strong anti-communist view or were
ignorant of the events.[10]

4.3.3 *From 1998 to 1999*

Previous claims regarding the right to know, the right to rectify victims' defamed
honor, the right to recover lost properties, and the right to proper burial continued
after the 1997 election of Korea's first opposition president, Kim Dae-Jung. The
victims' assertion of the right to know was initially met at the provincial level, but the
victims were not fully satisfied because the perpetrators were "national, not local,
authorities."[11] The *gyeoljahaeji* principle was therefore not fully met since the local
authorities investigated massacres committed by the national authorities. In addition, some demands were partially met by local civil society actors. For example,
activists embarked upon a healing project for the victims by organizing a province-
wide *gut* (a traditional shamanic ritual) to appease the souls of victims and heal those
left behind (Commemoration Committee 1998, 39). In April 1998, the *gut* lasted 11
hours and had 1,200 participants, including 700 victims. Furthermore, local activists

---

[9]   Interview, Kang Deok-hwan, Special Committee on 4.3 of the Jeju Provincial Council (October 16,
      2017).
[10] Ibid.
[11] Interview, Park Gyeong-hun, director of the Jeju Culture and Art Foundation (October 16, 2017).

found an important court document that recorded the names of 1,650 persons who had disappeared during the events. Most victims had been court-martialed or executed without due process. The document detailed personal information and the place where they had been executed, which was important information for the bereaved families to have proper funerals.[12] Families of the disappeared had been deprived of a funeral or a grave for over fifty years since they had no information at all.

New frames also emerged. On the one hand, since it was the "fiftieth anniversary" of the events, the concept of *huinyeon* (jubilee) was introduced. It was a Catholic priest who first suggested the frame as the fiftieth year is "a year of forgiveness and reconciliation."[13] The notion was foreign to most victims, and some rejected the idea of forgiveness and reconciliation. Thus, the frame was not popular among victims and activists. On the other hand, human rights were also introduced. Activists hosted the International Conference on Peace and Human Rights in 21st Century East Asia in August 1998. Six hundred scholars and activists participated, including prominent figures like Nobel Peace Laureate José Ramos-Horta; Fazel Randera from the South African Truth and Reconciliation Commission; and a Japanese senator, Den Hideo. The conference "drew national attention to the Jeju 4.3 events," and a strong link was established between the Jeju 4.3 events and human rights.[14] It was a watershed event that framed the events as a case of massive human rights violations. Other frames that had been strong in the previous five decades, such as *pokdong* (rebellion) or *hangjaeng* (uprising), were no longer visible in public discourse. The link with human rights was timely because the term was important under President Kim Dae-jung, who was himself an icon of democracy and human rights under dictatorship (see also Chapter 5). While campaigning for the presidency, Kim had stressed that he would enact a comprehensive human rights law and establish a National Human Rights Commission when elected.

Clashes occurred between victims and opponents during the enactment of the special law to create a truth commission, and diverse claims were exposed in the process. The ruling party's draft bill contained most of the demands that victims and activists had raised during the negotiation process. First, victims defined the events as "human rights violations by the state" and asked to change the beginning date of the event from April 3, 1948, a day of an armed uprising, to May 1, 1947, a day on which police illegally shot civilian protestors. These demands contained bereaved families' claims that they had the right to restore victims' honor by denying false accusations of being communists or communist sympathizers. Second, victims also claimed the right to reparations (*baesang*) for them and for their family members.

---

[12] Interview, Yang Dong-yun, president of the Provincial Solidarity for the Investigation of the Truth and Restoration of Honor for the Jeju 4.3 Events (May 4, 2011).
[13] Ibid.
[14] Interview, Park Chan-sik, head of the Special Investigation Team under the Jeju 4.3 Peace Foundation (October 18, 2017).

The conservative opposition, however, adamantly refused to allow any reparations language in the bill. For the opposition party, codifying reparations in the law meant acknowledging past state responsibility before conducting any official investigation at the national level. They objected to reparations because it was "practically difficult" to make reparations to many victims from a limited national budget.[15] Responding to this challenge, victims forfeited reparations and adhered to the new definition of the events. Some described this as "a strategic concession" and viewed reparations as a "deferred agenda."[16]

Second, the negotiated bill had to go through the voting process. Conservative politicians resorted less often to anti-communist logic under the Kim Dae-jung administration. In discussing the events, terms representing these views were seldom used. Instead, new claims were invented to obstruct or delay the process. These included claims of "insufficient evidence," "a historic event that should not be judged from the current political viewpoint," or "a task for historians, not politicians" (National Assembly 1999). Anti-communism claims did not fade away entirely, however. For example, National Assembly member Kim Yong-gap, a renowned conservative politician, claimed that the events were "armed riots … by communists," which "rejected the free, legitimate, and democratic South Korean government" (National Assembly 1999, 13). This claim, however, was ineffective, at least within the National Assembly, even among the opposition party members, and the special law was passed with a consensus.

Despite changes in the overtones of counterclaims in established institutions like the National Assembly, anti-communist logic still prevailed among conservative groups, including conservative journalists and academics, retired generals, former ministers and lawmakers, former police and secret agents, and veterans. Rhee In-su, the adopted son of Rhee Syngman, was a prime example. Starting in 1997, he even mobilized the law by filing civil and criminal lawsuits against progressive newspapers like the Hankyoreh and Jemin Ilbo. These newspapers sought out untold stories from witnesses and revealed the illegality of harsh counterinsurgency operations in the Jeju 4.3. events. Rhee In-su sought the correction of reports that President Rhee had unconstitutionally declared martial law. In his brief, he claimed that "Rhee's honor has been defamed" by the false newspaper articles.[17] His was the beginning of a series of legal challenges against victims and activists, some of which asserted similar rights claims – the right to restore someone's honor – but from the opposite side. Despite the enactment of the Special Law at the turn of the century, oppositional forces were adamant and grew more vociferous after the creation of the Jeju Commission.

[15]   Interview, Byeon Jeong-il, former lawmaker (May 10, 2011).
[16]   Interview, Yang Jo-hun (October 17, 2017).
[17]   Interview, Kim Jong-min (October 19, 2017).

4.3.4 *From 2000 to 2017*

Immediately after the passage of the Special Law, opponents began attacking it in the media. The conservative magazine *Weolgan Chosun* released opinion pieces by Lee Jin-wu, a former National Assembly member and lawyer, and Lee Hyeon-hee, a conservative historian, claiming that the National Assembly had made a fatal mistake by passing the Special Law. Here, two claims were made. First, the Jeju 4.3 events were not human rights incidents as claimed but a "communist rebellion" instigated by the communist North and the Soviet Union to overthrow the new democratic government. Second, they claimed that the Special Law challenged the legitimacy of the nation by "betraying the military and police" and accusing them of being criminals (J. Lee 2000). The next step was to use their right to constitutional appeal in the Constitutional Court (see Chapter 6). Fifteen conservative leaders, including retired generals and former ministers and congressmen, filed an appeal to the Constitutional Court to make the Special Law void. A similar appeal was submitted by 322 retired generals who had held commanding positions during the counterinsurgency operations in Jeju.

The constitutional appeals had three purposes. First, the retired generals wanted to abolish the Special Law and obstruct the Jeju Commission's activities. Second, opponents wished to exert maximum pressure on the prime minister, who was heading the Commission, to reflect their position. Third, they wanted to provide support for conservative commissioners and investigators in the Commission to echo their views. In 2001, the Constitutional Court dismissed both appeals and rejected their admissibility in the court.[18] The majority – seven out of nine judges – dismissed the case and claimed that the Special Law was properly enacted through democratic procedures to support the principle of liberal democracy.

The commission spent two-and-a-half years collecting documents and conducting interviews and released the report in 2003. Roh made an apology in 2003 after the release of the report, which marked the first apology issued by the head of state regarding past abuses. The political atmosphere, however, drastically changed with the election of Lee Myung-bak in 2007. With the return of the conservative regime, opponents initiated several lawsuits against the state and the Commission to nullify many of their previous efforts. Two additional lawsuits were filed in the Constitutional Court against the final report of the Commission and the presidential apology. They claimed that "the basic order of liberal democracy," which is stipulated in the constitution, was jeopardized by the Commission's activity. Consequently, claimants asserted that their basic constitutional rights, such as the right to equality and the right to pursue value and happiness, had been gravely infringed. Moreover, they claimed that their "basic human dignity," which again was officially upheld in the constitution, was violated by the Commission's report and the presidential apology.

[18] 2000Heonma238; 2000Heonma302.

Seven additional lawsuits were filed against the Jeju Commission chair and regarding the decisions in the victims' screening process, the final report, and the damages inflicted upon society by the Commission. It was Kim Jong-min, a special investigator in the Commission, who vigorously defended the Commission and its achievements against these conservative legal challenges.[19] Jeju society also fought hard against these lawsuits. While the victims' association – Jeju 4.3 Huisaengja Yujokhoe – was most active in these efforts, all of Jeju society, including the provincial government and social movement groups, expressed its opposition. Victims and activists maintained the frame that the Jeju 4.3 events were human rights violations, as inscribed in the Special Law.[20] Consequently, most of the opponents' lawsuits were dismissed or lost (J. Kim 2017), but the court sometimes expressed concern over the Jeju Commission's activities and recommended that it not treat communist party executives, insurgent leaders, and those who committed murder or arson as victims (J. Kim 2017, 912).

Victims and activists were not only reactive against the conservative challenge but also proactive. When the conservatives filed a constitutional appeal supposedly signed by 147 people, the victims' association closely examined the document and found that in many cases the signers' personal seal (equivalent to a signature) was identical. They then interviewed the supposed signatories of the petition and found that, of the 147 names, 130 were people from Jeju whose names had been forged. All these efforts ended in victory in court against the conservative group (J. Kim 2017). Sometimes the victims' association not only took defensive action but also initiated lawsuits against the conservatives. For example, Pastor Lee Seon-gyo published an article in 2008 that labeled the Jeju 4.3 Peace Museum "the riot museum," referred to the final report as "the fake report," and called the 13,564 victims "rioters" (J. Kim 2017). Victims and activists sued Lee for defamation.

Nonlegal attempts were also made to undermine the Jeju Commission's official findings. Immediately after President Lee's inauguration, the conservative group known as the New Right activists established the Textbook Forum to rewrite history, including relating to the Jeju 4.3 events, to reflect the traditional anti-communist view. This led to the publication of the *Alternative Textbook for Modern and Contemporary History of Korea* in 2008 (Gyogwaseo Poreom 2008). At the same time, opponents interfered with the opening of the Jeju 4.3 Peace Museum in 2008. The conservatives, especially the veterans' association, lobbied the prime minister to delay or cancel the museum opening. They also urged Park Se-jik, a prominent conservative politician who served as Seoul mayor, to appeal directly to the prime minister.[21] Once again, the locals, including the governor of Jeju province, local elites, victims, and activists, strongly resisted the pressure. Victims claimed that the Jeju 4.3 events were already established as being true by the Commission's report

---

[19] Interview, Kim Jong-min (October 19, 2017).
[20] Ibid.
[21] Interview, Yang Jo-hun (October 17, 2017).

and the presidential apology. A similar pattern of suppression and local resistance continued under the Park Geun-hye administration.

4.4 ADAPTATION AND CONTESTATION IN RIGHTS CLAIMING

As explained earlier in the chapter, rights claiming is based upon shared interpretations of a problem and collective action to solve it. In the Jeju case, these shared interpretations appeared in the form of naming the Jeju 4.3 events differently over time and were contested along partisan lines. Different understandings of the events led to different demands in the collective actions of victims and opponents. Table 4.1 provides a summary of the various rights claims made by victims and opponents and their characteristics.

Table 4.1 shows that rights claims are diversified when the counterclaims, which usually are supported by the state, are strong. The diversification and effectiveness of claims also depends on the favorable opening of the opportunity structure.

In the Jeju case, we can witness the changes of rights claims by both victims and opponents. The period between 1947 and 1992 is marked by the total suppression of

TABLE 4.1 *Different rights claims made by victims and opponents in the Jeju 4.3 case*

Year	Opportunity Structure	Key Claims of Victims	Key Claims of Opponents
1947–92	*Totally closed* (Anti-communist regimes)	4.3 victims being innocent civilians * Claims were passive and defensive in nature	4.3 events being a communist rebellion * Claims resonated strongly with anti-communism
1993–97	*Partially open* (The civilian government of Kim Young-sam)	4.3 event being a popular uprising, democratic movement, unification movement, or anti-US movement * Claims diversified but only at the local level	4.3 events being a communist rebellion but open to healing and reconciliation * No further development in claims
1998–99	*Fully open* (President Kim Dae-jung and his emphasis on democracy and human rights)	4.3 events being major human rights (*ingwon*) violations * Claims strongly resonated with the regime	4.3 events being historical events with insufficient evidence * Anti-communism disappeared from public forum
2000–17	*Mixed* (Progressive and conservative regimes)	Reparations and commemoration should follow * Claims partially resonated with different regimes	Opponents started to claim that their constitutional rights were infringed by activities of the Jeju Commission * All claims were dismissed

victims' claims by the state. The opportunity structure was quite closed for the victims, and mobilizing structures were relatively weak and localized. Any claims from victims and their families were systematically suppressed, and victims remained generally submissive and passive. Even under these circumstances, however, a few activists brought up the past atrocities when they could. Claims made by victims and sympathizers focused on the term *yangmin* (innocent civilians), and counterclaims made by the state centered around *bangong* (anti-communism). The victims' claims were passive and defensive in nature, while anti-communism resonated strongly with key national policy objectives at the time. For the state and opponents, counterclaims were easy and straightforward. Under the subsequent anti-communist regime, they simply had to raise the flag of *bangong* (anti-communism) to counteract victims' demands. According to their logic, those killed were communists, or sympathizers who had been opposed to building the new state – the Republic of Korea – and thus deserved no rights in that state.

Compared to the highly resonant frame of anti-communism, victims' claims of *yangmin* were not universal but particularistic rights claims. Claiming that a particular victim was not a communist is a claim of special, not general, rights. Moreover, victims at this time did not act collectively, and their claims for special rights were expressed in an individual, not collective, manner. Often, students and activists also claimed the victims' right to know the truth (*jinsang gyumyeong*, revealing the truth) and the rights to justice and retribution (*chaegimja cheobeol*, punishing those responsible), but the victims themselves seldom openly supported these claims.

The period between 1993 and 1997 was marked by strong local activism by victims at the Jeju Provincial Council. Victims' claims were now more developed and diverse than before. They no longer passively defended their innocence but actively demanded various rights, such as the right to know, the right to restore victims' honor, the right to recover lost properties, and the right to properly bury their ancestors. These claims were made possible by the rise of an alternative framing of the Jeju 4.3 events as *minjung hangjaeng* (popular uprising) or *sageon* (events). On the other hand, the state's claims remained almost identical and relied on the logic of anti-communism. Interestingly, however, with democratization, new claims, such as *chiyu* (healing) and *hwahae* (reconciliation), briefly appeared from anti-communist victims to individualize and silence victims of state violence. The diversification sometimes led to in-group competition such as victim-against-victim or activist-against-activist narrative. Overall, victims' claims started to become effective at the local level, but the opponents' counterclaims were still strong, especially at the national level.

The year 1998 was critical for victims, since Kim Dae-jung, who had consistently pledged himself to finding the truth and restoring victims' honor, was elected to the presidency. Victims and activists concentrated their efforts on the enactment of a special law, and the locus of activism moved from Jeju to Seoul. The main targets of activism became politicians and lawmakers at the national level. Various rights claims were again raised, and new concepts such as *huinyeon* (jubilee) emerged. Importantly, with the fiftieth anniversary commemorations, all these claims converged into a highly effective umbrella concept of *ingwon* (human rights). Human rights, defined by one scholar as "the rights that one has simply because one is a human being," (Donnelly 2003, 1) are a prime example of a frame that is inclusive, flexible, and broad in scope to cover all human beings as the ultimate holders of rights. In reality, however, the zone of application for this particular concept was not always universal and inclusive.

The most important change in the late 1990s was the use of the human rights frame, which had a lasting impact. Victims and activists made efforts to rename, redefine, and reframe the Jeju 4.3 events and civilian massacres to advance and achieve certain desired goals of the movement. This framing process occurred throughout a series of debates and events. The human rights frame, which became popular with the inauguration of Kim Dae-jung, was applied to the Jeju 4.3 events to understand the associated state violence and atrocities. This reframing process intensified during the commemoration project organized by the 4.3 Research Institute (Commemoration Committee 1998). The human rights framework was fully developed in the course of debate and negotiation during the enactment process against opponents. The codification of the Jeju 4.3 events as human rights violations by the state in the Special Law was the most important change.

Because of Korean's progressive presidency, the state was no longer openly antagonistic toward the Jeju victims. Instead, other counterclaims, such as *"jeunggeo bulchungbun"* (insufficient evidence) or *"yeoksajeok sageon"* (past events), were invented to hinder progress. At the same time, anti-communist logic still prevailed among conservative opponents. Hence, framing shifted in response to the political opportunity structure liberalizing. With the inauguration of President Kim Dae-jung, who, for his entire political life, had been falsely accused of being a communist, anti-communism lost its standing in political language. When the two sides clashed during election campaigns in 1998 and 1999, the victims' claims overwhelmed those of opponents, and the Special Law was finally passed.

With the passage of the Special Law in 1999, opponents started to use more diverse means, such as the media, public protests, civil and criminal lawsuits, administrative lawsuits, and constitutional appeals to obstruct the Commission's work and counter victims' claims. Old claims about "communist riots" persisted at the societal level, but new claims were also invented. It was this period when opponents' rights claims started to become multifaceted. This new diversification of opponents' claims mirrors the diversification of the victims' claims in the 1990s with the arrival of the first civilian president. From the two examples, we can infer that new frames develop and flourish when counterclaims are formidable. Various attempts were made to attack the claims of those with elite allies, such as anti-communism in the 1990s and human rights in the 2000s.

In particular, in their constitutional appeal, opponents started to claim that their constitutional rights had been infringed, including the right to equality and the right to pursue values and happiness (J. Kim 2017, 905). For example, they claimed that, because of the Commission's activity, their right to pursue liberal democratic values had been seriously violated. Thus, the situation was reversed. It was the opponents who tried to change the status quo by diversifying their rights claims, and it was victims and activists who wanted to maintain their achievements by holding closely to the human rights frame. In this process, human rights, the principle proclaimed in the Special Law, became a critical concept in fighting many challenges.[22] Interestingly, opponents' new claims, although universal and general, did not succeed. Courts consistently held that the opponents' proclaimed rights had not been infringed.[23] In a series of lost cases, opponents ironically bolstered the legitimacy of the Special Law and the Commission's activities.

Seventy years of activism and counter-activism around the Jeju 4.3 massacres show that new claims emerged and diversified under two conditions: first, when the counterclaim seem formidable with a strong support from the current regime, and second, despite the strong support, new political opportunity structure, often associated with the rise of resistance from civil society, opens up.

4.5 CONCLUSION

Rights claims around transitional justice are often contested. The Jeju case shows that the diversity and effectiveness of rights claims are affected by the opportunity structure and framing processes. This finding has an important empirical lesson for South Korea since addressing past atrocities was and still is a dynamic and complicated issue in Korea. Since Kim Young-sam's "civilian" (*munmin*) administration began in 1993, Korea has made serious efforts to address the past atrocities in the name of "correcting history" (*yeoksa baro sewugi*). Even more progress was made under the administrations of Presidents Kim Dae-jung and Roh Moo-hyun. Twelve truth commissions and reparations committees were set up under their tenures. However, the public – both supporters and opponents – seemed to start to feel fatigue about "the Republic of Commissions" (*wiwonhoe gonghwaguk*) (Park and Kim 2007) and questioned whether all these past-correcting measures could achieve their goals within the context of a limited budget. Commissions consequently faced backlash under the conservative regimes of Presidents Lee Myung-bak and Park Geun-hye. The nature of the returned suppression can be divided into actions taken by the government and the legislature, on the one hand, and the society, on the other. It also includes attempts to close down the commissions or make the

---

[22]   Article 1 of the Special Law specifically states, "the purpose of this Act is to contribute to promoting human rights, developing democracy and national unity by ascertaining the truth about the Jeju 4.3 Incident and restoring honor of the victims of this Incident and their bereaved families."

[23]   Constitutional Court, 2009Heonma147 (November 25, 2010).

commissions ineffectual, and attacks by the conservatives, tampering with the commission's findings.

The story, however, did not stop there. The Candlelight Revolution in December 2016 led to the impeachment of President Park. Since May 2017, the new progressive regime led by President Moon Jae-in has rekindled efforts to address past atrocities. In July 2017, the government announced a list of 100 policy tasks; the third-highest priority on the agenda was "resolv[ing] historical issues in a way that meets the expectations of the people" (Cheong Wa Dae 2017). President Moon publicly promised to find the person responsible for giving the command to shoot civilians during the 1980 Gwangju democratic movement. The prosecutorial office, defense ministry, and intelligence agencies simultaneously started to examine their past wrongdoings. In March 2018, the chief prosecutor issued an apology for the past abuses of his office and visited Busan to apologize to the father of Park Jong-cheol, a torture victim whose death ignited the June democratic uprising of 1987 (S. Kim 2018).

Based on this chapter's analysis of how the Jeju 4.3 events have been framed and counter-framed, it makes sense to expect that conservatives' future return to the presidency could usher in a less favorable political opportunity structure for rights claiming related to past state abuses of power. The Jeju case reveals that the Jeju Commission and victims faced difficult times under the conservative Lee and Park administrations. However, even under these regimes, the human rights frame was highly effective. Not many people expected the declaration of April 3 as a national Memorial Day to be possible under the subsequent regime, given that it required a progressive revision of the law in June 2013 (Law 11995/2013). With the revision, the victim screening process was again opened and progressed rapidly. Applications were on the table before June 2013 but could not be processed. A historical decision was made in May 2014 at the eighteenth plenary meeting of the commission, where 200 additional victims and 28,173 family members were acknowledged.

Nevertheless, lawmakers started negotiating with the ruling party after being urged by the victims. The ruling party reluctantly agreed to the revision because President Park had promised it during her campaign after also being pressured by victims, local campaign strategists, and politicians, some of whom associated her with her father's past abuses of power. The victims consistently pressed the presidential office and the ruling party to fulfill this promise after Park's election, leading to the law's revision in June 2013. This example suggests that even if the regime changes in the future, the trajectory of past developments will be difficult to change.

The Jeju case demonstrates that a complex process of rights claiming and counterclaiming shaped seventy years of a dynamic transitional justice process in South Korea. Right claims by both sides are not made in a vacuum but within a thick layer of existing discourses and narratives, which are empowered by the power structure of the society. In the course, an interesting dynamic of claim diversification and frame resonance was observed depending on the contour of opportunity structure in a particular time and space.

REFERENCES

Arrington, Celeste L. 2019. "The Mechanisms behind Litigation's 'Radiating Effects': Historical Grievances against Japan." *Law & Society Review* 53(1): 6–40.

Benford, Robert D., and David A. Snow. 2000. "Framing Processes and Social Movements: An Overview and Assessment." *Annual Review of Sociology* 26: 611–39.

Choi, Yeong-hun. 1994. "Guksa gyogwaseo gaepyeonan yongeo jeongui nollan" [Controversies over the changes of terms in history textbooks]. *Donga Ilbo*, March 20, 1994.

Commemoration Committee. 1998. *Je-50-junyeon jeju 4.3 haksul munhwa saeop baekseo* [White paper on the work of the Commemoration Committee]. Jeju: Commemoration Committee.

Dae, Cheong Wa. 2017. "100 Policy Tasks: Five-Year Plan of the Moon Jae-in Administration." Accessed October 31, 2018. https://english1.president.go.kr/dn/5af107425ffod.

Donga Ilbo. 1994. "Jinbosagwan gangnyeok bipan" [Severe criticism over progressive view of history]. *Donga Ilbo*, March 22, 1994.

Donnelly, Jack. 2003. *Universal Human Rights in Theory and Practice.* 2nd ed. Ithaca: Cornell University Press.

Gyogwaseo Poreom. 2008. *Daeangyogwaseo geunhyeondaesa* [Alternative textbook for modern and contemporary history of Korea]. Seoul: Giparang.

Hart, H. L. A. 1955. "Are There Any Natural Rights?" *Philosophical Review* 64(2): 175–91.

Jeju Commission. 2002a. *Jeju 4.3 sageon jaryojip 3* [Jeju 4.3 events archive, vol. 3]. Seoul: Jeju Commission.

  2002b. *Jeju 4.3 sageon jaryojip 4* [Jeju 4.3 events archive, vol. 4]. Seoul: Jeju Commission.

  2003. *Jeju 4.3 sageon jinsang josa bogoseo* [Report of the truth about the Jeju 4.3 events]. Seoul: Jeju Commission.

Jeju Provincial Council. 1997. *Jejudo 4.3 pihae josa bogoseo* [Report of the victims of Jeju 4.3]. Jeju: Jeju Provincial Council.

Keck, Margaret E., and Kathryn Sikkink. 1998. *Activists Beyond Borders: Advocacy Networks in International Politics.* Ithaca: Cornell University Press.

Kim, Gyeong-hun. 1993. "4.3 Hapdongwiryeongje: Wae musan doeeonna?" [Why did the negotiation for the united memorial service fail?]. *Weolgan jeju* [*Monthly Jeju*], May 1993.

Kim, Hun Joon. 2014. *The Massacres at Mt. Halla: Sixty Years of Truth Seeking in South Korea.* Ithaca: Cornell University Press.

Kim, Jong-min. 2017. "Beopjeonge seon 4.3" [4.3 in the courtroom]. In *Jeju 4.3 70-nyeon: eodumeseo bicheuro* [The 70th anniversary of Jeju 4.3: from darkness to the light], edited by Jeju 4.3 Peace Foundation, 883–993. Jeju: Jeju 4.3 Peace Foundation.

Kim, Seung-yeon. 2018. "Top Prosecutor Offers Apology to Father over Son's Torture Death in 1987." *Yonhap News Agency*, March 20, 2018. www.yna.co.kr/view/AKR20180320137400051.

Ko, Chang-hun. 1989. "4.3 Minjung hangjaengui jeongaewa seonggyeok" [The process and characteristics of the 4.3 popular uprising]. In *Haebang jeonhusaui insik 4* [A study of the Korean liberation era, vol. 4], edited by Jang-jip Choi, 245–340. Seoul: Hangilsa.

Lee, Hyeon-hee. 2000. "Jeju 4.3 sageonui bonjireul dasi malhanda" [Re-stating the true nature of the Jeju 4.3 events]. *Weolgan chosun*, April 2000.

Lee, Jin-wu. 2000. "Gukguneul baesinhan daehanminguk gukoe" [The National Assembly that betrayed the Korean Army]. *Weolgan chosun*, April 2000.

McAdam, Doug, John D. McCarthy, and Mayer N. Zald, eds. 1996. *Comparative Perspectives on Social Movements: Political Opportunities, Mobilizing Structures, and Cultural Framings*. Cambridge: Cambridge University Press.

Ministry of the Interior and Safety. 2018. "Jeju 4.3 sageon huisaengja singo mit gyeoljeong hyeonhwang" [The number of applications and decisions of victims of the Jeju 4.3 events]. Accessed October 31, 2018. http://pasthistory.go.kr/.

National Assembly. 1999. *Je-208-hoe gukoe bonhoeui hoeuirok Je-22-ho* [Minutes of the 208th National Assembly, no. 22]. Seoul: National Assembly. http://likms.assembly.go.kr /record/mhs-40-010.do#none.

Park, Sin-hong, and Yeong-hun Kim. 2007. "Wiwonhoe gonghwaguk" [Republic of commissions]. *Joongang Ilbo*, December 7, 2007. https://news.joins.com/article/2972037.

Park, Weon-sun. 1994. *Gukga boanbeop yeongu 1: Gukga boanbeop byeoncheonsa* [A study of the National Security Law, vol. 1, The development of the National Security Law]. Seoul: Yeoksa Bipyeong.

Reus-Smit, Christian. 2013. *Individual Rights and the Making of the International System*. Cambridge: Cambridge University Press.

Robinson, Michael E. 2007. *Korea's Twentieth-Century Odyssey*, 6th ed. Honolulu: University of Hawai'i Press.

Seo, Jung-seok. 1999. *Jo Bong-am-gwa 1950-nyeondae (Ha)* [Jo Bong-am and the 1950s, vol. 2]. Seoul: Yeoksa Bipyeong.

Shin, Gi-Wook. 2006. *Ethnic Nationalism in Korea: Genealogy, Politics, and Legacy*. Stanford: Stanford University Press.

Shue, Henry. 1996. *Basic Rights: Subsistence, Affluence, and U.S. Foreign Policy*. Princeton: Princeton University Press.

Smith, Jackie. 2002. "Bridging Global Divides? Strategic Framing and Solidarity in Transnational Social Movement Organizations." *International Sociology* 17(4): 505–28.

Yang, Jeong-sim. 2008. *Jeju 4.3 hangjaeng: Jeohanggwa apeumui yeoksa* [The Jeju 4.3 Uprising: A history of resistance and pain]. Seoul: Seonin.

5

Advancing Human Rights, Advancing a Nation

Becoming a Seonjinguk *via the National Human Rights Commission of Korea*

Soo-Young Hwang

5.1 INTRODUCTION

Each state's desire for international legitimacy is "historically contingent, context based, and intersubjective" (Flowers 2009, 26). South Korea likewise pursued international legitimacy by acting in internationally "appropriate" ways and participating in the international human rights regime at a specific moment in its national development. Due to decades of Japanese colonial rule, US military occupation, and dictatorship after the Korean War, South Korea had weak internal sovereignty. Especially during the decades of authoritarian rule in South Korea, its political elites, lacking domestic legitimacy, relied heavily on outside recognition; the regime was thus often more concerned with its international reputation than with its own citizens' opinions of it (D. C. Kim 2006). The recognition or approval of other countries – especially of rich, advanced countries – became central to South Korea's intersubjective national identity. The *seonjinguk* discourse in Korea grew out of a Eurocentric development model that made hierarchical distinctions between *seonjinguk* (developed countries) and *hujinguk* (underdeveloped countries), and Korea rejected its own previous *hujinguk* identity in its attempts to "catch up" with or become *seonjin* (J. Kim 2011, 2012). The *seonjinguk* identity emerged as "the most influential discursive framework for the interpretation of Korean national identity in the world" (John 2015, 41). Literally, *seonjinguk* translates as "forward-going country," or advanced country. In Korea, the term *seonjinguk* is a notion that has been historically constructed over decades. It has justified Korea's effort to "catch up" with more advanced or *seonjin* states in a wide range of areas, from economic growth to social development to foreign policy to human rights policy. Korea's striving for *seonjinguk* status coincided with the increasing standardization of human rights and the norms related to national human rights institutions (NHRI) worldwide in the 1990s, which influenced the development of rights in Korea. Korean political elites' desire to become a *seonjinguk* – with varying definitions – played a determinant role in the advancement of rights in Korea, especially as analyzed through the establishment, consolidation, and diminishment of the National Human Rights Commission of Korea (NHRCK).

The establishment of NHRIs raises the question of why states create and comply with NHRIs, which are designed to act as watchdogs over a state's behavior and thus may limit the state's freedom of action. Worldwide, the number of NHRIs keeps climbing. There were over 120 NHRIs around the globe as of 2019 – a fifteen-fold increase since the 1990s, with more than 5 new NHRIs being created each year (Kjaerum 2003, 5). How can we understand this global proliferation of NHRIs? Scholarship on NHRIs has primarily analyzed "why and under what conditions human rights institutions are created by states" (Goodman and Pegram 2011, 3); previous studies mainly focused on the influence of international organizations (Cardenas 2003; Pegram 2015; Pohjolainen 2006; Reif 2000; Sidoti 2011) or the influences of nonstate actors when explaining the creation of NHRIs (D. W. Kim 2009; Renshaw and Taylor 2008). These studies have generally presumed that states comply with the global norms on NHRIs because they are "coerced" or "influenced" by external agents – that they bow to pressure from inside or outside the country. But this position overlooks the state's agency and provides limited insights into a case like the NHRCK, where the state and its identity also played an important role. The universalization of liberal democracy and human rights as global standards enhanced the status of NHRIs, which rose to global prominence in the 1990s (Goodman and Pegram 2011; Koo and Ramirez 2009). Since that time, the creation of an NHRI has gradually become a way for countries to show how "legitimate" they are; NHRIs are seen as signifying good democratic governance and good human rights records (Reif 2000), thus explaining the critical function of establishing the NHRCK in South Korea.

This chapter contends that a state's adoption of a NHRI can only be sufficiently explained by taking seriously the importance of the state's desired identity, especially in cases where state compliance was not only "coerced" or "influenced" but also voluntary. This chapter examines Korea and the NHRCK, focusing on its relation-ship to Korea's *desired* national identity, which is central to the shaping and reshap-ing of its national interest, state policies, and human rights discourse and policies. This chapter claims that the creation of the NHRCK is related to Korea's aim to be recognized as a *seonjinguk*. Korea's desired identity was the core value that prompted domestic agents, including political leaders and activists, to adopt the international human rights norms that NHRIs represent and enforce. In addition to these domes-tic agents, the international community, which strongly supported the push for an independent and credible NHRCK, effectively appealed to Korea's desire to be recognized as a "model country," a "human rights state," and a "regional leader" when encouraging Korea to comply with international norms on NHRIs.

By tracing the two distinctive periods of the NHRCK – its rise (from 2001 to 2007) and its weakening (from 2008 to 2012) – this research demonstrates the Korean state's motives in its interactions with global human rights norms, which it accepted or disregarded according to policy preferences. This case study highlights the importance of answering the question of why states voluntarily adopt NHRIs. As the Korean case shows, external pressure was important, but only to a certain extent, and only when it aligned with domestic policy preference. The case of the NHRCK also demonstrates how human rights discourse was introduced and transformed in South Korea. Although the level of effectiveness differs over time, the NHRCK functioned as a remedy-seeking institution for human rights violations, a watchdog against the government, and an advocate for the implementation of international human rights laws and standards domestically. This chapter assesses the NHRCK's role as a key stakeholder in advancing rights discourses at home and abroad by taking into account its relationship to Korea's desired identity to become a *seonjinguk*. The chapter will provide a brief note on methodology; analyze how Korea pursued *seonjinguk* status in relation to rights during three definable periods of the NHRCK: its establishment (1993–2002), consolidation (2003–07), and diminishment (2008–12); and conclude with observations of the NHRCK's direction under the last two Korean presidents.

5.2 METHODOLOGY

This study examined official documents from the Korean government and from the international human rights community to see whether and how the establishment of Korea's NHRI was connected to the concept of *seonjinguk*. The government documents included statements made at international meetings, public statements from Korean presidents, and records of the National Assembly of Korea discussing the NHRCK. These government records indicate that support for adopting global human rights norms, including norms on NHRIs, was often linked to the idea of Korea's becoming a "human rights *seonjinguk*" (*ingwon seonjinguk*). Statements and reports from domestic NGOs and the international human rights community, including international NGOs and the UN, show how external pressure from these organizations, which leveraged Korea's desire to seek international legitimacy, affected change domestically over time. In addition, interviews were conducted to fill in the gaps of textual analysis and to offer a more in-depth, ethnographical account of the story of the NHRCK to show how the desire to be a *seonjinguk* in terms of human rights advancement contributed in the establishment, consolidation, and diminishment of the NHRCK.

5.3 THE ESTABLISHMENT OF THE NHRCK (1993–2002)

The enactment of the National Human Rights Commission of Korea Act and the establishment of the Commission serve as momentum to help Korea become a human rights seonjinguk.

—President Kim Dae-jung, October 9, 2001 (NHRCK 2009)

The views expressed herein are the author's and do not necessarily reflect the views of the United Nations.

[The establishment of the NHRCK] is the realistic and indisputable institutional mechanism by which Korea becomes a human rights seonjinguk.

— First Chairperson of the NHRCK, Kim Chang-guk (Kim 2001)

Korean human rights activist groups planted the seeds of the NHRCK while participating in the World Conference on Human Rights in Vienna in 1993, where global norms on NHRIs were discussed (NHRCK 2002, 5). These Korean NGOs returned to Korea eager to establish a NHRI. However, it took years for the Korean NHRI agenda to be realized. The breakthrough came from presidential candidate Kim Dae-jung, who promised in December 1997 to establish an NHRI if he was elected.[1] After winning the election, President Kim included "passing the Human Rights Commission Act and establishing the National Human Rights Commission" as one of his administration's "One Hundred Main National Tasks" (NHRCK 2002, 6). Although Kim Dae-jung was committed to establishing an NHRI, the details did not come easily. The first problem was deciding who would take the lead in designing the institution. The Ministry of Justice was tasked with drafting legislation for the proposed NHRI, which catalyzed a long and contentious struggle between the government, the ruling party, and NGOs for an independent NHRI. The government had to amend the Ministry of Justice's draft bill several times (Y. Cho 2000, 2). The Ministry of Justice's strength and potential ability to limit the fledgling NHRCK's independence prompted opposition to its role in designing the institution from the international human rights community, including the UN, and domestic human rights NGOs.

International human rights NGOs campaigned for an NHRI that met international standards, especially the Paris Principles adopted in 1993 by the UN General Assembly, which address the role, composition, status, and functions of NHRIs. Amnesty International actively engaged Kim's administration. Amnesty International's letters reveal that the organization leveraged Korea's desire to be the foremost human rights *seonjinguk* in the region (Amnesty International 1998a, 1998b, 1998c, 1999). After the Ministry's draft proposal was published in September 1998, for example, Amnesty International's Secretary-General, Pierre Sane, issued an open letter urging the president to reconsider the proposal, criticizing various elements of it:

> The draft legislation prepared by your Ministry of Justice does not in its present form conform to international human rights standards. It would result in a commission that lacks independence and investigative powers and does not have the authority to enforce its recommendations. It will also have a very limited mandate. If the legislation is adopted in this form, there is a serious risk not only of establishing a poor human rights commission but also of undermining the credibility of your

---

[1] For the role played by domestic NGOs in persuading Kim Dae-jung to pursue an NHRI, see Baek (2002, 34).

human rights reform program. . . . The draft law was drawn up by the Ministry of Justice in secret, without any consultation with human rights experts in South Korea. (Amnesty International 1998c)

Sane's letter also provided insight into why the government had decided to enact the problematic law on December 10, 1998, the fiftieth anniversary of the Universal Declaration of Human Rights. It stated that "we understand the symbolic import-ance of this date and your desire to show the South Korean people and world that South Korea has developed into a country which respects human rights," and it encouraged the government to postpone the adoption of the law, saying, "in this way, you will leave an important human rights legacy for all South Koreans." Here, Amnesty International purposefully and effectively appealed to Korea's desire to be recognized as a good human rights country by demanding that it comply with widely accepted international human rights standards. Amnesty International's advocacy was one of the key determinants in changing the government's plan. Its efforts also created space for the activities of Korean human rights NGOs, who were diffusing the international norms of credible, independent NHRIs.

During this struggle, the Ministry of Justice attempted to push through its draft bill with the UN's endorsement rather than with domestic support. In January 1999, the Secretary of Legal Affairs to the President, a former prosecutor, Park Joo-sun, met with staff of the Office of the United Nations High Commissioner for Human Rights (OHCHR) in New York regarding the creation of the Korean NHRI. He reported to the president that the UN experts supported the Ministry of Justice-drafted NHRCK bill. Brian Burdekin, the former Special Advisor on National Institutions to the UN High Commissioner for Human Rights, remembers the incident clearly:

> I remember the national institution building process in Korea very well. It was very unusual to see a ministry, the Ministry of Justice, tirelessly trying to get the institution in the way they wanted, even if the president was keen to have the institution in a different way – not to mention NGOs and the UN wanting it a different way. I also remember that a representative of the Korean government flew all the way to New York, met with one OHCHR officer (who did not specialize in National Institutions), and tricked her so that they could report to the president that the Ministry's proposal had the UN endorsement. It became a huge issue because it was simply not correct. I actually had to threaten a senior representative of the Korean Ministry of Foreign Affairs that, unless they corrected this information, I would fly to Seoul and hold a press conference and announce that the Ministry of Justice was deliberately misleading the government and the public about the real position.[2]

As this incident demonstrates, government officials from the Ministry of Justice were keener to obtain international recognition than to gain the consent of domestic

---

[2] Interview, Brian Burdekin (April 6, 2011).

constituencies. Burdekin's remarks insinuate that the Ministry officials may have thought that the issue would be more easily resolved at the domestic level after UN endorsement.

While little progress was made toward the establishment of an NHRI, another international voice joined the NGOs appealing to Korea's identity, interests, and desire to be *seonjinguk*: in October 1999, the UN High Commissioner for Human Rights, Mary Robinson, visited Seoul. Human rights advocate Lee Seong-hoon says that Robinson influenced President Kim:

> In creating an NHRI, each country goes through a different process and different variables come into play. . . . I think the international variables were quite critical in the creation of the NHRCK – the international opinion, especially, shifted the course of discussion over the independence of the institution. One of the critical moments was when the UN High Commissioner for Human Rights, Mary Robinson, met with the president, Kim Dae-jung, in October 1999 in Seoul. I believe the president must have been puzzled about the struggle between his trusted staff and his long-time supporters – human rights activists. At the meeting, the president asked Mary Robinson her views about how the Korean NHRI should be shaped. Mary Robinson answered that if the institution turned out to be a private foundation, the institution would not have legitimacy in the eyes of the inter-national community. Mary Robinson's timely and straightforward intervention was crucial in shifting President Kim's mind toward creating an independent institution.[3]

According to sociologist Koo Jeong-Woo, "the domestic human rights movement might not have been able to effectively pressure the government to commit to creating an independent and well-funded national institution if the movement had not been tied to the formation of the world human rights movement that was led by human rights IGOs and INGOs" (Koo 2011, 93). The cumulative endeavors of both the domestic and the international human rights community, including the UN, were largely successful, appealing as they did to the country's desire to be a *seonjin* human rights state.

However, the government and the ruling party decided to postpone the adoption of the Ministry of Justice version of the bill, and negotiations over the NHRCK bill remained largely inactive until an unexpected event made the Ministry of Justice give in. On October 13, 2000, the Nobel Committee announced that President Kim Dae-jung would be the Nobel Peace winner of 2000. This announcement changed the course of the negotiations, and the ruling party realized that "it would not look good [at home and abroad] if the Korean government were to enact human rights laws that are opposed by human rights NGOs" (Hankyoreh 2000b). Korean media also started to pay attention, wondering whether President Kim's Nobel Peace Prize

---

[3] Interview, Lee Seong-hoon (September 16, 2010).

would change the positions of the politicians and the Ministry of Justice now that Korea's international reputation was at stake (Hankyoreh 2000a, 2000b).

Attorney Cho Yong-hwan, one of the key drafters of the NGO-initiated NHRCK bill and the key negotiator with the Ministry of Justice, concurs that the announcement of the Nobel Prize Committee was the beginning of the end of the three-year struggle with the Ministry. Cho explains:

> The Ministry was increasingly isolated. Amid negotiations, the Nobel Prize Committee's announcement was instrumental in finally ending the long back-and-forth over the status of the NHRCK. The Ministry finally gave in because it could not afford to let the world see Korea as a country where a Ministry was fighting against the domestic and international human rights communities.
>
> It was quite rare, the amount of international attention the NHRCK received in the establishment process. I believe international human rights communities, especially Amnesty International and the UN OHCHR, saw Korea as a good human rights model that had achieved democratization in a rapid period, and thought that it could serve as an example for other Asian countries. President Kim's international fame helped.[4]

After President Kim received the Nobel Peace Prize in October of 2000, it was decided that a government-drafted bill from the National Assembly would best minimize the influence of the Ministry of Justice in the establishment of the NHRCK (D. W. Kim 2009, 228–29). The ruling party National Congress for New Politics began debating the new bill on February 27, 2001, establishing an independent and effective NHRCK with Korea's desired *seonjinguk* status. During the debates, the main drafter of the act, Assemblywoman Lee Mi-kyung, stressed that efforts to advance human rights should continue:

> With the trend of internalizing human rights enforcement within countries, the international community is paying more and more attention to each country's human rights situation; however, South Korea has not yet escaped from its negative human rights image from previous human rights violations under the authoritarian regimes of the past. Therefore, it is our historical mandate to build and realize a *seonjin* democratic society where human dignity, rules, and human rights are respected without discrimination and without human rights violations. (M. Lee 2001, 21)

This amended bill, which was largely in compliance with the Paris Principles, institutionalized the NHRCK as an independent governmental body with a broad mandate; it was formally adopted and became effective on May 24, 2001. The NHRCK was finally launched in November 2001 and became operational with the appointment of the first chairperson. The Commission's mandate was broad enough to protect the fundamental human rights of all individuals, including non-Koreans residing in Korea (Articles 1 and 4), and guaranteed the NHRCK's

---

4 Interview, Cho Yong-hwan (October 1, 2010).

independence (Article 2). It also imposed pluralism, one of the key components of the Paris Principles, on the composition of the Commission: four or more of the commissioners must be women, and commissioners could be either selected by the National Assembly or nominated by the President of the Republic of Korea or by the Chief Justice of the Supreme Court (Article 5). The Act provided the Commission the power to make recommendations to improve or rectify policies and practices (Article 25) and to present opinions to courts and Constitutional courts (Article 28). The Commission also had the authority to visit and inspect government facilities to protect the rights of people in those facilities (Articles 24 and 31).

5.4 THE CONSOLIDATION OF THE NHRCK (2003–07)

The Republic of Korea will make a new beginning as a model human rights country, and we will absolutely become a human rights seonjinguk. . . . It is meaningful in many aspects for Korea to host this Conference. I would like to think of this as an indication that the international community is recognizing Korea as a country of human rights and democracy.

—President Roh Moo-hyun's opening remarks at the 7th International Conference of National Human Rights Institutions September 14, 2004, Seoul (Presidential Secretariat 2005, 319)

The long process of establishing and launching the NHRCK took place during Kim Dae-jung's administration, but the NHRCK developed into a credible institution with solid standing under the next president, Roh Moo-hyun. Under President Roh, the process of changing Korea's image from that of an undemocratic developing country to that of an advanced democratic country accelerated, in part through economic growth, and in part through Roh's attempt to obtain moral legitimacy at the regional and international levels by proactively internalizing globally accepted human rights norms. During this period, numerous policies aimed to show the world that Korea was a human rights country and one of the "good" rich, developed countries. Thus, Korea's promotion of the NHRCK, an act that seemingly restrained the state's power, actually enabled Korea to effectively *strengthen* its standing in the international sphere by reinventing itself as a human rights *seonjinguk*.

The Roh administration's desire to join the *seonjinguk* club is clearly visible in its emphasis on human rights (including promoting the NHRCK), which became a priority policy issue during his tenure.[5] President Roh's statements exemplify how deeply human rights were embedded in the country's attempts to become a *seonjinguk*:

---

5 However, it should be noted that Roh's administration took a cautious approach to North Korean human rights issues that have been more of a political agenda rather than a human rights issue in Korea.

Korea has become the world's twelfth most prosperous country, overcoming the aftermath of the war. Freedom, human rights and democracy are bursting into full blossom after defeating the long oppression of dictatorship.

We cannot delay the adoption of an Employment Permit System for foreign labor any longer. . . . If we were to drive those who came to Korea with a Korean dream into becoming criminals, we could not be regarded in the world's eyes as a legitimate human rights state.

We [Koreans] need a collaborative effort to safeguard world's peace, security and human rights. We need to live up to our responsibility as a legitimate actor in the international community. (Presidential Secretariat 2004, 37, 284, 614)

The Roh regime's focus on human rights (including the promotion of the NHRCK) as a means of pursuing international legitimacy is particularly well evidenced in the president's remarks at the 7th International Conference for National Human Rights Institutions, which was hosted by the NHRCK in September of 2004. Roh states that the creation of the NHRCK was a turning point in Korean human rights history, marking the moment that Korea began to deal with human rights issues that had accumulated over the past decades. He affirms that he will lead Korea to be a "human rights *seonjinguk*" and that it will become a "model human rights state" by resolving its past human rights violations. He further asserts that the NHRCK's hosting of the conference means that "the international community is regarding Korea as a country of human rights and democracy" (Presidential Secretariat 2005, 320–21).

Over time, Roh's regime showed increasing confidence in Korea's status as a democratic human rights state. His statements, toward the end of his term, increasingly reiterate that the world is recognizing Korea as a democratic human rights *seonjinguk*:

It is different now. Korea has sufficient ability to keep our safety and pride. We have a strong military no country can overlook, and it is supported by the world's twelfth largest economic power. We are recognized as a legitimate democratic human rights state.

We have grown to have enough capacity to protect ourselves. We have become recognized by the world as a democratic human rights state, in which revival of dictatorship is unimaginable.

We are recognized as a democratic human rights state by the world. We still have a long way to go, but at least all of those shameful phases such as dictatorship [and] torture . . . are all in the past.

Your home, Korea, has now become a country you can feel proud of everywhere. We have the twelfth largest economy in the world; [we] have power to defend ourselves; and we are recognized as a democratic human rights state by the world. The [country's] reputation in the international community is high enough to elect a Korean UN Secretary-General. (Presidential Secretariat 2008, 112, 340, 390, 497)

Furthermore, the inauguration speech of the NHRCK's fourth chairperson, Ahn Kyung-hwan, also presents Korea's ambition to become a human rights *seonjinguk*.

> The Republic of Korea is praised by the international community as being the only country that has achieved both democratization and economic development in a short period of time after independence. The fact that one small country, which the UN built upon ashes of war, produced the chief of the UN demonstrates the current status of the Republic of Korea in the international community. ... We should let the world know about the human rights achievements made in Korea. Furthermore, we should build a stable foundation to leap toward being a *seonjinguk*, leading the world in the field of human rights by sharing responsibility for *hujinguk* (underdeveloped and developing countries). (Ahn 2006)

Under Roh, the NHRCK expanded and grew into an independent institution with a clear direction and voice, actively speaking up on various human rights issues in Korea, making recommendations to various government bodies, and handling an increased number of human rights cases. Between 2001 and 2007, the NHRCK handled 38,531 counseling cases, with the number increasing each year, from 7,738 in 2005 to 8,311 in 2006 and 10,693 in 2007 (NHRCK 2007, 46). In 2006, NHRCK processed a total of 34,382, cases, including 4,187 complaint cases, 10,737 counseling cases, and 19,558 general cases. The NHRCK's case-handling capacity drastically improved over the years; the 2006 total saw an increase of 1,045 cases over 2005 and an increase of 10,000 cases over 2004 (NHRCK 2006, 43–44).

The NHRCK had the strong support of the government during this time; there was a general culture of accepting the NHRCK's recommendations – a culture that cannot be forced and must rely on the goodwill of the recipients of those nonbinding recommendations. This culture is demonstrated by the high acceptance rate of NHRCK recommendations by the various government bodies they were presented to, including relevant ministries, competent courts, and legislative bodies. The cumulative acceptance rate for NHRCK recommendations between 2001 and 2008 was 89.1 percent (T. Kim 2009).

The issues covered by the NHRCK recommendations were often highly political and sensitive (Y. Chung 2011, 209). NHRCK recommendations covered the NEIS (National Education Information System), migrant workers, the *hoju* (family registry) system,[6] and a bill on the amendment to the Terror Prevention Act (NHRCK 2003, 14). One of the highlights was when the NHRCK issued a public statement opposing the president's decision to deploy troops to Iraq, arguing that the decision violated the values and principles of human rights (NHRCK 2003, 35–36).[7] To everyone's surprise, President Roh supported the Commission's right to publish a differing view, even one that publicly embarrassed the president by saying, "It is the

---

[6] See Eunkyung Kim (Chapter 3) on the household register's relation to women's rights in Korea.
[7] At the tenth anniversary of the NHRCK, experts agreed that the Commission's opinion opposing the war in Iraq was one of the top five agendas set by the NHRCK.

role of the government to be in charge of all matters related to foreign affairs and security, but the body that deals with human rights protection and promotion may have different views on these issues, as the government may leave things out" (Presidential Secretariat 2004, 554–55). Despite the NHRCK's opposition, the National Assembly passed the president's proposal and deployed troops. However, the NHRCK's political gamble, and President Roh's supportive reaction to it, increased the NHRCK's confidence and cemented its status as an independent and legitimate organization. It also showed that *seonjin* Korea respected human rights and guaranteed the independence of its NHRI, even in highly political and contentious situations.

The NHRCK actively engaged in international cooperation, taking up a leadership role in both international and regional bodies (e.g., International Coordinating Committee of National Institutions for Promotion and Protection of Human Rights (ICC) and Asia-Pacific Forum of National Human Rights Institutions (APF)) and assisting in the establishment of NHRIs in other countries. Through these efforts, the NHRCK became a credible and legitimate institution at both the domestic and international levels. Also, under Roh's administration, several Koreans occupied high-level positions at the UN, including UN Secretary-General and UN Deputy High Commissioner for Human Rights. In 2006, Korea was elected as one of the inaugural members of the UN Human Rights Council.[8]

Despite its many accomplishments, the NHRCK faced challenges such as staffing (many staff members were bureaucrats with no background in human rights) and internal politics (internal struggles between commissioners and the Secretariat outweighed those between the NHRCK and government bodies). The biggest challenge to the NHRCK, which persists into the present day, is its weak institutional standing. The original proposal to establish the Commission as a constitutional body was not accepted, and the Commission's functions and status are therefore based on a single document, the NHRCK Act. As the Commission's status is not firmly rooted in law, its consolidation, development, and success depend on government will, as seen next.

5.5 THE DIMINISHMENT OF THE NHRCK (2008–12)

There is no hope for the situation that the NHRCK is in now.

– Minbyeon (2010)

Whereas the NHRCK enjoyed autonomy and legitimacy domestically and internationally under Kim Dae-jung and Roh Moo-hyun, the inauguration of

---

[8] According to the government's self-assessment, it was "a demonstration that Korea has secured its reputation as one of Asia's leading promoters of human rights and a democratic nation and represents recognition in the international community that Korea played a constructive role in the Commission on Human Rights, the predecessor body of the Human Rights Council" (MOFAT 2007, 120).

a conservative administration headed by Lee Myung-bak ushered in a period of retrenchment for the NHRCK. Continuing internal issues, such as office factions and disagreements about appointments, also contributed to its decline (D. Kim 2010). The new administration's attempts to weaken the NHRCK – some successful and some unsuccessful – began immediately after the 2008 election. These attempts include downsizing and bringing the NHRCK under the office of the president. However, both domestic NGOs and international human rights actors, including the UN, the ICC, and international human rights NGOs, pressured President Lee to reinstate the strong, independent NHRCK. These voices appealed to Korea's desire to be *seonjinguk*, a tactic that had succeeded before but did not succeed with Lee.

This rhetoric did not work because the Lee administration redefined what it meant to be *seonjinguk* according to its own conservative political identity and preferences. The Lee government and its conservative allies not only attempted to reverse the "leftist" policies of the past decade (Y. Kim 2014, 161) but also modified Korea's desired national identity. This new national identity reinterpreted the concept of *seonjinguk* from comprehensive socioeconomic growth that included human rights to focusing purely on economic growth. Like other administrations, the Lee Myung-bak administration sought international legitimacy by becoming a *seonjinguk*, but the means of achieving this goal were quite different. Even had President Lee not actively weakened certain human rights in Korea, his kind of neoliberal *seonjin* state would have not been compatible with human rights. The privatization of public policies dissolved the minimum level of social rights that had previously been protected and exacerbated the already-extreme inequality in Korean society (J. S. Kim 2012, 61). In general, economic and social inequality worsened under Lee (Y. Kim 2014, 151), as did civil and political rights, including freedom of opinion and expression, freedom of assembly and association, and the freedom of the media. These rights may have been seen as hindrances to becoming *seonjinguk* (J. Park 2011). Some argue that Lee's administration attempted to discredit general human rights discourse in total rather than sectorally. Korean democratic values, including respect for procedure, protection of freedom of expression, and appropriate use of state power, were greatly reduced over the five years of Lee's rule (J. S. Kim 2012, 74–77).

Some critics state that human rights are often disregarded in the name of "law and order," a notion that was introduced and emphasized by Lee Myung-bak's government (S. Lee 2008). Several scholars argue that both the rule of law and respect for human rights have decreased during Lee's administration who stressed "order" (T. Chung 2009). In the lead-up to the Korea G20 meetings, a series of newspaper articles ran, arguing that "the way to become a *seonjinguk*" was through establishment of "law and order" (*beop jilseo*). While civil society organizations spoke out against the government's suppression of freedom of association and assembly around the G20 summit, this series advocated that Korea should stop the "*hujinguk*"-style protests if it aimed to be a *seonjinguk*, making its point by referring to the cases of other advanced countries, such as Japan and Germany (S. Park 2010; Yoo 2010). NHRCK Chairperson Ahn stated:

> I would like to comment on the new Administration's emphasis on "law and order." In a democratic society, law and human rights should not compete with each other, but they should run together like the two wheels of a bicycle. Therefore, it is a setback to downgrade human rights in the name of law in a democratic society, and it would mean the retrenchment of human rights. (Ahn 2008)

The different policy preferences of Lee's administration had a direct impact on the NHRCK. Attempts to weaken the NHRCK started as soon as Lee Myung-bak was elected and were interpreted as initiatives to restore the "lost decade" of progressive rule (B. Cho 2011, 176). The first action was an attempt to remove the NHRCK's independence and place it under the supervision of the president's office. Faced with this strong and immediate opposition from the international and domestic human rights communities (Amnesty International 2008; ANNI 2008; Arbour 2008; J. S. Kim 2012, 60), the government withdrew this plan and replaced it with another: to weaken the NHRCK by reducing its staff by 21 percent (B. Cho 2011, 196–97). In July of 2009, the NHRCK was further weakened with a change of chairperson; Chairperson Ahn resigned to protest the staff reduction, and Lee seized the opportunity to appoint someone who shared his ideas: Hyun Byung-chul.

By appointing Hyun Byung-chul, a law school professor who had no human rights background, President Lee rendered the NHRCK like a government branch that served the administration's objectives rather than independently promoting human rights. The NHRCK, therefore, lost its power to intervene in various urgent human rights issues in South Korea such as regressing freedom of expression, labor rights, forced eviction caused by development projects, poverty, as well as educational rights (B. Cho 2011, 176). Instead, the NHRCK's new focus on serving the executive's political agenda can be seen in its increased activities on North Korean human rights issues. In principle, the NHRCK Act does not mandate that the NHRCK work on human rights issues in North Korea, but Chairperson Hyun proactively changed the institution's focus to comply with the president's preference (T. Chung 2011, 166). For example, the budget allocated for North Korean human rights issues doubled during Lee Myung-bak's time (T. Chung 2011, 170).

The NHRCK's status declined after Lee Myung-bak's inauguration. Lee's lack of support for the NHRCK reverberated across the government: The acceptance rate for NHRCK recommendations declined drastically in all areas, including human rights violations, discrimination cases, and policy advice. For example, the acceptance rate of policy advice, which had been 75 percent during the previous two progressive administrations, dropped to 38 percent under Lee (B. Cho 2011, 182). The plummeting rate implies that the culture of acceptance withered as government bodies no longer respected the NHRCK's authority (Shin 2011). In addition, the NHRCK did not put itself forward as a candidate for the chairmanship of either the ICC or the APF, losing its very likely appointments to these important positions. The standing committee of the NHRCK reached a unanimous agreement "not to put up a representative for South Korea in the upcoming elections being held at the annual general meeting of the Asia–Pacific Forum of National Human Rights Institutions (APF) on August 3" because "we need human and material resources in order to carry out the role of the chair nation successfully, but NHRCK's capacity has been diminished due to layoffs" (Hankyoreh 2009).

It is not unusual for an NHRI to weaken after a change in administration. Governmental political preferences also shape the destiny of NHRIs in "other wealthy, developed states with stable democracies," such as in Australia when the budget of the Australian Human Rights Commission was cut drastically between 1996 and 1999 under the conservative government (Renshaw and Fitzpatrick 2012, 176–77). However, the extent of the NHRCK's decline after the conservatives' return to the Blue House in Korea was quite extraordinary. The case of the NHRCK, which experienced drastic ups and downs depending on the party in power, shows that NHRIs do not function in a political vacuum – they are highly susceptible to domestic policy preferences. Lee's administration marginalized the NHRCK by downsizing and compromising its independence. By the end of Lee's term, the NHRCK had also lost its reputation with both domestic and international human rights actors.[9] Civil society members had almost given up on reviving the NHRCK. For example, a long-standing human rights lawyers' network, Minbyeon-Lawyers for a Democratic Society (see Chapter 8), criticized Lee's administration, saying:

> From the beginning of the current administration, the Korean government ignored human rights, considering the concept of human rights to be a rebellious idea. The Korean government did not welcome the fact that the independent human rights body had been established by the recommendation of the UN – that the NHRCK belonged neither to the legislative branch, the judicial branch, nor the administrative branch. (Minbyeon, 2010)

5.6 CONCLUSION AND FUTURE DIRECTIONS

This chapter analyzed Korea's desired *seonjinguk* identity to show how international human rights norms on NHRIs were first widely diffused and accepted in the country but changed over time, becoming less accepted as the Korean domestic context changed. The study marshaled evidence to show that the establishment of an NHRI is not an end to the story of how human rights norms are adopted. The changing domestic context must also be examined in order to fully understand the

[9]   In a survey conducted in 2011, 80 percent of participating experts gave negative feedback on the Korean government's leadership in human rights, saying that the human rights situation of Korea had deteriorated, and the Korean government did not apply human rights considerations in its policies. One of the major reasons given for the poor leadership human rights record was the weakened authority of the NHRCK (NHRCK 2011, vii–ix).

permanent institutional arrangement that exists between a state and its NHRI – how the state's interests shape and change its policies, how and when the relationship does and doesn't work, and most of all, why states enter into this arrangement voluntarily.

Further research would be needed to describe the desired identity of the Park Geun-hye administration and its relationship to the *seonjinguk* concept, given Park's anomalous and nontransparent governance approach, which led to her impeachment in March 2017 (N. Kim, 2017). In the weeks leading up to the impeachment, hundreds of millions of Koreans protested for weeks on the streets of all major cities in Korea, demanding that she step down and restore democracy. The demonstrations were orderly and peaceful, and they were made up of common people who participated voluntarily rather than the activists who had led such political mobilizations in the past (Tharoor 2017). It is believed that the success of this "people power" built the confidence of the Korean people, making them feel like citizens of a real democratic country (Dudden 2017). In other words, it may have enabled Korean citizens to transform their intersubjective identities: Instead of constantly seeking recognition or endorsement from others, they no longer required outside recognition, transitioning from advancing human rights for others to advancing human rights for themselves.

Moon Jae-in, who was sworn in as the nineteenth president of Korea on May 10, 2017, is a former human rights lawyer who served in the cabinet of former president Roh Moo-hyun. Moon and his election represent the hope to restore democracy and normalize the country after Park's impeachment. One of his political commitments is to strengthen the NHRCK – a promise that the Commission welcomed (NHRCK 2017). Moon introduced several specific measures to restore the NHRCK, including an assessment of government bodies' acceptance rates for NHRCK recommendations to ensure that government bodies are again taking the NHRCK seriously (K. Kim 2017). He also appointed Choi Young-ae, a prominent human rights activist and a former Secretary-General of NHRCK, as the new chairperson in August 2018.

Positive signs of revitalization of the NHRCK have been observed. The NHRCK created an independent Reforms Committee, which made recommendations to improve its independence and effectiveness while recognizing how the NHRCK, especially for the last ten years, served political power, not the people (NHRCK 2018). Under Choi's leadership, the NHRCK has actively taken up human rights issues in South Korea, including sensitive political issues, such as Korea's restrictive refugee policy and collective bargaining and the freedom of association.[10] Further studies on Moon's definition of *seonjinguk*, which appears to distance itself from the former growth-centered economic development conception and focus on the

---

[10]   On December 21, 2018, NHRCK Chairperson Choi criticized the Ministry of Justice for its refugee application screening policy amid the nonacceptance of Yemeni refugees. On December 25, 2018, the Commission also recommended that the government ratify ILO Conventions No. 87 and No. 98, which relate to the freedoms of association and collective bargaining.

livelihoods of people and their rights, are expected to offer an interesting real-time study of how domestic political contexts affect the revitalization of global human rights norms and mechanisms in Korea.

The case of NHRCK demonstrates the importance of delving into the domestic context in which NHRIs exist. This domestic context – the national interest and identity, which is constantly constructed, deconstructed, and reconstructed – is where norms are diffused and reshaped over time. In addition, the Korean case shows the malleability of international human rights norms when the domestic political terrain changes. Similar in-depth studies on NHRIs in particular countries, each based on the host state's unique identity, will not only help understand how changing national interest shape and shift human rights policies but it also will enrich our understanding of NHRIs and contribute to the body of empirical studies of theories on compliance.

REFERENCES

Ahn, Kyung-hwan. 2006. "Chwiimsa" [Inauguration speech]. October 20, 2006. www .humanrights.go.kr/site/main/index001.

2008. "Segye ingwon seoneon 60junyeon ginyeomsa: "Teingwon hyangsangeuro gukgaui pumgyeogeul nopija" [Statement in celebration of the 60th anniversary of the Universal Declaration of Human Rights – Let's improve national class by enhancing human rights]. December 10, 2008. www.humanrights.go.kr/site/main/index001.

Amnesty International. 1998a. "A Human Rights Agenda for South Korea." www.amnesty.org /download/Documents/152000/asa250051998en.pdf. Accessed May 4, 2017.

1998b. "Proposed Standards for a National Human Rights Commission." www.amnesty.org /download/Documents/152000/asa250161998en.pdf. Accessed May 4, 2017.

1998c. "Letter from Amnesty International's Secretary-General, Pierre Sane." www .amnesty.org/download/Documents/152000/asa250371998en.pdf. Accessed May 4, 2017.

1999. "Open Letter to President Kim Dae-jung." April 9, 1999. Amnesty International. www .amnesty.org/download/Documents/144000/asa250171999en.pdf. Accessed May 4, 2017.

2008. "Grave Concerns for the Future Independence of the National Human Rights Commission of South Korea." January 18, 2008. Amnesty International. www .amnesty.org/download/Documents/52000/asa250012008eng.pdf. Accessed May 4, 2017.

ANNI (Asian NGOs Network on National Human Rights Institutions). 2008. "Asian NGOs Condemn South Korea's Plan to Control Its National Human Rights Commission." January 22, 2008. www.forum-asia.org/?p=7389.

Arbour, Louise. 2008. "Korea: Letter from the High Commissioner for Human Rights Regarding the Independence of the National Human Rights Commission of Korea." Forwarded Statement no. AHRC-FST-006–2008 to Lee Kyung-sook. www .humanrights.asia/news/forwarded-news/AHRC-FST-006–2008.

Baek, Woon Jo. 2002. "Daehanminguk gukgaingwonwiwonhoe beobui ipbeop gwajeonge gwanhan yeongu" [Study on the legislative process of the National Human Rights Commission Act of Republic of Korea]. Ph.D. dissertation, Inha University.

Cardenas, Sonia. 2003. "Emerging Global Actors: The United Nations and National Human Rights Institutions." *Global Governance* 9: 23–42.

Cho, Baeki. 2011. "Gukgaingwonwiwonhoe guseongui munjejeomgwa gaeseonbangan" [Problems of the composition of the NHRCK and ways to improve]. In

Gukgaingwonwiwonhoe seollip 10junyeon daetoronhoe [Conference on the occasion on the 10th anniversary of the NHRCK], 176–96. Seoul: Korea Human Rights Foundation.

Cho, Yong-Whan. 2000. "Gukgaingwon giguui gukjejeok baljeongwa hangugui daean" [National human rights institution: international development and proposal for Korea]. MA thesis, Seoul National University.

Chung, Tae-uk. 2009. "Gukgaingwonwiwonhoeui dongnipseonggwa jikjeryeong gaejeongui munje" [The independence of National Human Rights Commission of Korea (NHRCK) and the Chief Commissionerial Decree (Presidential Decree) on the reorganization of the NHRCK]. *Minju Beobhak* 40: 11–43.

Chung, Tae-uk. 2011. "Gukgaingwonwiwonhoe 10nyeonui byeonhwa: bukhan ingwon munjereul jungsimeuro" [Change in the NHRCK over ten years – centered on North Korean human rights issues]. In *Gukgaingwonwiwonhoe seollip 10junyeon daetoronhoe* [Conference on the occasion on the 10th anniversary of the NHRCK], 165–74. Seoul: Korea Human Rights Foundation.

Chung, Young-Sun. 2011. "Gukgaingwonwiwonhoeui dongripseonge daehan bipanjeok gochal" [Critical review of the independence of the NHRCK]. In *Gukgaingwonwiwonhoe seollip 10junyeon daetoronhoe* [Conference on the occasion on the 10th anniversary of the NHRCK], 197–219. Seoul: Korea Human Rights Foundation et al.

Dudden, Alexis. 2017. "Revolution by Candlelight: How South Koreans Toppled a Government." *Dissent Magazine*, Fall 2017. www.dissentmagazine.org/article/revolution-by-candlelight-how-south-koreans-toppled-a-government.

Flowers, Petrice R. 2009. *Refugees, Women, and Weapons: International Norm Adoption and Compliance in Japan.* Stanford: Stanford University Press.

Goodman, Ryan, and Thomas Pegram, eds. 2011. *Human Rights, State Compliance, and Social Change: Assessing National Human Rights Institutions.* Cambridge: Cambridge University Press.

Hankyoreh. 2000a. "Ingwonwi gukgagigu chujin" [The Human Rights Commission of Korea to be created as a state institution]. November 2, 2000. www.bigkinds.or.kr/news/newsDetailView.do?newsId=01101001.20001102000000104&fbclid=IwAR3TNfKv8MqTGXg6wwyJoiH8UOSELv3__KLb8VNAr9Z4lUUncG03m2Iz430.

2000b. "'Ingwonwi gukgagiguro gyeollon nana 3nyeonran' Maedeup Dangye Nobelsangui Him?" [The Human Rights Commission of Korea will end up being created as a state institution? The power of the Nobel Prize ends the 'three-year controversy'?]. November 2, 2000. www.bigkinds.or.kr/news/newsDetailView.do?newsId=01101001.20001102000000509&fbclid=IwARokXrPEaEzooLjW77yEYUeQ4LLIhPvlDwehYWuNlm3IBa9oYuGxj1CeXrw.

2009. "[Editorial] Heeding Resigning Commissioner's Advice for Soft Power." *Hankyoreh*, July 10, 2009. http://book.hani.com/arti/english_edition/e_editorial/365056.html.

John, Jojin V. 2015. "Globalization, National Identity and Foreign Policy: Understanding 'Global Korea'." *The Copenhagen Journal of Asian Studies* 33(2): 38–57.

Kim, Chang-suk. 2001. "Doum doeneun gukgagigu mandeulgetda [We will make a helpful governmental institution]." *Hankyoreh*, November 7, 2001. http://h21.hani.co.kr/arti/society/society_general/3818.html.

Kim, Dong Chun. 2006. *1997nyeon ihu hanguk sahoeui seongchal* [Introspection of Korean society since 1997]. Seoul: Gil.

Kim, Dong Wook. 2009. "Institutionalizing Human Rights: The United Nations, Nongovernmental Organizations and National Human Rights Institutions." Ph.D. dissertation, Political Science, University of Wisconsin.

Kim, Doosik. 2010. "Lee Myung-bak jeongbuhaui gukgaingwonwiwonhoe, wigiinga gihoeinga?" [The National Human Rights Commission under MB government: How to turn crisis into opportunity?]. *Law and Society* 39: 49–74.

Kim, Jong Seo. 2012. "Lee Myung-bak jeongbu 5nyeonui beop, ingwon, minjujuui" [Law, human rights and democracy during five years under Lee Myung-bak administration]. *Minju Beopak* 50: 55–88.

Kim, Jongtae. 2011. "The Discourse of sonjin'guk: South Korea's Eurocentric Modern Identities and Worldviews." Ph.D. dissertation, University of Illinois at Urbana-Champaign.

2012. "The West and East Asian National Identities: A Comparison of Discourses of Korean Seonjinguk, Japanese Nihonjinron, and Chinese New Nationalism." In *Globalization and Development in East Asia*, edited by Jan Nederveen Pieterse and Jongtae Kim, 80–97. New York: Routledge.

Kim, Ki-hong. 2017. "President Moon, Restoring Fallen Human Rights in Korea." *BreakNews*, May 25, 2017. www.breaknews.com/sub_read.html?uid=510840.

Kim, Nan. 2017. "Candlelight and the Yellow Ribbon: Catalyzing Re-Democratization in South Korea." *The Asia-Pacific Journal: Japan Focus* 15–14-5 (July 15, 2017).

Kim, Tae-gyun. 2009. "NHRCK 8 Year Cumulative Acceptance Rate 89.1%." *Yonhap News*, November 24, 2009.

Kim, Yung-myung. 2014. "Hanguk minjujuuiui baljeongwa toebo: Roh Moo-hyun jeongbu wa Lee Myung-bak jeongbu" [The development and decay of Korean democracy: A comparison of Roh Moo-hyun and Lee Myung-bak governments]. *Hanguk Jeongchi yeongu* 23(3): 137–62.

Kjaerum, Morten. 2003. "National Human Rights Institutions Implementing Human Rights." In *Human Rights and Criminal Justice for the Downtrodden*, edited by Klaus Slvensky, 631–54. Leiden: Martinus Nijohff Publishers.

Koo, Jeong-Woo. 2011. "Origins of the National Human Rights Commission of Korea: Global and Domestic Causes." In *South Korean Social Movements: From Democracy to Civil Society*, edited by Gi-Wook Shin and Paul Y. Chang, 77–95. New York: Routledge.

Koo, Jeong-Woo, and Francisco O. Ramirez. 2009. "National Incorporation of Global Human Rights: Worldwide Expansion of National Human Rights Institutions, 1966–2004." *Social Forces* 87(3): 1321-53.

Lee, Mi-kyung. 2001. "On the National Human Rights Commission of Korea Act." *National Assembly Records*, February 27, 2001. http://likms.assembly.go.kr/record/mhs-40-010.do?classCode=2&daeNum=20&commCode=BA&outConn=Y#none.

Lee, Suk-i. 2008. "Beopjilseo oechimyeo ingwon gyeongsihaneun Lee Myung-bak jeongbu" [Lee Myung-bak's disregard of human rights and promotion of legal order]. *Sisain*, December 15, 2008. www.sisain.co.kr/?mod=news&act=articleView&idxno=3435.

Minbyeon-Lawyers for a Democratic Society. 2010. Press Statement on the Resignation of Two Standing Commissioners of the National Human Rights Commission of Korea. November 18, 2010.

MOFAT (Ministry of Foreign Affairs and Trade, Republic of Korea). 2007. *Diplomatic White Paper*. Seoul: Republic of Korea.

NHRCK. 2002. "National Human Rights Commission of the Republic of Korea Annual Report 2002." www.humanrights.go.kr/site/program/board/basicboard/view?

currentpage=2&menuid=002003003001&pagesize=10&boardtypeid=7017&board
id=7000233.

2003. "National Human Rights Commission of the Republic of Korea Annual Report
2003." www.humanrights.go.kr/site/program/board/basicboard/view?currentpage=2&
menuid=002003003001&pagesize=10&boardtypeid=7017&boardid=7000297.

2006. "National Human Rights Commission of the Republic of Korea Annual Report
2006." www.humanrights.go.kr/site/program/board/basicboard/view?currentpage=2&
menuid=002003003001&pagesize=10&boardtypeid=7017&boardid=7000685.

2007. "National Human Rights Commission of the Republic of Korea Annual Report
2007." www.humanrights.go.kr/site/program/board/basicboard/view?currentpage=2&
menuid=002003003001&pagesize=10&boardtypeid=7017&boardid=7001181.

2009. "Chok Kim Dae-jung jeon daetongryeonggwa ingwonwi" [Late President Kim Dae-
jung and the NHRCK]. http://webzine.humanrights.go.kr/user/sub/right_view.do?
no=16859&magazine=2009.09*10.

2011. "Public Survey on the Perception of Human Rights 2011." http://humanrights.go.kr
/site/program/board/basicboard/view?currentpage=11&menuid=001003001004&page
size=10&boardtypeid=16&boardid=603763.

2017. "NHRCK Welcomes the Commitment to Reinstate the Commission's Reputation."
www.humanrights.go.kr/site/program/board/basicboard/view?boardtypeid=24&boardid
=7601114&menuid=001004002001.

2018. *Gukga ingwonwi hyeoksin wiwonhoe gwongo* [Recommendations of NHRCK –
Reforms Committee]. http://humanrights.go.kr/site/program/board/basicboard/view?
menuid=001004002001&boardtypeid=24&boardid=7602376.

Park, Joo-min. 2011. "Pyohyeonui jayue gwanhan gukgaingwonwiwonhoeui yeokal mit geu
byeonhwa" [NHRCK's role and its changes with regard to freedom of expression]. In
Gukgaingwonwiwonhoe seollip 10junyeon Daedoronhoe [Conference on the Occasion of
the 10th Anniversary of the NHRCK], 2–25. Seoul: Korea Human Rights Foundation.

Park, Sang-bong. 2010. "Teukbyeolgihoek: seonjingugeuro ganeun gil, beopjilseo chulcheo –
dogilui jipoewa siwi" [G20 special edition: in becoming seonjinguk – establishment of
law and order: association and assembly in Germany]. *Future Korea*, April 20, 2010. www
.futurekorea.co.kr/news/articleView.html?idxno=19613.

Pegram, Thomas. 2015. "Global Human Rights Governance and Orchestration: National
Human Rights Institutions as Intermediaries." *European Journal of International
Relations* 21(3): 595–620.

Pohjolainen, Anna-Elina. 2006. *The Evolution of National Human Rights Institutions: The
Role of the United Nations*. Copenhagen: The Danish Institute for Human Rights.

Presidential Secretariat. 2004. *Roh Moo-hyun daetongryeong yeonseol munjip* [Collection of
President Roh Moo-hyun's statements] Vol. 1 (February 1, 2003–January 31, 2004), edited
by Presidential Secretariat.

2005. *Roh Moo-hyun daetongryeong yeonseol* munjip [Collection of President Roh Moo-
hyun's statements]. Vol. 2 (February 1, 2004–January 31, 2005), edited by Presidential
Secretariat.

2008. *Roh Moo-hyun daetongryeong yeonseol munjib* [Collection of President Roh Moo-
hyun's statements]. Vol. 5 (February 1, 2007–January 31, 2008) of *Collection of President
Roh Moo-hyun's Statements*, edited by Presidential Secretariat.

Reif, Linda C. 2000. "Building Democratic Institutions: The Role of National Human Rights
Institutions in Good Governance and Human Rights Protection." *Harvard Human
Rights Journal* 13: 1–69.

Renshaw, Catherine, and Katrina Taylor. 2008. "Promoting and Protecting Human Rights in the Asia Pacific; the Relationship Between National Human Rights Institutions and Non-Governmental Organisations." *Human Rights Defender* 17 (2): 5–7.

Renshaw, Catherine, and Kieren Fitzpatrick. 2012. "National Human Rights Institutions in the Asia Pacific Region: Change Agents under Conditions of Uncertainty." In *Human Rights, State Compliance, and Social Change: Assessing National Human Rights Institutions*, edited by Ryan Goodman and Thomas Pegram, 150–180. Cambridge: Cambridge University Press.

Shin, Jin-ho. 2011. "Malbal an meokineun ingwonwi" [Non-acceptance of the NHRCK]. *Segye Ilbo*, December 12, 2011. www.segye.com/newsView/20111211002785.

Sidoti, Chris. 2011. "National Human Rights Institutions and the International Human Rights System." In *Human Rights, State Compliance, and Social Change: Assessing National Human Rights Institutions*, edited by Ryan Goodman and Thomas Pegram, 93–123. Cambridge: Cambridge University Press.

Tharoor, Ishaan. 2017. "South Korea Just Showed the World How to Do Democracy." *Washington Post*, May 10, 2017. www.washingtonpost.com/news/worldviews/wp/2017/05/10/south-korea-just-showed-the-world-how-to-do-democracy/?utm_term=.28456a885d27.

Yoo, Dong-yul. 2010. "Teukbyeol gihoek: seonjingugeuro ganeun gil, beopjilseo chulcheo – Hujinjeok jipoesiwi, ijen sarajyeoya handa" [G20 special edition: in becoming seonjinguk – establishment of law and order: hujinguk style association and assembly should stop]. *Future Korea*, March 19, 2010. www.futurekorea.co.kr/news/articlePrint.html?idxno=19552.

6

The Constitutional Court as a Facilitator of Fundamental Rights Claiming in South Korea, 1988–2018

Hannes B. Mosler

6.1 INTRODUCTION

The Constitutional Court has facilitated rights claiming by South Korean citizens in that it has promoted the development of rights, rule of law, and citizens' legal consciousness. Rule of law is fundamental to a functioning liberal democracy (Diamond and Morlino 2004; Morlino 2010; O'Donnell 2004), and the constitution of a given polity represents the basic framework within which all laws must be applied. Since in South Korea (hereafter, Korea) the Constitutional Court is the last arbiter of constitutional norms, it plays a central role in maintaining rule of law, particularly when it hears grievances against the state voiced by citizens through constitutional complaints. The guarantee of individuals' fundamental rights is only one function, albeit a central one, of an entire set of interrelated duties of constitutional courts in liberal democracies, such as Korea. Other functions include protecting and legitimizing the constitution and its values, constraining state powers, promoting and fostering political peace and social integration, and disseminating constitutional values. All these functions are mainly realized through constitutional review (Häberle 2014, 26; Kranenpohl 2004; Seo 2014), which allows courts to interpret, supplement, renew, and often even create fundamental rules and principles for the polity.

The existing literature on constitutional adjudication in Korea is mostly informed by the discipline of constitutional law and includes studies that focus on the characteristics of the Constitutional Court and constitutional adjudication (Ginsburg 2009; J. Kim 2010), major decisions (Ginsburg 2003b; Jeon 2016; Lee 2014; West and Yoon 1992; Yoon 2010), caseload statistics and changes in the Court's performance over time (Nam 2003; Song 2001; 2005), and the development and state of fundamental rights (D. Choi 2014; S.-D. Kim 2017; Naumann 2010; Shin 2011). Other studies assess the Constitutional Court from a comparative perspective, relating its evolution to other institutions in the Asian region and to the high courts of countries such as the United States, Germany, France, and Austria (Ginsburg 2003a; Yeh 2009; Yeh and Chang 2011).

Most accounts are positive, noting the Constitutional Court's processing capacity of an enormously increasing caseload as well as its wise decisions regarding fundamental matters, which have contributed to the consolidation of democracy since 1988 (Ginsburg 2009). In addition, opinion polls routinely show that, for the citizenry, the Constitutional Court is one of the most trusted political institutions (Constitutional Court 2015). At the same time, the Court is characterized as "reactive and cautious" in that it "rarely directs its decisions against the political majority's preferences or sentiments, especially when it involves some of the most hotly contested issues" (Yeh and Chang 2011, 827–29). To address such shortcomings, some scholars call for reforms such as extending justices' terms, strengthening democratic checks and balances in justice appointments, expanding the scope of eligibility for justice candidates, or adding a comprehensive review of statutes to the court's competencies (D. Choi 2008; J. Kim 2005).

This chapter updates the literature by investigating how the Korean Constitutional Court has been developing as a formal institutional mechanism for rights claiming. After summarizing the scope of discretion of the Constitutional Court, this chapter addresses two main questions: First, how successful have citizens been in making use of the Constitutional Court's competencies? This section analyzes caseload statistics from the Constitutional Court between 1988 and 2019 to assess which of its functions have been used to what extent, as well as to gauge the effectiveness of the different roads to constitutional adjudication. Second, how has the Constitutional Court protected and extended citizens' fundamental rights? This section qualitatively examines the Constitutional Court's salient decisions regarding major social issues such as gender equality, sexual autonomy, and freedom of conscience. These topics are relatively understudied among Constitutional Court cases, despite recently having developed into major sociopolitical issues. In addition, these issues have not only been repeatedly subject to constitutional adjudication in Korea but are also often addressed in other democracies. They thus provide a good yardstick for evaluating how the Korean Constitutional Court handles such rights claiming.

6.2 THE CONSTITUTIONAL COURT'S SCOPE OF REVIEW

As part of its democratization, Korea became the first Asian country to establish a Constitutional Court as a specialized court in 1988 and modeled it after its German counterpart (Constitutional Court of Korea 2008, 52). Korea's Constitution has been amended nine times since the foundation of the Republic in 1948, and constitutional review institutions have differed in their design and discretion accordingly.[1] Through these constitutional revisions, the list of enumerated basic rights has

---

[1]   In 1948, following the US-American model, the Supreme Court was designed to refer cases to a temporary Constitutional Committee for constitutional review (1948 Constitution Art. 81). In 1960, the Second Republic briefly introduced an independent Constitution Court, modelled after the one of the Federal Republic of Germany, though lacking individual constitutional complaint procedures

changed little since the 1948 Constitution, which was modeled after the German Weimar Constitution.[2] Thus, the Constitution has always provided for the protection of citizens' fundamental rights as expressed in Article 10: "It shall be the duty of the State to confirm and guarantee the fundamental and inviolable human rights of individuals." But realizing and extending these fundamental rights only became possible after the Constitutional Court's establishment in 1988 (Ginsburg 2003b, 213; S.-D. Kim 2017, 76; Lee 2014, 2).

Korea's Constitutional Court drew on the design of the German Federal Constitutional Court (and Korea's own predecessor during the Second Republic), and thus belongs to the European model of a special court that has the exclusive power to review legislation and state agency actions. The modern concept of constitutional review is rooted in the necessity to control against the possible malfunctioning or misuse of the rule of law. Toward this objective, the Constitutional Court's main types of proceedings are to make decisions (*simpan*) on impeachment, dissolution of political parties, competence disputes between state organs, judicial review of statutes, and constitutional complaints (see Table 6.1). These categories of constitutional adjudication are crucial for protecting the maintenance and functioning of the democratic order and thus guarantee fundamental rights to citizens and adjudicate on the constitutionality of laws and real acts (*Realakte*) of the state. All these competencies can be understood as part of the Constitutional Court's responsibility to safeguard the rule of law directly or indirectly.

TABLE 6.1 *Types of Proceedings at the Constitutional Court of Korea*

Types of Proceedings	Legal Basis		Case Codes
	Const.	CCA[3]	
Impeachment	§ 111 (3)	§ 48	HEON NA
Party dissolution	§ 111 (4)	§ 55	HEON DA
Competence dispute	§ 111 (2)	§ 61	HEON LA
Judicial review of statutes	§ 111 (1)	§ 41	HEON GA
Constitutional complaint	§ 111 (5)	§ 68	-
– *(non-)acts by public power*		(1)	HEON MA
– *legal statutes*		(2)	HEON BA

Source: Compiled by the author based on the Constitution of the Republic of Korea and the Constitutional Court Act.

(1960 Constitution Art. 83–3; see Mosler 2015; 2017a). These competencies were shifted first to the Supreme Court in 1963 (Constitution Art. 102) and later to a Constitutional Committee that was controlled by Park Chung-hee (1972 Constitution Art. 109). An analogous Constitutional Committee existed during the Fifth Republic but was rarely used (1980 Constitution Art. 112).

2   Even the first Constitution of the Provisional Government in 1919 enumerated the rights to equality, freedom, and political participation (see S.-D. Kim 2017, 63–67).

3   *Heonbeopjaepansobeop* (Constitutional Court Act), Act No. 4017 (1988).

Impeachment is a means of defense against an incumbent's violations of the constitution or other laws or betrayal of the trust of the people, and thus it guarantees and enforces core principles of democracy, such as the rule of law, separation of powers, and popular sovereignty.[4] *Dissolution of a political party* is another instrument the Constitutional Court can use – upon the National Assembly's request – if a political party's purposes or activities are contrary to the democratic basic order (Constitution, Art. 8).[5] *Disputes between state agencies*, disputes between state agencies and local governments, and disputes between local governments involve issues regarding jurisdictions. The basic power structure of state organization is laid out in the constitution, and more detailed and concrete regulations are fixed in related legal statutes. By adjudicating competence disputes, the Constitutional Court fulfills its responsibility as the final arbiter. The competence dispute procedure is based on the principles of separation of powers and minority rights. The most frequent types of adjudication the Constitutional Court conducts are *judicial review of statutes* (i.e., deciding on the constitutionality of a legal provision upon referral by another (lower) court) and particularly proceedings on *constitutional complaints* (i.e., deciding on whether the constitutionally granted rights of an individual have been violated).

A person's fundamental rights can be infringed upon constitutionally in two ways: by the effect of a statute invoked in a court trial or by the (in)action of any other public agency.[6] Constitutional adjudication in the former case is defined as the examination of a statute's unconstitutionality (*wiheon beomnyul simpan*) and concerns statutes that are a precondition of a given ongoing court proceeding (Constitution Art. 111(1); Constitutional Court Act (CCA) Art. 41(1)). The examination of unconstitutionality presupposes, however, that the court viewed the statutes as contradicting the constitution, and thus requested such a review by the Constitutional Court (CCA Art. 41(5)).[7] Requiring other courts to examine a statute's legality before initiating constitutional review keeps filings in check, securing efficiency and effectiveness of constitutional adjudication. At the same time, the constitution anticipates the possibility of a court misjudging the (un)constitutionality of a statute, thereby possibly depriving a person's fundamental right, and accordingly provides for the alternative remedy of direct claims-making (Art. 111(5)). Parties to a case can thus request such a referral (CCA Art. 41(1)), and if the court refuses to comply, a person may directly lodge a complaint to the Constitutional Court for judgment on the constitutionality of the statute in question (*heonbeop sowon simpan*; CCA Art. 68(2)). The *Regulation of Constitutional Court*

---

4   See Mosler (2017b) on impeachment.

5   See Mosler (2016) on the first and hitherto only dissolution case.

6   Violation of personal rights by other persons – natural or legal – is covered by civil and criminal law, and thus is not part of this enumeration here.

7   The Minister of National Court Administration at the Supreme Court must send the referral "without delay" to the Constitutional Court, and thus has no authority to review or examine the case (*Wiheon beomnyul simpanjecheongsageone gwanhan yegyu (jaeil 88–3)*), Established Trial Regulation No. 1716 (2019).

Case Filing (RCCF)[8] defines this route of constitutional appeal as a *type 2* complaint: the unconstitutionality examination of a legal statute (*wiheonsimsahyeong*; RCCF Art. 3(2), sentence 6).

Most constitutional complaints, however, belong to *type 1* complaints, that is, complaints for rights relief (*gwolligujehyeong*) in cases of infringement of fundamental rights by the (in)action of a public agency (RCCF Art. 3(2), sentence 5) belonging to the legislature, judiciary, or executive. In other words, this route is taken if fundamental rights were violated as a result of nonfeasance or omission in legislation, presidential decrees, ministerial ordinances, administrative omission or nonfeasance, and other authoritative real acts (*gwollyeokjeok sasilhaengwi*) – for example, resolutions or procedures – by agencies of the executive. All other legally available means of administrative and judicial relief must first be exhausted (subsidiarity principle). While this route explicitly excludes cases of fundamental rights infringement because of a legal statute invoked in an ongoing court trial (CCA Art. 68(1)), it allows individual petitions in judicial cases where a court applied a legal statute that was already declared unconstitutional by the Constitutional Court.

The Constitutional Court's discretion to rule on individual constitutional complaints is particularly important for understanding how citizens can leverage the constitution to remedy grievances against the state. Unlike the United States, for example, neither ordinary courts nor the Supreme Court[9] possess the discretion for constitutional review. Unlike the German case, no local constitutional courts exist to conduct constitutional review. In Korea, ordinary courts may only assess whether a statute in question might violate the Constitution and then accordingly refer cases to the Constitutional Court. Korea's Supreme Court only has the discretion to decide upon constitutional infringement regarding "the constitutionality or legality of administrative decrees, regulations or actions, when their constitutionality or legality is at issue in a trial" (Constitution, Art. 107).[10] Constitutional complaints are the most powerful mechanisms for the legal protection of constitutional rights because they allow citizens to directly appeal to the Constitutional Court and demand remedy for their grievances due to infringement of fundamental rights (Dannemann 1994, 142). The constitutional complaint proceeding has a dual function of guaranteeing the *subjective* fundamental rights of an individual while also bolstering the *objective* constitutional order by controlling for unconstitutional execution of public power (Häberle 2014, 26; Sung 2012, 1330).

---

[8] *Heonbeopjaepanso sageonui jeopsue gwanhan gyuchik* (Constitutional Court Regulation) No. 372 (2016).

[9] See later for some minor exceptions.

[10] Due to unclear legal regulations and competing interpretations thereof, the two courts have been frequently in conflict with each other over differing views on each other's competencies (see Ginsburg 2003a, 239–42).

6.3 CITIZENS' USE OF THE CONSTITUTIONAL COURT: A QUANTITATIVE ASSESSMENT OF CASELOAD PATTERNS

Annual filings with the Constitutional Court have continuously risen, from 425 cases in 1989 to 924 cases in 1999, and 1,487 cases in 2009 to 2,427 cases in 2018 (see Figure 6.1), thus reaching an accumulated number of 37,463 filings in total as of August 2019 (see Table 6.2). Already, this steady annual growth – with caseloads almost doubling every decade – demonstrates how actively Korean citizens have made use of the Court (see Figure 6.1). Although caseloads fell by one-third in 2008, the growth trend had recovered by 2017.

The largest share of cases (97 percent) have concerned direct petitions by individual citizens. Approximately 1.6 percent of cases are successful.[11] This pattern closely resembles the statistics of the Federal Constitutional Court of Germany, as does the success ratio.[12] Despite the low success rate, the Constitutional Court in Korea seems to fulfill its function of a "wailing wall" (Blankenburg 1998) for citizens to have at least a channel through which they can express their grievances. In this way, the Constitutional Court is also a "seismograph" for social problems (Kranenpohl 2004, 43). Moreover, the mere fact that a legal statute or act by public authority can

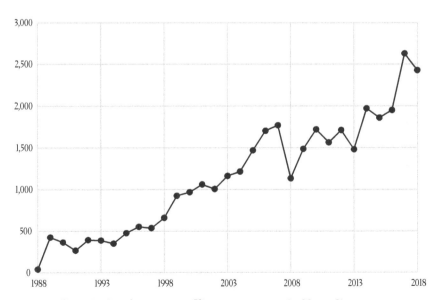

FIGURE 6.1 Constitutional court case filings per annum (1988–2018).
Source: Compiled by author; based on Constitutional Court statistics (www.ccourt.go.kr)

---

[11] The success ratio divides successful cases (512) by all filed cases (31,744) of constitutional complaints.
[12] The share of constitutional appeals at the German Federal Constitutional Court is 96.6 percent, with a success rate of 2.3 percent (Bundesverfassungsgericht 2018, 1).

TABLE 6.2 *Constitutional Court Case Filings (Sept. 1988–Aug. 2019)*

Types of Proceedings	Cases Filed	Share	Decisions*			Not Reviewed	Pending
			Unconstitutional (A)	Constitutional (B)	A + B		
Impeachment	2	0.005%	1	1	2	0	0
Party dissolution	2	0.005%	1	0	1	1	0
Competence dispute	109	0.3%	19	22	41	61	10
Judicial review of statutes	979	2.6%	388	347	735	196	48
Constitutional complaint	36,371	97.0%	1,301	9,933	11,234	24,070	1,067
– *(non-)acts by public power*	28,929	77.2%	899	7,679	8,578	19,716	635
– *legal statutes*	7,442	19.8%	402	2,254	2,656	4,345	432
Sub-Total (a)**	**37,341**	**99.7%**	**1,689**	**10,280**	**11,696**	**24,266**	**1,115**
Sub-Total (b)***	**8,412**	**22.5%**	**790**	**2,601**	**3,391**	**4,541**	**480**
Total	**37,463**	**100%**	**1,710**	**11,303**	**12,013**	**24,328**	**1,125**

Source: Compiled by author; based on Constitutional Court statistics (www.ccourt.go.kr)

* "Unconstitutional" includes modified decisions such as "unconformable," "conditionally unconstitutional," and "conditionally constitutional"; "Constitutional" includes "upholding," "constitutional," and "rejected"; "Not reviewed" includes "dismissed," "other," and "withdrawn" (see next).

** Sub-total (a) excludes cases of impeachment, party dissolution, and competence dispute.

*** Sub-total (b) comprises "judicial review" and "constitutional complaint" on legal statutes only.

become subject to constitutional scrutiny contributes to safeguarding fundamental rights a priori (see Dannemann 1994, 152).

With 1,125 cases pending as of August 2019, the Constitutional Court has thus far decided on a total of 36,338 cases, the majority of which (24,325 cases or 70 percent) were dismissed (*gakha*), not reviewed due to other (*gita*) reasons, or withdrawn (*chwiha*) by the claimant, and thus were not considered for substantial deliberation on their merits.[13] The other 12,013 cases were either found unconstitutional,[14] upheld (*inyong*) (1,710 cases), or found constitutional (*hapheon*) (11,303 cases). In other words, the Constitutional Court concurred with claims of fundamental rights infringement in 14.2 percent of cases. Analyzing the 12,013 cases with substantial decisions[15] allows for the assessment of the Constitutional Court's performance and meaning as a rights claiming mechanism for citizens. The following paragraphs provide an examination of how much and how successful different routes to the Constitutional Court as the last arbiter for fundamental rights claims have been so far. After comparing the two main proceedings of judicial review and constitutional complaints, I compare cases of review of legal statutes by referral with those by way of individual complaint. The section concludes with a deeper look into the largest group of cases: constitutional complaints against public prosecutors.

6.3.1 *Specific Judicial Review of Statutes versus Constitutional Complaints*

First, it is important to consider decisions on cases that were referred to the Constitutional Court by lower courts in relation to those that were brought before the Court directly by constitutional petition. This allows for comparing the standard route of claims through court referral (CCA 41(1)) vis-à-vis direct individual complaints (CCA 68 (1), (2)), and thus illuminates the role of the Constitutional Court in rights claiming processes by individuals. With 11,234 cases by complainant petition (93.9 percent) versus 735 cases by court referral (6.1 percent), it becomes clear how extensively citizens have made use of the constitution appeal system. Of the 11,234 constitutional complaints, 1,301 cases (11.6 percent) were found unconstitutional or were upheld, while 9,933 cases (88.4 percent) were ruled constitutional. Meanwhile, among the cases referred by lower courts, 52.8 percent (388 cases) were ruled unconstitutional, while 47.2 percent (347 cases) were found constitutional. It is not surprising that the share of successful cases by court referral (52.8 percent) is far larger than those of complainant petitions (11.6 percent) since the courts possess more extensive expertise and can be expected to judge the unconstitutionality of a matter in a possibly objective fashion, while directly affected individuals are prone

---

[13] Submissions are "dismissed" when formal requirements of the procedure are not fulfilled and "rejected" when the submission's contents are inadequate.

[14] This includes modified decisions rendering issues unconformable (*heonbeop bulhapchi*), conditionally unconstitutional (*hanjeong wiheon*), and conditionally constitutional (*hanjeong hapheon*).

[15] This excludes cases of impeachment, party dissolution, and competence disputes.

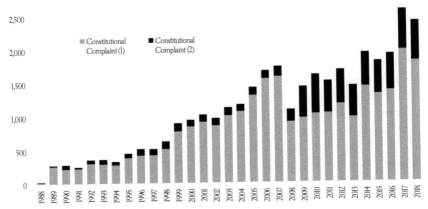

FIGURE 6.2 Constitutional complaints (CCA Art.68 [1] + [2]) filed per year (1988–2018).
Source: Compiled by author; based on Constitutional Court statistics (www.ccourt.go.kr)

to base their assessments on emotions, and because the complainant petitions include cases of fundamental rights infringement due to legal statutes (*type 2*) as well as those due to (non-)acts by state agents (*type 1*) (see Figure 6.2).

6.3.2 *Specific Judicial Review of Legal Statutes: Referral versus Complaint*

While the previous paragraph investigated to what degree citizens make use of the constitutional complaint system per se, for a more nuanced analysis, in this section only cases regarding judicial review of legal statutes are considered. Of the total 3,391 cases, only 735 (21.7 percent) were referred to by lower courts to be reviewed, while 2,656 (78.3 percent) were brought before the Constitutional Court by way of constitutional complaint. In other words, most requests for constitutional review were initiated by directly affected individuals. Of all reviews on claims' merits, less than a quarter were found unconstitutional or upheld (790 cases; 23.3 percent), whereas most cases were ruled constitutional (2,601 cases; 76.7 percent).

Among the 735 review referrals from lower courts, 388 (52.8 percent) were ruled unconstitutional, while 347 (47.2 percent) were found constitutional. Thus, if we assume that the Constitutional Court's decisions are always correct, the lower courts' performance appears questionable because only about half the cases they referred to the Constitutional Court were actually found unconstitutional.[16] As for those 2,656

---

[16] If cases were added that were not considered for review by the Constitutional Court, this ratio would become even worse. For a similar assessment at an earlier stage, see Song (2005). It is known that the workload of the courts is overwhelming, which may serve as further explanation for the phenomenon. An alternative explanation could be that, in ambiguous or borderline cases, the lower courts would rather defer to the Constitutional Court than risk issuing an unconstitutional ruling. I thank the two editors for their insights on these points.

cases that reached the Constitutional Court by individual complaint for a decision on their merits, 402 (15.1 percent) were found unconstitutional, while 2,254 (84.9 percent) were ruled constitutional. As already noted, it is not surprising that the success ratio of constitutional complaints is much lower compared to those submitted by lower courts.

However, the low rate of successful complaints does not mean review referrals on the constitutionality of legal statutes are dispensable. Of the 790 cases regarding legal statutes that were ultimately found unconstitutional, no less than 402 cases (50.9 percent) were filed through the route of constitutional complaint. Put differently, about half the statutes the Constitutional Court has ruled unconstitutional since 1988 were not recognized as such by the lower courts. This shows how important the alternative route of direct constitutional complaint is for remedying fundamental rights infringements. If citizens were exclusively dependent on lower courts' assessments, every second grievance stemming from unconstitutional legal statutes would not have been remedied.

6.3.3 *Constitutional Complaints against Public Authorities: The Case against Prosecutors*

This section focuses on constitutional complaints against acts of state authority. Of 8,578 decisions, the Constitutional Court ruled 899 cases (10.5 percent) constitutional or upheld, while 7,679 cases (89.5 percent) were ruled unconstitutional. Based on accumulated numbers as of August 2019, the largest portion of complaints against state actions concerned cases related to the executive branch (61.3 percent),[17] while filings challenging (in)action by the legislative (18.5 percent), the judicative (10.7 percent), and other entities (9.6 percent) occurred far less frequently. As Figure 6.3 illustrates, these executive-related cases also help account for the drop in overall caseloads at the Constitutional Court in 2008. Meanwhile, other categories' case rates have been slowly increasing and, at face value, do not correlate with the changes in the executive-related caseload.

Figure 6.4 shows the development of cases based on a breakdown of the executive-related category and makes clear what the actual source of the 2008 decline is: cases in which citizens challenged decisions by a prosecutor to indict (*giso*), not to indict (*bulgiso*), or suspend the indictment of (*gisoyuye*) a suspect. The strongly increasing trend of filings regarding executive powers (mostly prosecutors) up to 2007 almost halved and maintained that level for nearly a decade, only to rise again in 2016. Unlike comparable prosecution services in other countries, prosecutors in Korea enjoy far-reaching discretion – even including the authority to decide to indict or not to indict an alleged culprit (see Mosler 2018).

---

[17] These 14,613 cases represent 61.3 percent of all cases filed with the Constitutional Court between 2001 and end of August 2018.

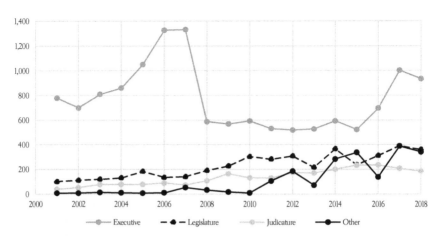

FIGURE 6.3 Constitutional complaints against state acts according to domains (2001–18).[18]
Source: Compiled by author; based on Constitutional Court statistics (www.ccourt.go.kr)

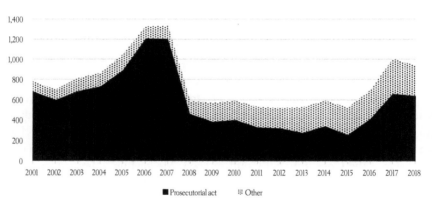

FIGURE 6.4 Breakdown of executive-related cases according to subject of complaint (2001–18).
Source: Compiled by author; based on Constitutional Court statistics (www.ccourt.go.kr)

There have always been many cases where people have felt that their indictment was not justified, that their indictment was suspended (*gisoyuye*) yet the alleged offense remained on their criminal record, or that an alleged perpetrator was acquitted due to lack of evidence (*muhyeomui*). In 1973, at the height of President Park Chung-hee's dictatorship, alternative ways for relieving grievances

---

[18] Statistical data on the different objects of case filings are available from 2001 onward only.

regarding the misuse of civil servants' power were limited, with almost no way to appeal against prosecutors' (in)activity. This void in the legal structure was filled by establishing an appeal system in 1988 via CCA Article 68(1), which led to the marked increase in constitutional petition filings regarding prosecutorial actions.[19] In 2007, portions of the Criminal Procedure Code[20] (Art. 60) were amended to again include the possibility to request dismissal (*jaejeongsincheong*) of such (non)indictments at lower courts, which immediately led to a dramatic drop in CCA Article 68(1) petitions to the Constitutional Court concerning cases of nonindictment (*bulgiso*) of the accused from 2008 onward. According to the principle of subsidiarity laid out in CCA Article 2, Section 3(1), the Constitutional Court can only consider cases that have exhausted all other means of grievance relief, and since the revised Criminal Procedure Code provides those means, a large share of abrogation requests were handled by lower courts. Nonetheless, the reform was not exhaustive, and thus there are cases that are not covered, which explains why cases filed with the Constitutional Court continue to account for a significant share of the caseload.[21]

6.4 FUNDAMENTAL RIGHTS CLAIMS BEFORE THE COURT

Some key decisions regarding the right to gender equality,[22] sexual autonomy, and freedom of conscience illustrate well the development of constitutional review over time in Korea. These issues have not only been addressed for decades, they were also repeatedly subject to constitutional adjudication. In Korea, as in other advanced industrialized democracies, these issues have become increasingly important and thus serve as a significant sample of constitutional adjudication regarding funda-mental rights claims. Cases related to gender equality involve questions of national-ity, military conscription, and the head-of-household system. Sexual autonomy encompasses issues of adultery, abortion, and homosexuality. Meanwhile, the Constitutional Court's evolving decisions on conscientious objection speak directly to the issue of freedom of conscience. Hence, this section sheds light on the continuities and changes in argumentation in the Constitutional Court's rulings to examine how it protected and extended citizens' fundamental rights.

---

[19]   In April 1989, for the first time, the Constitutional Court made explicit that nonindictment decisions by the prosecutor's office could additionally become the object of constitutional petitions (88Heonma3, April 17, 1989).

[20]   *Hyeongsasosongbeop*, Act No. 8730 (2007).

[21]   Between 2013 and 2017, more than 1,600 cases were filed, of which around 200 were decided in favor of the claimants (Im 2017). In addition, despite an overall slight growth in annual numbers of the remaining categories, namely, the category of "other" has been increasing most prominently from less than 10 cases in 2001 to almost 400 cases in 2017. Among cases regarding those related to grievances over public power, (in)action petitions concerning administrative measures (*haengjeongcheobun deung*) have been showing a steady growth since 2008.

[22]   For a general overview, see H. Choi (2012).

6.4.1 Gender Equality

In July 1997, the Constitutional Court decided that Article 809(1) of the Civil Code[23] that prohibits marriage between two persons who have the same family name and come from the same patrilineal ancestry (dongseongdongbon) ran contrary to the Constitution.[24] The decision's reasoning drew on the right of sexual self-determination, the right to pursue happiness, and the principle of gender equality. In August 2000, the Court also argued that to base questions of nationality on patrilineality (bugyejuui) – that is, that a foreigner who marries a Korean man would receive the Korean nationality, while a foreigner who marries a Korean woman would not (Nationality Act, Art. 2(1))[25] – violated the right to equality.[26] In the same vein, in February 2005, the Court ruled that an offspring prohibited from adopting the mother's family name but forced to use the father's surname did not conform with the Constitution (buseongjuui; Civil Code, Art. 781(1(1))) because it violates constitutionally granted personality rights, personal dignity, and gender equality.[27]

In December 1999, the Constitutional Court decided that provisions of the Act on Supporting Discharged Soldiers (Art. 8(1), 8(3), Art. 9)[28] violated the constitutional right to equality because only male citizens were obliged to serve in the army and thus exclusively enjoyed the privilege of receiving extra credit points (gasanjeom) when taking public servant exams.[29] In February 2006, the Court similarly ruled that provisions of the Cordial Reception and Support Act for Patriots and Veterans (Art. 31)[30] – which awarded extra points to family members of patriots or veterans – were unconstitutional.[31] While the majority of justices in a later decision in November 2010 rejected an appeal against the Military Service Act (Art. 3(1)),[32] which stipulates that only men have the constitutional duty of military service and that women may only apply to serve, one dissenting opinion argued that this norm represents discrimination and a violation of the right to equality, and thus was unconstitutional.[33]

One of the most well-known decisions with respect to promoting gender equality was the verdict in 2005 that ruled the male head-of-household system (hojuje) (Civil Code, Art. 781(1))[34] discriminated against women regarding legally registering

---

[23] Minbeop, Act No. 4199 (1990).
[24] 90Heonga70 (March 11, 1993).
[25] Gukjeokbeop, Act No. 5431 (1997).
[26] 97Heonga12 (August 31, 2000).
[27] 2003Heonga5 etc. (December 22, 2005).
[28] Jedaeguninjiwone gwanhan beomnyul, Act No. 5482 (1998).
[29] 98Heonma363 (December 23, 1999).
[30] Gukgayugongja deung yeu mit jiwone gwanhan beomnyul, Act No. 7104 (2004).
[31] 2004Heonma675 etc. (February 23, 2006).
[32] Byeongnyeokbeop, Act No. 9620 (2009).
[33] 2006Heonma328 (November 25, 2010).
[34] Minbeop, Act No. 7427 (2005).

family members, inheritance rights, and the status of offspring.[35] Here, the Constitutional Court made clear that national traditions and family values (see Chapter 3) can be superseded by the constitutional imperative of gender equality.

6.4.2 *Adultery*

Another development regarding gender equality to overcome traditional stereotypes was the decision on Article 241 of the Criminal Code[36] that punished adultery (*gantongjoe*) with up to two years imprisonment. In the Court's first ruling regarding adultery in 1990, it decided in a seven to two vote against the unconstitutionality of Article 241 by arguing that it was important to maintain virtuous sex morals (*seol-lyanghan seongdodeok*), monogamy, the institution of marriage for the sake of guaranteeing family life, protecting married couples' duties of sexual faithfulness, and preventing social illnesses due to adultery.[37] Hence, the bench asserted that punishing adultery did not violate sexual self-determination, human dignity, or the right to pursue happiness. In a complementary opinion, one justice added that even though the normative power of criminalizing adultery had weakened due to changes in society's and citizens' awareness, adultery nonetheless retained the "quality of an anti-social crime" (*beomjoejeok bansahoeseong*) and thus the article cannot be said to violate the Constitution.[38] This decision was upheld with no additional argumentation in 1993.[39] In its third dealing with the matter in 2001, the Court again maintained its basic verdict. This time, however, one justice explicitly dissented, repeating earlier critics by stressing that adultery is a question of morals belonging to the private life of a person and is thus not to be determined by the state.[40] What is more, referring to the key arguments of the hitherto dissenting opinions, the Court's majority concluded by urging the legislature to seriously consider abolishing Article 241 in reference to changes in "our legal consciousness (*uriui beobuisik*)."[41] In other words, despite its conservative decision regarding the Article's constitutionality as such, the Court quite plainly indicated that criminalizing adultery was slowly but surely becoming outdated in light of present Korean standards and thus reverted the issue to the National Assembly.

Seven years later, in 2008, an even stronger shift in the Court became apparent. Only four justices decided for the constitutionality of Article 241, and they repeated the argument that legislative change was needed to alleviate the problem of intruding into and criminalizing private matters.[42] Meanwhile, four justices asserted that

---

[35]   2001Heonga9 etc. (February 3, 2005). See Yang 2013.
[36]   *Hyeongbeop*, Act No. 4040 (1988).
[37]   89Heonma82 (September 10, 1990).
[38]   *Id.*
[39]   90Heonga70 (March 11, 1993).
[40]   *Id.*
[41]   2000Heonba60 (October 25, 2001).
[42]   2007Heonga17 etc. (October 30, 2008).

the Article was unconstitutional, and one justice decided criminalizing adultery was nonconforming with the Constitution (*heonbeopbulhapchi*). Because striking down the Article would have required a minimum of six judges to find it unconstitutional, the Court's four to five verdict failed again to initiate its abolition. Yet the incremental change in judicial thinking was clear.

Finally, in 2015, the Constitutional Court ruled seven to two that the Article on adultery excessively encroached upon sexual self-determination and privacy, and thus was unconstitutional.[43] The majority of the bench argued that, in light of values, norms, and changes in Korean society regarding the institution of marriage and the right to sexual self-determination, "[t]here is no longer any public consensus regarding the criminalization of adultery." In addition, many advanced countries have abolished adultery from their criminal law. While adultery might still be immoral, acts that occur in the private sphere and are neither harmful to society nor violate other individuals' legal interests should not be encroached upon excessively by the state. The fact that adultery charges have often been misused by spouses in divorce suits or by others to blackmail women was added as another reason for abolishing the statute. In conclusion, the bench contended that "the provision at issue violates the constitution for infringing on the right to sexual self-determination and secrecy and freedom of privacy."

In November 2009, the Court had already resorted to a similar reasoning regarding sexual autonomy when, with a six to three vote, it struck down Article 304 of the Criminal Code that had punished a person for inducing a woman who was not prone to an obscene act (*eumhaengui sangseup eomneun bunyeo*) into sexual intercourse under false promises of marriage or engagement fraud (*honinbingjaganeumjoe*).[44] First, the Court reasoned that sexual relationships and activities are private matters and thus should not be regulated by law or even criminalized unless they are proven to exert an evil influence on society.[45] What is more, many other countries either did not have such regulations or had abolished them. Second, the argumentation contended that punishing such sexual relations excessively restricts men's fundamental rights, such as the right to sexual self-determination and the right to privacy.[46] Third, criminalizing premarital sexual relationships denies not only women's right to sexual self-determination but also stigmatizes all other women who have multiple partners as women "prone to obscene acts." The norm thus denies women's sexual autonomy "under the guise of protecting women, by treating them as not being mature enough to have the capacity to voluntarily make such a decision."[47]

---

[43] 2009Heonba17 etc. (February 26, 2015).
[44] 2008Heonba58 etc. (November 26, 2009).
[45] *Id.*
[46] *Id.*
[47] *Id.*

In a seven-to-two vote seven years previously, the Court had ruled the provision constitutional on reverse premises.[48] Even then, the majority opinion presupposed that women could in fact decide when to have sex with someone and that this matter belonged to the private realm that, in principle, should not be transgressed by criminal law. At the same time, the Court reasoned that in cases wherein men deliberately approach women to have sex under the pretext of marriage, women "easily fall for it," which necessitates restriction by criminal law.[49] This is corroborated by referring to the particular "meaning of marriage in our society" that can make it "extremely difficult for unmarried women to firmly protect their sexuality" and can lead to the violation of women's sexual self-determination.[50] Having reasoned this way, it is noteworthy that, similar to the 2001 adultery ruling mentioned earlier, the Court called for consideration about whether to uphold the idea of criminalizing fraudulent engagements in the future.[51] Put differently, the Court appears to have changed its stance on sexual self-determination in the early 2000s, although this shift in perception translated into divergent ruling only toward the late 2000s.

6.4.3 Abortion

Another major question of sexual self-determination regards women who decide to have an abortion (*naktae*), which was, according to the Criminal Code (Art. 270(1)), punishable by up to one year of imprisonment (or a fine of 2 million won). In August 2012, the Constitutional Court ruled four to four to uphold the constitutionality of the provision.[52] The opinion argued that, aside from the fundamental duty to protect the life of the embryo, not punishing the termination of pregnancy would lead to rampant abortions. Moreover, the justices reasoned that because the Mother and Child Health Act (Art. 14)[53] allowed for abortion in exceptional cases, the provision's prohibition on early-stage abortions for social or economic reasons did not violate the Constitution by excessively restricting the right to self-determination.[54] The four dissenting justices countered by stressing that to prohibit and punish abortion at any stage of the pregnancy – in particular, the first fourteen weeks – infringed upon the principle of minimal violation of basic rights, and thus, they found the provision unconstitutional on the grounds that it violated the right to self-determination. Therefore, and drawing on established law in countries such as Germany, the United Kingdom, and Japan, one justice demanded that legislative measures be taken to change Korea's law such that pregnant women could decide to

---

[48] 2001Heonba70 (June 27, 2002).
[49] Id.
[50] Id.
[51] Id.
[52] 2010Heonba402 (August 23, 2012).
[53] *Mojabogeonbeop*, Act No. 9333 (2009) and Presidential Decree No. 21618 (2009).
[54] 2010Heonba402 (August 23, 2012).

have an abortion in an early stage and in a medically safe environment.[55] In other words, while ultimately upholding the prohibition of abortion due to personal beliefs, half the bench argued for applying at least a similar standard of self-determination as in other advanced countries' regulations.

Since 2017, the Constitutional Court has again heard a case related to Article 269 of the Criminal Code that punishes abortion. Calls for liberalizing abortion arose in fierce debates in the media, public, and government agencies around the first scheduled hearing of the case in mid-2018. The Ministry of Justice's opinion submitted to the Constitutional Court clearly echoed abortion opponents' reasoning, but the Ministry of Gender Equality and Family argued for abolishing the provision that criminalized abortion and violated the right to freely decide on reproduction (Yi 2018). Even the testifier on the side of the interested party argued that the present law was too restrictive and should be extended to at least allow abortion due to personal reasons up to twelve weeks of pregnancy.

Surveys also confirmed public support for legalizing abortion. In a recent poll, 21 percent said abortion must be strictly prohibited, while 74 percent said it should be allowed (Gallup 2016).[56] Only respondents older than fifty years showed less inclination toward legalization, indicating generational shifts in values. A similar tendency could be observed in the press, where editorials' headlines illustrated that, with the exception of conservative religious outlets such as *Catholic Times* or *Christian Today*, most mainstream news outlets, irrespective of their political stances, opposed the criminalization of abortion or at least called for debating the issue in society since most developed countries were more liberal concerning abortion (see Joongang Ilbo 2018; Seoul Sinmun 2018).

Even justices at the first public hearing seemed open to if not explicitly inclined to argue for the abolition of the Article criminalizing abortion (Yeo 2018), which anticipated the Court's later seven-to-two vote ruling Article 269 nonconforming to the Constitution, and thus overturned the 2012 precedent. Four of the seven justices who voted for constitutional nonconformity argued that a pregnant woman's safety is crucially connected with the fetus' safety, and the notion of "protection of the fetus" (*taeaui saengmyeong boho*) only has meaning if the pregnant woman is also protected as a person. The four justices found that Article 269 gave "absolute and unilateral superiority" to public interest in protecting fetal life, violating the principles of proportionality and balance of interests as well as infringing upon the right to self-determination of a pregnant woman.[57] The other three justices, while

---

[55] *Id.*

[56] Interestingly, these findings resemble those from 1994, when 26 percent were strictly against and 72 percent were in favor of legalizing abortion. This might be explained by the fact that, in the mid-1990s, only roughly half the interviewed people (48 percent) were aware that there was a law prohibiting abortion in the first place, while in 2016, the vast majority (73 percent) knew of its existence. Moreover, back then, most people (78 percent) thought of abortion as a kind of murder, while today, only merely half (53 percent) of respondents would say so (ibid.).

[57] 2017Heonba127 (April 11, 2019).

basically concurring, emphasized that the provision was unconstitutional because it clearly violated pregnant women's right to self-determination during the first trimester of pregnancy and thus the Constitution.[58] Article 269 lost its effect at the end of 2020, because the National Assembly did not change the law accordingly.

6.4.4 *Homosexuality*

While the Court recently rendered the previous landmark cases in favor of protecting sexual autonomy for heterosexuals, it has not yet ruled in favor of sexual minorities' rights. For example, in all three decisions on the topic since 2002, the Constitutional Court held that Article 92 of the Military Criminal Code[59] was constitutional in stipulating punishment for anal intercourse – that is, "sodomy (*gyegan*) or other indecent acts (*chuhaeng*)" – between military service members of the same sex. Judging these rulings, the key issues the bench repeatedly deliberated on were the questions of the freedom of sexual self-determination, discrimination based on homosexuality, and violations of the privacy of one's private life.

In its first verdict in 2002, the Court ruled six to two that the provision was limited to military personnel, and thus the protection of a sound life and military discipline had priority and *not* individuals' sexual freedom.[60] The Court also stressed that the term "indecent acts" was deliberately vague in order to encompass a variety of "abnormal (*byeontaeseong*) sexual gratification acts" (ibid.). The two dissenting justices challenged the majority opinion in two ways. First, they reasoned that the expression "indecent act" indeed may not be overly ambiguous in its meaning as such, but the provision did not specify whether force must be involved in order to apply punishment. Second, Article 92 did not clearly state whether it mattered if the act involved a person outside the military or persons of the opposite sex, or if the act was not known to any other person and thus could not raise feelings of aversion (*hyeomogam*).[61] Concerning homosexuality and referencing provisions of the National Human Rights Commission Act (Art. 30, Item 2),[62] the justices stressed that values were changing in Korea, as in other advanced countries, regarding sexuality and homosexual acts (see Chapter 12). Moreover, they rejected the argument that homosexual acts could in any way harm the maintenance of the military's combat readiness.[63]

In a five-to-four decision in 2011, the Court again confirmed the constitutionality of Article 92.[64] The majority opinion echoed its earlier decision by stressing that irrespective of whatever indecent act had taken place, the importance of

---

[58]   *Id.*

[59]   *Gunhyeongbeop*, Act No. 5757 (1999).

[60]   2001Heonba70 (June 27, 2002).

[61]   *Id.*

[62]   *Gukgaingwonwiwonhoebeop*, Act No. 6481 (2001).

[63]   2001Heonba70 (June 27, 2002).

[64]   2008Heonga21 (March 31, 2011).

maintaining discipline and combat readiness in the military was the highest priority. The higher interest of protecting the state trumped everything else, including sexual self-determination and freedom as well as secrecy of one's private life. Article 92 did not infringe on homosexuals' equality rights just because of "the higher possibility that, relative to the general society, abnormal sexual acts (*bijeongsangjeogin*) [in the military] involve individuals of the same sex."[65] The three dissenting justices contended that it was impossible to use sodomy as a standard for deciding the obscenity (*eumlan*) of an act, and that there was no criteria in place for gauging an act's degree of obscenity.[66] The judges once more pointed out that the provision was contradictory in that it punished any obscene act regardless of whether it happened by force or by consent.[67]

The third decision in 2016 did not contain any substantially new arguments on either side but was rendered by a vote of five to four, indicating a slow shift toward more balanced opinions within the Court.[68] The verdict came at a time when the provision in question had been changed as a result of revisions to the Criminal Code regarding sexual violence and terminology (Legislation and Judiciary Committee 2013, 7). The term "sodomy" was replaced by "anal sex (*hangmunseonggyo*)" in the 2013 revision of the Military Criminal Code such that the new provision read: "a person having had conducted anal sex or other indecent acts is punished with two years or less imprisonment." The simple exchange of terms for essentially the same act did not change the fundamental problem that the provision discriminated based on homosexuality. While one could argue that anal sex could occur between men as well as between a man and a woman, sexual intercourse between women was not explicitly regulated.

Since the 2009 revision of the Military Criminal Code, the provision had been diversified into eight sub-provisions, each of which dealt with a particular form of sexual violence. These reforms took into account most other objections of dissenting justices regarding the status of the persons involved, the place of the act, and whether or not coercion was involved. However, the indecent act provision still does not differentiate between cases of mutually consented and coerced anal sex. Despite the fact that the basic issue has not been resolved, the Court's rulings clearly shifted toward problematizing discrimination based on homosexuality and the legal contradictions arising due to changing values at home and abroad. This is still an area of law likely to change in light of the fact that in most countries' militaries – even the United States – sexual intercourse between two persons of the same sex is only punished if coercion is involved (Dunham 2011). As Kim and Hong (Chapter 12) note, the UN Committee on Economic, Social and Cultural Rights (CESCR) has also repeatedly expressed concern at the criminalization of same-sex acts and

---

[65] *Id.*
[66] *Id.*
[67] *Id.*
[68] 2012Heonba258 (July 28, 2016).

recommended changing the relevant provision in the law accordingly (Human Rights Watch 2017).

6.4.5 *Conscientious Objection*

According to the South Korean Military Service Act, men aged eighteen to thirty-five must serve in the military for twenty-four to twenty-eight months and are punished by up to three years imprisonment if they fail to do so, irrespective of their consciences. In 2004, the Constitutional Court decided in a seven-to-two vote that the Military Service Act (Art. 1(1)) did not violate the Constitution by failing to provide alternative forms of civil service to conscientious objectors.[69] The Court's ruling that freedom of conscience is an important fundamental right, yet not so important that it would legitimize legislation that might impede state security, consists of three main strands. First, the bench asserted that the freedom of consciousness (Constitution, Art. 19) involves only the right to demand that the state possibly consider and protect the individuals' consciousness, but it cannot be grounds for rejecting one's legal duties or demanding alternative civil service.[70] Second, regarding the precarious security situation on the Korean peninsula, the introduction of an alternative civil service is only possible after North and South Korea have settled into peaceful coexistence.[71] Third, social consensus is necessary before the introduction of an alternative civil service so that social cohesion is not undermined by perceptions of unequal burden sharing in the fulfillment of military duties. At the same time, the opinion both refers to the major share of countries and international tendencies that opted for accepting conscientious objectors and urges the legislature to "seriously examine whether our society has now matured to such a degree that it shows understanding and tolerance towards conscientious objectors," and "after having passed through serious social debate the state must find a solution."[72] The bench went so far as to argue that if there exists a way to protect freedom of conscience by "allowing reductions or exemptions in punishment or disciplinary action" in cases of refusing to serve the military, then such a way should be considered.[73]

The two dissenting justices argued that, by introducing an alternative civil service, the problem of punishing persons who object to military service could assuage his conscience in the context of religious beliefs, but that such a person would be burdened with enormous disadvantage. Moreover, Korea's military size was sufficient, so that conscientious objectors' nonparticipation would hardly harm combat readiness. In addition, the judges argued that many other countries that have

---

[69] 2002Heonga1 (August 26, 2004).

[70] *Id.*

[71] *Id.*

[72] The recommendation to consider legislative reform was disputed by one justice who, in his separate opinion, argued that this was not a desirable solution because it ran counter to the principle of separation of powers (2002Heonga1 (August 26, 2004)).

[73] 2002Heonga1 (August 26, 2004).

established an alternative service have been successful in ensuring only genuine conscientious objectors are exempted from carrying weapons.

In August 2011, the Constitutional Court deliberated on conscientious objection for the third time and again decided by a seven-to-two vote that the Military Service Act was not unconstitutional.[74] Only in June 2018 did the Constitutional Court finally rule that moral and religious beliefs are valid reasons to refuse military service.[75] In a six-to-three decision, the Court argued that the Military Service Act was unconstitutional because Art. 5(1) does not offer alternative forms of civilian service to conscientious objectors. Unlike preceding opinions, it was argued that fairness regarding military duty is sufficiently possible in the event that the state introduces respectful, objective mechanisms to prevent the misuse of an alternative civil service. The Court also emphasized that having objectors work in services that contribute to security in a broad sense and to the public good is better than interning them in prisons. Moreover, the Court contended that fourteen years ago, it recommended that the legislature examine the possibility of introducing an alternative civil service. In the meantime, cases in which other courts acquitted conscientious objectors have sharply risen such that this matter cannot be delayed any longer, and the "state has the duty to eliminate a situation of fundamental rights violation."[76] Ultimately, the Court demanded that the government and the parliament introduce the option of performing alternative services and thus declared the provision in question void in the event that the law was not revised accordingly by the end of 2019.[77]

6.5 CONCLUSION

This chapter raised the question of how the Constitutional Court in Korea has been developing as an institutional mechanism for fundamental rights claiming. The answer was addressed in two sections dealing with patterns in the quantity of rights claims and the quality of evolving decisions on major issues, respectively. The first section shed light on the court's caseload statistics regarding how successful citizens have been in making use of various proceedings at the Constitutional Court. While all the Constitutional Court's five competencies have been utilized, the overall caseload growth was mostly driven by constitutional complaints against public acts particularly concerning grievances toward public prosecutors. The continuously growing caseload resembles those of comparable countries' constitutional courts' caseload patterns and shows, in quantitative terms, the continuing importance of this institutional mechanism for fundamental rights claims, especially those filed by

---

[74] 2006Heonma788 (August 30, 2011). Later in 2004, in another ruling, the majority decision had been upheld in the court's second ruling on conscientious objectors (2004Heonba61 etc. (October 28, 2004)).

[75] 2011Heonba379 etc. (June 28, 2018).

[76] *Id.*

[77] 2011Heonba379 etc. (June 28, 2018); On December 31, 2019, the National Assembly enacted *Byeongyeokbeop*, Act No. 16852 (2019).

individual citizens. Thus, the Constitutional Court in Korea additionally functions as an authority to which citizens can turn to as a last resort to make their complaints heard. Moreover, the power of the Constitutional Court to scrutinize statutes or acts by public authorities is crucial for guaranteeing individuals' basic rights, as has become increasingly apparent since the end of the 2000s. It can be attributed to citizens' burgeoning consciousness regarding the law in general and fundamental rights in particular, an increasing need to appeal to the courts due to mounting complexity in politics, society, and the economy, and citizens' growing legal mobilization skills.[78]

The second section traced developments in selected landmark decisions, mainly focusing on issues regarding gender equality, sexual autonomy, homosexuality, and freedom of conscience. The analysis shows that the Constitutional Court is reacting cautiously to changes in society's preferences or sentiments. Although limited to the cases examined, it can be argued that the Court has followed a pattern of increasingly liberal or progressive interpretations regarding perceptions in society that have been drastically changing in regard to issues of patrilineality, women and adultery, and military-related gender discrimination. Even understanding and tolerance regarding conscientious objectors have spread in public discourse, despite the fact that military service is closely linked to the always-sensitive topic of national security. The only issue that has not yet settled are opinions regarding homosexuality, which is still strongly contested particularly by religious conservatives (see Chapter 12). Although this chapter did not establish a causal relationship, rulings on sexual minorities' rights suggest a connection between pockets of Conservative countermobilization in Korean society and a reluctant Constitutional Court. Put differently, rather than promoting its own agenda, the Court reacts to political and social demands and thus has coevolved alongside a progressing society that has been changing its norms and values. That does not mean that the Court is passive. On the contrary, through its reactive and cautious conduct, which, if necessary, includes recommending as well as demanding remedies from the government or the legislature, it has positioned itself as a politically and socially respected, effective facilitator of change during the last thirty years. In this way, the Constitutional Court, as a mechanism for fundamental rights claims, has contributed to rights development, the rule of law, and citizens' rights consciousness.

REFERENCES

Blankenburg, Erhard. 1998. "Die Verfassungsbeschwerde: Nebenbühne der Politik und Klagemauer von Bürgern." *Kritische Justiz* 31: 203–18.

---

[78] This is in line with the observations regarding "legal opportunity structures" (Chapter 7) and the development of "public interest lawyering" (Chapter 8) in Korea.

Choi, Dai-Kwon. 2008. "Minjujuuiwa beopchijuui; heonbeopjaepanui jeongchihak" [Democracy and the rule of law: The politics of constitutional adjudication]. *Heonbeop nonchong* 19: 177–223.

2014. "The State of Fundamental Rights Protection in Korea." In *Current Issues in Korean Law*, edited by Laurent Mayali and John Yoo, 87–124. Berkeley: Robbins Collection Publications.

Choi, Hee-Kyoung. 2012. "Heonbeopgwa jendeoe gwanhan gochal" [A study on the constitution and gender]. *Ewha Law Journal* 17 (2): 1–31.

Constitutional Court of Korea. 1998. *Heonbeopjaepanso 10-nyeonsa* [Ten years Constitutional Court]. Seoul: Constitutional Court of Korea.

2008. *Heonbeopjaepanso 20-nyeonsa* [Twenty years Constitutional Court]. Seoul: Constitutional Court of Korea.

2015. "'Saeropda, haegyeolhada, gungmineul wihada', bigdeiteo bunseogkeul tonghae bon heonbeopjaepanso 27-nyeon" ["Fresh, to solve, for the people," looking into 27 years of the Constitutional Court through big data analysis]. www.ccourt.go.kr/cckhome/kor/ccourt/pressrelease/selectPressrelease.do?searchClassSeq=220.

Dannemann, Gerhard. 1994. "Constitutional Complaints: The European Perspective." *International and Comparative Law Quarterly* 43: 142–53.

Diamond, Larry, and Leonardo Morlino. 2004. "The Quality of Democracy. An Overview." *Journal of Democracy* 15 (4): 20–31.

Dunham, Will. 2011. "Obama Hails end of U.S. Military Restrictions on Gays." *Reuters*, September 20, 2011. www.reuters.com/article/us-usa-gays-military-idUSTRE78J3W P20110920.

Gallup. 2016. "Naktae gwallyeon insik" [Perceptions regarding abortion]. *Gallup*, October 20, 2016. www.gallup.co.kr/gallupdb/reportContent.asp?seqNo=784.

Ginsburg, Tom. 2003a. *Judicial Review in New Democracies. Constitutional Courts in Asian Cases*. Cambridge: Cambridge University Press.

2003b. "Rule by Law or Rule of Law?" In *Judicial Review in New Democracies*, edited by Tom Ginsburg, 206–46. Cambridge: Cambridge University Press.

2009. "The Constitutional Court and Judicialization of Korean Politics." In *New Courts in Asia*, edited by Andrew Hardin and Penelope Nicholson, 145–57. New York: Routledge.

Gukhoesamucheo. 1960. "Heonbeopgaejeongan gichowiwonhoe sokgirok" [Minutes of the Constitutional Amendment Bill Committee]. May 4, 1960.

Häberle, Peter. 2014. *Verfassungsgerichtsbarkeit – Verfassungsprozessrecht. Ausgewählte Beiträge aus vier Jahrzehnten*. Berlin: Duncker & Humblot.

Human Rights Watch. 2017. "South Korea. Events of 2017," *Human Rights Watch*, www.hrw.org/world-report/2018/country-chapters/south-korea.

Im, Sun-hyeon. 2017. "Bulgisocheobun chwisohaedalla … heonbeopsoweon haemada 300-geon isang" [More than 300 cases filed for requesting the cancelation non-indictment by prosecution]. *Yonhap*, October 12, 2008. www.yonhapnews.co.kr/bulletin/2017/10/12/0200000000AKR20171012113200004.HTML.

Jeon, Jeong-hyun. 2016. "Political Functions and Dilemma of the Korean Constitutional Court." *Korea Observer* 47(3): 461–492.

Joongang Ilbo. 2018. "Naktaejoe pyeji, sahoejeok nonui sijakhaja" [Let's start talking about the abolition of the crime of abortion]. *Joongang Ilbo*, May 25, 2018, https://news.joins.com/article/22654181 (accessed January 2, 2019).

Kim, Jongcheol. 2005. "Heonbeopjaepanso guseongbangbeopui gaehyeongnon" [Reform proposal for the Constitutional Court's constitution method]. *Heonbeophak Yeongu* 11 (2): 9–48.

2010. "The Structure and Basic Principles of Constitutional Adjudication in the Republic of Korea." In *Litigation in Korea*, edited by Cho Kuk, 114–34. Cheltenham, UK: Edward Elgar.

Kim, Sang-cheol. 1988. "Heonbeopjaepanui hwalseonghwabangan (ojeontoronyoji)" [Activation proposals for constitutional adjudication (morning discussion)]. *SNU Beophak* 29 (3/4): 46–59.

Kim, Seung-dae. 2017. "Gibongwonui pyeoncheon" [The evolution of fundamental rights]. *Hyeondaesagwangjang* 9: 62–81.

Kranenpohl, Uwe. 2004. "Funktionen des Bundesverfassungsgerichts. Eine politikwissenschaftliche Analyse." *Aus Politik und Zeitgeschichte*, B 50–51: 39–46.

Lee, Kang-kook. 2014. "The Past and Future of Constitutional Adjudication in Korea." In *Current Issues in Korean Law*, edited by Laurent Mayali and John Yoo, 1–13. Berkeley: Robbins Collection Publications.

Legislation and Judiciary Committee, Chairperson of the 2013. Beopjesabeopwiwonhoe Hoeuirok [Minutes of the Legislation and Judiciary Committee], 5th meeting, March 4, 2013. http://likms.assembly.go.kr.

Morlino, Leonardo. 2010. "The Two 'Rules of Law' between Transition to a Quality of Democracy." In *Rule of Law and Democracy*, edited by Leonardo Morlino, and Gianluigi Palombella, 39–63. Leiden/Boston: Brill.

Mosler, Hannes B. 2014. "Judicialization of Politics and the Korean Constitutional Court: the Party Chapter Abolition Case." *Verfassung und Recht in Übersee*, Heft 3: 293–318.

2015. "Legal Translations 'Made in Korea'." In *Lost and Found in Translation*, edited by Eun-Jeung Lee and Hannes B. Mosler, 115–64. Frankfurt am Main: Peter Lang Academic Publishers.

2016. "Das Verbot der Vereinten Progressiven Partei in der Republik Korea." *Zeitschrift für Parlamentsfragen* (ZParl) 47 (1): 176–94.

2017a. "Deutsch-koreanische Geschichte im Licht verfassungsrechtlicher Übersetzungen." In *Facetten deutsch-koreanischer Beziehungen – 130 Jahre gemeinsame Geschichte*, edited by Eun-Jeung Lee and Hannes B. Mosler, 57–92. Frankfurt am Main: Peter Lang Academic Publishers.

2017b. "The Institution of Presidential Impeachment in South Korea, 1992–2017." *Verfassung und Recht in Übersee*, Heft 2: 111–34.

2018. "Democratic Quality and the Rule of Law in South Korea: The Case of the Prosecution." In *The Quality of Democracy in Korea: Three Decades after Democratization*, edited by Hannes Mosler et al., 73–120. Basingstoke: Palgrave Macmillan.

Nam, Puk-hyeon. 2003. "Beomnyului ipbeopgwajeong siljewa heonbeopjaepansoe uihan wiheonyeobu gyeoljeongui sanggwangwangye" [The correlation between the legislation process and unconstitutionality decisions by the Constitutional Court]. *Law and Society* 24: 213–55.

Naumann, Kolja. 2010. "Die verfassungsgerichtliche Entwicklung des Grundrechtschutzes in der Republik Korea." *Jahrbuch des öffentlichen Rechts der Gegenwart* 58: 685–712.

O'Donnell, Guillermo. 2004. "Why the Rule of Law Matters." *Journal of Democracy* 15 (4): 32–46.

Seo, Ki-seok. 2014. "Heonbeopjaepanui uiuiwa yeokhal" [The meaning and role of constitutional review]. *Beobyeon* 43: 62–67.

Seoul Sinmun. 2018. "Heonjae, naktaejoeui hyeonsiljeok goeri jiksihaeya" [The Constitutional Court has to face the discrepancy between criminalizing abortion and reality]. *Seoul Sinmun*, May 25, 2019. www.seoul.co.kr/news/newsView.php?id=20 180525031025&wlog_tag3=naver.

Shin, Woo Cheol. 2011. "Uri heonbeopsaeseo 'gibongwon'ui uimi" [The meaning of "fundamental rights" in Korean constitutional history]. *Yeoksa Bipyeong* 96: 61–108.

Song, Ki-Choon. 2001. "Heonbeopjaepanso simpansageonnugyepyoe natanan beobweonui heonbeoppandanui sujunbunseok" [An analysis of the Constitutional Court's decisions based on the court's caseload statistics]. *Public Law* 29 (4): 243–63.

———. 2005. "Heonbeopjaepanso simpansageon tonggyebunseok" [A time series analysis of the case statistics of the Constitutional Court of Korea]. *Public Law* 34 (2): 83–115.

Sung, Nak-in. 2012. *Heonbeophak* [Constitutional law], Paju: Beommunsa.

West, James M., and Dae-Kyu Yoon. 1992. "The Constitutional Court of the Republic of Korea: Transforming the Jurisprudence of the Vortex?" *The American Journal of Contemporary Law* 40 (1): 73–119.

Yang, Hyunah. 2013. "Colonialism and Patriarchy: Where the Korean Family-Head (hoju) System Had Been Located." In *Law and Society in Korea*, edited by Hyunah Yang, 45–63. Northampton: Elgar.

Yeh, Jiunn-Rong. 2009. "The Emergence of Asian Constitutionalism: Features in Comparison." *NTU Law Review* 4 (3): 39–53.

Yeh, Jiunn-Rong, and Wen-Chen Chang. 2011. "The Emergence of East Asian Constitutionalism: Features in Comparison." *The American Journal of Comparative Law* 59 (3): 805–39.

Yeo, Hyeon-ho. 2018. "Heonjaeseo 6-nyeonmane beoreojin 'naktaejoe' gyeongnon ... hapheon gyeoljeong bakkwil ganeungseong" [After six years heated debate at the Constitutional Court again on the 'crime of abortion', possibilities of change of decision]. *Hankyoreh Sinmun*, May 24, 2018. www.hani.co.kr/arti/society/society_general/846123.html.

Yi, Eseudeo. 2018. "Yeogabu, 'naktaejoe pyejihaeya' heonjae uigyeon jechul, jeongbu bucheo cheoeum" [MGE submits 'abolish abortion crime' to Constitutional Court, first government agency to do so]. *Joongang Ilbo*, May 23, 2018. https://news.joins.com/article/22645945.

Yoon, Dae-Kyu. 2010. *Law and Democracy in South Korea*. Seoul: IFES.

7

Rights Claiming through the Courts

Changing Legal Opportunity Structures in South Korea

Celeste L. Arrington

7.1 INTRODUCTION

People in democratic polities have various channels through which to remedy rights violations and make sure laws are faithfully implemented. Besides voting, they can raise public awareness via media attention or public events, publish reports, protest, join or support an interest group, contact bureaucrats, lobby elected officials, or file lawsuits, just to name a few options. These options offer different ways for people to assert their rights and remind the state or other parties of their associated duties (Burke 2000, 1261–62). In cases of a lone individual or small group of rights claimants, litigation may seem like the only path forward if they fail to capture politicians' or the public's attention (e.g., Zemans 1983). However, the complex rules, procedures, and anticipated costs of litigation can be daunting. Judicial processes are often more structured than other channels. Hence, examining changes in legal rules and procedures that render the courts more or less attractive for rights claiming helps answer a core question: To what extent and how has civil litigation become an institutional mechanism for rights claiming in South Korea (the Republic of Korea, ROK)?

Sociolegal scholarship offers useful tools for approaching this question. As one recent review notes, studies of legal mobilization analyze rights claiming that entails "the use of law in an explicit, self-conscious way through the invocation of a formal institutional mechanism" (Lehoucq and Taylor 2020, 168). Legal mobilization can involve individual disputing or collective litigation to assert rights or remedy rights violations. To understand when people mobilize the law, scholars recently coined the term "legal opportunity structure" (LOS). Like the concept of political opportunity structures, it describes the relatively stable but "not necessarily formal or permanent" features of legal and judicial systems that encourage or discourage people from litigation (Andersen 2006; Evans Case and Givens 2010; Hilson 2002; Tarrow 1994, 85; Vanhala 2012, 2018a; Wilson and Rodriguez Cordero 2006). The LOS concept is useful for pinpointing which factors might affect the incentives that Korean citizens face when considering rights claiming via litigation. The concept generally includes rules governing access to the courts and the costs and rewards of litigation, existing laws, judicial precedents, and sometimes the presence of resources and allies for the litigation process (Lejeune 2017; Vanhala 2018a, 384–85). While researchers have examined the Korean Constitutional Court and politically significant rulings (e.g., Ginsburg 2003; Kim and Park 2012), few studies have taken stock of the lower visibility changes to judicial procedures, rules, and statutes that have gradually but significantly cumulated to transform the incentive structures that Koreans face when contemplating legal mobilization. This chapter's analysis indicates that Koreans have benefited from a liberalizing structure of legal opportunities and improved potential for rights protection via the courts.

On balance, Korea's structure of legal opportunities has grown more favorable for rights claiming, especially in the past twenty years, despite perceptions that the conservative presidencies of Lee Myung-bak (2008–13) and Park Geun-hye (2013–17) ushered in a period of judicial retrenchment, such as in cases involving workers' rights (see Chapter 9), and alleged political interference in the judiciary during Park's administration (Jo 2018). This chapter suggests that rights claimants, activist lawyers, partisan politics, and international factors are driving some of the changes in the structure of legal opportunities. However, this trend could reverse, and improved access to courts does not necessarily guarantee improved rights protection. In addition, greater access to civil litigation is not uncontroversial in Korea. Media commentary criticizes the growing number of lucrative "planned lawsuits" (*gihoek sosong*) by tens of thousands of plaintiffs (Beomnyul Sinmun 2013). And lawmakers' debates about some statutory rights expansions, such as anti-discrimination rights for people with disabilities (see Chapter 10), are filled with concerns about encouraging litigiousness.[1] Nonetheless, by investigating factors that have helped liberalize the structure of legal opportunities, this chapter argues that creative and effective legal mobilization is facilitating further rights claiming by building up experienced networks of activists and that the infrastructure for legal mobilization is growing more institutionalized with the emergence of public interest law firms and foundations (see further Chapter 8).

For several reasons, the concept of legal opportunity structures is useful for analyzing litigation as an institutional mechanism for rights claiming. First, the LOS framework resonates with older research that had noted how structural factors, such as rules on standing (who has the right to sue) or cost shifting, affected litigation rates. Haley (1978), for example, argued that court delays and costs, few lawyers, and limited remedies – as opposed to cultural values – best explained Japanese citizens' apparent reluctance to use the courts. Political and bureaucratic elites in Korea, as in Japan, had incentives to create similar barriers that constrained access to the legal system and the extent to which litigation could be used to push policy change

---

[1]   On the Disability Discrimination Act, Minutes of Health and Welfare Committee, Mtg. No. 265, 2 (February 7, 2007).

(Ginsburg 2002; Upham 1987). To such older institutional analyses, the LOS concept helpfully adds perceptual and contingent elements from social movements studies. Shifts in legal opportunity structure create opportunities for action, rather than directly cause action (Andersen 2006, 215). Opportunities must be recognized and seized, which is why, as Goedde (Chapter 8) elaborates, "support structures" of lawyers, advocacy organizations, and funding are important (Epp 1998).

Second, therefore, the LOS concept encourages researchers to pay more attention to claimants' interpretations of structures and the agency of those acting within institutional constraints to creatively use, stretch, and even alter those constraints. How rights claimants use the law shapes other potential claimants' perceptions of opportunities, as well (Cichowski 2016, 893). As a concept, legal opportunity structure builds on the consensus in social movements studies about the need to replace the false dichotomy of structure versus agency with dynamic analyses of their recursive interactions (McAdam, Tarrow, and Tilly 2001). Indeed, my research suggests that citizens are recognizing and using legal opportunities, and sometimes even prying open new opportunities, in pursuit of rights.

Third, by disaggregating the "legal system" to highlight which rules and procedures matter for rights claiming, the LOS concept helps illuminate institutional *changes* instead of taking legal institutions as given (see also Evans Case and Givens 2010; Vanhala 2018b). Building on the Western-centric LOS literature, this chapter analyzes how changes in the legal opportunity structure have been transforming Koreans' experiences with the law and the possibilities for private litigation regarding statutory rights in the democratic era.

After a brief historical summary, this chapter discusses key changes in the structure of legal opportunities in Korea since the 1990s and what has driven these changes. Rights claiming can occur in the context of civil, administrative, constitutional, or criminal cases. Mosler (Chapter 6) covers the Korean Constitutional Court, and Hwang (Chapter 5) discusses claims-making via the National Human Rights Commission of Korea, which increasingly occurs in conjunction with civil or constitutional claiming. This chapter focuses on rights claiming via civil litigation. I examine factors affecting the use of both individual and collective private litigation. In Korea, collective litigation is called *jipdan sosong*, which is technically different from the American-style class action in that rulings only apply to those individuals listed as plaintiffs, rather than to an entire class of victims not named on the complaint. Due to the number and complexity of rules and civil procedures that could be analyzed, I eschew comprehensiveness and instead highlight several that are emphasized in the LOS literature and by participants in Korea. First is the legal stock, which encompasses existing statutes and judicial precedents that constrain how people can frame their claims, how persuasive those claims are, and how disputes are adjudicated (Andersen 2006). Although civil law systems like Korea do not adopt the principle of *stare decisis* (i.e., judicial precedents are not binding), courts still do often reference prior rulings (Fon and Parisi 2006). Kwon (2007, 137) calls prior rulings "de facto binding" in Korea, and Korea is becoming more of a hybrid legal system due to heavy US influence. The second are procedural rules, which are numerous. The most significant for rights claimants considering litigation are standing rules, fee-shifting rules, the statute of limitations, and the burden of proof. Standing rules determine who can bring cases to court. Statutes of limitations affect when claims can be brought, relative to when the alleged injury or rights violation occurred. Finally, rules on who bears the costs of litigation affect the potential risks and rewards of legal mobilization.

These dimensions of legal opportunity structure are not the only factors affecting rights claiming through the courts. For instance, "political disadvantage" may drive groups to the courts, as opposed to conventional channels of political participation (Cortner 1968; Javeline and Baird 2007; Zackin 2008). The presence of lawyers in a movement or the structure and resources of an organization may also push toward judicial remedies (Scheppele and Walker 1991; Vanhala 2018a). Yet structural barriers to legal mobilization, which are often technical and obscure rules or procedures, deserve greater attention for their broader consequences (see also Arrington 2021). This chapter examines Korea's legal opportunity structure, drawing on original interviews conducted with lawyers, activists, and judges, research in news media and court archives, and Korean legal scholarship.[2] By way of conclusion, the chapter offers hypotheses about what might be driving these changes to guide future research. I briefly discuss partisan politics, judges' innovations, international factors, and the ideas and demands of rights claimants and their lawyers.

7.2 A BRIEF HISTORY OF IMPEDIMENTS TO LITIGATION IN KOREA

As a relatively new democracy and an East Asian case that went from having low rates of litigation in the twentieth century to becoming something of a juggernaut in terms of the growing role of law and courts in politics since its democratization in 1987, Korea represents an ideal case for investigating changes in legal opportunity structures. Historically, legal mobilization was highly constrained in Korea. Before 1987, authoritarian regimes stacked courts with allies, passed laws to legalize abuses of power, and sought to restrict citizens' access to justice through institutional means like imposing high filing fees or capping the number of people allowed to pass the bar exam each year (e.g., Ginsburg 2004; Kwon 2010). Korea's transition to democracy in 1987 was accompanied by significant institutional changes, including to aspects of the legal and judicial systems. The creation of the Korean Constitutional

---

[2] This chapter utilizes twenty-five semi-structured anonymized interviews that I conducted in Korean with lawyers, judges, and activists between 2009 and 2017. After each interview, I reconstructed the conversation in writing; the quotes are my translations from Korean based on my memory and notes. The chapter also draws on interpretive analysis of contemporary texts, such as news articles, blogs, movement newsletters, and lawyers' internal strategy documents to illuminate how people perceived their options for rights claiming and legal institutions.

FIGURE 7.1 New civil lawsuits filed, first instance.

Court in 1988, for example, opened a new avenue for rights claiming that was untainted by the authoritarian past. As Mosler (Chapter 6) details, many citizens perceive this as a more accessible institutional mechanism and avidly file claims with the Constitutional Court. The Korean Constitutional Court saw its caseload rise by nearly fivefold between 1996 and 2016.[3] In the 1990s, civil litigation rates rose rapidly, and since about 2001 the rate has remained stable (see Figure 7.1).[4] These data include a great variety of private and public causes, only some of which involve rights claiming. One explanation for these rising litigation rates is the past few decades' diverse or less visible changes to the rules governing access to the courts and litigation procedure, as well as statutory reforms and changes in the legal profession. This chapter takes stock of these changes.

Early studies of the institutional factors impeding or facilitating litigation in Korea emerged as a reaction to cultural arguments. In a landmark study, Hahm Pyong-choong (1986) posited that legal mobilization was antithetical to Korean culture because Koreans scorned litigation, had myriad informal dispute resolution mechanisms, and lacked legal consciousness. Like Kawashima's (1967) theory about Japanese people's antipathy toward litigation, Hahm argued that Korean culture valued harmony and conflict avoidance. Critics soon countered that claims-making occurred even among disadvantaged groups like women in the late Joseon era (see Chapter 1) and in the colonial period (see Chapter 2), that conflict avoidance is common even in the supposedly litigation-happy United States, that Hahm's methodology was flawed, and that he overlooked institutional disincentives to litigation (M. S.-H. Kim 2012, 56–57; C. Lee 1998; Yang 1989). As Kawashima and others have noted, litigation is generally a last resort. But Koreans also faced institutional

---

[3]   Data from Korean Constitutional Court website, www.ccourt.go.kr (accessed February 20, 2018).
[4]   Calculated from data available in the *Sabeop Yeongam* [Judicial Yearbook], various years.

hurdles, which included the high legal fees that could be charged by Korea's tiny private bar (limited by state quotas, not raised until 1981), delays in the court process, the lack of justiciable rights, and authoritarian interventions in the judiciary (Yang 1989, 895). Hahm's critics recommend avoiding cultural essentialism in favor of examining the structures and institutions – often state-imposed – that shape people's incentives and their perceptions of legal mobilization. This chapter builds on such early institutional analyses, adding insights from LOS studies about how claimants perceive and exploit legal opportunities.

Korea's democratization in 1987 engendered dramatic openings in political and legal opportunity structures in Korea. These have understandably received more scholarly attention than the subtler shifts in the structure of legal opportunities that have occurred *since* the transition, especially in the past two decades (but see Yoon 2010, 21–47). Although the courts in democratic Korea retained a reputation for being more bureaucratic, centralized, and conservative compared to the Constitutional Court,[5] the structure of legal opportunities for litigation has liberalized. Numerous new statutes regarding minorities have created justiciable rights (e.g., Yoon 2010, chaps. 12–14). The most researched and ambitious post-democratization reforms to the legal and judicial systems increased the number of private attorneys, altered legal education, and introduced a lay-judge system for serious criminal cases (e.g., Choi and Rokumoto 2007; Ginsburg 2004; Kage 2017). As with similar judicial reforms in Japan, one of reformers' stated aims was to increase citizens' access to justice and democratize criminal procedures. Korea's historically low number of attorneys per capita had contributed to expensive and scarce legal representation, and the reforms steadily reduced the number of citizens served by each attorney (see Figure 7.2).[6] In addition, the state-administered bar exam and the subsequent Judicial Research and Training Institute (JRTI) were criticized for restricting lawyers' backgrounds and perspectives, and for inculcating a prostate bias among judges, prosecutors, and lawyers who studied together at the JRTI for two years. In 2009, Korea introduced law schools, which became mandatory for aspiring lawyers. The bar exam operated parallel to the law schools but was abolished in 2017, after its abolition was unsuccessfully challenged in the Constitutional Court, and the JRTI ceased training legal professionals after the 2019 class finished (K. Lee 2018a). Also, the Korean Law School Association and the Ministry of Education have implemented a scholarship system for law students based on their tax-reported income to counter accusations that law schools' high tuition fees impede access for lower income applicants. The full impact of these changes in legal training has yet to be realized, but anecdotal evidence indicates increased competition for jobs and pay, as well as the diversification of the legal profession.[7]

[5] For example, Interviews, activist D (May 28, 2015), and law professor A (July 26, 2013).
[6] Data compiled from the annual reports of the Japan Federation of Bar Associations and the Korean Bar Association, and from Japan's Ministry of Justice.
[7] Interview, law professor C (July 24, 2013).

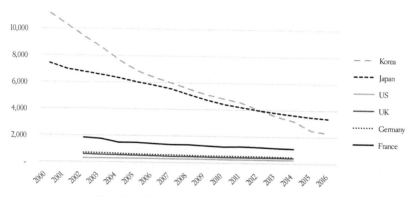

FIGURE 7.2 Number of citizens served by each lawyer, comparative.

Litigation, including for private rights enforcement and public interest litigation, contributed significantly to democratic consolidation. Yet relatively few studies in English go beyond politically salient cases to analyze the more incremental and less visible changes in Korean courts' rules and procedures, particularly during the past two decades (e.g., J. Kim 2008). Meanwhile, Hong (2011, 97–98) discusses law as part of the structure of political opportunities faced by the People's Solidarity for Participatory Democracy (PSPD), which pioneered litigation for policy change, but he does not examine rules governing which disputes go to court, how disputes are adjudicated, or what remedies are available.

Outside the realm of civil law, Kim Joongi (2009) writes about how reforms such as sentencing guidelines improved the consistency of judicial enforcement of laws related to campaign finance and elections to combat corruption by public officials. And Ginsburg (2001) examines revisions to the Administrative Procedure Law, which opened opportunities for checking the bureaucracy by creating a dedicated administrative court, lowering the requirements for administrative lawsuits, and expanding public comment forums for proposed rules and statutes. Many analyses of the role of courts in Korean politics understandably seek evidence of the rule of law and of democratic consolidation. Indeed, South Korean governments have explicitly aimed to "democratize the judiciary" with major reforms to expand the private bar, change legal education, and introduce juries for serious criminal cases. The smaller procedural changes that are detailed later occurred in the context of and were overshadowed by these broader reforms. Yet they have cumulated to significantly reshape citizens' experiences with the law.

Once Korea's presidency returned to the conservatives with the election of Lee Myung-bak in 2007, however, the legal opportunity structure was perceived as constricting. Polls revealed that the number of Koreans who expressed trust in the courts (but not the Constitutional Court) fell from a low of 8 percent to 3.1 percent from 2008 to 2014.[8] Even before conservatives recaptured the Blue House, progressives had bemoaned how many former judges and prosecutors were becoming attorneys with heightened influence in court, which stacked judicial outcomes against marginal groups and helped the attorneys command higher fees – a phenomenon called *jeongwan yeu* (Kim and Hwang 2007). Additionally, the number of defamation cases rose under Presidents Lee and Park Geun-hye even more than under progressive President Roh Moo-hyun, with observers concluding the courts were helping to erode press freedoms rather than protecting rights (Haggard and You 2015, 169–71). Rifts within the legal professions deepened as Korea descended into the Choi Soon-sil scandal and President Park's impeachment in 2016–17. One lawyer criticized conservative elites' efforts to eviscerate the truth commissions (see Chapter 4) and related retrials of former political dissidents.[9] In the wake of Park Geun-hye's impeachment, the Supreme Court's chief justice was also accused of stalling on politically sensitive cases, keeping a blacklist of progressive judges, and working behind the scenes to rein in the Constitutional Court to curry favor with President Park to advance his preferred restructuring of the judiciary (Kang 2018; K. Lee 2018b).

Nevertheless, Korean citizens continued to turn toward the courts, signaling an accelerated version of changes in governance that are happening in democracies worldwide. The trend has been called the judicialization, juridification, or legalization of politics (e.g., Barnes and Burke 2015; Hirschl 2011; Vallinder 1994). Citizens are demanding and achieving greater access, transparency, and accountability from their governments, often through the courts (Cain, Dalton, and Scarrow 2003; Cichowski 2006). In these processes, courts can be more responsive than traditional democratic institutions, and judicial checks on other branches of government are especially valued in new democracies (Ginsburg 2003). Indeed, Korean courts have played important roles in political conflicts, including those related to presidential impeachment, state liability for authoritarian-era abuses, and corruption involving public officials (see Chapter 6). In analyses of the judicialization of politics in Korea, the focus has been on high-visibility cases and the Constitutional Court (J. Kim 2008; Kim and Park 2012). However, as Ramseyer (1985, 605–06) noted with regard to Japan, private litigation can serve the public interest when it deters rights abuses or controls state misconduct. Private litigation has had public benefits in that it enhanced enforcement and supplemented state agencies' regulatory efforts, albeit to a lesser extent in Korea than in the United States (Farhang 2010; Kagan 2001). It has also revealed information that informed related policy debates, added impetus for policy change, or supplemented quasi-judicial institutional mechanisms for rights claiming such as ombudsmen or the National Human Rights Commission of Korea (NHRCK), as detailed by Hwang (Chapter 5). Yet changes in the legal

---

[8]   August 2014 Realmeter polling.
[9]   Interview, lawyer E (July 13, 2012).

opportunity structure that affect the likelihood of civil litigation remain understudied. This chapter, therefore, turns to how the legal opportunity structure has changed in Korea in the past two decades.

7.3 CHANGES IN THE STRUCTURE OF LEGAL OPPORTUNITIES IN KOREA

This section traces recent changes in Korea's structure of legal opportunities, including rule changes, new or revised statutes, and judicial reinterpretations or innovations. The discussion is not intended to be exhaustive, but rather to offer a basis for beginning to theorize about sources of institutional change. Prior scholarship on legal opportunity structures (albeit primarily focused on Western contexts), Korean legal scholarship, and my interviews with Korean lawyers, judges, and activists guided the selection of procedural and substantive changes to highlight. On balance, interviews and anecdotal evidence suggest that such changes are altering people's perceptions about rights claiming via litigation, but the changes are too obscure and intertwined to be amenable to public opinion polling. It is important to note that although the evidence indicates a more open legal opportunity structure, this trend could reverse and result in judicial retrenchment (Staszak 2015). However, the evidence presented here reveals that institutional changes continued to enhance access to the courts even during the two conservative administrations of Lee Myung-bak and Park Geun-hye. The changes – often low-visibility and incremental – concern barriers to entry, the adjudication process, and judicial remedies that have cumulated to facilitate rights claiming via civil lawsuits.

7.3.1 *Lower Barriers to Entry*

Historically, costs and long duration were significant deterrents to rights claiming via litigation. Recognizing that the private bar's small size made lawyers expensive, barriers to entry were a major concern of the Judicial Reform Council in 2003–04, as it debated increasing the number of lawyers and enhancing legal aid (Yoon 2010, 220–25). In addition, the major revisions to Korea's Civil Procedure Act (KCPA) in 2002 aimed primarily to make trials more efficient, as well as shift Korea away from the German model toward more interactive and adversarial US-style civil procedure. The revisions increased the importance of pretrial conferences, in which the parties and the lead judge would discuss the case and plan ways to make the trial speedier. Further revisions in 2008 required early first hearings (Art. 258(1)) (Kwon 2007, 128). The other reductions in barriers to entry discussed in this section include changes to the lawsuit filing process, looser interpretation of the statute of limitations, and some changes to group litigation.

First, in 2010, Korea introduced an Electronic Litigation System (ELS).[10] The new law's declared purpose was to "enhance the swiftness and transparency [of civil procedure], thereby contributing to realizing people's rights." Complaints may now be filed over the Internet. The new system also expanded the range of material admissible in court to include images, videos, and sounds (Baik 2015, 223–24). With its reduced filing fees compared with paper-based filing, it became popular. Parties to lawsuits can now receive emails about developments in their case and can track their case's status online more easily than before. In addition, new online templates for complaints reduced the need to hire lawyers. The increased number of cases, however, also raised concerns about overburdened courts and high appeal rates due to litigants' dissatisfaction with rulings (Kim and Min 2017).

Second, the relatively short duration of the statute of limitations in Korea was long seen as impeding litigation. It is three years from when the victim becomes aware of the tortious act and ten years from when the tortious act was committed (KCPA Art. 766). It has been waived or relaxed for certain cases. In the 1990s, special legislation was enacted, waiving the statute of limitations to allow the prosecution of former presidents Chun Doo-hwan and Roh Tae-woo (Ginsburg 2002, 784). The statute of limitations was abolished altogether in 2011 for sexual assault or violence against children and in 2015 for first-degree murder (Im 2012). And Korea's first public interest law firm, Gonggam, helped pass a law in 2011 that abolished the statute of limitations on documents related to international adoptions.[11] A landmark Supreme Court ruling in 2011 also waived the statute of limitations regarding compensation claims by bereaved families of victims of state crimes, notably the police killings of thousands affiliated with the National Guidance League (*Bodo yeonmaeng*) in Ulsan in 1950 (R. Kim 2011). More than 500 leprosy survivors who suffered due to forced vasectomies and abortions through the 1980s cited this interpretation of a limitless claim period in cases of state crimes when they filed six collective lawsuits over alleged violations of their rights to happiness, self-determination, dignity, and private life in 2011 (Arrington 2014; Yonhap News 2017). The Supreme Court ruled in the leprosy plaintiffs' favor in 2017. Partially successful litigation by persons with mental disabilities who were enslaved in salt farms decades ago similarly aimed to "persuade the judges to waive or reinterpret the statute of limitations."[12] However, anecdotal evidence indicates that such looser interpretations have not been uniformly applied. In some cases of past state abuse, the court used stricter interpretations of the statute of limitations and limited damage awards, even when truth commissions had already recognized the plaintiffs as victims.[13] The clearest changes to the statute of limitations occurred via legislation on particular issues, but

---

[10] *Minsasosong deungeseoui jeonjamunseo iyongdeunge gwanhan beomnyul* (Act on the Use of Electronic Documents in Civil Litigation etc.), Act No. 10183 (2010).

[11] Interview, lawyer B (May 27, 2015).

[12] Interviews, lawyer F (September 12, 2017) and activist A (September 14, 2017).

[13] Interview, judge A (May 29, 2015).

plaintiffs' lawyers routinely emphasize that their clients long lacked or were unaware of their right to bring claims.

Finally, procedures for group litigation have changed at the margins. Most group litigation in Korea takes the form of a collective lawsuit, wherein the rulings apply to all plaintiffs who joined the lawsuit with common causes (KCPA Art. 65). Unfortunately, the Korean term *jipdan sosong* is commonly used for both collective litigation and class actions. However, genuine class action (i.e., a person can sue on behalf of an entire class of alleged victims who do not have to join the suit) only became available in Korea in 2005, and its use is limited to securities cases so far. PSPD spearheaded the campaign for the Securities-Related Class Action Law to address minority shareholders' rights in the aftermath of the Asian Financial Crisis.[14] But one lawyer who helped draft the law notes, "it's usually difficult to get district court approval for class action, and the defendant can challenge the court's approval before the case even goes to trial."[15] To date, lawyers report that the law has been used in fewer than ten cases.

In terms of liberalizing standing rules, gains have been incremental. With the 2007 revisions to the Framework Act on Consumers, consumer rights organizations became eligible to file group lawsuits on behalf of consumers who suffered legally or factually identical damages.[16] But the provision remains largely untested because faster remedies are available through the Consumer Dispute Settlement Commission and the Korea Fair Trade Commission. NGOs can also file complaints with the NHRCK. On balance, reforms have lowered barriers to entry for civil litigation.

7.3.2 *More Favorable Adjudication Procedures*

Enhancing procedural justice has been a reform goal because, in the past, Korean courts' adjudication procedures posed numerous hurdles to claimants. The process was like "dripping water," with oral hearings happening only every few months (Baik 2015, 229). Judges had to revisit the facts of the case each time, and the sporadic pace clashed with the frequent rotation of judges. Despite the KCPA's provisions for oral argument (Art. 134), Korean judges historically weighted documents more than witnesses and oral arguments (Kwon 2007, 132). The courts' reliance on paper documents seemed to impede citizens' ability to understand and participate in adjudication processes. Due to Korea's lack of discovery procedures, plaintiffs also struggled to access enough evidence to prove rights violations. Substantive and procedural changes have sought to alleviate these challenges.

For example, the KCPA overhaul in 2002 aimed at increasing procedural efficiency by instituting pretrial conferences and concentrating trials. Pretrial

---

[14] *Jeunggwongwallyeon jipdansosongbeop* (Securities-Related Class Action Act), Act No. 7074 (2004).
[15] Interview, lawyer A (May 22, 2015).
[16] *Sobijagibonbeop* (Framework Act on Consumers), Act No. 7988 (2006).

procedures were supposed to give judges a chance to dismiss or correct incomplete complaints expeditiously, but the standards for evidence were unclear (J. Lee 2014, 122–23). And criticisms soon emerged about delays and violations of procedural rights (J. Lee 2014, 116–17). Moreover, because the conferences reduced the importance of oral arguments, which in practice often occurred in the conferences rather than in the public courtroom, the Supreme Court began recommending more dynamic argumentation (Kwon 2007, 142).

Oral arguments with active discussions and some of the broader judicial reforms of the 2000s, such as juries for serious criminal offenses, aimed to make Korean courtrooms more open and participatory. One judge explained that many judges "try to hear more from the plaintiffs and from all parties to the lawsuits in the past ten years to increase public trust in the courts."[17] He said he calls more witnesses and explains things more carefully now in oral hearings. The move toward electronic records also enabled judges to use PowerPoint in the courtroom. Disability rights lawyers, meanwhile, have fought to enhance accommodations for people with disabilities in the courtroom, including sign language interpreters, captioning, and simpler presentation of points.[18] As JaeWon Kim noted (Chapter 10), the Korean Supreme Court also published Guidelines for Judicial Assistance for Persons with Disabilities in 2013, but its implementation has been uneven (Committee on the Rights of Persons with Disabilities 2014, 2).

Other procedural innovations resulted from negotiations between plaintiffs' lawyers and judges. For example, judges have agreed to some lawyers' requests that they visit the actual site of alleged rights violation. In the state compensation lawsuits by more than 500 leprosy survivors subjected to forced vasectomies and abortions, the judges visited the leprosarium hospital on Sorokdo, and news photographs showed judges listening to a plaintiff's testimony while standing around an operating table (Ock 2016). They also held a moment of silence at a shrine on Sorokdo to commemorate the victims (Heo 2016). In litigation over the inaccessibility of intercity buses, plaintiffs' lawyers similarly persuaded judges to ride a bus to experience the challenges people with disabilities face.[19]

For lawsuits regarding sensitive or stigmatizing issues, Korean courts have introduced some innovations to protect the parties' privacy (Arrington 2019). Anyone with a complaint's number can look up the plaintiffs' names and other details online. Hence, Korean attorneys often closely guard case numbers and ask reporters to conceal their clients' names. In civil cases related to sexual violence, courts have started limiting the use of parties' names. One activist reported a small-scale change: "[T]he prosecutor in the recent Dogani case [involving sexual abuse of disabled minors in 2011] used witnesses' real names only once, as the judges required. After that, he called them 'witness' in court to minimize their exposure. I think he became

---

[17]   Interview, judge A (May 29, 2015).
[18]   Interview, lawyers K and L (May 28, 2015).
[19]   Interview, lawyer I (September 11, 2017).

aware of privacy rights and stigma through his wife's work as a lawyer with sexual violence victims."[20] Disability rights advocates also report that some judges are more aware of the issue of secondary victimization from the court process.[21] The Supreme Court began redacting names and addresses from the limited number of rulings made available online starting in 2013 (Won 2016, 82–83).

In addition, provisions to shift the burden of proof away from plaintiffs made it easier to satisfy evidentiary standards, thus enhancing the prospects for private rights enforcement. For instance, Korea's Supreme Court has ruled in several cases to relax the KCPA's high bar for tort liability. Art. 750 requires proof of (1) intention or negligence, (2) an unlawful act, (3) plaintiffs' losses or injuries, and (4) a (proximate) causal relationship between the unlawful act and the injuries. Negligence, intention, and causation are usually hardest to prove. However, in an environmental pollution lawsuit in 2000, the Supreme Court accepted the logic of probability regarding indirect exposure and multiple causal factors instead of direct causation. The court ruled that "requiring victims to present rigid scientific evidence of the causal relationship in environmental lawsuits may in effect lead to a complete denial of judicial remedies."[22] Korea's 2002 Product Liability Law waived the expectation that plaintiffs prove a product's defects (Y. D. Lee 2003, 174). Subsequent rulings reaffirmed the relaxed or shifted burden of proof. Also, courts accepted epidemiological evidence – showing substantial probability based on comparisons of populations, rather than direct causation – in cases related to HIV-tainted blood products and smoking, but the Supreme Court still ultimately ruled in 2014 that tobacco producers were not liable for lung cancer-related claims.[23]

Finally, since Korea lacks strong discovery mechanisms for persuading defendants to release information, societal actors are increasingly using freedom of information requests. Under KCPA Art. 344, plaintiffs must specify each document they request to see from the defendants, who can also refuse to reveal the documents. Originally passed in 1996, the Act on Disclosures of Information by Public Agencies was amended to include online information in 2004.[24] Any individual or group can request information disclosure.[25] Between 2006 and 2016, the number of requests rose from 151,000 to 756,000 (MOIS 2016, 17). Not all succeed though. Gonggam lawyers, for instance, have requested information regarding refugee acceptance guidelines and the Sewol ferry sinking, but they have been rejected for national security reasons. And lawyers have complained that the information disclosure law has too many loopholes, and requests can take as short as a month or as long as two to

---

[20] Interview, activist C (July 22, 2013).
[21] Interview, activist A (September 14, 2017).
[22] Supreme Court 2000da65666 (October 22, 2002). Cited in S. G. Lee (2016, 83).
[23] Supreme Court, 2008da17776 (September 29, 2011) for HIV-tainted blood products. Seoul High Court, 2007na18883 (February 15, 2011) and Supreme Court 2011da22092 (April 10, 2014) for tobacco.
[24] *Gonggonggigwan jeongbggonggaebeop* (Act on Disclosures of Information by Public Agencies), Act No. 7127 (2004).
[25] Open Information Portal, www.open.go.kr/ (accessed March 4, 2018).

three years.[26] Still, one official commented that "it seems that lawyers are getting much better and more specialized at such requests."[27]

7.3.3 *Better Potential Remedies*

To round out this analysis of changing legal opportunity structures, let me turn to expected outcomes. Rewards in civil cases in Korea have historically been capped by judges, limiting the attractiveness of private litigation for rights claims. The KCPA stipulates that the losing party pays in civil disputes (Art. 98), and the court has discretion in cases of partial defeat (Art. 101) (Baik 2015, 225–28). The KCPA permits only awards for actual damages, and punitive damages (*jingbeoljeok sonhaebaesang*) were considered anathema to the social order (Kwon 2007, 141). Even the amount that a losing party owes was limited. However, the unpredictability of award sizes has increased, which prior literature indicates creates incentives for litigation rather than bargaining in the shadow of the law (Haley 2002, 132–33). Ninety percent of Korean lawyers surveyed supported the idea of punitive damages, albeit only in specific areas like environmental law, North Korean migrants, and product liability (Son 2016). Disability rights activists unsuccessfully sought to insert punitive damages into Korea's 2007 Disability Discrimination Act (see Chapter 10).[28] The option of punitive damages, which are technically still limited to triple damages, for unfair practices by large corporations was introduced in 2011 and has not been used to date (see further T. Kim and Kim 2016, chap. 4). In April 2017, the Product Liability Law was amended to include triple damages and a lower burden of proof.[29] Legal mobilization related to the 500 plus deaths caused by humidifier disinfectants made by Oxy had pressured lawmakers to adopt legislation providing both class action and punitive (triple) damages (Kwak 2016, 2017). The center-left party and an NGO coalition, including PSPD, backed these reforms. Still, litigation is rarely lucrative, and observers remain concerned about clogging the courts. To cope with rising litigation rates and backlogs, mediation and alternative dispute resolution mechanisms have grown in usage. While they are beyond the scope of this chapter, some, such as the National Human Rights Commission of Korea (see Chapter 5), have been effectively combined with litigation. The fact that most rulings and settlements are not publicly available constrains their value as precedents that inform subsequent rights claiming (Park and Youm 2017). But networks of lawyers are spreading and institutionalizing knowhow. And low visibility adjustments like those discussed in this chapter have cumulated to render the structure of legal opportunity relatively more open than twenty years ago.

[26] Email with Patricia Goedde. Interview, lawyer B (May 27, 2015).
[27] Interview, official A (July 23, 2013).
[28] *Jangaein chabyeolgeumjibeop* (Act Prohibiting Discrimination against People with Disabilities), Act No. 8341 (2007). Interview, lawyer J (September 12, 2017).
[29] *Jejomul chaegimbeop* (Product Liability Law), Act No. 14764 (2017).

7.4 CONCLUSIONS: BEGINNING TO EXPLAIN CHANGES IN THE STRUCTURE OF LEGAL OPPORTUNITIES

In sum, this chapter has traced how incremental changes in civil procedure, statutes, and the rules governing access to the courts and dispute adjudication have gradually liberalized the structure of legal opportunities in Korea in the past two decades, facilitating rights claiming. In part, lawmakers' and judges' choices account for these changes, but a full explanation requires looking at the demand side of the equation, too. Lawyers with advocacy organizations, knowhow, and funding have helped societal groups perceive, use, and sometimes even pry open legal opportunities.

By way of concluding, this section elaborates on four factors that help account for some of the changes in the legal opportunity structure discussed earlier: the demands and ideas of rights claimants and their lawyers, judges' behavior and beliefs, partisan politics, and international factors. The relative importance of each factor varies across issue areas and stages in the litigation process. It is beyond the scope of this chapter to prove causation; these factors deserve further research. Here, I build on existing scholarship to suggest potential hypotheses.

First, a full understanding of changes in the legal opportunity structure requires looking at the societal actors who are bringing innovative lawsuits to court. For example, Vanhala (2012) showed how environmental NGOs in the United Kingdom successfully pressured courts to liberalize standing and alter the cost structures of litigation, despite losing their cases. An increasingly institutionalized infrastructure for legal mobilization in Korea – detailed by Goedde (Chapter 8) – has spurred some of the changes in the legal opportunity structure discussed earlier and has equipped societal actors to better recognize and utilize these changes. Epp's (1998) comparative research demonstrated that groups seeking to use the courts for rights claiming depend on "support structures" comprising advocacy organizations, funding, and especially rights-advocacy lawyers. This infrastructure of public interest law firms and foundations, issue-specific legal expert associations, and funding for reform litigation has helped not just to recognize legal opportunities but sometimes also to forge opportunities. Lawyers are important change agents, but not the only drivers of liberalizing legal opportunities. They also interact with plaintiffs, judges, activists, journalists, and government officials in the process of rights claiming and rights enforcement. Still, growing legal opportunities are more likely when experienced lawyers play an entrepreneurial role and can recognize, use, and pry open legal opportunities.

A second set of potential explanations highlights judges' behavior and beliefs. Such accounts explore judicial activism and are often concerned with the ways in which a "juristocracy" is detrimental to democracy because judges are rarely elected or accountable (Goldstein 2004). However, judges may also innovate at the margins in ways that matter, gradually shifting interpretations of procedural doctrine or rendering previously controversial issues more mainstream (Ginsburg and

Matsudaira 2012; T. M. Keck 2009, 159). In some cases, such judicial innovation can undermine the accessibility of courts and deter rights claiming (Dodd 2018, chaps. 8–10; Staszak 2015). But Korean judges have at times signaled receptivity to rights claims, reshaping people's perceptions about the potential rewards of litigation. The signals judges send can be subtle as they often occur via low-visibility procedural cases. To recognize such shifts in legal opportunities, lawyers' expertise is essential.

A third set of explanations focuses on politicians as change agents and partisan competition as the motive. Legislators may pass laws or create new rules that establish new justiciable rights or render private enforcement of rights via litigation an important mechanism for policy implementation. According to the existing scholarship, politicians may encourage recourse to the courts to avoid taking a position on controversial issues (Whittington 2005); to constrain the next party in power (Hirschl 2004); or to cope with stalemates and fragmentation in political systems (Kagan 2001; Kelemen 2006). These studies indicate that moments of impending turnover in the party in power or a divided government would be accompanied by legislative actions that open legal opportunities. Such was the case with the enactment of the Disability Discrimination Act in 2007, which was passed just before conservatives recaptured the Blue House (see Chapter 10).

Fourth, international factors constitute a final driver behind liberalizing legal opportunity structures. Transnational advocacy networks facilitate the diffusion of new rights and ideas about how to achieve them domestically (González-Ocantos 2016; Keck and Sikkink 1998). The process of ratifying international human rights treaties also "precommits governments to be receptive" to rights claims, provides resources for domestic rights mobilization, creates opportunities for enlarging the coalition of supporters, and raises expectations about state behavior (e.g., Simmons 2009, 144–46; Tsutsui and Shin 2008). Legal opportunity structures are more likely to open when rights claimants can cite an international treaty or foreign legal model for emulation. For example, a coalition of NGOs and lawyers across Europe promoted EU standards on racial equality to open national legal opportunities for strategic litigation (Evans Case and Givens 2010). International treaties and models have influenced Korean lawmakers and, indirectly, judges. The NHRCK's establishment, as Hwang (Chapter 5) details, was catalyzed by international norms. Yet on issues such as LGBTI rights, Korean lawmakers and judges have resisted international norms and pressure despite growing social acceptance (see Chapters 11 and 12).

There are several implications of this research. First, it highlights how the structure of legal opportunities, while relatively stable, does change. Such changes deserve greater scholarly attention. Most of the literature treats legal opportunity structures as given, as an explanatory variable. But this chapter examined changes in Korea's legal opportunity structure. Second, using the lens of legal opportunity structures focuses our attention on contingent factors and participants' perceptions of legal institutions. Future research might explore variation across types of cases (i.e., tort versus administrative lawsuits) in terms of how rights claimants perceive and leverage legal opportunities. Finally, this chapter points to the need for further research on the conditions under which legal opportunity structures are most likely to change. For instance, it suggests that ideas about procedural rights and judicial innovations can spread across issue areas domestically, as well as from foreign models or international treaties. More institutionalized support structures for rights claiming enable citizens to learn about and use such ideas to advance their own causes. Also, change depends on the openness of judges and the central authorities in the judicial system. Further research is needed to assess the relative weight of each of these factors for explaining continuity and change in Korea's legal opportunity structures. However, this chapter confirms the conclusions of Kwon (2007, 143), who found that there has been a "power shift from the public to the private." Korean citizens now have greater resources for rights claiming via the courts, and they face a more open legal opportunity structure for doing so.

REFERENCES

Andersen, Ellen Ann. 2006. *Out of the Closets and into the Courts: Legal Opportunity Structure and Gay Rights Litigation*. Ann Arbor: University of Michigan Press.

Arrington, Celeste L. 2014. "Leprosy, Legal Mobilization, and the Public Sphere in Japan and South Korea." *Law & Society Review* 48 (3): 563–93.

2019. "Hiding in Plain Sight: Pseudonymity and Participation in Legal Mobilization." *Comparative Political Studies* 52 (2): 310–41.

2021. "Legal Mobilization and the Transformation of State-Society Relations in South Korea in the Realm of Disability Policy." In *Civil Society and the State in Democratic East Asia*, edited by David Chiavacci, Simona Grano, and Julia Obinger, 297–323. Amsterdam: Amsterdam University Press.

Baik, Kang-Jin. 2015. "Civil Disputes in Korea and the New Role of the Court." In *The Functional Transformation of Courts: Taiwan and Korea in Comparison*, edited by Jiunn-rong Yeh, 215–38. Göttingen: Vandenhoeck & Ruprecht.

Barnes, Jeb, and Thomas F. Burke. 2015. *How Policy Shapes Politics: Rights, Courts, Litigation, and the Struggle over Injury Compensation*. Oxford: Oxford University Press.

Beomnyul Sinmun. 2013. "Gihoek sosongui munjejeom, haru ppalli gaeseonhaeya" [The issues with strategic litigation, must be resolved soon]. August 21, 2013. www.lawtimes.co.kr/Legal-Opinion/Legal-Opinion-View?serial=77790.

Burke, Thomas F. 2000. "The Rights Revolution Continues: Why New Rights Are Born (and Old Rights Rarely Die) Symposium." *Connecticut Law Review* 33: 1259–74.

Cain, Bruce E., Russell J. Dalton, and Susan E. Scarrow, eds. 2003. *Democracy Transformed?: Expanding Political Opportunities in Advanced Industrial Democracies*. Oxford: Oxford University Press.

Choi, Dai-Kwon, and Kahei Rokumoto, eds. 2007. *Korea and Japan: Judicial System Transformation in the Globalizing World*. Seoul: Seoul National University Press.

Cichowski, Rachel A. 2006. "Introduction: Courts, Democracy, and Governance." *Comparative Political Studies* 39 (1): 3–21.

2016. "The European Court of Human Rights, Amicus Curiae, and Violence against Women." *Law & Society Review* 50 (4): 890–919.

Committee on the Rights of Persons with Disabilities. 2014. "Concluding Observations on the Initial Report of the Republic of Korea." CRPD/C/KOR/CO/1. UN Convention on the Rights of Persons with Disabilities.

Cortner, Richard C. 1968. "Strategies and Tactics of Litigants in Constitutional Cases." *Journal of Public Law* 17: 287–307.

Dodd, Lynda G., ed. 2018. *The Rights Revolution Revisited: Institutional Perspectives on the Private Enforcement of Civil Rights in the US*. Cambridge: Cambridge University Press.

Epp, Charles R. 1998. *The Rights Revolution: Lawyers, Activists, and Supreme Courts in Comparative Perspective*. Chicago: University of Chicago Press.

Evans Case, Rhonda, and Terri E. Givens. 2010. "Re-Engineering Legal Opportunity Structures in the European Union? The Starting Line Group and the Politics of the Racial Equality Directive." *JCMS: Journal of Common Market Studies* 48 (2): 221–41.

Farhang, Sean. 2010. *The Litigation State: Public Regulation and Private Lawsuits in the U.S.* Princeton: Princeton University Press.

Fon, Vincy, and Francesco Parisi. 2006. "Judicial Precedents in Civil Law Systems: A Dynamic Analysis." *International Review of Law and Economics* 26 (4): 519–35.

Ginsburg, Tom. 2001. "Dismantling the Developmental State-Administrative Procedure Reform in Japan and Korea." *American Journal of Comparative Law* 49: 585–626.

　　2002. "Confucian Constitutionalism? The Emergence of Constitutional Review in Korea and Taiwan." *Law & Social Inquiry* 27 (4): 763–99.

　　2003. *Judicial Review in New Democracies: Constitutional Courts in Asian Cases*. Cambridge: Cambridge University Press.

　　ed. 2004. *Legal Reform in Korea*. New York: Routledge.

Ginsburg, Tom, and Tokujin Matsudaira. 2012. "The Judicialization of Japanese Politics?" In *The Judicialization of Politics in Asia*, edited by Björn Dressel, 17–36. London: Routledge.

Goldstein, Leslie Friedman. 2004. "From Democracy to Juristocracy." *Law & Society Review* 38 (3): 611–29.

González-Ocantos, Ezequiel A. 2016. *Shifting Legal Visions: Judicial Change and Human Rights Trials in Latin America*. Cambridge: Cambridge University Press.

Haggard, Stephan, and Jong-Sung You. 2015. "Freedom of Expression in South Korea." *Journal of Contemporary Asia* 45 (1): 167–79.

Hahm, Pyong-choon. 1986. *Korean Jurisprudence, Politics, and Culture*. Seoul: Yonsei University Press.

Haley, John O. 1978. "The Myth of the Reluctant Litigant." *Journal of Japanese Studies* 4 (2): 359–90.

　　2002. "Litigation in Japan: A New Look at Old Problems." *Willamette Journal of International Law and Dispute Resolution* 10: 121–42.

Heo, Jae-hyun. 2016. "In the Place Where They Underwent Forced Surgeries, Hansen's Patients Testify." *Hankyoreh*, June 21, 2016. http://english.hani.co.kr/arti/english_edition/e_national/749110.html.

Hilson, Chris. 2002. "New Social Movements: The Role of Legal Opportunity." *Journal of European Public Policy* 9 (2): 238–55.

Hirschl, Ran. 2004. *Towards Juristocracy: The Origins and Consequences of the New Constitutionalism*. Cambridge: Harvard University Press.

　　2011. "The Judicialization of Politics." In *The Oxford Handbook of Political Science*, edited by Robert E. Goodin, 253–74. London: Oxford University Press.

Hong, Joon Seok. 2011. "From the Streets to the Courts: PSPD's Legal Strategy and the Institutionalization of Social Movements." In *South Korean Social Movements*, edited by Gi-Wook Shin and Paul Y. Chang, 96–116. London: Routledge.

Im, Sanggyu. 2012. "Gongsosihyo jedoui munjejeomgwa gaeseonbangan" [Issues with the statute of limitations and directions for reform]. *Beophak Noncheong* 32 (2): 295–315.

Javeline, Debra, and Vanessa Baird. 2007. "Who Sues Government?: Evidence from the Moscow Theater Hostage Case." *Comparative Political Studies* 40 (7): 858–85.

Jo, He-rim. 2018. "Judges Call for Prosecutorial Probe over Ex-Supreme Court Chief." *Korea Herald*, June 3, 2018. www.koreaherald.com/view.php?ud=20180603000237.

Kagan, Robert A. 2001. *Adversarial Legalism: The American Way of Law*. Cambridge: Harvard University Press.

Kage, Rieko. 2017. *Who Judges?: Designing Jury Systems in Japan, East Asia, and Europe*. Cambridge UK; New York: Cambridge University Press.

Kang, Jin-kyu. 2018. "Moon Asks Court to 'Self-Reform'." *JoongAng Daily*, September 14, 2018. http://koreajoongangdaily.joins.com/news/article/article.aspx?aid=3053178.

Kawashima, Takeyoshi. 1967. *Nihonjin No Hō Ishiki* [The legal consciousness of the Japanese]. Tokyo: Iwanami.

Keck, Margaret E., and Kathryn Sikkink. 1998. *Activists Beyond Borders: Advocacy Networks in International Politics*. Ithaca: Cornell University Press.

Keck, Thomas M. 2009. "Beyond Backlash: Assessing the Impact of Judicial Decisions on LGBT Rights." *Law & Society Review* 43 (1): 151–86.

Kelemen, R. Daniel. 2006. "Suing for Europe: Adversarial Legalism and European Governance." *Comparative Political Studies* 39 (1): 101–27.

Kim, Dohyun, and Seung Heum Hwang. 2007. "Career Patterns of the Korean Legal Profession." In *Judicial System Transformation in the Globalizing World: Korea and Japan*, edited by Dai-Kwon Choi and Kahei Rokumoto, 139–81. Seoul: Seoul National University Press.

Kim, Duol, and Heechul Min. 2017. "Appeal Rate and Caseload: Evidence from Civil Litigation in Korea." *European Journal of Law and Economics* 44: 339–60.

Kim, Jongcheol. 2008. "Government Reform, Judicialization, and the Development of Public Law in the Republic of Korea." In *Administrative Law and Governance in Asia: Comparative Perspectives*, edited by Tom Ginsburg and A. Chen, 129–54. London: Routledge.

Kim, Jongcheol, and Jonghyun Park. 2012. "Causes and Conditions of Sustainable Judicialization of Politics in Korea." In *The Judicialization of Politics in Asia*, edited by Björn Dressel, 37–55. Oxon: Routledge.

Kim, Joongi. 2009. "The Judiciary's Role in Good Governance in Korea." In *Transforming Asian Governance: Rethinking Assumptions, Challenging Practices*, edited by M. Ramesh and Scott Fritzen, 135–53. London: Routledge.

Kim, Marie Seong-Hak. 2012. *Law and Custom in Korea: Comparative Legal History*. Cambridge: Cambridge University Press.

Kim, Rahn. 2011. "Compensation Claim Period Limitless for Inhumane State Crimes." *Korea Times*, September 8, 2011. www.koreatimes.co.kr/www/nation/2020/12/113_94525.html.

Kim, Tae-ho, and Jeong-hwan Kim. 2016. *Gongik sosong jedoeui hyeonhwanggwa gaeseonbangan* [The status quo and future directions of public interest litigation policy]. Seoul: Judicial Policy and Research Institute.

Kwak, Jung-soo. 2016. "Why Have Korean Victims of Humidifier Disinfectant Not Received Compensation?" *Hankyoreh*, May 11, 2016. http://english.hani.co.kr/arti/english_edition/e_international/743377.html.

2017. "New System Would Seek Threefold Compensation from Companies That Make Harmful Products." *Hankyoreh*, January 6, 2017. http://english.hani.co.kr/arti/english_edition/e_business/777672.html.

Kwon, Youngjoon. 2007. "Litigating in Korea: A General Overview of the Korean Civil Procedure." *Journal of Korean Law* 7: 109–44.

2010. "Litigating in Korea: A General Overview of Korean Civil Procedure." In *Litigation in Korea*, edited by Kuk Cho, 1–30. Cheltenham: Edward Elgar Publishing.

Lee, Chulwoo. 1998. "Talking about Korean Legal Culture: A Critical Review of the Discursive Production of Legal Culture in Korea." *Korea Journal* 38 (3): 45–76.

Lee, Jinkyoo. 2014. "Effectiveness of Pretrial Disposition Reform: Interactions between Judicial Efficiency and Access to Justice." Ph.D. Dissertation, Seattle: University of Washington.

Lee, Kyung-min. 2018a. "Last Batch of Bar Exam Trainees Enter Training Center." *Korea Times*, March 2, 2018. www.koreatimes.co.kr/www/nation/2018/03/356_245018.html.

2018b. "Constitutional Court Cannot Review Supreme Court Rulings." *Korea Times*, August 30, 2018. www.koreatimes.co.kr/www/nation/2018/08/251_254783.html.

Lee, Sun Goo. 2016. "Proving Causation with Epidemiological Evidence in Tobacco Lawsuits." *Journal of Preventive Medicine and Public Health* 49 (2): 80–96.

Lee, Young-Dae. 2003. "Great Expectations: The Past, Present & (and) Future of Product Liability Laws in Korea Practitioner's Corner." *Journal of Korean Law* 3 (1): 171–80.

Lehoucq, Emilio, and Whitney Taylor. 2020. "Conceptualizing Legal Mobilization: How Should We Understand the Deployment of Legal Strategies?" *Law & Social Inquiry* 45 (1): 166–93.

Lejeune, Aude. 2017. "Legal Mobilization within the Bureaucracy: Disability Rights and the Implementation of Antidiscrimination Law in Sweden." *Law & Policy* 39 (3): 237–58.

McAdam, Doug, Sidney Tarrow, and Charles Tilly, eds. 2001. *Dynamics of Contention*. New York: Cambridge University Press.

MOIS. 2016. "Jeongbogonggae yeonchabogoseo" [Annual report on information disclosure]. Seoul: Ministry of the Interior and Safety. www.open.go.kr/.

Ock, Hyun-ju. 2016. "Hansen's Patients Testify at On-Site Court Hearing." *Korea Herald*, June 20, 2016. www.koreaherald.com/view.php?ud=20160620000936.

Park, Ahran, and Kyu Ho Youm. 2017. "Judicial Communication in South Korea: Moving toward a More Open System?" In *Justices and Journalists: The Global Perspective*, edited by Richard Davis and David Taras, 184–208. Cambridge: Cambridge University Press.

Ramseyer, J. Mark. 1985. "The Costs of the Consensual Myth: Antitrust Enforcement and Institutional Barriers to Litigation in Japan." *The Yale Law Journal* 94 (3): 604–45.

Scheppele, Kim Lane, and Jack Walker. 1991. "The Litigation Strategies of Interest Groups." In *Mobilizing Interest Groups in America*, edited by Jack Walker, 335–72. Ann Arbor: University of Michigan Press.

Simmons, Beth A. 2009. *Mobilizing for Human Rights: International Law in Domestic Politics*. Cambridge: Cambridge University Press.

Son, Hyeon-su. 2016. "Byeonhosa 10myeong jung 9myeong, 'jingbeoljeok sonhaebaesang jedo doip chanseong'" [9 in 10 lawyers support punitive damages system]. *Law Times*, June 15, 2016. www.lawtimes.co.kr/Legal-News/Legal-News-View?Serial=101154&kind=AE.

Staszak, Sarah. 2015. *No Day in Court: Access to Justice and the Politics of Judicial Retrenchment*. Studies in Postwar American Political Development. Oxford: Oxford University Press.

Tarrow, Sidney. 1994. *Power in Movement: Social Movements, Collective Action and Politics*. Cambridge: Cambridge University Press.

Tsutsui, Kiyoteru, and Hwa Ji Shin. 2008. "Global Norms, Local Activism, and Social Movement Outcomes: Global Human Rights and Resident Korean in Japan." *Social Problems* 55 (3): 391–418.

Upham, Frank K. 1987. *Law and Social Change in Postwar Japan.* Cambridge: Harvard University Press.

Vallinder, Torbjörn. 1994. "The Judicialization of Politics – A Worldwide Phenomenon: Introduction." *International Political Science Review* 15 (2): 91–99.

Vanhala, Lisa. 2012. "Legal Opportunity Structures and the Paradox of Legal Mobilization by the Environmental Movement in the UK." *Law & Society Review* 46 (3): 523–56.

2018a. "Is Legal Mobilization for the Birds? Legal Opportunity Structures and Environmental Nongovernmental Organizations in the United Kingdom, France, Finland, and Italy." *Comparative Political Studies* 51 (3): 380–412.

2018b. "Shaping the Structure of Legal Opportunities: Environmental NGOs Bringing International Environmental Procedural Rights Back Home." *Law & Policy* 40 (1): 110–27.

Whittington, Keith E. 2005. "'Interpose Your Friendly Hand': Political Supports for the Exercise of Judicial Review by the United States Supreme Court." *American Political Science Review* 99 (4): 583–96.

Wilson, Bruce M., and Juan Carlos Rodriguez Cordero. 2006. "Legal Opportunity Structures and Social Movements: The Effects of Institutional Change on Costa Rican Politics." *Comparative Political Studies* 39 (3): 325–51.

Won, Hoshin. 2016. "Measures to Realize Sustainable and Efficient Justice from the Perspective of Information and Communications Technology Focusing on the Korean Court Special Articles: SNU-JPRI-Berkeley." *Journal of Korean Law* 16: 67–92.

Yang, Kun. 1989. "Law and Society Studies in Korea: Beyond the Hahm Theses." *Law & Society Review* 23 (5): 891–901.

Yonhap News. 2017. "Top Court Orders Gov't to Compensate Lepers for Abuse." February 15, 2017. https://en.yna.co.kr/view/AEN20170215004600315.

Yoon, Dae-kyu. 2010. *Law and Democracy in South Korea: Democratic Development Since 1987.* Seoul: Kyungnam University Press.

Zackin, Emily. 2008. "Popular Constitutionalism's Hard When You're Not Very Popular: Why the ACLU Turned to Courts." *Law & Society Review* 42 (2): 367–96.

Zemans, Frances Kahn. 1983. "Legal Mobilization: The Neglected Role of the Law in the Political System." *The American Political Science Review* 77 (3): 690–703.

8

Public Interest Lawyering in South Korea

Trends in Institutional Development

Patricia Goedde[1]

8.1 INTRODUCTION

In mid-2018, the arrival of over 500 Yemeni citizens on Jeju Island, South Korea (hereafter Korea), provoked nationwide debate about whether they should be formally admitted as refugees or deported as threats to national security. Citizen rallies and petitions to the Presidential Blue House called for a more stringent refugee policy in the name of protecting the physical and economic security of Korean citizens.[2] South Korean refugee advocates spoke out tirelessly on behalf of the Yemeni, combating stereotypes and misperceptions of the Middle Eastern men who were being characterized as undocumented migrants out to usurp jobs, Muslim fundamentalists, potential criminals, rapists, and terrorists. These advocates include a new generation of public interest lawyers and groups who have intensively participated in media broadcasts and public lectures to explain refugee advocacy and why citizens fleeing war need protection, not expulsion. They are part of the Korea Refugee Rights Network, which includes lawyers from various organizations such as Gonggam Human Rights Foundation, Advocates for Public Interest Law (APIL), Immigrants' Advocacy Center Gamdong, Dongcheon Foundation, Nancen, and Dongheng, among others. This type of network illustrates how lawyers from different public interest law entities converge to advocate for rights protection and related causes.

Legal mobilization studies often include analyses of how lawyers help advocate for causes using rights framing, advocacy coalitions, and legal processes. Rights revolutions rely on the resources for sustained litigation, namely lawyers, advocacy organizations, and funding (Epp 1998, 18–22). Lawyers help mobilize the marginalized by framing grievances into rights entitlements, simultaneously raising rights consciousness for disempowered groups and the public in general (McCann 1994,

[1] This chapter is a modified version of the author's article "Public Interest Lawyering in South Korea: Trends in Institutional Development and Future Sustainability." 15 *University of Pennsylvania Asian Law Review* 52 (2019). This work was funded by the ROK Ministry of Education and National Research Foundation (NRF-2016S1A3A2925085).

[2] *Cheongwadae* (Blue House) Petition Website, petition on the Jeju asylum seekers, June 13–July 13, 2018, www1.president.go.kr/petitions/269548 (accessed May 5, 2020).

227–310; Scheingold 2004, 131–50). This has been called rights lawyering, cause lawyering, and public interest lawyering, among others. Global case studies on cause lawyering and legal mobilization recently began to emerge more consistently (Sarat and Scheingold 2005, 2006). However, it has taken longer to study the legal profession's role in Korean social movements and how lawyers have also been critical agents in advancing causes (but see Arrington and Moon 2020; Goedde 2008). Yang Kun was one of the first to call for the need to analyze the role of lawyers in the democratization of Korea (Yang 1989, 900). Other Korean legal scholars heeded this call by explaining the difficulty of human rights lawyering during the authoritarian regimes of Park Chung-hee and Chun Doo-hwan (Ahn 1994, 123–28; Kim 2001, 60–61). Supplementing a detailed history of how human rights lawyers pushed for various social causes through their institutional development and legal advocacy (W. Park 2003), Gonggam attorney Yeom Hyeong-guk has summarized the latest developments in public interest lawyering in Korea, particularly the new forms of public interest law groups (Yeom 2018, 25–49).

This chapter further informs the scholarship on public interest lawyering in Korea by addressing how public interest law groups have developed in form and methodology to complement the current needs of social movements since the early 2000s. It uses Epp's conception of support structures (i.e., lawyers, advocacy organizations, and funding) to assess Korean legal advocacy organizations in particular, especially in how they define their work and support their activities institutionally and financially. This chapter focuses on the different types of public interest law groups that have emerged, and why some patterns endure while new forms arise in other situations. What do public interest law groups have in common, and how do they distinguish themselves from each other? How do public interest law groups network among themselves for coalition advocacy and generate future public interest lawyers? Are current approaches institutionally sustainable or will public interest lawyering take new forms in the future? This chapter examines several public interest law entities since the early 2000s to identify patterns in institutional development and sustainability, especially in terms of legal mobilization and coalition advocacy, professional affiliations and networks, and the reproduction of public interest lawyers. Based on five interviews with at least one of the most senior lawyers of each key public interest law group (ten lawyers in total) and their annual reports, these case studies show how public interest law organizations network, collaborate, and generate more public interest lawyers. They thus trace the dynamics of rights advocacy mechanisms in Korea.

The next section reviews the history and discourse of public interest lawyering in Korea. I then introduce and compare the pioneering nonprofit public interest law group, Gonggam, and its successors, explaining what accounts for their similarities and differences, and how they fund their activities. The chapter then turns to public interest law groups created by private law firms: Dongcheon Foundation initiated by Bae, Kim & Lee (*Taepyeongyang*, or BKL), and Duroo by Jipyong LLC. It analyzes their relationships with the original nonprofit public interest law groups like Gonggam. Finally, the chapter delves into the issue of sustainability, given the challenges of operating public interest law groups, and analyzes how certain public interest law actors not only network and collaborate on certain causes but also work to train a new generation of public interest lawyers.

8.2 A BRIEF HISTORY OF PUBLIC INTEREST LAWYERING IN KOREA

Rights lawyering in Korea began in the colonial era, when a small number of Korean lawyers (as well as a few Japanese lawyers) represented those arrested for resistance by Japanese authorities (W. Park 2003, 70–74). The outbreak of the Korean War, its aftermath, and political struggles gave rise to a few examples of lawyers defending opposition parties and newspaper publishers. Aside from such male activist lawyers, Yi Tae-yeong became the first female lawyer in Korea in 1952 and strove to combat gender discrimination in the existing family law, later founding the Korean Legal Aid Center for Family in 1956 (Yang 1998, 126). Around this time, another lawyer, Yi Byeong-nin led efforts to form a bar association independent from the state, later becoming president of both the Seoul District Bar and the Korean Bar Association in 1964. Considered the godfather of "human rights lawyers" (*ingwon byeonhosa*), Yi Byeong-nin and his colleague Han Seung-heon inspired other lawyers by defending dissident college students arrested in the 1974 Mincheong Hangnyeon case during the Park Chung-hee administration.

Such lawyers of the 1970s were called the "first-generation" human rights lawyers, and they mentored the "second generation" of human rights lawyers who mainly defended workers protesting for better labor conditions. Yi Byeong-nin's death in 1986 motivated about thirty lawyers to covertly form the group Jeongbeophoe (Lawyers for the Realization of Justice, or *Jeonguisilcheon beopjoinhoe*) to handle cases brought against the state (Minbyeon 1998, 26; W. Park 2003, 357). Jeongbeophoe could not operate openly since it could not register with the state, so it functioned publicly as the Human Rights Committee of the Korean Bar Association. This institutional affiliation offered a degree of protection when bringing cases against the state in the 1980s. Jeongbeophoe transformed into Minbyeon (Lawyers for a Democratic Society, or *Minjusahoereul wihan byeonhosa moim*) in 1988 as democratization allowed nongovernmental organizations to register with the state. With fifty-one cofounding members, Minbyeon was active in its early years taking on cases of protestors accused of violating the National Security Act and the Assembly and Demonstrations Act (Minbyeon 1998, 80, 101, 128).[3]

Legal advocacy patterns began to change in the 1990s. Democracy opened up space for the emergence of civil society, civil and political rights protection

---

[3] For reference to the current laws, see *Gukgaboanbeop* (National Security Act), Act No. 13722 (2016) and *Jiphoe mit siwie gwanhan beomnyul* (Assembly and Demonstration Act) Act No. 13834 (2016).

improved, and attention turned to the socioeconomic concerns of the growing middle class. Minbyeon membership increased yearly, but its newer members began to align with and advise nongovernmental organizations in the areas of environmental protection, labor rights, consumer rights, women's rights, and economic rights. Minbyeon-affiliated lawyers' cases shifted from criminal defense litigation toward proactive civil litigation for diversified rights (Goedde 2011).

In 1994, Minbyeon cofounding member Park Won-soon helped establish the People's Solidarity for Participatory Democracy (PSPD), an influential NGO that monitored and litigated in reaction to government and conglomerate actions on various issues, from social welfare to shareholders' rights. He enlisted other Minbyeon members to join PSPD subcommittees and litigate on the behalf of affected citizens, thus mainstreaming the tactic of legal mobilization for policy change. He also framed their work as "public interest law" (*gongik beop*), borrowing this phrase from American discourse when talking about protecting citizens' rights. "Public interest lawyer" (*gongik byeonhosa*) is thus a relatively new expression in Korea, having evolved from the concept of human rights lawyering, which was the more prevalent discourse since the 1970s (Goedde 2009). This shift in discourse implies changes in the larger landscape of rights advocacy in Korea, from a focus on dissidents' civil and political rights to citizens' socioeconomic rights.

Park Won-soon later formed a charity organization called the Beautiful Foundation, through which a young attorney named Yeom Hyeong-guk approached Park about wanting to practice public interest law despite not knowing how to start. Park proposed that Yeom join the Beautiful Foundation, which later created Korea's first nonprofit "public interest lawyers' group," Gonggam (meaning "empathy"). Four more lawyers joined on a full-time, salaried basis (Kim Yong-su, So Rami, Jung Jung-hoon, and Hwang Pill-kyu) for Gonggam's official launch in 2004.

Public interest law should be differentiated here from legal aid, which is defined as assistance provided by the state. Bar associations continue to offer legal assistance, and government offices have legal aid available through the Ministry of Justice, Korean Legal Aid Corporation, court system, and city and district offices. Pro bono usually implies unpaid legal services provided by private lawyers or law firms but may also be provided by a lawyer in any capacity. "Human rights lawyering" retains left-leaning political connotations, unlike the more neutral "public interest lawyer." However, it is gaining more usage again given the mainstreaming of human rights discourse in Korea and lawyers' regular participation in international human rights mechanisms. Indeed, Gonggam recently changed its name and legal status to "Gonggam Human Rights Foundation" (partly for grant-making and governance purposes), and other public interest law groups refer to their respective work as falling under human rights law.

8.3 GONGGAM AND NEWER PUBLIC INTEREST LAW GROUPS: A MODELING EFFECT?

Gonggam pioneered a new type of nonprofit public interest law group in Korea, and a few others have followed in its footsteps. This section introduces three main organizations (Gonggam, Korean Lawyers for Public Interest and Human Rights (KLPH), and APIL), and discusses how they came into being, their target areas, how they imitate or diversify from each other, their funding sources, and the continued viability of this organizational form.

Gonggam has developed solidly over the years and now has ten lawyers. It became independent from the Beautiful Foundation in 2013, three years later to become a foundation in its own right.[4] As expressed in its mission statement, Gonggam's main purpose is to protect social minority rights (*sosuja gwolli*). Its main areas of practice cover migrant women victimized by violence, people with disabilities, migrants and refugees, laborers, poverty and welfare, and public interest law in general. Gonggam originally characterized its work into four major areas: (1) legal service projects for NGOs, (2) public interest lawsuits and legal reform, (3) development of public interest law programs and brokering pro bono activities, and (4) research. While public interest lawyering in Korea started off being largely related to collective litigation, this is not the mainstay of what Gonggam does. In its early stage, one attorney explained:

> Impact litigation has been the stated goal, but in reality, it is [both] impact litigation and legal assistance. One-third to one-fourth is litigation work. The rest is legal assistance, writing manuals, and doing research. Gonggam has about 40 cases per year (including all court levels).[5]

In addition, Gonggam cooperates and networks with other governmental, human rights, and professional organizations at both the domestic and transnational levels to advance the impact of their legal activities – and, by extension, often also rights. Gonggam is explicit about its brokering role, trying to match clients with private lawyers willing to take on pro bono cases. Gonggam has since expanded into international human rights promotion and public interest law education and advancement. It also launched the in-house Transnational Human Rights Institute in April 2019 on its fifteenth-year anniversary.

As the first public interest law group in Korea, Gonggam's learning curve was steep. In 2006, it made a fact-finding trip to the United States to "find a good role model for Gonggam."[6] They visited about twenty organizations and attended conferences in New York, Washington, DC, Los Angeles, and San Francisco. From the trip, Gonggam gained many ideas about project development and management,

---

[4] See www.kpil.org. The legal status of a foundation confers certain tax status for its grant-making role.
[5] Interview G090407 (April 9, 2007).
[6] *Id.*

sponsorships, funding, potential pro bono arrangements, and gathered many samples of legal manuals. During its early years, senior Minbyeon lawyers questioned how long Gonggam would survive:

> Gonggam is a pioneer group. Minbyeon and PSPD are watching Gonggam carefully as the first nonprofit public interest law group. At first, they were a bit skeptical, saying, "Let's see how long Gonggam lasts." Now they are surprised to see that we are still here, going strong in our fourth, fifth year.[7]

The lawyer continued, "We would like Gonggam to be a model for other public interest law groups." They faced challenges, such as financial viability and having a small team trying to handle immense legal work. Yet, they sustained their efforts at litigation, consulting for NGOs representing minority communities, forwarding cases to Minbyeon attorneys and law firms, and initiating discourse about public interest law at the Judicial Research and Training Institute (JRTI). And indeed, Gonggam became a model for other public interest law groups, such as those described next. While commonalities exist in terms of overlapping mandate areas, legal mobilization tactics, and financial donor models, each group distinguishes itself from Gonggam in some of their specializations and institutional design.

8.3.1 *Korean Lawyers for Public Interest and Human Rights*

Korean Lawyers for Public Interest and Human Rights (*Huimangeul mandeuneun beop*, abbreviated as *Huimangbeop* or "hope" and "law") was founded in 2011, starting with six lawyers and later expanding to nine.[8] The interviewed lawyer explained that they researched what kind of entity they wanted to become, looking carefully at Gonggam.[9] KLPH's mandate areas are driven primarily by its lawyers' specializations, which are LGBTI issues, disability rights, business and human rights, and the rights of assembly and protest. Their group is notable for having Korea's first transgender lawyer, Park Han-hee, who works on transgender rights.

KLPH does not have many cases, but the ones it takes on entail heavy workloads and long hours.[10] These are usually impact cases, so the lawyers simultaneously work with plaintiffs, hold or present at seminars, and draft documents. They take not just individual cases but also those for framing and strategic positioning to set precedents.[11] These can include some criminal cases representing human rights defenders who have been jailed, as well as civil cases regarding disabilities and LGBTI rights. Additionally, the organization files many petitions to the National Human Rights Commission of Korea because it is fairly easy to do so

---

[7] *Id.*
[8] See www.hopeandlaw.org.
[9] Interview H021117 (November 2, 2017).
[10] *Id.*
[11] *Id.*

(see Chapter 5).[12] It also files legislative and Constitutional Court petitions (see Chapter 6) and submits reports to UN human rights bodies.

As the lawyer explained, each issue area has a coalition of movement organizations. For example, KLPH is a member of the Korean Transnational Corporations Watch to help monitor Korean corporate accountability abroad, especially in relation to labor exploitation, which falls under its issue areas of business and human rights.[13] For LGBTI rights, it is a member of Rainbow Action, a network of LGBTI advocacy NGOs (see Chapters 11 and 12). For disabilities, it links with Disability Discrimination Acts of Solidarity in Korea (DDASK) (*Jangaein chabyeol geumji chujin yeondae*), and one of its attorneys is on the board of directors for the Korean Disabilities Law Association (*Jangaeinbeop yeonguhoe*) (see Chapter 10).[14] Under the progressive Moon Jae-in administration, it started to work with the government on national action plans for improved human rights protection, and looks forward to more collaborations between the government and civil society organizations on new laws and revisions.

8.3.2 *Advocates for Public Interest Law*

Attorney Kim Jong-chul created APIL (*Gongikbeop senteo eopil*) in 2011, and it has expanded to five lawyers.[15] APIL differentiates itself from Gonggam, viewing the latter as a more general public interest law group.[16] APIL sees itself as protecting "the most vulnerable of the vulnerable,"[17] their five specific mandates being refugees, detained migrants, trafficked victims, stateless persons, and victims of multinational Korean companies. Their mission is to give legal assistance to noncitizens most at risk. Also included in APIL's focus areas are children and transgender people. APIL's first priority is legal reform in these focus areas.[18] They have many cases but limited resources, so they pursue impact litigation, taking types of cases not litigated before for the potential to set legal precedent.[19] APIL often obtains informal referrals from P'Nan and Nancen, two of the most active NGOs in Korea that assist refugees.[20]

In terms of networking, APIL works with Gonggam, Dongcheon Foundation (discussed below), and Immigrants' Advocacy Center Gamdong on immigration matters, usually as part of the Korea Refugee Rights Network. They are involved with a number of networks, both local and transnational (e.g., Korean Transnational Corporations Watch, Asia Pacific Refugee Rights Network (APRRN), Cotton

---

[12]   *Id.*
[13]   See ktncwatch.net.
[14]   *Id.*
[15]   See apil.or.kr.
[16]   Interviews A241017a and A241017b (October 24, 2017).
[17]   *Id.*
[18]   *Id.*
[19]   *Id.*
[20]   See www.pnan.org and nancen.org.

Campaign, and Good Electronics).[21] APIL often actively contributes their research and findings in NGO reports to both UN treaty bodies and the Universal Periodic Review (UPR) process concerning the Korean government's human rights records. APIL once served as the coordinating NGO for a UPR report, which entailed gathering and translating all NGO contributions for a joint report via Google Doc.[22] The coordinating NGO has usually been a larger organization, such as Minbyeon, PSPD, or KOCUN (Korea Center for UN Human Rights Policy). The APIL lawyers noted that Korea is unique in being this organized, even being questioned by the UN Secretariat in Geneva on whether all Korean NGOs cooperate so well given counterexamples from other countries.[23] Meanwhile, unlike Gonggam, APIL did not have separate administrative staff until late 2018, meaning that all lawyers juggled both casework and office responsibilities. But like Gonggam, APIL takes interns from law schools locally and from abroad to help with research, translations, and writing. While administration can detract from substantive work, direct personal communication from lawyers has allowed innovative and personalized approaches, such as making use of social media and online videos regarding their clients, causes, and themselves via Facebook, Twitter, and Instagram.

8.3.3 *Funding*

The institutional sustainability of public interest law groups relies on revenue for the basic operation of an office, including rent, overhead costs, salaries, research and project funding, computers, printing, travel, and so on. As is common across Korean NGOs, public interest law groups strongly depend on the donor model to provide a significant amount of income from citizens who become "members" and donate a small monthly contribution ranging between 10,000 won and 100,000 won (approximately $8–83), which counts as a tax write-off.

As a nonprofit public interest law firm, Gonggam has been dependent on private voluntary donations. In its early years, one lawyer explained:

> Funding is a huge challenge. Before there was seed money, some JRTI money, and funding from law firms. Now it is about one-third from individual contributors, one-third from companies, and one-third from law firms.[24]

The increase in funds was a result of various campaigning efforts. For example, JRTI trainees were asked to pledge 1 percent of their income to Gonggam. Gonggam attorneys also regularly asked for donations at lawyers' conferences. Over a decade later, Gonggam's 2019 budget is now 1,118,258,000 won (approximately $933,000) with individual donations accounting for 70 percent, companies and other groups

---

[21] See, for example, aprrn.info and www.cottoncampaign.org.
[22] Interviews A241017a and A241017b (October 24, 2017).
[23] Id.
[24] Interview G090407 (April 9, 2007).

for 18 percent, law firms for 10 percent, and interest and other sources for the remaining 2 percent (Gonggam 2019, 62).

According to their 2019 annual reports, the revenues and membership percentages of APIL and KLPH are significant but fall behind Gonggam. APIL had revenue of 737,846,000 won ($615,500) with individual and group donations counting for almost all (APIL 2019, 20). KLPH had revenue of 570,223,000 won ($475,600) with individual donations accounting for over 82 percent (KLPH 2019, 72). The latter does consistently well, relying on donor pledges by JRTI and law school alumni and colleagues. It also saves on rental costs by operating in a city-subsidized building, a Seoul city initiative to help the sustainability of social enterprises and NGOs.[25] Additionally, attorney Park Han-hee's salary is funded by Gongmyeong, a public interest fund set up by more than seventy graduates of the sixth-year entering class of Seoul National University Law School (S. Park 2017). As one of its lawyers said, a main success of this fund is just being able to survive as an entity, considering Korea's influential movement against sexual minorities' rights (see Chapters 11 and 12).[26]

On the institutional side, funding works in a cascading fashion as public interest law groups, law firms, and law firms' pro bono centers provide financial support for each other, thus illustrating mutual reliance in terms of both financial and human resource support. For example, given the size and the nearly $1 million budget of Gonggam, it is now in a position to give grants of its own to smaller public interest law groups and fund fellowships for young lawyers (discussed next). As indicated in annual reports, Dongcheon Foundation and Jipyong have also contributed to APIL, while Gonggam, APIL, KLPH, Dongcheon Foundation, and Jipyong have all donated to smaller public interest law entities.

8.3.4 *NGOs and Other Public Interest Law Entities*

The Gonggam model is difficult for many entities to follow. Gonggam's senior lawyers explained that its model is unique: It has the "premium" of having been around the longest, being the biggest, and being very well networked.[27] While APIL and KLPH are relatively effective, funding challenges make it difficult for other attorneys to build an independent office with more than one or two persons. Nonetheless, a number of smaller-staffed public interest law groups have been created, such as Immigrants' Advocacy Center Gamdong (*Ijumin jiwon gongik senteo gamdong*), Wongok Law Office, Boda Law Office, Neighborhood Lawyer's Café (*Dongne byeonhosa kape*), Migrant Center "Friend" (*Ijumin senteo chingu*), and Minbyeon's Public Interest and Human Rights Litigation Center (*Gongik byeollon senteo*).[28]

[25] Author's visit to Seoul Innovation Park (November 2, 2017).
[26] Interview H021117 (November 2, 2017).
[27] Interview G261017 (October 26, 2017).
[28] See gamdong.love.org, blog.naver.com/wongoklaw, bodalaw.net, dongbyun.tistory.com, chingune .or.kr, and minbyun.or.kr/?page_id=42901 (accessed July 6, 2020).

More commonly now, a single lawyer joins an NGO or other entity. As of the end of 2017, around forty lawyers had joined NGOs in this manner.[29] KLPH concurred that the new model seems to be one attorney per NGO or small law firm focusing on a single type of cause, as Gamdong does with migrants.[30] In the 1990s and 2000s, several NGOs had a single lawyer or more, as was the case with the Korea Federation for Environmental Movement (KFEM) and Green Korea United or with PSPD, Citizens' Coalition for Economic Justice (CCEJ), and older NGOs like the Family Legal Aid Center. The NGOs that lawyers have joined in recent years are more diverse, covering issues related to migrants and refugees (Nancen), children and students' rights (Ban Ollim, Save the Children), digital rights (OpenNet), youth and sexual minorities (LGBTI Youth Crisis Center), and social enterprises (Deoham).

Meanwhile, it is difficult to have public interest law groups outside Seoul given that most financial donors are in Seoul.[31] For example, Gwangju's only nongovernmental public interest law group is Dongheng (*Gongik byeonhosawa hamkkehaneun donghaeng*, also known as Lawyers for Public Interests), which is a two-member group that formed in 2015, focusing on women, migrants, and people with disabilities. While Gwangju has a substantial history of civil society movements and activities, it does not have as active a donor society as Seoul. The centralization of public interest law groups in Seoul means that legal mobilization elsewhere involves government legal aid programs and local bar associations, such as the Korea Legal Aid Corporation or government "village lawyers" who visit urban and rural district offices. As a nationwide trend, city and provincial governments have also opened legal aid offices, such as Seoul City's Human Rights Center for People with Disabilities, Seoul Social Welfare Public Interest Law Center, and Gyeonggido Human Rights Center for People with Disabilities. Universities like Seoul National University and Korea University have also established Human Rights Centers, usually hiring an in-house lawyer, with other universities throughout Korea quickly following suit.

8.4 THE PRIVATE LAW FIRM'S PRO BONO MODEL

The pro bono requirement for lawyers is relatively new in Korea. Both the Attorney-at-Law Act and the Korean Bar Association regulations were amended in 2000 to add a public service requirement.[32] The exact term used in the Act and by the bar associations is *gongik hwaldong* (*gongik* meaning public good, benefit or interest, and *hwaldong* meaning activity, action, or operation). Attorneys are required to

---

[29] Interview G261017 (October 26, 2017).
[30] Interview H021117 (November 2, 2017).
[31] Interviews G261017 (October 26, 2017), *id.*
[32] *Byeonhosabeop* (Attorney-at-Law Act), Act No. 1154 (1962), amended by Act No. 6207 (2000), art. 27. *Daehan byeonhosa hyeobhoe hoechik* (Korean Bar Association Rules) (1952), amended (2000), art. 9(2).

perform thirty hours of public service annually unless they have less than two years' practice or are over sixty years old.[33] Local bar associations have the option to reduce the requirement to twenty hours, as the Seoul Bar Association has done. Each hour not performed may be atoned for by paying a penalty between 20,000 won and 30,000 won (roughly $25) as determined by the local bar association, thus making it easy to evade this requirement. It should be noted that pro bono is a loose term and not always applied in a private law firm setting for clients who cannot afford the standard fee. Lawyers may also be said to be doing pro bono work for nonprofit organizations, legal aid groups, and other indigent clients.

In the last decade, in-house lawyers often affiliated with Minbyeon and senior Gonggam members have urged major private law firms in Seoul to prioritize pro bono work. Three years after the addition of the bar's public service requirement, PSPD surveyed twenty-five law firms, finding that eight had started acknowledging pro bono hours as part of the required billable hours (Yoo, Lee, and Baek 2016, 10). A year later, PSPD surveyed thirty-eight law firms, this time finding that among nine firms, many had or were planning to implement various pro bono support systems, including designating coordinators, creating public interest law centers, formulating regulations, and funding.

The momentum for institutionalizing pro bono services has continued. One of the largest law firms in Seoul, Bae, Kim & Lee LLC (BKL) was the first to establish a public interest law foundation, Dongcheon Foundation, in 2009. Since then, other major law firms in Seoul have followed suit. As of late 2017, these include Duroo of Jipyong LLC (nine lawyers), Kim & Chang (two lawyers), Yulchon (two lawyers), Sejong (one), Hwawoo (one), Won (one), and Dongin (one) (Yeom 2018, 30). Given these groups' proliferation, Gonggam initiated the Law Firm Public Interest Network in 2016, with Yeom Hyeong-guk chairing its first few years. Representatives of approximately a dozen private law firms meet monthly to share their pro bono casework and activities, which can vary but often overlap (e.g., disabilities, migrants and refugees, children, youth, women, elderly, multicultural families, social welfare, social enterprises, people with Hansen's disease, and international human rights issues).

The Law Firm Public Interest Network has also benchmarked US models, specifically the Pro Bono Institute's "Law Firm Pro Bono Challenge" (Yoo, Lee, and Baek 2016, 7, 11).[34] Both BKL and Jipyong have taken this standard seriously and surpassed both the Korean and Seoul Bar Associations' requirements of thirty pro

---

[33] *Gongik hwaldong deunge gwanhan gyujeong* (Korean Bar Association Regulation on Public Interest Activity), Regulation No. 54, June 26, 2000, *amended* Feb. 5, 2018, art. 3. Korean Bar Association Rules, July 19, 2000, amended Feb. 27, 2017, art. 9(2).

[34] Among the principles calling for institutional commitments to pro bono activities, one is that a major law firm should make its best efforts to contribute annually at least 3–5 percent of the firm's total billable hours or 60 to 100 pro bono hours per attorney to pro bono work (Pro Bono Institute 2017). This would exceed the 50-hour per attorney/year recommendation set forth under the American Bar Association's Model Rules of Professional Conduct (§6.1).

bono hours per year. In 2018, 323 out of 431 attorneys (75 percent) participated in Dongcheon's pro bono activities, and its average number of pro bono hours was 56.6 hours per participating attorney (BKL-Dongcheon LSR Report 2018, 2–3). In the same year, Duroo likewise demonstrated high pro bono participation with 139 out of 144 attorneys (96.5 percent) contributing an average of 54 hours (Jipyong Duroo Pro Bono CSR Report 2018, 4–5). As pro bono leaders, BKL and Jipyong have institutionalized such activities by having their lawyers commit above and beyond the required pro bono hours and by creating public interest law centers.

8.4.1 *Dongcheon Foundation*

Dongcheon Foundation pioneered an institutionalized form of public interest lawyering under the auspices of private law firms when it was established in 2009.[35] One of the top-ranked law firms in Korea, BKL has been the most aggressive in promoting a pro bono culture internally and setting a higher bar for Korean lawyers in general. BKL's Pro Bono Committee was established in 2002, expanding the number of its subcommittees progressively through the years to cover refugees, North Korean settlers, people with disabilities, women/youth, social enterprises, and welfare. In 2009, partners Noh Yeong-bo and Yoo Wook decided to take the institutional step of creating a separate nonprofit foundation, Dongcheon, by hiring a full-time attorney, Yang Dong-soo, to head and coordinate pro bono projects. Since its inception, Dongcheon has been consistently involved in litigation, research, and training, keeping up with its missions of promoting the social responsibility of law firms and associates, providing legal assistance to social minorities, supporting civil society organizations, and cultivating public interest lawyers and advocates (BKL-Dongcheon LSR Report 2017, 12–13). This ties in directly with BKL's commitment to pro bono.[36] In its first year, Dongcheon Foundation coordinated pro bono cases with BKL lawyers, started an annual refugee legal aid training program, and granted scholarships and awards to students and local public interest advocacy groups (BKL-Dongcheon LSR Report 2017, 53).

Since its establishment, Dongcheon Foundation has been involved not only in such substantive legal matters but also in promoting a pro bono ethic within the Korean legal profession. To this end, Dongcheon Foundation has regularly held international and domestic symposia on the state of public interest law issues globally and in Korea, and it forged connections with groups such as the Global Network for Public Interest Law (PILnet).[37] It has held competitions for public interest law projects by law school students and has been proactively involved with public interest law clinics at law schools such as Sungkyunkwan University, Korea

---

[35] See bkl.or.kr.
[36] See BKL "Pro Bono" at www.bkl.co.kr/front/law/about/society.do?lang=eng#.XwMR31UzbX4 (accessed July 6, 2020).
[37] See www.pilnet.org.

University, and Yonsei University. Since 2012, Dongcheon Foundation has also hired attorney fellows on two-year contracts to train them in public interest law practice, with a total of eight fellows to date.

Dongcheon's influence and centrality among public interest law entities have continued to grow. For example, in 2016, it established the Dongcheon Legal Center for Nonprofit Organizations, which matches lawyers to NPOs in an advisory capacity. In 2018, it donated 113,989,000 won ($98,500) to thirty-four nonprofit organizations (BKL-Dongcheon LSR Report 2018, 39). Staff-wise, Dongcheon Foundation has three full-time lawyers, two attorney fellows, and four administrative personnel. The existence of Dongcheon Foundation inspired other large law firms to open their own pro bono centers.

8.4.2 *Duroo*

Founded in 2000, Jipyong is also a leading law firm in Seoul with over 160 attorneys.[38] It had a public service committee from the firm's creation due in part to the background of then managing partner, Cho Yong-hwan, who is one of the original Minbyeon members. He created Duroo in 2014 as a separate legal entity to work on public interest law cases and activities.[39] One of the original members of Gonggam, partner Kim Youngsoo, has headed Duroo since its inception. Another partner, Im Sung-taek, is also a Minbyeon member and heavily involved with the disability rights movement (see Chapter 10).

As of 2020, Duroo has eleven full-time lawyers who also work directly with Jipyong lawyers on cases. Its subject areas are disabilities, social enterprises, international activities, education, and general cases. Duroo has also worked with Dongcheon Foundation on some lawsuits, such as regarding express bus accessibility for people with disabilities and accommodation for the hearing impaired to watch movies. Since matching cases to lawyers can be difficult for urgent or time-consuming cases, Duroo has referred cases to NGOs and Dongcheon Foundation or BKL lawyers.[40] Connections with other public interest law groups depend on the issue. For example, lawyers on cases concerning youths work with NGOs assisting the youth. Similarly, Duroo cooperates with Deoham, a social enterprise NGO now led by Yang Dong-soo, who was formerly at Dongcheon Foundation. Besides casework, Duroo also has research projects commissioned by the National Human Rights Commission of Korea, with subjects such as disabilities' facilities and prisoners' children.

Duroo is operationally different from Dongcheon Foundation as the latter seems more independent from the law firm and has a fellowship program, hiring lawyers to train them as public interest lawyers.[41] Duroo seems to view Dongcheon lawyers as

---

[38]   See www.jipyong.com.
[39]   See duroo.org.
[40]   Interviews D231017a-d (October 23, 2017).
[41]   *Id.*

being less active on case litigation with BKL lawyers and acting more as coordinators, unlike Duroo whose lawyers work directly with Jipyong lawyers and receive training in the process.[42] However, Duroo lawyers do not view themselves as competing with Dongcheon Foundation, but instead as learning from each other.[43]

With the backing of their respective law firms, Dongcheon Foundation and Duroo have strong institutional viability. In its 2019 annual report, Dongcheon Foundation reported revenue of roughly 853,594,000 won ($712,000) with 80 percent coming from outside donors and BKL lawyers. Gonggam was financially on par with Dongcheon Foundation in 2016, but surpassed Dongcheon Foundation's revenue in 2017. As for Duroo, Jipyong's Public Interest Committee decided from the outset that 1–2 percent of the law firm's profits would go to Duroo,[44] which translated to an income total of 432,334,000 won in 2019 ($387,000) (Duroo 2019, 7).

8.5 LEGAL MOBILIZATION AND COALITION ADVOCACY

Overall, the public interest law groups and pro bono centers described in the previous section pursue very similar forms of legal mobilization, which encompass legal consulting, litigation, legislative advocacy, coalition/network building, training, and education. These similarities are evident in all their annual reports, as the organizations categorize their work not only into direct legal assistance such as litigation and consulting but also research, training, and networking. The public interest law firms (i.e., Gonggam, KLPH, APIL) share further commonalities not just in terms of mobilization methods but also in their overlapping mandates, their donor model for funding (common among NGOs), and the fact that virtually all are located in Seoul. All acknowledge Gonggam as the pioneer model, but they differentiate among each other in some ways. Specifically, APIL claims to represent the most vulnerable minorities, whereas KLPH has four specific mandates and is a noted leader in LGBTI rights.

Dongcheon Foundation and Duroo share many of the same legal mobilization methods and mandates as Gonggam, APIL, and KLPH but have stronger institutional backing from their respective law firms in terms of funding, office space, and in-house lawyers who are available for pro bono work. What may look like a bifurcation in public interest law vehicles (founded by private law firms versus not) is not necessarily so considering that they often network and collaborate on the same causes and cases, for example, in the areas of refugees, migrants, disabilities, and social enterprises. While many mandates overlap among the public interest law groups, the public interest lawyers do not report viewing each other as competitors given the shortage of public interest lawyers to begin with.[45] Rather, lawyers from the

[42] *Id.*
[43] *Id.*
[44] *Id.*
[45] Interviews A241017a and A241017b (October 24, 2017) and D231017a-d (October 23, 2017).

different public interest and pro bono groups coalesce into specific movement coalitions, meeting through NGO networks, bar or Minbyeon committees, or as needed for casework or UN reporting.

Resource pooling is also evident, as public interest law groups may refer cases to each other when one lawyer cannot handle a case at the time or alone. Minbyeon and Gonggam frequently play such a role brokering cases out to their network of attorney members or contacts. With the establishment of Dongcheon Foundation and Duroo under the auspices of large law firms, they can forward cases to their respective in-house lawyers as well. On the one hand, creating more public interest law firms on the scale of Gonggam and KLPH appears difficult, indicating that such public interest law firms are unsustainable. However, Gonggam, Dongcheon Foundation, and Duroo have become the institutional powerhouses behind public interest law work, operating as financiers, brokers, and generators of cause networks as they have largely captured the institutional "market" in public interest law service, discussed next.

8.6 PROFESSIONAL AFFILIATIONS AND NETWORKING

While each public interest law entity has a small number of lawyers, the networking among these groups and with relevant NGOs allows for more efficient and effective legal mobilization per cause. Given JRTI or law school alumni connections, Minbyeon membership, bar membership, and coalition networks, this means that the public interest law community is a tightly concentrated network. In addition to multiple memberships, migration between public interest groups and NGOs occurs frequently, resulting in the cross-pollination of knowledge and expertise. While Minbyeon has historically been the dominant network, a newer one of self-identified public interest lawyers is emerging via new professional networks such as Han Madang Public Interest Lawyers' Association (*Gongik byeonhosa moim hanmadang*) and through the new Seoul Bar Association Pro Bono Center.

The most common thread among public interest lawyers is their alumni connections, mainly through the JRTI or their respective law schools. The JRTI alumni network is strong, with the vast majority being graduates of Seoul National University. School ties are strong among same-year graduates but also on a senior–junior (*seonbae–hubae*) level. These connections have historically linked judges, prosecutors, and lawyers across the civil service and public sector (West 1991, 26), but apply to the burgeoning public interest law sector as well. Other affiliations cement these bonds even further, such as through Minbyeon, bar committees, or Han Madang.

The Minbyeon lineage is evident in the leadership of the late Seoul mayor Park Won-soon (PSPD), the Beautiful Foundation, Gonggam, Cho Yong-hwan and Im Sung-taek (both of Jipyong), and Yeom Hyeong-guk (Gonggam, Han Madang, Seoul Pro Bono Center). Concurrent Minbyeon membership is apparent among the lawyers of the public interest law groups and pro bono centers. For example, nearly all lawyers of Gonggam and KLPH are Minbyeon members. Everyone in KLPH met through Minbyeon.[46] For KLPH, having Minbyeon's support is a strategy since Minbyeon's brand name can help a coalition with a statement, such as on a proposed bill (e.g., see Chapter 12 regarding anti-discrimination legislation).[47] In APIL, two out of five are in Minbyeon.[48] APIL's senior lawyer Kim Jong-chul had also led the Korean Bar Association's Human Rights Committee for two years. One of the non-Minbyeon lawyers of APIL said she did not feel it necessary to join because she was already doing public interest law work.[49] As for Dongcheon Foundation and Duroo, almost everyone is also a member of Minbyeon (the one non-Minbyeon Duroo lawyer saying "not yet").[50] Minbyeon membership is on a sliding scale, discounted for public interest lawyers.

Besides Minbyeon, Han Madang is a newer network of public interest lawyers, which meets every other month. The number of members has reached 100 as of March 2018 though not all attend the bimonthly meetings. For instance, APIL and KLPH interviewees stated that they were too busy with their own activities to participate consistently.[51] Attorney Yeom Hyeong-guk of Gonggam is the most senior among the group, so by default he is the informal leader.[52] The lawyers communicate with each other in a Telegram chat group.

To illustrate how tightly intertwined these networks are: attorney Yeom is also the director of the Seoul Pro Bono Center, having founded it in 2016 under the auspices of the Seoul Bar Association. The purpose is to match pro bono cases to lawyers. The online membership registry has not worked as well as intended yet.[53] Instead, it organizes an offline roundtable discussion once a year with NGOs and existing and new lawyers on rotating topics such as migrants, refugees, the homeless, disabled, women, social enterprises, and so on. Usually around fifty participants attend.[54] Attorney Yeom is based full-time at Gonggam but visits the Seoul Pro Bono Center office once or twice a week.

Nonlawyer affiliations also help. For example, APIL benefits from a strong Christian network. While some of its lawyers are Christian, APIL does not have a formal affiliation with a religious group.[55] However, many church members donate to APIL through word of mouth and personal introductions.[56] Sometimes APIL refers cases to members of the more progressive Christian Lawyers Federation,

---

[46]   Interview H021117 (November 2, 2017).
[47]   *Id.*
[48]   Interviews A241017a and A241017b (October 24, 2017).
[49]   *Id.*
[50]   Interviews D231017a–d (October 23, 2017).
[51]   *Id.*; interviews A241017a and A241017b (October 24, 2017).
[52]   Interview G251017 (October 25, 2017).
[53]   *Id.*
[54]   *Id.*
[55]   Interviews A241017a and A241017b (October 24, 2017).
[56]   *Id.*

such as general types of cases involving refugees (e.g., criminal, traffic) or those who cannot afford to pay for a lawyer.[57] APIL also does outreach with church groups, giving lectures about refugee advocacy.

Networking between lawyers and NGOs is further cemented as lawyers become in-house counsel and converge with other lawyers and activists per cause. The migration of public interest lawyers and fellows to different public interest law groups and NGOs as seen throughout this chapter speaks to the general difficulty of building a long-term public interest law career at one organization, instead propelling lawyers to other NGOs and public interest law groups while still retaining their former linkages and relationships. This helps to perpetuate the networking effect and builds comprehensive public interest law expertise, but it also means that there are not enough sufficiently paid jobs for public interest lawyers. Nonetheless, all of the aforementioned public interest law groups and pro bono centers participate in training the next generation of public interest lawyers about human rights and pro bono ethics.

8.7 REPRODUCTION AND RECRUITMENT OF PUBLIC INTEREST LAWYERS

As mentioned earlier, legal education is a vital part of the activities of public interest law groups and pro bono centers, based on their annual reports. These include community lectures, law school clinic participation, annual academic programs and workshops, and the provision of fellowships for new or young lawyers. Awareness programs are also publicized for the general public, including many talks and campaign events usually announced online via their homepages, Facebook, Twitter, Instagram, and so on.

Gonggam and KLPH have taken the lead in training young lawyers and future generations of rights advocates. Gonggam runs an annual three-day Human Rights Summer Camp for undergraduates, covering an array of human rights topics led by local and international experts. KLPH offers an annual two-day Human Rights Academy for law school students and first- and second-year lawyers, which also counts as continuing legal education for practicing lawyers. It is purposefully different from Gonggam's program as KLPH wanted to provide for young public interest lawyers training that they themselves did not have as lawyers starting out in their career.[58] Many of the other public interest lawyers also often give workshops and lectures to the public, NGOs, and law schools.

Over the years, Gonggam has hosted research fellows, including law students, law graduates, and young professionals, many of whom have left to become leaders in their fields. Currently, Gonggam provides fellowships to young lawyers who want to join NGOs. The fellowship program is in conjunction with NOW (*Nau*), a network

---

[57]   *Id.*
[58]   Interview H021117 (November 2, 2017).

of fifty lawyers who donate funds for this very purpose. Gonggam's fellowship program pays half the salary of a public interest lawyer who joins an NGO. Gonggam has funded public interest law fellowships, including at the LGBTI Youth Crisis Center and NGOs in Gwangju and Busan.

Dongcheon Foundation hires attorney fellows, on average two per year, as part of its staff to provide early-career training. Duroo also did but ended the fellowship program after having difficulty placing their fellows with permanent jobs.[59] Existing public interest law groups and pro bono centers struggle to recruit and pay new lawyers, which explains why public interest lawyers often join NGOs directly or form one to three-member organizations. However, the continuing centralization of resources in Seoul raises the issue of whether public interest lawyering will be successful throughout the nation, particularly in other major cities and rural areas dependent more on government legal aid.

Meanwhile, law schools and student associations have cooperated with public interest law groups and pro bono centers to advance human rights education and training at the graduate level. For example, the legal clinics of Sungkyunkwan University, Yonsei University, and Ewha University have worked with Dongcheon Foundation on refugee advocacy projects (Goedde 2014, 367–71). Under my supervision, Sungkyunkwan University has collaborated with Dongcheon since 2011. Other law school clinics and human rights centers, such as Seoul National University and Korea University, frequently liaise with public interest law groups and pro bono centers, especially given alumni relations. The public interest law groups and pro bono centers try to connect with law students outside of Seoul as well. Dongcheon Foundation has held small grant competitions nationwide for law students to create and run public interest law projects. Each law school also has a Public Interest and Human Rights Law Student Association, which is part of a nationwide law student association called In:Yeon. Meanwhile, Duroo, Gonggam, and others offer short externships for law students to experience some time working with them over academic breaks (in addition to internships for often prelaw students). As these examples illustrate, public interest lawyers and keen law students continue to cultivate and sustain professional interest in various social movements, human rights, and a general pro bono ethic.

8.8 CONCLUSION

The nature of Korean public interest lawyering in the new millennium focuses increasingly on the rights of social minorities as opposed to the civil and political rights of citizens that were emphasized in the 1980s or the socioeconomic rights emphasized in the 1990s. New legal institutions and mechanisms have developed accordingly in the past decade and a half to respond to the unaddressed grievances of

---

[59] Interviews D231017a-b (October 23, 2017).

various minority communities. As in the 1980s and 1990s, lawyers continue to be critical agents in strategizing and mobilizing the law for social movements and human rights causes. Collaboration occurs across NGO networks, including public interest law entities, to form unified domestic coalitions per rights issue, leveraging various legal tactics both domestically and internationally. Coalition advocacy occurs through these concentrated, synergistic networks where different lawyers' groups pool their legal knowledge and expertise and tap their respective committees on an ad hoc basis to strategize litigation and legal methods. This happens not just locally but also on a transnational level. Human rights and public interest lawyers have protested, litigated, drafted laws and amendments, reported via UN human rights mechanisms, and networked with NGOs and each other to strengthen rights protections for Korean citizens and noncitizens (see Chapter 13).

Gonggam has set an undeniable precedent in its design and leadership for the NGO community, but it cannot fulfill every legal need. Instead, its senior lawyers have been instrumental in creating new public interest law networks among both law firms and young lawyers. Institutionally, the public interest lawyers' groups and pro bono centers assist one another through case referral, collaborative litigation, outsourcing to in-house counsel, funding projects, and legal training. As such, they serve as the "support structures" for rights-promoting mobilization.

While such work seems to evidence a vibrant and intact ecosystem for public interest lawyering, the sustainability of this form must be probed. With the difficulty of expanding or replicating existing public interest law entities, the emerging trend is for solo or duo nonprofit practice, single lawyers to be embedded within or to advise an NGO, or for law firms to hire one lawyer to constitute their pro bono center. This is not an entirely new dynamic given that many Minbyeon lawyers in the past advised NGOs, and that law firms had civic-minded lawyers who volunteered their legal services, often with these two roles overlapping. However, the large law firms that have emerged in Korea in the past two decades have more lawyers who can offer their time and services, especially in fulfillment of their annual pro bono requirements. They also have gained a vested interest in bolstering their image as a corporation interested in social responsibility. Meanwhile, nonprofit public interest law groups can capitalize on these law firms by asking for their free expertise, funding, and name brand for certain projects and cases when their resources are limited.

Challenges continue, with the fundamental question being whether minorities nationwide are finding adequate representation through existing public interest law groups and mechanisms. The new forms of public interest law entities lean toward impact litigation, meant to make systemic improvements for many. Such legal mobilization can sideline or overlook the smaller, quotidian claims of social minorities, particularly migrants outside the capital. As Kim and Hong illustrate (Chapter 12), cases regarding noncitizens, sexual minorities, and victims of racial discrimination are particularly frustrating and time-consuming without adequate legal and policy frameworks in place to structure potential administrative or court victories. For example, the continuing low acceptance rate of refugees means that pro bono lawyers are likely to lose their clients' cases from the beginning, disincentivizing them to take refugee cases.

The centralization of public interest law entities in Seoul is also problematic. While the most urgent cases filter up through NGOs to public interest law groups, these are mostly for cases that arise in Seoul. With most lawyers being physically based in Seoul, it means most public interest lawyers are also in Seoul rather than throughout the nation. Further connections for referrals may need to be explored between nonprofit public interest law entities and government legal aid offices. Improving the pro bono ethic among existing law firms, bar associations, law school students, and recent graduates is another strategy to investigate. Nonetheless, the public interest law community and the increasing number of self-identified "public interest lawyers" (as well as law school students who aspire to become public interest lawyers) attest to an undiminished spirit of rights advocacy within the legal profession.

REFERENCES

Ahn, Kyong Whan. 1994. "The Growth of the Bar and the Changes in the Lawyer's Role: Korea's Dilemma." In *Law and Technology in the Pacific Community*, edited by Philip S. C. Lewis, 119–34. Boulder: Westview Press.

Arrington, Celeste L., and Yong-il Moon. 2020. "Cause Lawyering and Movement Tactics: Disability Rights Movements in South Korea and Japan." *Law & Policy* Vol. 42 (1): 5–30.

Epp, Charles R. 1998. *The Rights Revolution: Lawyers, Activists, and Supreme Courts in Comparative Perspective*. Chicago: University of Chicago Press.

Goedde, Patricia. 2008. *How Activist Lawyers Mobilized the Law for Social and Political Change in South Korea: 1988–2007*. Unpublished Ph.D. dissertation. Seattle, WA: University of Washington.

———. 2009. "From Dissidents to Institution-Builders: The Transformation of Public Interest Lawyers in South Korea." *East Asia Law Review* Vol. 4: 63–89.

———. 2011. "Lawyers for Democracy (Minbyeon) and Its Legal Mobilization Processes Since 1988." In *South Korean Social Movements: From Democracy to Civil Society*, edited by Gi-Wook Shin and Paul Chang, 224–44. New York: Routledge.

———. 2014. "Globalized Legal Education, Human Rights Lawyering, and Institutional Form." *Clinical Law Review* Vol. 20 (2): 355–78.

Gonggam. 2013. *Urineun huimangeul byeollonhanda [We advocate hope]*. Seoul, Korea: Buki.

Kim, JaeWon. 2001. "The Ideal and the Reality of the Korean Legal Profession." *Asian-Pacific Law and Policy Journal* Vol. 2: 45–68.

McCann, Michael. 1994. *Rights at Work: Pay Equity Reform and the Politics of Legal Mobilization*. Chicago: University of Chicago Press.

Minbyeon. 1998. *Minbyeon baekseo [Minbyeon white paper]*. Seoul: Minbyeon.

Park, Soo-jin. 2017. "South Korea's First Transgender Lawyer Selected for Support from Alumni." *Hankyoreh*, May 8, 2017. www.hani.co.kr/arti/english_edition/e_national/793826.html.

Park, Won-soon. 2003. *Yeoksaga idueureul mujoero harira* [*History shall acquit them*]. Seoul: Durae.

Pro Bono Institute. 2017. Law Firm Pro Bono Challenge, The Commentary to the Statement of Principles 1. www.probonoinst.org/wpps/wp-content/uploads/Law-Firm-Challenge-Commentary-2017–1.pdf.

Sarat, Austin, and Stuart A. Scheingold, eds. 2006. *Cause Lawyers and Social Movement.* Stanford: Stanford University Press.

    2005. *The Worlds Cause Lawyers Make: Structure and Agency in Legal Practice*. Stanford: Stanford University Press.

Scheingold, Stuart A. 2004. *The Politics of Rights: Lawyers, Public Policy, and Political Change*. Ann Arbor: University of Michigan Press.

West, James. 1991. *Education of the Legal Profession*. Seoul, Korea: International Legal Studies, Korea University.

Yang, Hyunah. 1998. *Envisioning Feminist Jurisprudence in Korean Family Law at the Crossroads of Tradition/Modernity*. Unpublished Ph.D. dissertation. New York: New School for Social Research.

Yang, Kun. 1989. "Law and Society Studies in Korea: Beyond the Hahm Theses." *Law & Society Review* Vol. 23 (5): 891–901.

Yeom, Hyeong-guk. 2018. "Hangugui gongik byeonhosa hyeonhwanggwa jeonmang" [The current situation and prospects of Korean public interest lawyers]. In Minbyeon, *Hangugui gongik ingwon sosong* (2) [Korea's public interest / human rights litigation, Vol. 2]. Seoul: Beopmunsa.

Yoo, Wook, Lee, Hui-suk, and Baek, Min. 2016. "Ropeom gongikhwaldongui hyeon-hwanggwa gwaje" [Law firms' current status and tasks of public interest]. In *Ropeom gongik neteuwokeu [Law firm public interest law network]. Ropeom gongik hwaldong hwalseonghwa semina jaryojip [Law firm public service activities seminar resources]* 10 (November 7, 2016).

Reports / Websites

Advocates for Public Interest Law (APIL) Annual Report 2016, 2017, 2018, 2019 (www.apil.or.kr).

Bae, Kim & Lee LLC & Dongcheon Foundation, BKL-Dongcheon LSR Report 2016, 2017, 2018, 2019 (www.bkl.or.kr).

Gonggam Human Rights Law Foundation (Gonggam) Annual Report 2016, 2017, 2018, 2019 (www.kpil.org).

Jipyong Duroo Pro Bono Annual Report 2016, 2017, 2018, 2019 (www.duroo.org).

Jipyong Duroo Pro Bono CSR Report (2018).

Korean Lawyers for Public Interest and Human Rights (KLPH) Annual Report 2016, 2017, 2018, 2019 (www.hopeandlaw.org).

PART III

Mobilizing Rights for the Marginalized

9

From "We Are Not Machines, We Are Humans" to "We Are Workers, We Want to Work"

The Changing Notion of Labor Rights in Korea, the 1980s to the 2000s

Yoonkyung Lee

9.1 INTRODUCTION

On November 13, 1970, Jeon Tae-il set himself on fire in protest of labor exploitation at Peace Market garment factory and screamed "Respect the Labor Standards Act; We are not machines; Let us take Sundays off" (Y. Cho 1991).[1] The last words that Jeon left behind revealed the gruesome labor conditions that Korean workers were subjected to in despotic factories during the developmental authoritarian era. Fast forward to November 12, 2017, two workers of Finetek, a digital display manufacturer, climbed up a 75-meter-high chimney to begin a sky protest and hung a banner with an imprinted slogan, "We want employment security; Abolish evil labor laws."[2] Sky protest refers to a form of resistance staged by a single protester or a small number of protesters who isolate themselves in a risky place of high altitude, such as an industrial crane or a transmission tower, with the bare minimum living conditions (Y. Lee 2015).

During the forty-seven years that passed between these two protests, South Korea transitioned from a military dictatorship to a vibrant democracy with its economy soaring from a labor-intensive exporter to a high-tech global powerhouse. The guarantee of basic labor rights and the respect of human dignity – what Jeon demanded back in the 1970s – may have improved, but not equitably for everyone in the labor market decades later. With the neoliberal restructuring of the economy and concomitant labor law reforms since the 1990s, the labor force has been exposed to an internal stratification and heightened insecurity and precariousness. As the sky protest by Finetek unionists illustrates, Korean workers assert their rights to secure

[1] In a petition letter to President Park Chung-hee, Jeon wrote "our demands include a reduction of working hours from 14 hours to 10 to 12 hours per day; permission to take at least two Sundays off per month; requirement for a professional medical exam; a 50% raise of the daily wage of 70–100 won for our sewing machine assistants (*sidagong*). These are not over-the-bar demands but the minimum request as a human being" (Y. Cho 1991, 300–01).

[2] Finetek closed its factory in Gumi in 2013, opened a new one in Asan in 2016, and closed it again a year later. Workers were laid off without proper compensation.

employment by contesting existing labor laws and resorting to an extreme form of protest.

This chapter defines labor rights as workers' claims to certain entitlements, which workers themselves view as the minimal conditions for their survival and reproduction. Based on this conceptual approach, this chapter chronicles the changing notion of labor rights for Korean workers between the transitional period of the 1980s and the neoliberal decade of the 2000s and identifies novel forms of contention that workers use to press for their rights. The immediate grievances of Korean workers emanate from their drastically different lived experiences in the workplace where job insecurity and precarity have soared compared to previous decades. Yet, insecure employment with diminishing protections is hardly exclusive to Korean workers; it is a common shift found in labor markets in both developed and developing economies around the globe (Standing 2011; Weil 2014). Still, the specific manifestations of neoliberal labor conditions vary depending on local practices and institutions (Rudra 2008). Through their interactions with employers and state authorities who impose specific restrictions on labor rights, workers develop distinctive rights claims and rights-pursuing methods that resonate with the broader working population in the nation.

Because rights are defined and codified in laws, the construction of labor rights claims involves contestation over the making, interpretation, and implementation of labor laws. A noteworthy development in Korea in recent decades is that both the government and corporations are increasingly relying on laws and litigation to deny labor rights and to undermine labor movements. In response, workers assert their rights by contesting the partial interpretation and ineffective enforcement of laws. In this process, workers' central claims converged on "We are workers and we want work" as a way of affirming their worker status and entitlement to basic labor rights and employment security. This implies that the specific modes of labor rights articulation are shaped by interactions among workers, employers, and state institutions.

The following discussion begins with my theoretical approach to explain the making of labor rights, which builds on a constructivist perspective to the working class' rights consciousness (Thompson 1963; Koo 2001) and critical legal theories on the recursivity of laws and rights (Halliday and Carruthers 2007; Liu and Halliday 2009). This is followed by a brief historical account of the construction of labor rights in the 1980s by highlighting the labor conditions in despotic factories during the export-oriented industrialization era, the methods that authoritarian states and firms employed to repress workers' mobilization, the connection built between labor and the pro-democracy movement, and the politics of labor law reforms in the post-democratic transition period. Against this historical background, the third section describes the neoliberal restructuring of the labor market since the late 1990s and its consequences for altering the laboring experiences of Korean workers. Divided between regular and irregular workers, central rights claims have diverged depending on one's location within the labor market. The fourth section focuses on how employers and state authorities use labor laws and litigation as a tool to constrict the rights claims and undermine labor unions. A close examination of the contestation over "worker status recognition" and "lawful labor strike" is presented to illuminate how workers contest the rights discourse through specific rights-pursuing strategies in the 2000s. In the final section, I offer concluding thoughts on the implications of the specific modes of labor rights articulation in Korea.

This chapter builds upon various sources of empirical data that I have collected during my field research in Korea over three summers (2016–18), which varied from four to eight weeks in length. The sources include participatory observation of labor protests, recorded oral histories of labor activists archived at the Korea Democracy Foundation, published memoirs of union leaders, labor-related statistics, and the Korea Labor Institute's public surveys on industrial relations.

9.2 THEORIZING THE CONSTRUCTION OF LABOR RIGHTS

How do workers understand and articulate their rights? This chapter considers workers' conceptions of labor rights to be an integral component of class consciousness or class identity, which is context-specific and expressed in diverse ways. In his classic study *The Making of the English Working Class*, E. P. Thompson moved away from the deterministic approach of traditional Marxist scholars and suggested a concept of class that is formed through an active and relational historical process. He demonstrated that class consciousness is not an essentialist value that is automatically shared by "proletarians of all nations," but premised in the concrete lived experiences of workers in the specific sociohistorical context (1963, 9–12). Scholars investigating labor movements in Asia have advanced a similar constructivist approach to understand specific manifestations of working-class identity.[3] Hagen Koo (2001) demonstrated that class interests are not determined by the actors' position in the economic structure but that they are contingent upon cultural and political processes embedded in the developmental trajectories. He explained how the cultural contempt of manual labor, especially by young female workers, and the systematic exploitation of labor in despotic factory regimes shaped the core demands of Korean workers, which converged on "humane treatment and justice" in the 1970s and the 1980s (H. Koo 2001, 16).

This chapter takes the concrete lived experiences in the workplace as the primary ground from which workers' grievances and rights claims are generated. If grievances are workers' identification of specific problems that outrage them in their working experience (Jasper 1997), they contribute to the development of "rights

---

[3] For Taiwanese labor, see Ming-sho Ho (2014). For Chinese labor, see Ching Kwan Lee (2007), Eli Friedman (2014), and Diana Fu (2017).

consciousness."[4] Rights consciousness is an important component of class identity as it implies that an aggrieved individual or group begins to show increasing awareness of rights and willingness to claim redress on the basis of rights (Li 2010; Lorentzen and Scoggins 2015). In the process of redressing labor grievances, workers implicate their entitlements to certain rights, press for the guarantee of those rights, and protest when those rights are violated. Through this iterated process, workers form a shared class identity centered on a rights discourse.

Rights consciousness is cultivated not only from workers' collective complaints emanating from laboring experiences on the shop floor but also from their interactions with other social actors such as employers and state authorities. To borrow Thompson's language, "class is a social and cultural formation (often finding institutional expression) which cannot be defined abstractly, or in isolation, but only in terms of relationship with other classes" (1963, 357). Among other class actors, corporations and the government have the most direct relationship with labor because they define and regulate production relations and labor laws. Employers rely on diverse methods of managing the labor force to extract productivity and compliance (Hall and Soskice 2001). The state, too, plays a varying role in intervening in the labor market via industrial policy and labor laws. It is through interactions with employers and state institutions that workers articulate and claim certain aspects of labor rights more than others.

In this sense, rights claims are often made and contested around labor laws. Rights, defined as "an imperative, nondiscretionary requirement to protect one's personhood, dignity, and autonomy" (Harel 2005, 191), are inscribed in laws and acknowledged and enforced by relevant institutions. This process necessarily involves conflicts over which rights and whose interests are written in laws and how the rights are interpreted and enforced. Therefore, "law is politics" (Kairys 1982) and lawmaking is reflective of contested perspectives on what the rights entitlements should be for various actors in the society.

Labor laws constitute a particularly conflictual arena because they concern the fundamental axis of class conflict in capitalist democracies. To follow T. H. Marshall's conceptualization of citizenship, labor rights fall under the category of social citizenship, which addresses the inequality of the class system by inserting workers' rights into economic welfare and security (1950). Labor rights prescribe the basic welfare of workers and a fair distribution of wealth and power, while labor laws regulate the employment relationship against the (imagined) pure market logic (Fudge 2007; Collins 2011). The inscription of labor rights into laws involves state intervention into the sphere of market interactions among private actors. Employers whose interests lie in market efficiency and the maximization of capital accumulation would like to see the least intervention by the law and political

---

[4] Snow and Soule (2010, 24) propose that "mobilizing grievances" are sufficiently serious to spur collective action.

institutions. In contrast, workers would stress that labor rights are fundamental rights that possess constitutional force in a liberal political order (Collins 2011). Contestation is inevitable because labor laws represent the subtle (im)balance of the principles of capitalism and those of democratic entitlements.

Critical legal theories highlight this contestation by approaching laws not as the outcome of a consensual agreement but rather a provisional statement reflective of arguments (Tushnet 2005). Recursivity in law is commonly found because there is always a gap between rights written in law and rights in practice. Lawmaking also involves ambiguity and inconsistencies because the interpretation and implementation can be contradictory and disputable (Halliday and Carruthers 2007; Liu and Halliday 2009). Therefore, contestation over rights claims takes place not only in terms of which rights need to be included in the law but also in terms of how those rights are interpreted and enforced in reality. Uncovering the inconsistencies between rights in writing and rights in practice can be a way of asserting workers' rights by challenging state officials and employers to be "prisoners of their own rhetoric" (Scott 1985, 263). Therefore, the process of formulating core claims of labor rights involves political conflict over what constitutional rights (or social citizenship) for workers are and whether the lawful rights are guaranteed and implemented impartially.

Informed by a constructivist approach to the formation of class identity and critical legal theories on the recursivity of rights, the following sections examine how structural conditions in the labor market generate the primary grievances of workers, how these grievances enlighten workers' rights consciousness, and how workers' interactions with employers and state institutions, which revolve around labor laws, shape the core claims of labor rights in the 1980s and the 2000s, respectively. It also compares different forms of collective action that workers take to assert their rights between these two periods.

9.3 THE MAKING OF LABOR RIGHTS AND DEMOCRATIC TRANSITION IN THE 1980S

Despotic factory regimes under the authoritarian developmental state provided the basis of workers' demands for the guarantee of basic labor rights and humane treatment in workplaces in the 1980s. Because the authoritarian state and repressive institutions were at the forefront of depriving labor rights and suppressing workers' mobilization, Korean labor activism during this period was radicalized and labor issues were included in the pro-democracy movement's central agenda, not like women's rights that were rather sidelined (see Chapter 3). Yet, labor rights were framed as basic human dignity that a democratic government should guarantee, not as a radical class issue because of the strong anti-communist ideology that governed the Korean society.

The authoritarian developmental state pursued export-driven industrialization by mobilizing "cheap labor" from rural areas to industrial manufacturing in the

1960s–1980s. Because capital accumulation in export-oriented, labor-intensive manufacturing relies on the squeeze of labor costs, Korean employers relied on labor exploitation such as long hours, long workweeks without proper holidays, low wages, forced overtime work, lack of basic sanitary or safety facilities, and verbal and physical violence on the shop floor. By invoking cultural contempt toward manual labor performed by workers with low levels of education, particularly female workers, corporations justified their treatment of workers like machines, not human beings (H. Koo 2001).

The military regime buttressed this production system with repressive labor laws, security apparatuses, and ideological indoctrination. The autocratic state was keen to control labor to keep labor costs low for the success of labor-intensive export manufacturing as well as to preempt the political mobilization of workers against the regime. Labor laws under Park Chung-hee (1961–79) and Chun Doo-hwan (1980–87) placed severe constraints on independent organizing of industrial workers and their rights of collective action. The Trade Union Act of 1985 and the Labor Dispute Act of 1986 required more than thirty employees sign a labor union registration form to be approved by state agencies (which could reject the registration for a variety of reasons), confined union organizing to the company level to deter industrywide or nationwide organizing, maintained the principle of single unionism to prevent autonomous unions from forming against the existing pro-management union, required permission from state agencies for labor strikes to avert workers' collective action, prohibited third-party involvement in union affairs to preempt solidarity building with other social actors, and empowered district offices to change union leaders or to order union dissolution (Lee and Kang 2013).[5] These measures were intended to preclude the formation of an autonomous labor movement against the state-sponsored Federation of Korean Trade Unions (FKTU), which was placed under the tight control of the authoritarian state. In short, labor laws during this period were not a legal document to protect workers but to restrict them in any possible way.

Furthermore, the military regime deployed the Korean Central Intelligence Agency (KCIA) along with the police to curtail union activism and labor rights. The KCIA assigned hundreds of intelligence agents who specialized in anticommunist missions to supervise union cadres in key industrial sites (Ogle 1990). According to a testimony by a female union leader in 1978, "electing a union leader was not a matter to be dealt by the management but by the KCIA. When our leader was elected, the KCIA began to actively repress" (C. G. Lee 2018). In addition, the

---

[5]   The Trade Union Act disallowed the use of union funds for any political activity and banned anyone who is not a union member, such as laid-off unionists, lawyers, or politicians, from assisting union affairs (Y. C. Kim 1994). The Trade Union Act (*Nodong johapbeop*) and the Labor Dispute Act (*Nodongjaenge-ui jojeongbeop*) were later combined as a single law: *Nodong johap mit nodong gwangye jojongbeop* (Trade Union and Labor Relations Adjustment Act), Act No. 5310 (1997), amended as Act No. 15849 (2018).

authoritarian state mobilized various ideological tools like nationalism, anti-communism, Confucian hierarchy, familism, and military-style disciplining to coerce workers' acquiescence. Korean workers were framed as "industrial warriors" fighting for national economic growth; advocating for labor rights was deemed a pro-North Korean, pro-communist act; employers were domineering fathers and employees were obedient children; and the shop floor was organized and disciplined like a military unit by top-down order and physical violence (S. Cheong 2005; Y. Kim 2005). In the 1970s, factory *Saemaeul* campaigns also sought to institutionalize work discipline and ideological inculcation within the labor force (O. Lee 1990).[6]

Such direct involvement of the state and security apparatuses in industrial relations contributed to Korean workers' understanding of the linkage between inhumane treatment experienced in workplaces and political repression imposed by autocratic forces. Pro-democracy dissident groups also played an important role in the formation of early labor movements (H. Koo 2001). Pro-democracy activists, particularly after the self-immolation of Jeon Tae-il, strived to build an alliance with the labor movement by stressing the connection between "labor liberation" (*nodong haebang*: workers being liberated from exploitation and repression) and the political democratization in Korea.[7] A large number of student activists and religious groups with progressive theological orientations reached out to workers by becoming "disguised workers" and opening night schools in factory towns.[8] Through these interactions, activists intended to raise workers' awareness of and sense of entitlement to labor rights and ultimately to facilitate the development of industrial workers' class consciousness (H. Koo 2001). A female factory worker who began attending one of the dissident-run night schools (*yahak*) in the late 1970s recollected that she began to "open her eyes to the notion of labor rights (*nodongja gwonik*) in the night school classes."[9]

In the 1980s, the primary grievances of Korean workers laboring in despotic factories were expressed in the crude language of "We are not machines, we are

---

[6] The *Saemaeul* (New Village) movement was a massive program that the Park Chung-hee regime pursued to modernize rural areas in the 1970s. With the *Saemaeul* campaign in factories, slogans such as "Workers are our family members" and "Factory work is my work" were posted on the shop floor, while both female and male workers were constantly disciplined through rules unrelated to work, such as hair and outfit regulations, verbal abuse, and military-style beating (Y. Kim 2005, 59–87). Workers were also sent to *Saemaeul* training programs to receive boot-camp-style physical training and education on anti-communism and national security (S. Cheong 2005).

[7] Dissident intellectuals envisioned democratization as a historical project of resurrecting the subjectivity of *minjung* (the common people), the repressed and exploited people under developmental authoritarianism (N. Lee 2007).

[8] Churches of various denominations were involved in the incipient stage of union movements and the Urban Industrial Mission and Young Catholic Workers were most active in reaching out to factory workers (Ogle 1990).

[9] Interview with Bae Ok-byeong. Oral History Archive of the Korea Foundation of Democracy: http://archives.kdemo.or.kr/oral-archives/view/170, listened on March 1, 2018.

humans" and evolved into a rights consciousness that demanded basic respect as a human being in workplaces as well as minimum conditions to survive, such as a subsistence wage and safe working conditions. Furthermore, because managerial despotism in factories was buttressed with labor-rights-restricting laws and outright repression by authoritarian regimes, another important rights claim centered on the freedom of association, that is, the right to form labor unions. Workers perceived the creation of an autonomous labor union as a crucial aspect of labor rights because the state-sponsored FKTU monopolized union representation (B. You 2005). Speaking about her participation in union activities in the 1970s and the 1980s, a female worker recollected that "by joining the [independent] union, I learned about the causes of poverty, about my rights to be treated as an equal human being, about my rights to speak out on the shop floor" (C. G. Lee 2018).

In the summer of 1987, right after the eruption of nationwide pro-democracy protests that successfully pressured the Chun Doo-hwan regime to concede to political liberalization, workers across industrial towns exploded with demands for wage increases, humane treatment, and the right to organize an independent union. During the Great Workers Struggle, about 2.7 million workers (out of a total of 4.6 million industrial workers at the time) across 4,000 unionized and ununionized shop floors participated in a variety of collective actions, such as sit-ins, strikes, rallies, and street demonstrations (H. Cho 1998, 275–76). Such a collective action helped render labor law reforms one of the key agendas of political democratization. Major amendments to labor laws occurred in 1987 and 1989.[10] These revisions improved the freedom of association for workers by relaxing conditions for organizing a labor union, particularly among previously restricted public employees. The amendment eliminated several anti-labor clauses instituted under military dictatorships, such as the prohibition of unions' political activities, the prohibition of third-party involvement in union affairs, and the power of district offices to change union leaders or to order union dissolution (Y. Choi et al. 2000). Included in the 1988 revision was the expansion of the application of the Labor Standards Act to firms employing five or more employees.

Gradually, in the democratic era, Korean workers gained more freedom to form labor unions and access to multiple institutional venues to address their grievances and assert labor rights. Countering the monopoly of the conservative FKTU, the Korean Confederation of Trade Unions (KCTU) was formed in 1995 as a second national labor center and was legally recognized in 1998. The Korea Tripartite Commission (now renamed to Economic and Social Development Commission) was established in 1998 to facilitate tripartite consultations among the representatives of the government, employers, and workers. Finally, the Democratic Labor Party was formed in 2000, signaling the presence of labor in legislative politics in the

---

[10]   Amendments were made to the Labor Standards Act, the Trade Union Act, and the Labor Dispute Act in November 1987 with additional presidential enforcement orders in April 1988.

2000s. This progressive party raised labor and redistribution as important political issues to be addressed in the formal political process.[11]

In summary, the notion of labor rights in the 1980s was centered on "getting the basics right" for workers who were deprived of humane treatment and organizational representation in their workplaces. The common slogans shouted during the Great Workers Struggle included "We are humans, too," "Do not repress our unions," and even "Free hair style" (H. Cho 1998).[12] Workers argued that they were not machines, but humans entitled to basic rights and dignity as well as to the freedom of association to press for their labor rights. This was also a negotiated version of labor rights discourse because speaking directly about "labor" or "class" was extremely constrained under a highly anti-communist ideological environment in South Korea. The language of class (*gyegeup*) was used in underground circles but rarely appeared openly in workers' protests during this period (You 2005).

Workers asserted these rights through collective actions like strikes and sit-ins, by forming an independent union, and bargaining with management to rewrite collective agreements. Because labor repression was imposed by the state and state-authored labor laws, the labor and pro-democracy coalition aimed at labor law revisions to inscribe basic labor rights in legal documents. With political democratization in 1987, Korean workers were able to take the first step of asserting their rights. However, this political opportunity to institutionalize labor rights into social rights of citizenship (Marshall 1950) was short-lived as neoliberal globalization soon restructured the economy and the labor market.

9.4 NEOLIBERAL RESTRUCTURING OF THE LABOR MARKET AND CHANGING LABOR RIGHTS CLAIMS SINCE THE 1990S

Since the 1990s, both the government and corporations have pursued neoliberal globalization of the Korean economy by deregulating capital movements, transforming Korean capital into global capital, and reorganizing the labor market for greater flexibility (see Chapter 5). Labor market restructuring was accelerated in the aftermath of the Asian Financial Crisis (1997–98) as the International Monetary Fund required increased "flexibility" in employment relations as a condition of its bailout package. Labor law amendments in 1997 and 1998 reflected these deregulatory orientations. On the one hand, the revised labor law granted improved collective labor rights by introducing clauses that allow teachers' unions and public employees' unions, political activities by labor unions, and the legal standing of the KCTU

---

[11] Factional strife within the party precipitated its organizational decline and the demise of its political relevance in electoral politics in the 2010s.

[12] "*Urido saramida*" "*Nodongjohap tanap mara*," and "*Dubal jayuhwa*." Workers' request for the freedom of hairstyle reflects the extent to which factories were run like a military unit. Male workers were required to maintain a buzz cut in many manufacturing workplaces. Otherwise, factory managers or guards would forcefully cut workers' hair.

(Y. Choi et al. 2000).[13] However, these pro-labor clauses were an excuse or exchange to introduce relaxed conditions for massive layoffs and precarious employment such as substitute, fixed-term, part-time, and agency workers (Y. Choi et al. 2000).[14] While these legal changes were presented as a tripartite social pack in 1998, rank-and-file members of the KCTU viewed the agreement as a betrayal of the labor cause and voted out the national union's leadership.

Due to a rising stratification and precarity in employment relations, specific laboring experiences and risks that workers face today greatly vary depending on their location in the labor market. As workers are divided by their employment statuses, their immediate grievances diverge, and labor rights claims center on different entitlements in the 2000s.[15] The central concern for full-time workers (regular workers or *jeonggyujik*) is the right to work or employment security against massive layoffs and factory closings. For irregular workers (*bijeonggyujik*), the key issues are the recognition of worker status and conversion into regular employment.

Most workers employed in large corporations with a full-time status are organized into labor unions, and their major concern is job security. In the name of business rationalization, employers easily decide on massive layoffs and plant closures while reorganizing their production and service systems with a highly complex hierarchy of subcontracting and outsourcing. As the revised Labor Standards Act[16] has relaxed conditions for large-scale job cuts, corporations can engage in massive layoffs and force workers into voluntary retirement under the misleading name of "honorable retirement." Because reemployment of laid-off workers (especially if they are middle-aged) is highly unlikely, regular workers campaign to sustain their employment. However, when labor unions protest massive job cuts with militant strikes, the court often rules these strikes as "unlawful" collective action under the amended Trade Union Act[17] of 2001, which removed "massive layoffs" from the lawful reasons for labor strikes.[18] The Act stipulates that labor unions are allowed to go on strike only when conflict arises on issues of collective bargaining, such as wages, working hours, welfare, and unfair labor practices. The court's narrow interpretation of lawful strikes provides the legal basis for corporations to pursue a specific union-busting legal strategy as will be discussed in the following section.

---

[13] Multiple unionism, one of the KCTU's demands, was agreed but its implementation was deferred to 2002.

[14] The amended clause in the Labor Standards Act allows massive layoffs for managerial reasons, including mergers and acquisitions. The specific form of contingent labor was termed "dispatch workers" (*pagyeon geulloja*).

[15] As with the different demands from workers in variant employment statuses, Erin Chung (Chapter 13) also shows how migrants' rights claims are divergent depending on their visa status.

[16] *Geullo gijunbeop*, Act No. 5510 (1998), amended as Act No. 16415 (2019).

[17] *Nodongjohap mit nodonggwangye jojongbeop* (Trade Union and Labor Relations Adjustment Act), Act No. 6456 (2001), amended as Act No. 15849 (2018).

[18] According to an analysis of 408 labor strike case rulings by the Supreme Court between 1990 and 2015, 349 cases (85.5 percent) judged the strike as unlawful, whereas only 59 cases (14.5 percent) saw the strike as lawful (J. Kang 2015).

With frequent instances of massive layoffs and the under-provision of full-time jobs with employment protections, the self-employed have increased to account for one-third of the working people in Korea (Statistics Korea 2020). Those who lose their jobs from corporations are often drawn into the already overcrowded service sector, such as the mom-and-pop stores in neighborhoods. People in one-person businesses are not regarded as "workers," since they are categorized as "self-employed," but they are exposed to low income, high debt, and business insecurity (Y. Lee 2014). Therefore, regular workers who lose their employment in secure jobs claim that "layoff is death" to express their desperate circumstances (Lee and Kim 2017). A union activist who worked in an auto manufacturing company for thirty years attests that the introduction of massive layoffs destroyed the backbone of labor movements by narrowing regular workers' interests to keeping their jobs and wages (B. Lee 2017). This is an indication of the deep chasm between having a decent formal job in a corporation and falling into insecure and irregular work in industrial or service sectors.

In addition to massive layoffs and factory relocations, corporations have increasingly relied on irregular employment by creating a highly complex hierarchy of subcontracting and outsourcing since the late 1990s, when the revised Labor Standards Act relaxed conditions for precarious employment. The Kim Dae-jung government passed the Dispatched Workers Protection Act[19] in 1998 and authorized the use of labor dispatch agencies in thirty-two sectors with the exclusion of manufacturing. Firms across all sectors, regardless of legal restrictions, widely employ workers of subcontracted and outsourced units. Therefore, a labor force in one workplace is not only divided between regular and irregular workers directly employed by the lead corporation (*woncheong*) but also between workers in the lead company and those in subcontracted (*hacheong*) and outsourced (*weju*) firms that further divide their workers with long-term and short-term contracts. For instance, on the assembly line at Hyundai Automobile (where the law prohibits the use of dispatched workers), a full-time worker sets the right-side wheels, while an irregular worker of a subcontracted firm sets the left-side wheels (Hankyoreh 2010). They perform the same labor on the same shop floor under the managerial instruction of Hyundai Automobile, but their different employment statuses separate them regarding their wages, benefits, job security, and other rights claims.

In short, variegated forms of irregular jobs that include fixed-term, part-time, and specially employed workers (dispatched workers, subcontracted independent contractors, and home-based workers) have increased in number to constitute almost half of the Korean labor force since the neoliberal restructuring of the labor market in the 1990s (Y. Kim 2017).[20] The division between regular and irregular workers is

---

[19] *Pagyeon guelloja boho deunge gwanhan beomnyul* (Act on the Protection, etc. of Temporary Agency Workers), Act No. 5512 (1998), amended as Act No. 14790 (2017).

[20] Y. Kim's measure of irregular workers covers the aforementioned categories in addition to long-term part-time and seasonal workers, which the government's labor statistics does not include.

substantial because irregular workers are subject to low wages, job insecurity, discrimination, and lack of legal protections or organizational representation. Irregular workers are paid about 66 percent (12,076 won) of the hourly wage of regular workers (18,212 won) and are covered at a much lower rate than regular workers by social protection programs and other benefits (Ministry of Employment and Labor, Survey Report on Labor Conditions by Employment Types 2016). Furthermore, women and young workers – who disproportionately are irregular workers – are located at the bottom of the labor market hierarchy and exposed to greater work-related insecurities than male workers. This implies that the achievements of the labor movement for "humane treatment" in the early period of democratization were largely concentrated among unionized, full-time, male workers employed in large corporations (see also Chapter 3 on male dominance in Korea's democratization movement).

For irregular workers in Korea, rights claims are centered on worker status recognition and conversion to regular employment, wherein the employer is legally obliged to protect numerous rights. One source for workers to demand the recognition of worker status comes from the so-called in-house subcontractors, a form of indirect employment practiced by many corporations as noted in the case of Hyundai Automobile. Jennifer Chun notes that these indirect employment practices misclassify workers and "place them outside legally circumscribed employer-employee relations and thus outside the boundaries of existing rights and protections afforded to regular workers" (2009, 537). In-house subcontracting enables the lead corporations not only to save labor costs by using "cheap" irregular workers of subcontracted or outsourced units but also to obscure employment relations and conceal which employer is accountable for the provision or violation of labor rights. Prime examples of worker status claiming are the lawsuits brought by irregular workers at Hyundai Automobile and Kia Automobile, who claim that the extended use of in-house subcontractors is illegal and demand recognition of their actual employment relations with the lead company. On paper, these workers are hired by subcontracted firms, but on the shop floor they work side by side with workers of Hyundai or Kia for more than two years, the limit for indirectly contracted workers set by the 2007 Irregular Workers Protection Act.[21]

Another source for the struggle over worker status recognition comes from the misclassification of workers as independent contractors or self-employed. Irregular employment in Korea has a subcategory called "specially employed workers," who include golf game assistants, home study tutors, insurance sales agents, telemarketers, and freight truck drivers. Although their work involves employment

---

[21] The Irregular Workers Protection Act (*Bijeonggyujik bohobeop*) is a customary term that refers to the Fixed-term and Part-time Employees Protection Act (*Giganje mit dansigan geulloja boho deunge gwanhan beomnyul*) and the Dispatch Workers Protection Act (*Pagyeon geulloja boho deunge gwanhan beomnyul*). The litigation that began as early as 2004 is protracted, and even when lower courts uphold the claims of workers, corporations procrastinate with delaying tactics (Sisa News 2018).

relationships with a primary firm, current law denies their status as workers and excludes them from entitlement to labor rights. The aforementioned workers appeal to the court to vindicate their status as workers and claim their entitlements, as defined by labor laws (J. Chun 2013). However, the court denies their worker status, and their trade unions, most representatively the Freight Workers' Solidarity (*Hwamul yeondai*), are classified as extralegal unions for including nonworkers as union members (Labor Today 2011).

Because many irregular workers perform the same labor that regular workers do but with much lower wages, fewer benefits, and conveniently terminable contracts, they often demand their jobs be converted to permanent employment. One example appeared on a banner of the Finetek workers engaging in the sky protest discussed at the beginning of this chapter: "Abolish irregular employment" and "Conversion to regular employment." My participant observation of labor protests in the last several years confirms that employment security and the reduction of irregular jobs are the most repeatedly chanted slogans today. For example, protesting workers hold banners that say, "Layoff is death," "Abolish irregular employment," "Amend vicious labor laws," and "Respect three labor rights."[22]

Compared to the 1980s, Korean workers' rights claims are less homogenous and less political because workers are divided by their employment status in the labor market and face divergent laboring experiences and variegated grievances in the 2000s. The central concern for full-time workers is the right to employment security against massive layoffs and factory closings. For irregular workers, the cardinal claims are the recognition of worker status and the conversion into regular employment.

A 2017 survey of workers concerning industrial relations shows the changing priority of rights claims over the last thirty years (see Table 9.1). The importance of wages and working conditions diminished from 90.3 percent in 1989 to 47.4 percent in 2017. The decline of this category's importance between 2007 and 2017 is modest, which seems to be associated with the persistent presence of irregular workers and their dire material circumstances. The centrality of employment security among union activists, about which the question first appeared in the 2007 survey, rose from 13.6 percent in 2007 to 25.9 percent ten years later. This change reflects both regular workers' fear of massive layoffs and irregular workers' plea to escape chronic insecurity.

9.5 NEW METHODS OF LABOR REPRESSION AND NEW FORMS OF ASSERTING LABOR RIGHTS IN THE 2000S

Amendments to labor laws since the late 1990s have not only provided the legal basis for corporations to cut jobs and employ temporary labor at their convenience but also created opportunities to invent new methods of union busting. While the

---

[22] Three labor rights (*Nodong samgwon*) include the right to labor unions, the right to collective bargaining, and the right to collective action.

TABLE 9.1 *Survey on Industrial Relations: 1989, 2007, and 2017*

What is the central concern of labor unions?	1989	2007	2017
Wages and working conditions	90.3	59.5	47.4
Employment security	–	13.6	25.9
Protection of the disadvantaged	36.6	9.7	11.4
Institutional reform*		3.8	6.1

Note: The sample size is about 2,000, but the survey questions are not consistent across the three surveys. *In the 1989 survey, the answer choice was "Democratization of society," which was reframed as "Institutional reform" in the surveys conducted in 2007 and 2017.
Source: Korea Labor Institute, National Survey on Industrial Relations, 1989, 2007, and 2017. Retrieved from Korean Labor Institute www.kli.re.kr/kli/rsrchReprtView.do?key=14&pblctListNo=5346&schRsrchRealmNo=2 (accessed March 1, 2018). Cheong 2017 for the 2017 analysis.

authoritarian state was the central force of labor repression in the 1980s, as exemplified by the police's violent crackdown of labor strikes and the systematic involvement of KCIA agents in labor affairs, damage compensation litigation and the deployment of commercial security agents against labor unions have become a core strategy for employers in the 2000s. The introduction of multiple unionism and the removal of "massive layoffs" from the lawful reasons for labor strikes in the Trade Union Act opened ways for corporations to pursue these strategies.[23]

In 2003, the Korean Employers' Federation distributed "Employers' guidelines for labor strikes" to its member companies and advised for the active use of civil and criminal lawsuits against union activists (S. Kang 2007). Companies having independent labor unions began to contract industrial relations specialists, that is, public labor attorneys working with commercial security firms, to manage industrial relations and to design and execute plans for union destruction.[24] Taking advantage of the multiple union clause in the Trade Union Act, this strategy entails instigating violence and divisions within independent labor unions, setting up second pro-management unions, and deploying private security agents (*yongyeok pongnyeok*) to violently crackdown on workers' collective action. The number of both private security firms and public labor attorneys increased in the 2000s and a majority of them work on the side of employers (Hankyoreh 21 2012).[25] Ongoing investigations

[23] After years of a grace period, the multiple union clause in the Trade Union Act (*Nodong johapbeop*) went into effect in 2011, and employers and labor consulting firms took advantage of these legal clauses to destroy independent labor unions.

[24] There is also a historical precedent of inserting *gusadae* (battalion that saves the company, literally) into labor disputes in the 1980s and 1990s.

[25] The number of private security firms increased from 1,929 in 2000 to 5,337 in 2016 and the size of employment grew from 97,117 to 147,049 during the same period. The number of private security firms can be found at Korean National Police Agency, www.data.go.kr/dataset/3072328/fileData.do (accessed March 3, 2018).

on Hyundai Automobile and Samsung Electronics reveal that the central management units of these global corporations worked closely with the Korean Employers' Federation and industrial relations consultants to orchestrate and fund union destruction plans in their firms and subsidiaries (H. Ryu 2019).

Another routine strategy that employers and the government have adopted for union repression in recent years is damage compensation litigation (Y. Lee 2019). Because revisions to the Trade Union Act in 2001 reduced the lawful reasons for labor strikes, many episodes of workers' collective action are ruled unlawful, opening the way for criminal and civil litigation against labor unions. The Korean Criminal Act allows for heavy fines on unionists who engage in activities that "obstruct business," and both the government (Ministry of Justice) and corporations sue labor unions to compensate for the loss of revenue and other damages arising from work stoppage.[26] Since the early 2000s, damage compensation lawsuits that impose significant costs on labor unions and individual workers have been a common strategy of deterring labor rights claims, particularly targeting labor unions affiliated with the progressive KCTU. The court often upholds the claims made by corporations by presenting a narrow interpretation of lawful strikes even when the causes of the strike are multiple and not limited to massive layoffs. When labor strikes are ruled unlawful, firms proceed with lawsuits to claim damages. The amount of damage compensation filed against labor unions rose fivefold between 2002 and 2017 (from 34.5 billion won or USD30 million to 186.7 billion won or USD163 million), targeting thirty-nine unions in 2002 and sixty-five unions in 2017 (Sonjapko 2017). These unions form the core members of the Metal Unions Federation, which buttresses the KCTU. The potential threat of or actual litigation for damage compensation deters the exercise of workers' rights to collective action.

Moreover, in adjudicating lawsuits filed against labor, the court rules on the side of corporations more often than on the side of workers. According to a study of labor-related legal cases, there were 833 cases brought to the court between 1990 and 2015, and about 80 percent of these cases were resolved in favor of employers (J. Kang 2015; Kyunghyang 2015). Workers who undergo these legal procedures view juridical institutions (the law, employers' litigation, the prosecutors, and the court) to harbor an anti-labor bias and thus unlikely to provide a fair opportunity to redress violations of labor rights.

Under these economic and political circumstances, Korean workers' rights claiming methods have developed two distinctive features. First, workers' collective action tends to last for a long time without tangible outcomes. *Janggi tujaeng saeopjang* (long-term protest workplaces) emerged as a term to describe how workers' protests

---

[26] The "Public Security" team within the Prosecutors' Office is in charge of labor-related investigations and is known for over-applying the obstruction of business clause to union activists involved in labor strikes.

last for years and sometimes over a decade. Labor activists occupy the protest site for a prolonged period or rotate from site to site, engaging in multiple protest methods. Although workers' grievances are generated from their specific workplaces, workers move to politically symbolic sites for labor protest because they find it impossible to resolve the grievances at the local level or through formal channels. Many banners, camp-in tents, and protest-art structures observed in major locations in Seoul represent these long-term labor struggles, and these sites show slogans such as "Dismissal is murder," "Withdraw the damage compensation lawsuit," and "Let's live together."[27]

Another noteworthy development in recent labor contention is the protesters' reliance on extreme forms of resistance. Workers become easily deprived of access to their workplaces where they can stage a collective protest and thus have to look for alternative venues and methods. With plant closures and the deployment of commercial security forces to factory premises, regular workers are denied entry to the shop floor. For irregular workers, their status as dispatched workers or the contingent termination of their contract precludes the possibility of resorting to labor strikes in their workplaces (D. Cho 2012). Even when traditional forms of collective actions like disruptions of assembly lines or mass rallies are feasible, they often fail to produce meaningful results as employers respond with the aforementioned anti-labor strategies. Such a tilted terrain forces workers to resort to extreme repertoires, including self-inflicted and lonely tactics like hunger strikes, hair shaving, single-person protests, camp-in protests, and long marches of *samboilbae* (the three-steps-and-one-bow procession). Particularly distinctive is the rise of both the sky protest and protest suicides by workers in their resistance against labor repression in the 2000s.

Sky protest, as exemplified by the Finetek workers noted earlier in this chapter, has become a representative form of contentious action to assert labor rights, and its frequency has increased since the beginning of the 2000s. Between 1990 and 1999, there were only nine cases of sky protest, but this risky form of resistance soared to over 100 cases in the 2000s (Y. Lee 2015). Labor activists in most of the aforementioned long-term protest locations have chosen this method of protest as their last resort. Workers occupy a variety of high structures such as advertisement towers and power plant chimneys to gain attention to their acute grievances after other modes of protest have been exhausted. Sky protest symbolizes the protesters' desperation, determination, and self-sacrifice because they are choosing self-confinement in a highly unsafe place. Most of the sky protesters testify that they chose this method as the last resort at least to make their desperate circumstances known to a wider public (Kyunghyang 2013).

---

[27] They include unions of KTX women attendants, Dongyang Cement, Sejong Hotel, Asahi Irregular Workers, Cort-Cortech, Hydis, and HitecRCD. The slogans in Korean are as follows: "*Haegoneun sarinida*," "*Sonbaesosong cheolhoe*," and "*Hamkke salja*." See Byeon (2016).

One of the most extreme methods of labor resistance in Korea today is workers' ending their lives in defiance and frustration of labor repression. Like the rise of sky protests, the number of protest suicides committed by industrial workers increased in the 2000s (M. Im 2017). What lies behind the suicides is not only labor activists' frustration over the failed cause but also the extreme pressure resulting from damage compensation lawsuits, a targeted anti-labor tactic used by employers as described earlier. Several union activists mentioned unbearable financial burdens coming from damage compensation litigation in their suicide notes. Bae Dal-ho at Doosan Heavy Industry in 2003, Choi Kang-seo at Hanjin Heavy Industry in 2012, Bae Jae-hyeong at Hydis Electronics in 2015, and Han Gwang-ho at Yooseong (a supplier for Hyundai Automobile) in 2016, all committed suicide, leaving notes that described the brutality of the financial pressure caused by damage compensation lawsuits (J. Kim 2016).

The struggle of Ssangyong Motor workers that began with a labor strike against massive layoffs in 2009 is a prime example of a protracted protest workplace that involved all imaginable extreme tactics. The strike that lasted for about two months in 2009 was quelled by the brutal violence of a special weapons and tactics force and commercial security agents. This was followed by the imprisonment of twenty-two unionists and damage compensation lawsuits of 17 billion won or USD155 million (Y. Lee 2015). Lee Chang-geun describes his traumatic experiences in the 2009 strike at Ssangyong Automobile as "unfathomable pain becoming a collective memory" (Lee and Kim 2017, 157). In the aftermath of the strike, thirty individuals (twenty-seven Ssangyong workers and three spouses) lost their lives due to mental and physical stress caused by the extreme violence experienced during the labor strike, the financial burden of job loss and damage compensation litigation, and frustration over no rectification (S. Kim 2017). Among the thirty deaths, nine were by suicide. Union leaders went on hunger strikes, camp-in protests, *samboilbae* marches, and sky protests (for 7 months in 2012–13 and for 3.5 months in 2014–15), demanding the agreed reinstatement of workers who were placed on unpaid leave for almost ten years.[28]

Experiencing a highly stratified labor market, internal divisions, misclassification as nonworkers, job loss, and insecurity, Korean workers in the 2000s saw the right to employment and job security as the most important labor rights. Because numerous legal mechanisms are used to undermine labor rights, Korean workers invoke inconsistencies in labor laws (such as misclassification) or contend anti-labor clauses and pro-employer interpretations (such as the restriction on labor strikes and compensation litigation). In addition to their risky status in employment relations, workers encounter corporations and the government that

---

[28] In the summer of 2018, when another laid-off worker of Ssangyong committed suicide and reignited public attention to this protracted labor contention, the president of the tripartite commission persuaded Ssangyong management and labor unions to come to an agreement and reinstate all the remaining dismissed workers.

undermine labor rights through the means of litigation and the deployment of commercial security forces. Therefore, workers' rights-pursuing methods take more extreme forms with protracted longevity compared to their collective action in previous decades.

9.6 CONCLUSION

This chapter examined the changing notion of labor rights for Korean workers between the transitional period of the 1980s and the 2000s and identified novel forms of contention that workers use to press for their rights. In the 1980s, the primary grievances of Korean workers laboring in despotic factories were expressed in the existential language of "We are not machines, we are humans" and evolved into rights consciousness that demanded respect as human beings, a subsistence wage, and safe working conditions. Furthermore, because managerial despotism in factories was buttressed by rights-restricting laws and outright repression by authoritarian regimes, core rights claims centering on the freedom of association, that is, the right to form autonomous labor unions, resonated with the broader pro-democracy movement.

The neoliberal restructuring of the labor market since the late 1990s altered the laboring experiences of Korean workers by creating internal stratifications and employment insecurity. Divided by their employment statuses in the labor market and facing divergent laboring experiences, full-time workers emphasize their right to work or employment security against massive layoffs and plant closures, while irregular workers assert their worker status recognition and conversion into regular employment. Because corporations and the government increasingly rely on laws and litigation to restrict labor rights and undermine labor movements, workers are pessimistic about the redressability of their rights through formal institutions and instead pursue extreme forms of contention that are risky, self-tormenting, and protracted.

This chapter has highlighted how workers' rights claims are formed from their laboring experiences and through their interaction with employers and state institutions. Labor rights and labor laws are one of the most contested fields in capitalist democracies as they reflect the conflicting interests of profit-maximizing corporations and social-citizenship-demanding workers. For Korean workers, the democratic political opportunity to institutionalize social citizenship was brief and was soon replaced by a neoliberal shift that emboldened the power of corporations. Labor laws have been revised and routinely interpreted in favor of employers. As a result, corporations are able to reshape the labor market, exercise dominant control in employment relations, and invent new litigation methods to restrict workers' rights. In reaction, workers contest the contradictions of labor laws that deny or obscure the status of workers and that severely restrict workers' rights to collective action.

The denial of labor rights and union repression by corporations and state institutions were most pronounced under the conservative governments of Lee Myung-bak and Park Geun-hye (2008–17). The newly inaugurated Moon Jae-in government took several measures to address notable labor issues, such as the conversion of irregular workers into regular employment in the Seoul-Incheon International Airport in 2017, the reinstatement of female irregular workers who were dismissed from the Korea Train eXpress back in 2006, and the tripartite-commission-mediated agreement to reemploy Ssangyong's dismissed workers (G. Noh 2019). These are positive examples that show how government intervention can uphold workers' rights and bring a closure to long, protracted labor struggles in South Korea. Yet, the central government's interventions in industrial relations are ad hoc in nature and will not be a full answer to rights claims of Korean workers. Unless labor laws are amended and enforced to provide a substantive guarantee of basic labor rights as well as social rights, workers' contention may not subside even under the most liberal government in Korea. Asserting labor rights is and will be the most contested political action in polities where capitalist principles collide with democratic claims.

REFERENCES

Byeon, Baek-seon. 2016. "Long-term protest workplaces." *Labor and the World,* June 22, 2016. http://worknworld.kctu.org/ (accessed March 3, 2018).

Cheong, Heung-jun. 2017. "Nosagwangye gungminuisik josa" [Opinion survey of labor relations]. *Labor Review* (November): 47–60.

Cheong, Seung-kuk. 2005. "Resistance at the shop-floor in automobile manufacturing in the 1970s." In *1960-70nyeondae Nodongjaui jageopjang kyeongheomgwa saenghwal segye* [Workers' shop-floor experience and everyday life in automobile manufacturing in the 1960s and 1970s], edited by Gui-ok Kim, 127–57. Seoul: Hanwool.

Cho, Don-moon. 2012. *Bijeonggyujik juche hyeongseonggwa jeollyakjeok seontaek* [The formation of irregular worker subjectivity and strategic choice]. Seoul: Maeil nodong sinmun.

Cho, Hee-yeon. 1998. *Hanguk minjujuuiwa sahoe undong* [Democracy and social movements in Korea]. Seoul: Dangdae.

Cho, Yeong-rae. 1991. *Jeon Tae-il pyeongjeon* [A Single Spark]. Seoul: Dolbegae.

Choi, Young-ki, Kwang-seok Jeon, Cheol-soo Lee, and Beom-sang Yoo. 2000. *Hangugui nodongbeop gaejeonggwa nosa gwangye* [Labor law reform and Industrial relations in Korea]. Seoul: Korea Labor Institute.

Chun, Jennifer. 2013. "The struggles of irregularly employed workers in South Korea, 1999–2012," University of California-Los Angeles Institute for Research on Labor and Employment working paper, https://irle.ucla.edu/old/research/documents/Korea.pdf (accessed October 1, 2018).

———. 2009. "Legal liminality: the gender and labour politics of organising South Korea's irregular workforce." *Third World Quarterly* 30 (3): 535–50.

Collins, Hugh. 2011. "Theories of rights as justifications for labour law." In *The Idea of Labour Law*, edited by Guy Davidov and Brian Langille, 137–55. Cambridge: Oxford University Press.

Friedman, Eli. 2014. *Insurgency Trap: Labor Politics in Postsocialist China*. Ithaca: ILR Press.

Fu, Diana. 2017. *Mobilizing without the Masses: Control and Contention in China.* Cambridge: Cambridge University Press.

Fudge, Judy. 2007. "The new discourse of labor rights." *Comparative Labor Law and Policy Journal* 29 (1): 30–66.

Hall, Peter A., and David Soskice, eds. 2001. *Varieties of Capitalism: The Institutional Foundations of Comparative Advantage.* Oxford: Oxford University Press.

Halliday, Terence C., and Bruce G. Carruthers. 2007. "The recursivity of law." *American Journal of Sociology* 112 (4): 1135–202.

Hankyoreh 21. 2012. "Nojo eotteoke eopsaedeurilkkayot?" [How should I remove the labor union?]. October 8, 2012. http://h21.hani.co.kr/arti/society/society_general/33050.html.

Hankyoreh Sinmun. 2010. "Hyeondaecha bunsin nodongja" [Self-immolated Hyundai Auto worker]. November 23, 2010. www.hani.co.kr/arti/society/labor/450157.html.

Harel, Alon. 2005. "Theories of rights." In *Philosophy of Law and Legal Theory*, edited by Martin Golding and William Edmundson, 191–206. Hoboken: Blackwell Publishing.

Ho, Ming-sho. 2014. *Working Class Formation in Taiwan: Fractured Solidarity in State-Owned Enterprises, 1945–2012.* London: Palgrave Macmillan.

Im, Miri. 2017. *Yeolsa: bunnowa seulpeumui jeongchi* [Martyrs: the politics of wrath and sorrow]. Seoul: Owolui bom.

Jasper, James M. 1997. *The Art of Moral Protest.* Chicago: Chicago University Press.

Kairys, David. 1982. *The Politics of Law.* New York: Pantheon.

Kang, Jin-ku. 2015. "Nodongja urineun nodongbeop simpandeul" [Labor case rulings that make workers sob]. *Kyunghyang Sinmun*, July 5, 2015. http://news.khan.co.kr/kh_news/khan_art_view.html?art_id=201507052231485.

Kang, Seong-jun. 2007. "Recent cases of criminal and civil litigation against labor," unpublished paper (on file with the author).

Kim, Jibang. 2016. "Paeop sonbaeso" [Damage compensation lawsuits against labor strikes]. *Kukmin Ilbo*, October 27, 2016. http://news.kmib.co.kr/article/view.asp?arcid=0923634068.

Kim, Seung-seop. 2017. *Apeumi giri doeryeomyeon* [If pain is to be a path]. Seoul: Dongasia.

Kim, Yeong-su. 2005. *1960-70nyeondae Hanguk cheoldo nodongjadeurui nodong hyeonjanggwa nodong johap* [The shop-floor and labor unions of Korean rail workers in the 1960s and 1970s]. Seoul: Yeoksamunhwa yeonguso.

Kim, Yong Cheol. 1994. "State and Labor in South Korea: Coalition Analysis." Doctoral dissertation. Ohio State University.

Kim, Yoo-seon. 2017. "Bijeonggyujik nodongja gyumowa siltae" [The size and reality of irregular workers]. KLSI Issue Paper. www.klsi.org (accessed August 1, 2017).

Koo, Hagen. 2001. *Korean Workers: The Culture and Politics of Class Formation.* Ithaca: Cornell University Press.

Kyunghyang Sinmun. 2013. "Cheoltapeseo majihaneun nodongjeol" [Greeting the Labor Day on a pylon]. April 17, 2013. http://news.khan.co.kr/kh_news/khan_art_view.html?artid=201304302233465&code=940702.

2015. "Nodongbeop pankyeole nodongjaneun eopeotta" [No labor in labor court cases]. July 7, 2015. http://news.khan.co.kr/kh_news/khan_art_view.html?art_id=201507052232415.

Labor Statistics. http://laborstat.molab.go.kr/.

Labor Today. 2011. "Nojoseolip sinko" [Labor union registration submission]. November 23, 2011. www.labortoday.co.kr/news/articleView.html?idxno=107779.

Lee, Beom-yeon. 2017. *Wijangchwieopjaeseo neulgeun nodongjaro eoeon 30-nyeon* [Thirty years from a disguised worker to an old worker]. Seoul: Redian.

Lee, Chang-geun, and Hyeon-jin Kim. 2017. *Urineun gal gosi eopda* [We have nowhere to go]. Seoul: Alma.

Lee, Ching Kwan. 2007. *Against the Law: Labor Protests in China's Rustbelt and Sunbelt*. Los Angeles: University of California Press.

Lee, Chong-gak. 2018. "Interview with the union leader of Dongil bangjik in 1978." *Tongil News*, February 21, 2018. http://m.tongilnews.com/news/articleView.html?idx no=123850.

Lee, Kwang-tak, and Hyeon-ju Kang. 2013. *Nodongbeop jejeong 60-nyeoneui pyonggawa kwaje* [Sixty years of labor law: assessment and tasks]. FKTU report.

Lee, Namhee. 2007. *The Making of Minjung: Democracy and the Politics of Representation in South Korea*. Ithaca: Cornell University Press.

Lee, Ok-ji. 1990. "Labor Control and Workers' Resistance in Korean Textile Industry: 1945–1985." Doctoral dissertation. University of Wisconsin.

Lee, Yoonkyung. 2019. "Neo-Liberal methods of labour repression: Privatised violence and dispossessive litigation in Korea." *Journal of Contemporary Asia* 51 (1): 20–37.

———. 2015. "Sky protest: New forms of labor resistance in neoliberal Korea." *Journal of Contemporary Asia* 45 (3): 443–64.

———. 2014. "Labor after neoliberalism: The birth of the insecure class in Korea." *Globalizations* 11 (4): 1–19.

Li, Lianjiang. 2010. "Rights consciousness and rules consciousness in contemporary China." *The China Journal* 64: 47–68.

Liu, Sida, and Terence C. Halliday. 2009. "Recursivity in legal change." *Law and Social Inquiry* 34 (4): 911–50.

Lorentzen, Peter, and Suzanne Scoggins. 2015. "Understanding China's rising rights consciousness." *The China Quarterly* 223: 638–57.

Marshall, T. H. 1950. *Citizenship and Social Class*. Cambridge: Cambridge University Press.

Noh, Gwan-pyo. 2019. "Mun Jae-in jeongbu 1gi nodong jeongchaek pyeonggga" [Evaluating labor policy during the first term of the Moon Jae-in government]. KLSI Issue Paper 116–15: 1–18.

Ogle, George E. 1990. *South Korea: Dissent within the Economic Miracle*. Washington, DC: Zed Books.

Rudra, Nita. 2008. *Globalization and the Race to the Bottom in Developing Countries*. Cambridge: Cambridge University Press.

Ryu, Han-seung. 2019. *Hangugui nojo pagoe* [Labor union destruction in Korea]. Seoul: NPO.

Scott, James. 1985. *Weapons of the Weak*. New Haven: Yale University Press.

Sisa News. 2018. "Hyeondaecha beopwoneui pankyeoldaero" [Hyundai Automobile needs to abide by court rulings]. January 16, 2018. www.sisa-news.com/news/article.html? no=111217.

Snow, David A., and Sara A. Soule. 2010. *A Primer on Social Movements*. New York: W. W. Norton.

Sonjapko. 2017. "The 2017 Report on damage compensation seizure and labor repression cases." unpublished report (on file with the author).

Standing, Guy. 2011. *The Precariat: The New Dangerous Class*. New York: Bloomsbury USA.

Statistics Korea. 2020. "Economically Active Population Survey." http://kostat.go.kr/portal/eng/pressReleases/1/index.board?bmode=read&aSeq=381095.

Thompson. E. P. 1963. *The Making of the English Working Class*. London: Penguin Books.

Tushnet, Mark. 2005. "Critical legal theory." In *Philosophy of Law and Legal Theory*, edited by Martin Golding and William Edmundson, 80–89. Oxford: Blackwell Publishing.

Weil, David. 2014. *The Fissured Workplace*. Cambridge: Harvard University Press.

You, Beom-sang. 2005. *Hangugui nodong undong inyeom* [Ideologies on the Korean labor movement]. Seoul: Korea Labor Institute.

From Invisible Beneficiaries to Rights Bearers

How the Disability Rights Movement Changed the Law and Korean Society

JaeWon Kim[1]

10.1 INTRODUCTION

Leaving a five-page letter addressed to the mayor of Seoul, a thirty-four-year old Korean man using a wheelchair committed suicide in 1984. In the letter, he described how difficult it was for a wheelchair user to commute in the capital city of South Korea. He lamented that most restaurants and dining facilities in the city were not accessible for a person like him, and he particularly urged the city government to build barrier-free sidewalks and ramps. Major newspapers informed readers nationwide of his suicide note (Han 1984), and this tragic incident made the public aware of the hardships that wheelchair users faced every day. Predictably, the public soon forgot this problem, but the incident awakened some student activists to disability-related issues. Although not so visible at the time, the college students who mobilized to rectify the problem later became leading figures of the national coalition for the "right to mobility" (*idonggwon*) campaign in the 2000s (D. H. Kim 2007, 39).

Despite increased public awareness and remedial measures by the government, the right to move in the modern capital city remained elusive for people with disabilities at the turn of the millennium. In 2001, another tragic accident happened at a subway station in Seoul. The station's wheelchair lift malfunctioned, causing a woman to fall to her death and leaving her accompanying husband seriously wounded. It was not the first time. A similar accident had happened at another station two years earlier (You 2005, 18). The 2001 incident, however, triggered rights-centered mobilization by and for people with disabilities that achieved major legislative changes regarding accessible public transportation and accelerated the parallel movement for nondiscrimination protections for people with disabilities. For example, the Solidarity for the Right to Mobility (*Idonggwon yeondae*) formed after the fatalities in the subway and initiated a nationwide campaign to collect

[1]   I would like to thank the *Journal of Korean Law* for permission to reprint my article, "From Invisible Beneficiaries to Independent Rights-Holders," 19, no. 2 (August 2020). It has been slightly modified for this volume.

1 million signatures, making the right to mobility a visible public issue. The Solidarity also took the bold action of occupying subway stations, with mobility impaired members chaining themselves to the tracks and stairways (W. Y. Kim 2010, 213). By 2002, the Solidarity was able to secure the Seoul mayor's promise that all subway stations would be equipped with elevators. Since merely relying on the words of a politician would not guarantee permanent change, the Solidarity allied with the left-wing Democratic Labor Party to introduce a bill regarding accessible public transportation. Such efforts culminated in the enactment of a new law in 2005: the Act on the Promotion of Transportation Convenience of Mobility Disadvantaged Persons (W. Y. Kim 2010, 213).[2]

This chapter charts how waves of activism and legal reform in Korea transformed societal and governmental perceptions of disability to increasingly recognize and protect the rights of persons with disabilities. Intertwined struggles by disabilities groups, civic organizations, and lawyers raised public awareness of disability rights and pushed the National Assembly to enact or amend laws that significantly affected the lives of people with disabilities. This chapter traces rights-based mobilization leading to the Disability Discrimination Act (DDA) of 2007, as well as activism concerning rights to mobility and special education. While these legal reforms have enabled rights claiming by people with disabilities to an unprecedented degree in Korea, they remain targets of activism that aim to further develop and defend those rights and catalyze social changes that make those rights real for persons with disabilities.

These collective efforts to raise public awareness of disability rights and achieve legislation for disability rights helped make the invisible visible (see also Chapter 12). Persons with disabilities in Korea had long been confined in private homes or institutions. They had been viewed not as individual subjects holding civil liberties and fundamental rights, but rather as objects of pity to be cared for by family members or society. The prevailing public perception of and attitude toward people with disabilities reflected the charity or medical model, which understands a person with disabilities as a vulnerable "other" who needs caretaking and protection from family or society. Since persons with disabilities were not considered independent members of society, some form of paternalistic intervention by society to these "deviant members" was justified (Jackson 2018, 3). Meanwhile, the medical model of disability contrasts the deviant or deficient state of disabled persons with a healthy state of nondisabled persons. "Central tenets of the medical model of disability are that a person's 'impairment' can be diagnosed, cured, or at least rehabilitated, by modern medicine and/or medical technology" (Jackson 2018, 3). The model thus calls for paternalistic intervention by all-knowing medical professionals. Paternalism is common to both models (see also Lacy 2003). When introducing disability

---

[2] *Gyotong yakjaui idong pyeonui jeungjinbeop* ("Transportation Convenience Act"), Act No. 7382 (2005).

discrimination legislation in Canada, Cliona Kimber pointed out the persistent problem of paternalism:

> People with disabilities are also treated with a numbing paternalism. Little is expected of them, so that little is offered in the way of education, training, and opportunities. Even the smallest achievement is treated as a major accomplishment, in a manner offensive to the disabled person involved. Added to this is a feeling of guilt on the part of the able-bodied, that those with disabilities are suffering while the able-bodied person is not. (Kimber 1993, 166)

This problem of paternalism applies equally to Korea, if not more so. By demonstrating their existence in society, people with disabilities demanded not only fair treatment but also a fundamental shift of perspective toward the social and human rights model. The social model affirms that "disability arises from barriers within 'an oppressive and discriminating society' rather than [from] impairment per se. This shifts the onus of response away from the individual (to be cured) to society (to dismantle barriers that construct disability)" (Jackson 2018, 5). The 2006 UN Convention on the Rights of Persons with Disabilities (CRPD) took a step further by articulating a human rights model.[3] It "not only builds on the premise [of the social model] that disability is a social construct, but it also values impairment as part of human diversity and human dignity" and embraces civil and political, as well as social and economic, rights for all persons, regardless of their health or body status (Degener 2016, 43, 54).

The fundamental shift in approach to disabilities in Korea was manifest in the enactment of the DDA in 2007.[4] As Korea's first comprehensive legislation prohibiting discrimination was based on disabilities, this law incorporated the social and human rights models of disability. The DDA aimed not only to prevent discrimination but also to empower persons with disabilities as rights-bearing subjects who can enjoy the same liberties and entitlements as other abled people. Since the new legislation became effective in 2008, Korean disability communities and advocacy groups have actively utilized the law both in and out of the courtrooms. Also, well over half of all complaints at the National Human Rights Commission in recent years are related to disability (Jung 2008). The position and attitude of the judiciary gradually changed, too. Courts are now more responsive to disability rights claims and have even published the "Guidelines on Judicial Assistance for People with Disabilities" in 2013 to enhance access to justice.[5]

This chapter traces the fundamental shift from the charity/medical models to the social/human rights models of disabilities in the areas of education, licensing,

---

[3]   UN GA Doc. A/RES/61/106 (December 13, 2006) became effective May 2008.

[4]   *Jangaeinchabyeolgeumji mit gwolliguje deunge gwanhan beomnyul* (Act on the Prohibition of Discrimination against Persons with Disabilities, Remedy against Infringement of Their Rights, and so on or "Disability Discrimination Act"), Act No. 8341 (2007), amended as Act No. 16740 (2019).

[5]   The Office of Court Administration, Publication No. 32–9740029000587-01 (2013).

mobility, independent living, and employment (see also You and Hwang 2018). Activism by Korean disability communities, civic organizations, and lawyers helped raise public awareness and obtain better legal rights and claims-making options for people with disabilities. This chapter first surveys early historical incidents and activism before the DDA's enactment, and then it analyzes the major disability movements for the right to mobility and special education. It also discusses the influence of the Americans with Disabilities Act (ADA) and the CRPD on the enactment of Korean disability-related laws. The chapter then examines the out-comes of such movements, including prominently the DDA's enactment and its implications for judicial enforcement and remedies. The chapter concludes by pointing out the shortcomings of Korean disability-related legislation and suggests reform measures for a more inclusive and integrated Korean society.

10.2 EARLY RIGHTS CLAIMING

Activism and public discourses related to disabilities can be divided into two distinct eras in modern Korea: before and after the 2007 DDA enactment that marked a paradigm shift to the social/human rights models of disability. However, rights claiming and activism by people with disabilities remained sporadic and isolated until Korea's democratization in the late 1980s. During the centuries before the establishment of the Republic of Korea in 1948, kings and government officials are documented as granting people with disabilities special treatment out of sympathy. For example, people with disabilities were exempted from taxation and involuntary servitude. Those who mistreated or abused people with disabilities were also more severely punished (C. G. Jeong 2011, 426–27). Such special treatment, however, did not stem from any legal basis or recognition of the equal rights of people with disabilities.

As in many other countries, the first modern legislation for people with disabilities in South Korea was a consequence of warfare. Immediately after the outbreak of the Korean War in 1950, a law was passed to provide medical and financial support, as well as vocational training, for wounded soldiers and veterans. A similar law for injured police officers was enacted the following year (C. Y. Kim 2009, 51). Korean society, however, had to wait three decades to have legislation for people with disabilities who were neither military nor police personnel. In 1981, the Welfare Act for Mentally and Physically Disabled Persons was passed, and it was later renamed the Welfare Act for Persons with Disabilities in 1989.[6]

Regarding disability-related rights claiming and public discourse about rights, one can find a few isolated incidents before 2000. Early activism focused on the right to education, starting in the 1960s. At that time, almost all highly competi-tive or prestigious secondary schools required applicants to take a physical test,

---

[6] *Simsin jangaein bokjibeop*, Act No. 3452 (1981); renamed *Jangaein bokjibeop*, Act No. 4179 (1989).

which left applicants with physical disabilities unable to gain admission to such schools. Since there was no provision of reasonable accommodations for applicants with mental or learning disabilities, the intellectual aptitude test was an additional hurdle. In 1967, when a bright student was denied admission to Busan Junior High School just because of his physical disability, the families of students with disabilities and special education teachers mobilized to protest. The Korean Association of Special Education launched a campaign to change the physical test requirement for students with disabilities. Campaigners collected signatures from citizens nationwide. Reluctantly responding to the campaign, the Minister of Education promised that the government would provide an exclusive admission track for students with polio. Due to persuasive appeals and criticism, the Ministry of Education took the more permanent step of exempting junior and high school applicants with disabilities from the physical test in 1972 (Hong 2016, 388).

However, discriminatory practices remained within college admissions processes. In the 1970s, several students with strong academic records were denied entrance to private and state universities, including Seoul National University. After being denied admission to a major private university, one student with disabilities, who had an exceptionally high score on the entrance examination, filed a lawsuit against the university. Judicial victory in 1982 resulted in the student getting admitted to the university. Despite being a private lawsuit, the case is frequently praised as the beginning of legal mobilization for disability rights in South Korea (Hong 2016, 389).

Very few people with disabilities sought remedies for discrimination through the courts, however. Indeed, discrimination claims were not even taken to court when they occurred within the judicial branch. Famously, four well-qualified candidates were denied appointments as judges in 1982 solely because of their disabilities. Disabled person organizations campaigned to collect 1 million signatures to rectify such discriminatory practices. The Office of Court Administration reversed its decision and hired three of them (D. H. Kim 2007, 36). In general, compared to judicial claims-making, mass protests and large-scale campaigns were considered more effective means to fight against disability discrimination. During this period, rights had no place in the charity- and welfare-based understanding of disability and persons with disabilities.

10.3 THE MOBILIZATION OF PEOPLE WITH DISABILITIES

As with human rights in general (see Chapter 5), the international community has significantly influenced the Korean disabilities community, its activism, and legislative initiatives. Two international events in the 1980s are noteworthy in this regard: initiatives led by the United Nations and Seoul's hosting of the Olympic Games. In 1975, the General Assembly adopted its second declaration regarding disability, called the Declaration on the Rights of Disabled Persons.[7] The declaration was intended to promote social integration of persons with disabilities and to set standards for equal treatment and accessibility to services. The UN then designated 1981 as the International Year of Disabled Persons. In the following year, the General Assembly adopted the World Program of Action Concerning Disabled Persons (WPA) to achieve the goal of the full and active participation of persons with disabilities, rehabilitation, and the equalization of opportunities. To advance the goals of the WPA, the UN General Assembly dedicated the 1983–1992 decade to persons with disabilities (UN 2018).

Meanwhile, General Chun Doo-hwan and his followers seized power in 1980 after brutally suppressing the Gwangju Democratization Movement. Afraid of its lack of legitimacy, Chun's government proclaimed "the realization of a welfare state" as its foremost agenda. In 1981, it also officially designated April 20 as Disabled Person's Day and enacted the Welfare Act for Mentally and Physically Disabled Persons in the same year (D. H. Kim 2007, 39). While the law did not recognize people with disabilities as rights bearers, it gradually improved benefits and services for them. Conscious of international criticism of the military coup, Chun's administration subsequently worked to use the 1988 Summer Olympics and the Paralympics that were held immediately thereafter to showcase to the international community the administration's commitment to the welfare of disabled persons.

Due to the combined effects of UN activities and the Chun government's policies, several major disability organizations formed during the 1980s. The Korean Association of Parents of Disabled Persons (*Hangukjangaein hakbumohoe*) was set up in 1985. Disabled Peoples' International (DPI) established its Korean branch in the following year.[8] Those who had different disabilities, such as visual and hearing impairments, formed separate national organizations during this period, too. Ironically, many of the disability organizations that would play pivotal roles in the history of the Korean disability rights movement were established during a military government that severely violated citizens' civil and political rights (D. H. Kim 2007, 40).

As an outcome of citizens' struggles against the authoritarian regime of former generals, the June Democratic Uprising caused a new constitution to be adopted in 1987. The new constitution established the Constitutional Court (see Chapter 6), and associated reforms liberalized the legal opportunity structure in ways that facilitated claims-making (see Chapter 7). Although the 1987 Constitution is widely regarded as promoting and protecting human rights, it falls short on issues related to disabilities. Consisting of thirty articles, Chapter Two of the Constitution provides fundamental freedoms and rights in a highly detailed manner. However, it does not address the matter of disability at all. Article 11, a catchall provision on the equal

---

[7]   Declaration on the Rights of Disabled Persons, UN General Assembly res. 3447 (XXX), (December 9, 1975), www.ohchr.org/EN/ProfessionalInterest/Pages/RightsOfDisabledPersons.aspx.

[8]   See website at http://dpikorea.org/.

protection of law, specifies only gender, religion, and social status. The Constitution thus demonstrates lawmakers' and society's limited understanding of disability rights at the time. In fact, the Constitution only mentions disability once in Article 34, paragraph 5, and uses the term "physically disabled person" without mentioning any other disabilities. Article 34 deals with the state's responsibilities for social welfare. Thus, the Constitution does not recognize citizens with various disabilities as full members or rights-holding subjects. The drafters of the new constitution were presumably no different from the majority of South Koreans in viewing disability through the charity or medical lens.

The Korean disabilities communities saw the 1988 Seoul Paralympics as a critical event. They planned to press the government to take disability issues seriously before holding the international games, which the military government was eager to use to improve its reputation worldwide. People with disabilities launched the Campaign to Enact Two Major Laws (*Yangdae beoban tujaeng*) in early 1988. The first was a law to promote the employment of persons with disabilities via quotas. The second goal was to amend the Welfare Act for Mentally and Physically Disabled Persons. The movement wanted to make more provisions in the law mandatory, to create legal obligations. Meanwhile, other activist groups, such as those affiliated with the Research Institute for Disability Rights in Korea (RIDRIK) (*Jangaeu gwonik munje yeonguso*), took more radical strategies. One group occupied a church in downtown Seoul and staged a hunger strike. Their slogan was "Improving the quality of life for disabled people first, the Paralympics next!" They proclaimed their opposition to participation in the Paralympics unless the two legislative proposals were accepted (You 2005, 12).

The Ministry of Welfare held dialogues with the protesters and promised to help with their legislative goals. As a result, in August 1988, just two months before the opening of the Paralympic Games, Korea Differently Abled Federation (KODAF, or Jangchong) was formed as a national umbrella organization of various disabled people's organizations.[9] Through KODAF, the disabilities community could lobby National Assembly members for reforms more effectively. After the successful completion of the Paralympics, negotiations for the two legislative reforms produced some results. The Welfare Act was amended to include provisions covering state financial support for medical and educational expenses, along with subsidies for utility expenditure, among other benefits. The amended Act also started the official registration system for disabled persons, which classifies them based on a medical exam into one of six levels with associated benefits and services (You 2005, 12–13). Activists in subsequent decades argued that the grading system reflects the medical and welfare models of disability, rather than the social and human rights models.

As a second legislative success for Korea's disabilities movement, the long-debated Act for Promoting the Employment of Disabled Persons was finally enacted in

---

[9] See website at http://kodaf.or.kr.

January 1990.[10] Its main point of controversy was the size of companies that would be legally obliged to hire disabled employees under the Act. The Act was designed to gradually expand its applicability. The business community, however, argued that the law should first apply to companies with more than 300 employees and set a 1 percent hiring quota. By contrast, the original bill had required a 2 percent hiring quota for companies with more than 100 workers. Compromise produced a law that stipulated a 2 percent mandatory hiring quota for companies with more than 300 workers (D. H. Kim 2007, 47–48). These two legislative victories for Korea's nascent disabilities movement, while not advances in the rights of people with disabilities per se, did lay an essential foundation for subsequent rights-based mobilization.

10.4 FURTHER LEGISLATIVE REFORMS: INSTITUTIONAL LIFE AND SPECIAL EDUCATION

Although these outcomes were not entirely satisfactory, they and activists' experiences in the Campaign to Enact Two Major Laws led the Korean disability community to pay more attention to conditions in institutions for people with disabilities and special education in the 1990s. After the Korean War, many foreign aid agencies and Christian missionaries came to Korea and ran facilities for war orphans and the homeless. When most of them returned to their homelands in the mid-1960s, the Korean government allowed local religious organizations and civilians to take over and continue operating such facilities (D. H. Kim 2007, 50). Through the 1970 Social Welfare Enterprise Act, those who ran such facilities became eligible for financial support and subsidies from the government. Some of these enterprises, however, were later accused of corruption and moral hazard or found to have violated the human rights of those who were under their control. For example, investigative reporting revealed recently that staff at the Brothers' Home (*Hyeongje bokjiwon*) in Busan had abused thousands of children, vagrants, and people with disabilities who had been rounded up and institutionalized in the 1970s and 1980s (Kim and Klug, 2016). In addition, teachers at a school for the hearing-impaired repeatedly sexually assaulted students in the 2000s, as movingly depicted in the 2011 film Dogani ("The Crucible"), which led the National Assembly to pass legislation abolishing the statute of limitations for sex crimes against the disabled and children (R. Kim 2011). In the 1970s and 1980s, the government had wanted to avoid getting directly involved in caring for the homeless or persons with disabilities, and therefore shut its eyes to such abuse and corruption. Those who ran the facilities, moreover, were often influential locals, and thus well-connected with the very politicians, police, and agencies that were supposed to oversee them (D. H. Kim 2007, 51).

Activism to expose and remedy such corrupt and abusive practices began at rehabilitation and residential facilities for disabled persons. It was challenging to

---

[10]   *Jangaein goyong chokjin deunge gwanhan beomnyul*, Act No. 4219 (1990).

investigate such facilities because they were frequently isolated from the rest of society and pressing quotidian issues abounded at such institutionalized facilities. Yet a small band of activists with disabilities staged a sit-in protest at a big rehabilitation center in Seoul. It revealed long-standing corruption, including the director's misappropriation of public funds. The activists, as well as the disability community, came to realize that such corruption and abuse would not disappear without democratic and transparent management for such institutions. Though successful in informing the public of the seriousness of the corruption, the protests were not successful in achieving structural changes through legislation that made the management of such institutions more transparent and democratic (D. H. Kim 2007, 51–53).

Another problem the Korean disabilities community faced was NIMBY-ism (Not in My Back Yard). Many residents opposed building or operating a facility for disabled persons in their neighborhood. Even those who were sympathetic to people with disabilities feared that such facilities would negatively affect the market value of their real estate. Due to such sentiments, facilities were built outside of the city center, often in rural areas that were inconvenient to access. To be able to place such facilities in large cities such as Seoul so that the disabled could exercise their right to education, organizers had to compromise with local residents, such as by sharing part of the facility with them. Yet societal resistance to people with disabilities persists. In September 2017, for instance, residents in western Seoul protested the construction of a special education school, even though a court had ruled in 1996 that the detriment to neighbors of such schools was outweighed by the detriment of denying education rights to disabled students (Bak 2017).[11]

The disabilities community soon realized that persons with disabilities could not escape from second-class citizen status and claim their rights without receiving a proper education. Education is a potent vehicle for success in any society, particularly in Korea, where Confucian culture emphasized the value of education more than anything (Sorensen 1994, 11). Up until the end of the 1960s, however, the underlying policy of the Korean government had been exclusion and institutionalization rather than education for people with disabilities (D. H. Kim 2007, 57). Incrementally, some special accommodations were made for disabled students, such as abolishing the physical admissions exam after the petition drives and individual lawsuits discussed earlier in this chapter (Hong 2016, 388–89).

In the 1990s, however, activists mobilized to assert that students with disabilities were being treated as beneficiaries of special education services, not subjects with the right to education. The Alliance for the Welfare of Disabled Persons (*Jangaein bokji gongdaewi*) initiated a public hearing in April 1992 and organized workshops to highlight the flaws of extant laws, notably, the 1977 Act for Promoting Special

---

[11]   Seoul District Court, 1996Gahap158 (February 21, 1996).

Education.[12] The Alliance ultimately demanded a new law regarding the education of students with disabilities. Even with massive demonstrations nationwide for a new law, the Alliance failed to achieve its goal but had to accept amendments to the old law in 1994. The amended Act included some of the Alliance's demands, such as compulsory education for nine years, express provisions on integrated education, and individualized education, among others (D. H. Kim 2007, 59–61).[13] The goal of enacting a new law on special education and abolishing the old one was finally realized in 2007.[14]

Until the mid-1990s, it was common in South Korea to form disability organizations around the same or similar type of disability. This practice began to change as organizations or alliances formed for specific reforms. One of them was the Citizen's Solidarity for Promoting Reasonable Accommodations (*Jangaein pyeonui siseol chokjin siminyeondae*), which was established in 1997. It published a monthly magazine, *Free Space*, ran educational programs for young people with disabilities, and produced research papers on reasonable accommodations (but not yet rights) (D. H. Kim 2007, 89). In addition, women with disabilities started their own organization in 1998, launching many women-specific programs, including seminars, human rights camps, and various cultural events. The group became a national organization in the following year under the name of Korea Differently Abled Women United (KDAWU).[15] A decade later, some members of the KDAWU actively participated in the drafting of the UN Convention on the Rights of Persons with Disabilities, particularly on Article 6, a provision relating to the rights of women with disabilities (M. Y. Kim 2014, 119–21).

10.5 EMERGING LEGAL MOBILIZATION IN THE 2000S

In the 2000s, the disabilities movement in South Korea became noticeably more active and turned toward legal mobilization. Several changes in the Korean legal profession may have spurred this shift in rights claiming tactics toward the courts (see Chapter 8). First, the Attorney-at-Law Act, as amended in 2000, required all active members of the Korean Bar Association to provide thirty hours of pro bono activities per year.[16] In 2002, consequently, the big Seoul-based law firm, Bae, Kim & Lee (Taepyeongyang), established a pro bono committee and began providing legal representation for socially disadvantaged groups, including persons with disabilities. Other law firms soon followed. For example, another prominent Seoul-based law firm, Jipyong, created a public interest law foundation, Duroo. Although Duroo's

---

[12] *Teuksu gyoyuk jinheungbeop*, Act No. 3053 (1977).
[13] Revisions of the *Teuksugyoyuk jinheung beop*, Act No. 4716 (1994).
[14] *Jangaein deunge daehan teuksu gyoyukbeop* (Act on Special Education for Persons with Disabilities, etc.), Act No. 8483 (2007).
[15] *Hanguk yeoseong jangaein yeonhap*, website at kdawu.org.
[16] *Byeonhosabeop*, Act No. 6207 (2000), Article 27.

inception of 2014 was quite recent, it has been most active, hiring eight full-time lawyers and engaging the law in various areas of practice, including for persons with disabilities, children and youth, socioeconomic minorities, and international human rights advocacy.[17] Second, Korea's first full-time public interest law firm, Gonggam (literally, empathy), was launched in 2004, and it inspired several similar law firms dedicated to public interest law (Goedde 2009, 85). Gonggam made disability law one of its practice areas. Hope and Law (Huimangbeop), which was founded in 2012 and has nine attorneys (including a visually impaired one), also works closely with Gonggam and focuses on disability rights and sexual minorities.[18] Mounting awareness of disability rights within the legal profession was also evident in the Korean Bar Association's decision to add a separate chapter about the rights of people with disabilities to its annual Human Rights Report starting in 2001 (KBA 2001). A decade later, in 2011, lawyers, judges, prosecutors, and law scholars founded the Korea Disability Law Association (*Hanguk jangaein beop yeonguhoe*) to create a network for identifying test cases for litigation, advising on disability rights cases, researching foreign examples, and advocating for reforms. In addition to the enhanced availability of lawyers, the Korean public's growing rights consciousness and government reforms to enhance access to justice (see Chapter 7) contributed to this shift toward legal mobilization by and for people with disabilities.

As Mosler (Chapter 6) outlines, the Constitutional Court played a pivotal role after Korea's democratization in realizing the spirit of the Constitution and vindicating citizens' rights, which had long been neglected (Yoon 2010, 155–56). It also advanced disability rights. For example, several prominent Constitutional Court rulings in this era related to Korea's century-long practice of letting only persons with visual impairment run massage parlors. A group of persons without such impairment challenged the constitutionality of the relevant laws. The Constitutional Court initially rejected this challenge in 2003, but then reversed its decision three years later, holding that those laws violated the constitutional guarantee of the freedom of occupation (Art. 15), as well as Article 11's provision of equal protection before the law (J. W. Kim 2012, 222–23). The Court, however, reversed its decision once again two years later, holding, as it had in 2003, that the public interest of ensuring the livelihood of people with visual disabilities, according to Article 34 of the Constitution, was more important than protecting the general public's right to choose their occupation.[19] Since then, the Court has steadily supported the exclusive entitlement of persons with visual impairment. The Court's vacillation initially appeared to stem from minor legal technicalities. In fact, the Court may have been influenced by the increasingly active rights claiming by people with disabilities, supported by increasingly organized lawyers.

[17] Duroo, www.duroo.org/introduce/list.php.
[18] Huimangbeop, www.hopeandlaw.org/.
[19] Constitutional Court, 2006Heonma1098 (October 30, 2008).

10.6 THE RIGHT TO MOBILITY MOVEMENT

From its emergence, disability rights activism in Korea – as in many countries – targeted the physical environment because it prevented people with disabilities from participating in society as nondisabled citizens do (Kim and Jeong 2007, 107). Hence, Korea's 2005 enactment of the Transportation Convenience Act, with its articulation of a right to mobility (Art. 3), was another key victory. As discussed in the chapter's Introduction section, fatal accidents in the subway spawned the Solidarity for the Right to Move, which launched sit-ins, petition drives, and demonstrations that led to a bill in the National Assembly in 2004. The Solidarity then staged a sixty-eight-day sit-in outside the National Assembly. The bill became law in January 2005.

Its enactment is noteworthy because it overturned a 2002 Constitutional Court decision on the same issue.[20] When petitioners with disabilities challenged the government's failure to provide low-floor buses for mobility-disadvantaged persons, the Court refused to acknowledge that the government had a constitutional duty to provide accessible transportation. Instead, the Court merely recognized the "general responsibility" of the government to endeavor to promote the welfare of disabled persons. The fact that the 2005 law created legal obligations to provide accessible transportation marks a shift from the welfare model of disability toward the human rights model. The Transportation Convenience Act (Art. 3) legally acknowledged for the first time the right to mobility, stipulating that in order "to be guaranteed the right to pursue the dignity, value, and happiness as a human being, mobility disadvantaged persons shall have the right to use safely, conveniently, and without discrimination, all means of transportation, passenger facilities, and roads used by persons, other than the mobility disadvantaged persons."

In the late 1990s, moreover, discourse about and a movement for independent living (*jarip saenghwal*) emerged in Korea. DPI-Korea had introduced ideas about independent living in the United States, facilitated by the ADA, to Korea from Japan in the early 1990s (K. M. Kim 2008). The core ideas of the independent living movement resonated with the social and human rights models of disability: people with disabilities should be empowered to make choices in their lives because every person should have the right to participate in society. In 2007, the disability community fostered public debate about the "right to caregivers" or "the right to assisted living."[21] Rather than just waiting for volunteer service providers, they argued for legal entitlements, referring to Articles 10 and 12 of the Constitution, which guarantee self-determination and personal liberty, respectively. Their specific demands were for a government-sponsored system for personal assistance services (*hwaldong bojo*) for persons with severe disabilities. In 2009, SADD activists staged a sit-in rally for forty-three days. Some of them crawled along a major traffic-congested bridge for six hours, garnering considerable media attention (W. Y. Kim 2010, 214). As a result,

---

[20]   Constitutional Court, 2002Heonma52 (December 18, 2002).
[21]   *Jeonguk jangaein chabyeol cheolpye yeondae*, website at sadd.or.kr.

the government launched a pilot program for activity assistance starting in 2007, and the Act on Welfare of Persons with Disabilities was substantially amended in the same year to include new provisions to "support independent living" and personal assistance services. These legislative reforms occurred amid a nationwide movement for new legislation protecting disabled persons' fundamental nondiscrimination rights.

10.7 THE ENACTMENT OF THE DISABILITY DISCRIMINATION ACT

March 6, 2007, was a day the Korean disability community will never forget: the National Assembly finally passed the DDA. In April 2003, fifty-eight organizations had formed the Solidarity for Enacting the Disability Discrimination Act (*Jangchuryeon*, hereafter the Solidarity). Solidarity organizations are common in Korea's repertoire of collective action, but this mobilization among Korean disability groups marked an unprecedented degree of unity behind the goal of achieving nondiscrimination rights (Arrington and Moon 2020, 16–17). After holding its first public hearing in June 2003, the Solidarity organized numerous workshops and public hearings and pressed the National Assembly for new legislation by supplying its draft bill (DDASK 2007, 150–52). In 2006, as the NHRCK debated anti-discrimination legislation, the Solidarity added more contentious tactics, including a weeks-long sit-in at the NHRCK to demand a DDA. By combining legislative activism with the more direct-action tactics of the mobility rights movement, whose leadership was incorporated into the Solidarity in 2005 to spearhead its "struggle committee" (*tujaeng wiwonhoe*), the Solidarity catalyzed the unanimous passage of the DDA in April 2007. The DDA significantly advanced disability rights and moved Korea toward becoming a more inclusive and integrated society. The DDA is also Korea's first law incorporating the social model of disability, and thus shifted societal perceptions of disability.

10.8 RATIFYING THE UN TREATY

While the Korean disability community campaigned for the DDA, UN negotiations to create the CRPD blossomed. Following the proposal by Mexico in 2001, negotiations began for the first UN treaty on persons with disabilities (Sabatello and Schulze 2014, 6). From June 2003, a Korean delegation of over ten disability organizations actively participated in expert conferences, working group meetings, and the special committee for drafting the treaty (D. H. Kim 2007, 153–54). The Korean delegation's emphasis on multiple or intersectional discrimination against women and girls with disabilities was eventually reflected in Article 6 of the treaty. The fact that many leading figures in the Korean disabilities community had direct experience in this international lawmaking process was seen as an invaluable experience (M. Y. Kim 2014, 129–30). It awakened them to global disability issues and helped them forge transnational ties with disability activists, overcoming Korean activists' previously parochial focus.

In December 2006, the 61st UN General Assembly unanimously adopted the CRPD together with its Optional Protocol, which creates an individual complaints mechanism and empowers the UN Committee of the Rights of Persons with Disabilities to investigate complaints and issue recommendations to parties.[22] The Korean government ratified the Convention in December 2008, though it did not enter into the Optional Protocol. When Korea's DDA was drafted and negotiated, its basic concepts and provisions were influenced more by the 1990 ADA and its lessons than by the CRPD, though, because Korea's DDA and the CRPD were crafted nearly contemporaneously (DDASK 2007, 199–201). Although both the CRPD and the ADA were based on the social model of disability, the CRPD is viewed as more advanced in rights terms because its preamble recognizes disability as "an evolving concept" and understands that "disability results from the interaction between persons with impairment and attitudinal and environment barriers" (see also Degener 2016). Arguably, it would have been better had Korean policymakers adopted some newer aspects from the CRPD, such as the perspective of viewing persons with disabilities as "subjects with rights, who are capable of claiming those rights and making decisions for their lives based on their free and informed consent as well as being active members of society" (UN 2018, 2). Rather than wait for the CRPD's ratification, Korean activists felt a sense of urgency to enact anti-discrimination legislation before conservatives' widely anticipated return to the Blue House in the 2007 presidential election (Arrington and Moon 2020, 17). Still, National Assembly members were aware of and benchmarked the CRPD in the final stages of debate, which may have facilitated the DDA's unanimous adoption in spring 2007. And the DDA and Korea's ratification of the CRPD marks a significant departure from viewing people with disabilities as just objects of charity, patients, or social welfare recipients.

10.9 THE ENFORCEMENT OF DISABILITY-RELATED LAWS

Korea's DDA significantly advanced the rights of people with disabilities. Article 2 of the DDA defines disability expansively as "an impairment or loss of physical or mental functions that substantially limits an individual's personal or social activities for an extended period." The wording of this definition is like that of the ADA. The Korean law also adopts the American concept of reasonable accommodations.

---

[22] The following quotation is a part of Secretary-General Kofi Annan's speech: "Today promises to be the dawn of a new era – an era in which disabled people will no longer have to endure the discriminatory practices and attitudes that have been permitted to prevail for all too long. This Convention is a remarkable and forward-looking document." Available at https://news.un.org/en/story/2006/12/203222-lauding-disability-convention-dawn-new-era-un-urges-speedy-ratification.

Article 4.1(iii) of the DDA frames the failure to provide reasonable accommodations (*jeongdanghan pyeonui*) as indirect discrimination against persons with disabilities. Its definition of "discriminatory acts" also goes beyond just direct and indirect discriminatory actions to include advertising practices and discriminatory conduct against person(s) accompanying disabled people or guide dogs.

As for enforcement mechanisms, the DDA, in addition to monetary compensation and fines (Arts. 46 and 50, respectively), specifies several remedies for the first time. The primary complaint mechanism is the National Human Rights Commission, which may make recommendations in response to complaints filed by individuals or organizations (Arts. 38–42). The Minister of Justice may also issue an injunction to rectify discriminatory acts (Art. 43). An extraordinary remedy in this regard are the proactive relief measures aimed at preventing further recurrence of discriminatory acts (Arts. 43 and 48). In addition, Article 48 gives discrimination victims the right to bring a lawsuit, including in parallel with NHRCK complaints. When the DDA was being debated, the Solidarity had sought to incorporate punitive damages, shifting the burden of proof, class action, and proactive relief measures (Youm and Ku 2017, 358). However, only the last survived in the enacted law.

The Enforcement Decree of the DDA provides further details regarding reasonable accommodations. Specific reasonable accommodations required of an employer include installing or remodeling facilities or equipment, such as an entrance offering access to the place of work, ramps, and height-adjustable work tables, and modifying or adjusting working hours such as a change in work schedule and adjustment of sign-in and sign-out time (Art. 5). They also include means of communication, such as instructions or work guidelines for persons with disabilities (Art. 8). In addition, the Enforcement Decree prohibits discrimination at all stages of employment, as well as matters related to the labor rights of persons with disabilities, such as joining a labor union. Preemployment medical examinations aimed at investigating whether a potential employee has a disability are also prohibited.

After the DDA became effective in 2008, activists were initially disappointed that policymakers had written a law that channeled discrimination complaints to the NHRCK, but they have discovered ways of leveraging this institution alongside litigation. During the first eight months after the DDA came into force in 2008, the proportion of discrimination complaints received by the NHRCK that were related to disability leaped from 14 to 61 percent (NHRCK 2016, 137). Despite the backlog of cases due to the NHRCK's limited staff, complaints and associated recommendations from the Commission have helped to clarify the DDA's scope (CRPD 2014, 2). Furthermore, courts' attitudes and decisions regarding disability rights appear to be gradually changing since 2008 due to legal mobilization by people with disabilities. A 2010 ruling by the Seoul Central District Court is one example. Citing the DDA, the Court held that when investigating criminal suspects with disabilities, the investigating agency "must notify them in advance that they have a right to request accompaniment by their guardian" and also "must proactively ascertain the existence or degree of disabilities before investigation."[23] In another case in 2015 regarding employment, the Supreme Court ruled that it was illegal for a local government to discharge its employees who became disabled without reviewing alternative positions or considering possible task adjustments for them.[24]

Korean courts have not embraced their power to take proactive relief measures, which were modeled on the US Civil Rights Act of 1964.[25] Lawyers' active use of this provision, however, may be gradually influencing the judiciary. In a 2012 case where a woman with disabilities asked the court to order such proactive relief measures, the court ordered a subway station to build separate restrooms for disabled men and women and an elevator for transfers.[26] Besides, when persons with visual disabilities sought measures and monetary damages from a major airline company whose internet homepage was not accessible for them, the court facilitated a settlement agreement by urging proactive relief measures.[27] In other cases, however, the courts remain reluctant to exercise this new power to redress widespread discriminatory practices against people with disabilities.[28]

10.10 CONCLUSION

Like most other societies, Korean society long viewed disability as a medical problem or a personal tragedy. People with disabilities were considered objects of medical treatment, charity, and social welfare. The society and its legal system thus treated people with disabilities in paternalistic ways rather than as rights bearers. However, some persons with disabilities and their supporters began to raise their voices to protest such mistreatment and discrimination. They claimed that people with disabilities should be regarded not as objects but as subjects or rights holders. The long process of struggling for equal treatment for persons with disabilities finally resulted in changes in government policies and legislation, including the enactment of the DDA in 2007. The DDA is not just a new law; it is a comprehensive law that represents a significant paradigm shift in disability rights and associated discourses. The new social and human rights models of disabilities have replaced the charity and medical models (You and Hwang 2018). The enactment of the Transportation Convenience Act in 2005 also was an essential step toward creating a more inclusive and integrated society. People with disabilities publicly asserted the right to mobility (idonggwon): that they should not have to remain inside homes or institutions. By obtaining a law recognizing the right to mobility, persons with

---

[23]   Seoul High Court Judgment, 2009Gadan99509 (September 10, 2010).
[24]   Supreme Court, 2015Du45113 (April 12, 2016).
[25]   42 U.S.C. § 2000e-5.
[26]   Seoul Southern District Court, Conciliation Decision, 2012Gahap13003 (June 26, 2013).
[27]   Seoul Southern District Court, 2013Gahap102207 (September 30, 2013).
[28]   Seoul Central District Court, 2011Gahap38092 (August 30, 2013).

disabilities and other mobility-disadvantaged persons became more visible as they left previously isolated places, commuted to work, and participated more in society. They also gained new justiciable rights, a manual for improving disability rights in the judicial system in 2013, and backing from increasingly institutionalized networks of public interest lawyers.

Despite several legislative and judicial achievements that improved the rights of people with disabilities, South Korean society has more to do before it can become a truly inclusive and integrated society free from disability discrimination. There should be more initiatives to raise the public's awareness of disabilities. Mass media and public discourses still tend to regard disability as a personal misfortune and emphasize charity, cures, or other paternalistic interventions (see E. Kim 2016). Women and girls with disabilities have suffered more because of the lack of a "gender perspective" in the legal norms and governmental policies (UN 2014). The recent #MeToo campaign demonstrates that Korean women continue to be seriously exposed to sexual violence and harassment in homes, schools, institutions, and workplaces. Persons and children with mental or intellectual disabilities, including learning disabilities, are most poorly treated in Korean society, where cutthroat competition exists at every level of education, as the 2017 protests against the construction of a special education facility in Seoul (discussed earlier) demonstrated.

Insufficient societal understanding of disability rights will continue to constrain effective application and enforcement of Korea's improved legal rights for people with disabilities. As recently as 2016, a plurality of Koreans surveyed (42.2 percent) responded that the human rights of people with disabilities were still not respected (SSK Human Rights Forum-Hyundai Research 2016). Incremental changes, however, are improving the lives of people with disabilities. Even though current laws and legal practices are not entirely satisfactory, people with disabilities have grown active in making claims to defend and develop their rights. For example, the Moon Jae-in administration agreed to abolish the medically based classification system for disabilities in response to a five-year sit-in by people with disabilities, led by SADD, in the Gwanghwamun Metro Station (Kang 2017). The judiciary also shows a hint of progress. In September 2018, the Seoul High Court ordered the state to pay compensation to three of eight appellants with intellectual disabilities who had been forced to work in salt farms.[29] Disabilities groups' activism and criticism from the UN Committee on the Rights of Persons with Disabilities also helped prompt the December 2019 revisions to the DDA, which now mandates a fact-finding survey every three years.[30] Through such rights claiming and activism, people with disabilities are gradually reinforcing the law's transition from the medical/charity models of

---

[29] Seoul High Court, 2017Na2061141 (Nov. 23, 2018).
[30] Disability Discrimination Act, Act No. 16740 (2019).

disability toward the social or human rights models. They are also leveraging law and rights talk to demonstrate that they have equal value as rights bearers.

REFERENCES

Arrington, Celeste L., and Yong-il Moon. 2020. "Cause Lawyering and Movement Tactics: Disability Rights Movements in South Korea and Japan." *Law & Policy* 42(1): 5–30.

Bak, Se-hwan. 2017. "Disabled Students in South Korea Struggle to Find Right School." *Korea Herald*, September 17, 2017. http://news.koreaherald.com/view.php?ud=20170917000140.

CRPD. 2014. "Concluding Observations on the Initial Report of the Republic of Korea." CRPD/C/KOR/CO/1. UN Convention on the Rights of Persons with Disabilities.

DDASK. 2007. *Uriga ganeun giri yeoksada* [The path we have taken is history]. Seoul: Disability Discrimination Act Solidarity of Korea.

Degener, Theresia. 2016. "Disability in a Human Rights Context." *Laws* 5(3): 35–59.

Goedde, Patricia. 2009. "From Dissidents to Institution-Builders: The Transformation of Public Interest Lawyers in South Korea." *East Asia Law Review* 4: 63–90.

Han, Sam Hee. 1984. "A Person Using a Wheelchair Committed Suicide." *Chosun Ilbo*, September 22, 1984.

Hong, Seok Pyo. 2016. "Hanguk jangaein gongiksosongeui yeoksawa gwaje" [A history of the Korean public interest lawsuits on disability and remaining problems]. In *Jangeinbeop yeongu* [A study on disability law], edited by Taepyeongyang and Dongcheon, 385–441. Seoul: Kyungin Press.

Jackson, Mary Ann. 2018. "Models of Disability and Human Rights: Informing the Improvement of Built Environment Accessibility for People with Disability at Neighborhood Scale?" *Laws* 7(1): 10.

Jeong, Chang-geun. 2011. "Joseonsidae jangaein yesulgauijeonjaeyangsang" [The existential aspects of disabled artists in Joseon dynasty period]. *Journal of Korean Studies* 38 (September): 423–58.

Jung, Yeon-Soon. 2008. Human Rights Letter, The National Human Rights Commission of Korea. http://humanrights.go.kr/hrletter/08031/pop04.htm.

Kang, Haeryun. 2017. "A Small Victory for South Korea's Disability Rights." *Korea Exposé*, November 3, 2017. www.koreaexpose.com/small-victory-south-korea-disability-rights/.

KBA. 2001. *Ingwon bogoseo* [Human Rights Report]. Seoul: Korean Bar Association. www .koreanbar.or.kr/pages/board/view.asp?teamcode=&category=&page=3&seq=5118&ty pes=9&searchtype=contents&searchstr=%EC%9D%B8%EA%B6%8C%EB%B3%B4% EA%B3%A0%EC%84%9C (accessed March 10, 2020).

Kim, Chang Yeop. ed. 2009. *Naneun "nappeun" jangaein igo sipda* [I want to be a 'bad' person with disabilities]. Seoul: Samin.

Kim, Do Hyun. 2007. *Chabyeore jeohanghara: hangugui jangaein undong 20nyeon* [Resist discrimination: 20 years of the disability movement in Korea]. Seoul: Park Jong Cheol Publishing.

Kim, Eunjung. 2017. *Curative Violence: Rehabilitating Disability, Gender, and Sexuality in Modern Korea.* Durham: Duke University Press.

Kim, Jaewang. 2012. "Sigak jangaeinui siltaewa bisigak jangaein anmasa jagyeok jaehan" [The actual conditions of people with visual disability and the restriction of masseur member-ship for people with visual ability]. *Social Security Law Review* 1 (June): 215–48.

Kim, Kyung Mee. 2008. "The Current Status and Future of Center for Independent Living in Korea." *Disability & Society* 23(1): 67–76.

Kim, Mi Yeon. 2014. "Women with Disabilities: The Convention through the Prism of Gender." In *Human Rights and Disability Advocacy*, edited by Maya Sabatello and Marianne Schulze, 110–30. Philadelphia: University of Pennsylvania.

Kim, Myoung Su, and Jae Hwang Jeong. 2007. "Jangaein idong gweone gwanhan heonbeop jeok gochal" [A constitutional law study on the right to mobility for people with disabilities]. *Sungkyunkwan Law Review* 19 (December): 105–30.

Kim, Rahn. 2011. "National Assembly Passes 'Dogani Law'." *Korea Times*, October 28, 2011. www.koreatimes.co.kr/www/news/nation/2011/10/113_97529.html.

Kim, Tong-Hyung, and Foster Klug. 2016. "S. Korea Covered Up Mass Abuse, Killings of 'Vagrants'." *The Associated Press*, April 21, 2016. https://apnews.com/article/c22de3a565fe4e85a0508bbbd72c3c1b.

Kim, Won Young. 2010. "Jangaein undongi balmyeonghan gwolliwa geue daehan sabeop chegyeui suyonge daehan yeongu" [A study on the rights invented through movement for the disabled and its embodiment in Korean judiciary system]. *Public Interest & Human Rights* 8: 207–32.

Kimber, Cliona. 1993. "Disability Discrimination Law in Canada." In *Disability Discrimination Law in the United States, Australia, and Canada*, edited by Gerald Quinn, Maeve McDonagh, and Cliona Kimber, 165–220. Dublin: Oak Tree Press.

Lacy, D. Aaron. 2003. "Am I My Brother's Keeper: Disabilities, Paternalism, and Threats to Self." *Santa Clara Law Review* 44(1): 55–100.

NHRCK (National Human Rights Commission of Korea). 2016. *Jangaein chabyeol geumjibeop eehang jego mit jangaein ingwon jeungjineul wihan toronhoe* [Public hearing for enhancement of KDDA and improvement of people with disabilities rights]. Seoul: Hanhak Munhwa.

Sabatello, Maya and Marianne Schulze. eds. 2014. *Human Rights and Disability Advocacy*. Philadelphia: University of Pennsylvania Press.

Sorensen, Clark W. 1994. "Success and Education in South Korea." *Comparative Education Review* 38 (February): 10–35.

SSK Human Rights Forum-Hyundai Research. 2016. "National Human Rights Survey."

UN. 2014. "Concluding Observations on the Initial Report of the Republic of Korea." CRPD/C/KOR/CO/1.

UN. 2018. "The United Nations and Disability: 70 Years of the Work towards a More Inclusive World," available at www.un.org/development/desa/disabilities/wp-content/uploads/sites/15/2018/01/History_Disability-in-the-UN_jan23.18-Clean.pdf.

Yoon, Dae-kyu. 2010. *Law and Democracy in South Korea: Development since 1987*. Seoul: Institute for Far Eastern Studies, Kyungnam University.

You, Dong-chul. 2005. "Hanguk jangae undongui seonggwawa gwaje" [The achievements and assignments of Korea's disability movement]. *Social Welfare Policy* 21: 5–33.

You, Dong-chul, and Se Kwang Hwang. 2018. "Achievements of and Challenges Facing the Korean Disabled People's Movement." *Disability & Society* 33(8): 1259–79.

Youm, Hyun-guk, and Hyun-ju Ku. 2017. "Gwolli guje, sonhaebaesang mit beolchik deung" [Remedies, damages, and sanctions, etc.]. In *Jangaein chabyeol geumjibeop haeseolseo* [A Commentary on the Disability Discrimination Act], edited by the Korea Disability Law Association, 325–82. Seoul: Nanam Publishing.

11

The Politics of Postponement and Sexual Minority Rights in South Korea

Ju Hui Judy Han

11.1 INTRODUCTION

The question of progress for lesbian, gay, bisexual, transgender, and intersex (LGBTI) human rights in South Korea typically begins with a discussion of representation and visibility in the public sphere. One prominent case used as an example is the annual Queer Culture Festival in Seoul – also known as Seoul Pride or Seoul QCF – that has grown exponentially over the past few years, reaching an estimated 150,000 participants at its twentieth celebration in 2019. The timing of its phenomenal development into one of the largest pride gatherings in Asia coincided with the festival's change of location from the crowded streets of Sinchon to the open air plaza in front of Seoul City Hall in 2014, a coveted spot for all kinds of public events, including megaevents and mass rallies. The annual Seoul QCF now competitively selects dozens of rainbow-clad exhibition booths from social movement groups and arts and cultural producers and features congratulatory speeches and high-profile stage performances that celebrate LGBTI pride.

But what has also become increasingly visible in recent years is the opposition to LGBTI pride. Year after year outside the perimeter of the Seoul QCF, loud and outspoken protesters have come to vehemently oppose the celebration of LGBTI pride and demands for human rights. Thousands of anti-queer protesters, mostly Christian conservatives of Protestant persuasion, beat traditional Korean drums and shout religiously inflected epithets, hurling prayers of condemnation over the metal fence and police line that separate them from the Seoul QCF (J. Han 2015; W. Han 2018).

This spectacle of dueling mobilization has become an expected element of LGBTI visibility year after year. Though the anti-LGBTI contingent's size has dwindled in contrast to the growing scale of the Seoul QCF, hostile opposition nonetheless persists adjacent to the pursuit of LGBTI human rights. In fact, whereas LGBTI rights are arguably gaining greater public support and recognition as basic and fundamental human rights that ought to be extended to all (see Chapter 12), they have also sparked intense backlash from Christian conservatives who are not only intent on preserving what they define as tradition but also interested in pursuing policies that advance their own vision of social change (see J. Han 2018). It is also worth noting that the anti-LGBTI countermovement is comprised of diverse religious and political actors; most are evangelical and fundamentalist but not all are right-wing or from affluent megachurches (see Siu 2018).

Whereas the fraught space surrounding the Seoul QCF illustrates the ongoing contestations over the *place* of social change in South Korea, another set of questions has come to the fore in gender and sexual minority politics. These questions are about *time* and *timeliness*. Ongoing political actions and public expressions of discontent from LGBTI activists suggest that although there have been some positive signs of policy gains and expanded civil liberties, there is also a significant impasse. If anti-LGBTI conservatives have unsurprisingly tried to block social change, *liberals* have demonstrated a tendency to postpone them, arguing that sexual minority rights are temporarily premature, rather than permanently impossible. The prevailing idea is that it is "not yet" the right time to grant full human rights for gender and sexual minorities in South Korea, though it may be possible in the future, whenever that might be.

As a case in point, consider LGBTI struggles with the newly elected liberal government over gender and sexual minority rights in the wake of the Candlelight Protests in 2016–17 to impeach conservative President Park Geun-hye. LGBTI activists confronted not only conservative countermobilization but also resistance from liberal politicians, including President Moon Jae-in, a former human rights attorney who had publicly declared his opposition to LGBTI rights during his campaign. The LGBTI concerns were primarily over the criminalization and persecution of gay conscripts in the South Korean military and the urgent need for comprehensive anti-discrimination legislation (see Chapter 12), but progress seems to have been stalled even after the successful transition from conservative to liberal administration. LGBTI activists thus face twofold challenges: against intensifying conservative backlash, such as the highly visible protests mounted against the Seoul QCF, and against liberal reluctance to embrace gender and sexual minority rights.

In order to understand the present-day impasse and diagnosis of LGBTI rights as premature, this chapter discusses the persistent discourse of prematurity and postponement that has permeated LGBTI politics in Korea since the 1990s. I draw connections and distinctions between contemporary sexual minority student activism and leftist LGBTI activisms against so-called youth protection policies in the 1990s and early 2000s, highlighting key moments in the politics of death related to LGBTI rights and coalition-building. I then pair this history with the more recent instance of sexual minority activists' denunciation of liberal political deferral to examine what I call "a politics of postponement."

11.2 LGBTI STUDENT AND YOUTH ACTIVISM

Students have been at the forefront of mobilization for LGBTI rights. Consider QUV, which goes by the English name Solidarity of University Queer Societies in Korea or *Daehak cheongnyeon seong sosuja moim yeondae* in Korean. In important ways, QUV continues the tradition of youth and student activism as a key catalyst of social change. It is a national association of seventy-nine self-identified LGBTI groups at sixty-nine universities in every province in Korea and includes Anglican, Catholic, Protestant, and Buddhist schools and seminaries.[1] In 2016, the election of two out lesbian student leaders at prominent universities made headline news: Kim Bo-mi as the student government president at Seoul National University and Yi Ye-won as the vice president of Korea University's *Dongari yeonhapoe*, an association of student campus groups. Both were significant victories, especially when considering the historical importance of elected student leaders in previous social movements, such as the pro-democracy and disability rights movements (see S. Kim 2000; Lee 2007; Chang 2015; Chapter 10). They also signaled a major shift in the visibility of LGBTI rights activism. Kim Bo-mi has said in an interview that she sought the advice of older lesbian activists before deciding to run for office. "For the work that I have done and the work that I will continue to do," she said, "I certainly wanted to show that [being a] lesbian is not a stumbling block" (A. Cho 2016).

The trend has continued. In the following year, three self-identified sexual minority student leaders were elected: Han Seong-jin as vice president of undergraduates at KAIST, Ma Tae-yeong as president of the women's student government at Yonsei University, and Jang Hye-min as student government president at Kaywon University of Art & Design. In 2018, at the Anglican Sungkonghoe University in Seoul, an openly gay student named Baek Seung-mok was elected student government president. During his election campaign, Baek declared his vision to "create a university where everyone is treated equally without discrimination" (Gwak 2017). His policy platform included developing human rights guidelines, promoting gender neutral restrooms, implementing anti-violence and gender equality training for school officials, and increasing accessibility to accommodate those with disabilities.

These campus elections suggest that there has been measurable change in social acceptance and LGBTI political empowerment, and that these efforts continue. They also reflect the changing political landscape for student activism, one that no longer assumes leftist ideologies or labor solidarity as automatic political priorities. In many ways, they differ from the radical political contexts in which LGBTI student groups first emerged in the 1990s. The first gay and lesbian campus group called Come Together formed in April 1995 under the leadership of Seo Dong-jin, a well-known queer theorist and activist who was at the time a student at Yonsei University. Soon afterward that year, other groups formed: Maeum001 [Maum001] at Seoul

---

[1]   These numbers were last updated on September 3, 2019. From the QUV website. https://quvkorea
      .tistory.com/10?category=316133.

National University, Saramgwa Saram at Korea University, and Inhasiti [Inha City] at Inha University. Bringing together members of these fledgling groups, Daedongin (*Daehakdongseongaeja ingwonyeonhap*) formed in 1997 as a coalition of left-leaning university students who identified as homosexual, gay, or lesbian. As the group's name indicates, human rights (*ingwon*) were central from the start. To be sure, *dongseongaeja*, or "homosexuals," was the parlance of the time but throughout the 1990s and since then, terms like "lesbian and gay," "LGBTQ" or "LGBTI," or "sexual minority" have been used interchangeably, as they are throughout this chapter as well.

Many Daedongin members had become disillusioned by the heteronormative student activist culture and sought to work instead with like-minded activists by forging a different kind of radical political movement. Led by university students, including Jeong Yol, Yang Ji-yong, and Lim Tae-hoon, Daedongin represented a distinct gay and lesbian politics on the left. In contrast to the gay men's group Chingusai or the lesbian group Kirikiri that primarily focused on community networking and building social support without an ideological platform for societal change, Daedongin started explicitly as a leftist group and organized publicly around issues that were not narrowly defined as gender or sexual minority issues. One of its first political actions, for instance, was to join the widespread protests that became known as the General Strike of 1997, detailed below. In a column published on March 15, 1998, in the inaugural issue of *Dyke*, Daedongin's organizational newsletter, a subcommittee known as the Emergency Committee Against Distorted Media and AIDS Policy wrote, "We realized through our participation in the General Strike of 1997 that we cannot sit idly while women workers and others lose their status through mass layoffs. As *dongseongaeja* [gays and lesbians] we will continue to fight alongside workers against any form of bias or discrimination" (Daedongin 1998a, 16).[2] They called for solidarity among sexual minorities and workers in resisting undemocratic and capitalist exploitation and calling for equal rights.

11.3 LABOR, NATIONAL SECURITY, AND SEXUAL MINORITY ACTIVISM ON THE LEFT

From early in their activism, Korea's sexual minority activists linked LGBTI rights with other rights claims, notably by workers. The Korean Confederation of Trade Unions (KCTU) was founded in 1995, and just two years later in 1997, it led "the largest General Strike in the nation's contemporary history," at its height mobilizing over a million workers, students, and many others (Chun 2009). These protests had erupted in response to newly enacted labor laws that made it easier for companies to

---

[2] *Dyke* was the title of Daedongin's organizational newsletter, published six times between March 15, 1998 and July 2002.

lay off workers, legislation that was passed at a secret parliamentary session on December 26, 1996, that was attended only by ruling party legislators (see Chapter 9). What is often left out of discussions of the 1996 controversy, though, is that in addition to the new labor laws, the ruling New Korea Party passed a total of eleven laws, including a "pernicious new law ... that allows the country's notorious Agency for National Security Planning once again to spy on Korean citizens" (New York Times 1996). This was not a new law; Korea's National Security Law (NSL) has been in effect since 1948.[3] But importantly, the new amendments returned the investigative power over NSL cases to the National Security Planning Agency (NSPA), established in 1979 as the successor to the Korean Central Intelligence Agency (K. Cho 1997). The amendment strengthened the existing national security apparatuses to such an extent that an editorial in The New York Times called it "a damaging blow to South Korea's emerging democracy" as it would "more likely be applied against university students and other government critics" rather than any actual North Korean secret operatives and infiltrators (New York Times 1996). As a result, the widespread protests that ensued were in opposition to revisions to both labor laws and the NSL, mobilizing not only labor and student activists but also a wide range of human rights activists, including lesbian and gay groups like Daedongin, who rejected mass layoffs and demanded the release of political prisoners.

A discussion forum at Hanyang University in May 1998 drew explicit connections among lesbian and gay rights, the passage of the controversial labor and national security laws, the General Strike of 1997, and the emerging constellation of human rights activism of which Daedongin saw itself as a part. Daedongin organized the forum with the influential human rights group Sarangbang, the groundbreaking popular lesbian and gay magazine Buddy, gay men's group Chingusai, and several other university student groups. Daedongin recounted the details of this discussion in a May 15, 1998 editorial on the front page of the second issue of the organization's newspaper, Dyke.

Relatedly, an article in the same issue provides specific information and advice about the right to remain silent during a police investigation as it pertains to gays and lesbians. It used the example of an April 29, 1998 incident at a gay bar in Seoul in which undercover police officers coerced two bar patrons suspected of being underage minors to disclose their names and national identification numbers. The police also attempted to force the men to write statements of confession. A Daedongin activist who happened to be present at the scene intervened and advised the men of their right to remain silent and their right to decline to incriminate themselves. The police officers eventually left the scene, but not without causing a disturbance.

This incident was compounded by the fact that the bar patrons, including the Daedongin activist, were already reeling from another recent incident. There had been a raid at a gay bar on April 18, 1998, that led to a police chase of two men also

---

[3] Gukgaboanbeop (National Security Act), Act No. 3318 (1980), amended as Act No. 4704 (1994).

suspected of being underage. During the chase, one man fell down a flight of stairs, fracturing a leg and breaking his nose. Daedongin reports in the newsletter article, "Incidentally, the gay man who was injured on this day was a soldier and not a minor. He testified that he ran [from the police officers] because he was afraid of being outed [as gay] in the process of the police raid. He wishes he could take legal action against the police but has decided to hold off taking such action because of his status as a soldier" (*Daedongin* 1998b, 2). To Daedongin and its readers, these incidents in the community helped illustrate the connection between heightened national security enforcement and state violence in the form of anti-LGBTI policing.

11.4 YOUTH SUICIDES

In order to expand its political agenda and membership beyond the universities, Daedongin changed its name to Dongilyeon (*Dongseongaeja ingwonyeondae*) in 1998. Alongside various other gay and lesbian groups that formed during this time, Dongilyeon began to serve as a key voice for the gay and lesbian left. It grew significantly in membership and political capacity throughout the 2000s and 2010s. After seventeen years, it changed its name once more in 2015 to Haengseongin (*Haengdonghaneun seongsosuja ingwonyeondae*) in part to adopt the updated language of "sexual minorities" (*seong sosuja*) and reflect a wider range of gender and sexual diversity.[4] The continued inclusion of "human rights" (*ingwon*) in their name also shows what Lynette Chua (2015) has called a "vernacular mobilization of human rights." Korean LGBTI activists adopted the burgeoning discourse of human rights, cultivated new political communities, and actively participated in collective organizing alongside other social movement actors. The centrality of solidaristic action (*haengdong*) is also evident in their name. Whereas support-oriented groups like Chingusai (for gay men) and Kirikiri (for lesbians) emerged out of Chodonghoe, which was founded in 1994 as Korea's first albeit short-lived gay and lesbian group, Hangseongin traces its history to the radical left student activism of Daedongin that began in 1997 and continued as Dongilyeon.

Dongilyeon served as a refuge for many sexual minorities ostracized from other parts of their lives. O Se-in, a founding member of Daedongin and core member of Dongilyeon who had been kicked out of his family's home after coming out as gay, resorted to staying with friends or spending his nights at the Dongilyeon office. On May 17, 1998, O Se-in was found dead in the hallway outside the office in an apparent suicide. He took his life on May 17, which was becoming known in Korea as the International Day Against Homophobia (IDAHO).[5]

---

[4] Though the group's name changed from Dongilyeon to Hangseongin in 2015, their name in English has remained Solidarity for LGBT Human Rights of Korea.

[5] The tradition of the International Day against Homophobia, Transphobia and Biphobia began as a way to commemorate the 1990 decision of the World Health Organization to remove homosexuality

Similarly, Dongilyeon member Yook Woo-dang came to the group as a high school-age youth after experiencing violent harassment at school and lack of support at home. As a poet and a devout Catholic, he was well-liked for his irreverent yet heartfelt writings about identity, faith, and homophobia. Yook committed suicide at the age of 18, also outside Dongilyeon office, on April 25, 2003. He had participated in protests against the US war in Iraq, as part of Dongilyeon and the Joint Action of Homosexuals Against War (*Jeonjaengbandae dongseongaeja gongdonghaengdong*) throughout 2003, and in fact, many of Yook's friends in Dongilyeon learned about his death while attending a protest against the South Korean government's decision to dispatch troops to Iraq. Yook left his entire life savings of 340,000 won (approximately US$300) as a donation to Dongilyeon. In addition to his writings against war, his suicide note contained a blistering critique of religious homophobia and conservative Christianity. He wrote:

> Reckless prejudice and fucked up society are pushing countless sexual minorities off the edge of the cliff. Do they know how cruel and unbiblical that is? If my death results in the removal of gay websites from the government's list of banned and indecent media, and if my death could teach a lesson to those hypocritical Christians who say this and that about Sodom and Gomorrah, then my death would not have been in vain.[6]

It was a devastating discovery for activists who found O Se-in's and Yook Woo-dang's bodies. Jeong Yol, who had long been part of Dongilyeon since its fledgling days and served as its leader from 2002 to 2012, knew both young men well. "Yook Woo-dang's and O Se-in's suicides made us realize how important it was to support young people who identify as sexual minorities," he said, "[p]eople often ask why the two of them chose to commit suicide at the Dongilyeon office. But the answer is simple. They had nowhere else to go."[7] Dongilyeon offered, in other words, a space for both life and death.

11.5 PROTECTING YOUTH

Yook Woo-dang's reference to government censorship of online speech acts and Christian bigotry concerned the controversial mandate issued on August 25, 2000, by the now defunct Information and Communications Ethics Committee (predecessor to the current Korea Communications Standards Commission), which used to be under the Ministry of Information and Communication. Christian conservatives supported this mandate. Without warning, the Committee had decided that

---

from its International Classification of Diseases. Originally referencing just homophobia, transphobia was added to the name in 2009, and biphobia was officially added in 2015. In Korea, it has also become a day of annual commemoration for O Se-in and Yook Woo-dang, as well as others whose lives have prematurely ended.

[6] Excerpt (my translation) from Yook Woo-dang's suicide note. Author's personal archive.
[7] Interview in Seoul, July 26, 2017.

Exzone, a large gay community website known to be the first of its kind for Korean users, ought to be considered obscene and harmful to minors because of its subject matter – homosexuality (Kwon and Cho 2011). Established under the 1997 Juvenile Protection Act,[8] the Commission on Youth Protection subsequently followed the Committee's decision and added Exzone to the blacklist of media considered dangerous and harmful to youth.[9] This rendered all domestic and international gay and lesbian websites at risk for being placed on a list of sites deemed inappropriate for access by youth, a devastating blow to the growing gay and lesbian communities online and free speech rights. Activists saw the Internet as a critical tool for community-building and resource-sharing, especially for gay and lesbian youth who had little to no access to information or community.

Exzone served an invaluable function to thousands of anonymous users who logged in to meet one another and find communities in an overwhelmingly hostile social environment. What Exzone allegedly violated was Article 7 of the Juvenile Protection Act, which contained this clause: "Depiction of bestiality or the promotion of adultery, incest, homosexuality, sadomasochism, or other deviant sexuality, prostitution, and other sexual relations that are not tolerated by general social norms." Especially for *PC bangs* or Internet cafés – the once booming businesses that provided relatively private, around-the-clock computer access to paying customers – this meant that identification and monitoring software would have to be installed to prohibit underage users from accessing gay and lesbian websites, including websites designed to provide counseling and advocacy for gay and lesbian youth.

The Juvenile Protection Act made no distinction between the idea of homosexuality and the identities and practices based on nonnormative sexual orientations and nonconforming gender expressions. Nor did the legal prohibitions against "exposing" youth to homosexuality define what precisely constitutes homosexuality *in practice*. As in many other legal prohibitions against homosexuality, "homosexual" or *"dongseongae"* conveniently covered an ill-defined expanse of nonnormative genders and sexualities considered to be aberrant, undesirable, and harmful. All gay and lesbian websites, including those of educational, counselling, and advocacy organizations, would be required to prohibit minors from accessing their websites or be forced to shut down.

Understandably, the government's move to restrict online expression caused an uproar. As previously mentioned, the Internet was becoming essential for many aspects of social and political life, especially for gay and lesbian communities that were starting to experience phenomenal growth online. Not only Exzone but also sites like Ivancity and TG-Net, each with a thriving online community offering virtual meetings and facilitating in-person meet-ups, were becoming popular lifelines for lesbian and gay users throughout the country and in the Korean diaspora.

---

[8] *Cheongsonyeon bohobeop* (Juvenile Protection Act), Act No. 5297 (1997).
[9] The Korean name for the Committee is *Cheongsonyeon bohowiwonhoe*.

These online forums provided space for communication, which sometimes spurred increased rights consciousness. The new prohibitions struck a nerve as they were considered a flagrant attack against sexual minorities and their rights to free expression, and activists against censorship and obscenity laws in particular joined the cause (S-H. Yi 2013). The case of the Exzone ban brought to light the extent to which discrimination against gender and sexual nonnormativity could become codified into law under the guise of being dangerous and harmful to youth. The fight against such discrimination was framed as a matter of life or death, against premature deaths like that of Yook Woo-dang. Immediately following Yook's death, Dongilyeon's newsletter – now renamed the LGBT Paper – featured a bold front page that read, "Don't kill anymore. Immediately remove the discriminatory clauses against homosexuals in the Juvenile Protection Act" (see Figure 11.1).

The issue of youth suicide, the attempts to criminalize gay and lesbian bars, and prohibitions against community spaces online and offline were identified by Dongilyeon activists as nothing short of state-sanctioned death or increased vulnerability to death. This framing resonates with the idea of premature death, as

FIGURE 11.1 "Don't kill anymore. Immediately remove the discriminatory clauses against homosexuals in the Juvenile Protection Act." *LGBT Paper* (June and July, 2003).

articulated by Ruth Wilson Gilmore, a political geographer and prison abolition activist, whose influential definition of racism zeroes in on its fatal consequence: "the state-sanctioned or extralegal production and exploitation of group-differentiated vulnerability to premature death" (Gilmore 2007, 28).

Furthermore, it is worth considering the kinds of coalitional politics that animated Dongilyeon's focus on premature death. In discussing the work of Black lesbian writer and activist Audre Lorde, Grace Hong argues that Lorde articulated a set of coalitional politics "that is not based on the protection of self-interest or claims to injury, but on a critique of the uneven but connected dispersion of death and devaluation that make self-protective politics threaten to render others precarious" (Hong 2015, 5–6). Similarly, what Dongilyeon articulated – as in the image of its newspaper shown earlier – was not a narrowly cast identity politics based on rights preservation but a critique of the state's devaluation of a group of people in ways that prevented lesbians and gays from living fulfilling lives or living at all. Dongilyeon asserted that what threatened one vulnerable group would render other marginalized individuals vulnerable as well. Their activism promoted LGBTI rights not by excluding other rights claims but by bridging their claims with other groups' rights.

About a month before Yook Woo-dang's death, Dongilyeon and allied organizations had succeeded in obtaining from the National Human Rights Commission of Korea (NHRCK) a recommendation that the discriminatory language be removed from the Juvenile Protection Act. Specifically, the NHRCK pointed out that singling out homosexuality in such a way violated the Constitution's Article 10 ("Right to pursue happiness"), Article 11 ("Right to equality"), and Article 21 ("Freedom of expression").[10] Though not legally binding, the April 2003 recommendation was considered a significant gain for gay and lesbian rights, around which protests had been organized for several months.

Conservative Protestants vociferously disagreed with the NHRCK's recommendation and insisted that homosexuality goes against "mainstream social values" and that it should be considered harmful and dangerous, especially to youth.[11] The national flagship organization of evangelical Christians called Christian Council of Korea (CCK) issued a statement, noting that "Sodom and Gomorrah incurred God's wrath due to their immoral embrace of homosexuality" and that the catastrophic destruction that ensued was a direct consequence of homosexuality. CCK used this biblical story as a warning for Korean society. Though Yook's dramatic suicide had generated unprecedented media coverage and a surge in lesbian and gay political organizing, especially against religiously fueled homophobia, CCK did not capitulate. In the wake of Yook Woo-dang's death, Dongilyeon and several other gay and lesbian groups in alliance with progressive and reformist Christian groups held

---

[10]   News release. April 2, 2003. Resources database of the Korean Sexual-Minority Culture & Rights Center website. http://kscrc.org/xe/board_yNWI74/4890?ckattempt=1.

[11]   Christian Council of Korea (CCK)'s position is discussed here on the Korean Sexual Minority Culture and Rights Center website. http://kscrc.org/xe/board_hWwy34/770.

a commemorative service outside the CCK office. This coalition protested CCK's stance and demanded an apology and expression of condolence for Yook's death. A progressive Christian youth group called Hangiyeon (*Hanguk gidok cheongnyeon hyeobuihoe*, or Ecumenical Youth Council in Korea) delivered a letter to urge CCK to recognize their direct and indirect involvement in Yook's death, describing it as a "homicide at the hands of the Korean church" (Yang 2003). CCK refused. Dongilyeon protesters were told by an unsympathetic CCK representative that "[i]f you are a homosexual, you should be ashamed of yourself" (Im 2003). CCK maintained that Yook's death did not have anything to do with the conservative Christian stance on homosexuality or their opposition to the NHRCK's recommendation that homosexuality be removed from the Juvenile Protection Act.

The clause that defined homosexuality as a harmful influence on youth was eventually deleted from the Juvenile Protection Act in 2004. But the underlying suggestion that youth must be protected from gender and sexual nonconformity persists to this day in sex education curricula and public decency clauses in a variety of educational, legal, and political contexts. This can be seen in the ongoing debates over student human rights ordinances in a number of provinces and municipalities in South Korea (see Chapter 12). Christian conservatives have been the main force of opposition against these human rights ordinances. The idea that youth need protection from homosexuality still routinely appears in anti-LGBTI discourse, including slogans that claim that exposure to an LGBTI-affirming curriculum could lead an unsuspecting impressionable youth into *becoming* gay or lesbian, bisexual or transgender.

The discourse of "youth protection" – that youth need to be protected from premature exposure to "aberrant" and corrupting influences of nonnormative gender and sexual identities and expressions – is a familiar subject in queer politics. The conservative anti-LGBTI position asserts that nonnormative gender expressions and sexualities constitute perversion and moral indecency and that children and teenagers who are in the "formative stages" of adulthood must be protected from these corrupting influences. What is curious about this discursive claim of "youth protection" is that youth is a temporary marker. Would indecency and perversion be permitted once one matures beyond youth?

11.6 POLITICS OF POSTPONEMENT

Similar to the contentious political climate that characterized the General Strike and militant protests of the late 1990s and early 2000s when O Se-in and Yook Woo-dang took their lives, widespread protests throughout 2015 and 2016 raised hopes of progressive reforms, including regarding LGBTI rights. Multiple campaigns were being waged against the then president Park Geun-hye's nondemocratic rule, mass layoffs and unjust terminations, pervasive misogyny and violence against women, and against policies that endangered the lives of disabled people, as referenced in other chapters in this book. In the fall of 2016, the protest landscape in Seoul took a dramatic turn. The Candlelight Protests, the culmination of long-running protests and a fortuitous convergence of organized labor and anti-government protests scheduled in October, quickly gained momentum and kept growing in size through the winter and spring (see N. Kim 2017, 2018). By the time the seasonal smog blanketed the city in March 2017, the record-breaking mass protests and political upheavals resulted in the impeachment and removal of Park Geun-hye from the presidency. Subsequently, the special election held in May 2017 led to the inauguration of a liberal administration led by President Moon Jae-in, a former human rights attorney who had narrowly lost the election to Park back in 2012.

This was a jubilant time for many who opposed the conservative government and welcomed the liberal administration. There had been mass-scale candlelight protests in the past – most notably in 2002, after two fourteen-year-old girls were accidentally and fatally overrun by US military vehicles, and in 2008, against neoliberal policies such as the US-Korea Free Trade Agreement and the importation of US beef. But the Candlelight Protests in 2016–17 powerfully demonstrated that mass mobilization could yield what many referred to as *revolutionary* change (Hankyoreh Editorial 2017).

In the months leading up to the election, however, Moon had largely lost the support of sexual minority movements. Not only did Moon state to the progressive daily *Hankyoreh* in January 2017 that he valued traditional forms of family and marriage and therefore opposed same-sex marriage, but he also made it clear that he was no different from conservative candidates in his "opposition" to homosexuality (S.-A. Yi 2017; Y. Yi 2017; Yun 2017). As a parliamentarian, Moon had previously supported comprehensive anti-discrimination legislation bills in 2012 that included protection for gender and sexual minorities (see Chapter 12). As a presidential candidate, however, he made it clear during a nationally televised debate that his administration would oppose such anti-discrimination legislation. His conservative turn disappointed activists who had hoped to see sexual minority rights as part of the groundswell of changes presaged by the Candlelight Protests.

On the morning of February 16, 2017, a group of queer and trans activists convened a press conference to denounce Moon's position on homosexuality and comprehensive anti-discrimination legislation. They then rushed over to a public forum where Moon was to make an appearance. As the frontrunner in the presidential race, Moon was to announce his "blueprint for gender equality policy" at this forum. After waiting for Moon to finish the main part of his speech, during which he declared himself a "feminist president," the protesters disrupted the event. They suddenly stood up, each holding up A-4 size protest messages that read, "Human rights are a matter of life for sexual minorities" and "Sexual minority rights are not up for negotiation." They urged Moon to explain – and reverse – his position on human rights for sexual minorities.

This moment was captured in numerous photographs and on video. In a video recording edited and distributed by an independent online media project called Dot Face (.Face), one sees at the center Gwak I-gyeong [Kwak Ekyeong] and several other queer and trans activists, human rights attorneys, and disability activists disrupting the forum.[12] In a scene that has now become an indelible moment in queer political history in South Korea, Gwak shouts in a trembling voice:

> I am a woman and a lesbian. How is it that you can slice my human rights in half? How is it that my right to equality can be sliced in half? If you are the frontrunner for the presidency, please answer me. Why is it that in this policy of gender equality, you can not include equality for sexual minorities?[13]

Gwak is a longtime lesbian activist who worked closely with Jeong Yol in building Dongilyeon in the group's formative years. She also served as the group's leader after Jeong finished his term in 2012. As part of a small but influential cohort of left-leaning lesbian and gay activists who have been involved in labor, human rights, and feminist movements since the late 1990s, Gwak decided to work with organized labor after Dongilyeon. At the time of the protest against Moon, she was the Director of External Relations and Solidarity at the KCTU, a position that builds political ties among a wide range of issues and constituent communities beyond labor. One might describe this role as the face of South Korea's social movement unionism, such as detailed by Lee (Chapter 9). Her position was to facilitate the practice wherein labor unions engage not only in narrow workplace concerns or class mobilization but also connect labor with broader political struggles for human rights and social justice. Though Gwak I-gyeong is certainly not the only lesbian or gay activist in the labor movement, she is perhaps the best-known out lesbian activist who traverses across a wide range of queer-labor solidarity movement spaces. During the Candlelight Protests 2016–17, she also served on the core coordinating committee for the Emergency National People's Action for the Dismissal of Park Geun-hye.

The scene captured on video was widely shared on social media, but the video went viral not only because of the moving image of Gwak I-gyeong trembling with anger or the reason behind this political disruption. What was most remarkable about the protest was the response by Moon and the audience. Moon is heard telling Gwak, when she and others continued to press for his response, "[l]ater, I will give you a chance to speak later." Then, a few voices from the audience can be heard

---

[12] The infamous "Najung-e, Najung-e" [Later, Later] video taken on February 16, 2017, was edited and distributed by Dot Face (.Face). It is available on Youtube, at www.youtube.com/watch?v=fV5jfZSE3OA.

[13] Gwak uses the word *dongseongaeja* in her protest. Rather than translating it literally as "homosexual," I translated the first instance as "lesbian" because it referred to herself – and she identifies as a lesbian – and the second instance as "sexual minority" because that is the term that best captures the political subjectivity in question.

repeating Moon's words – "Later!" (*najung-e*). This catches on and before long, the audience chants in unison, "Later! Later! Later!"

It is a scene of a crowd silencing the voice of one, almost cheery chants that contrast the urgency of the protesters. Gwak and other protesters are seen in the video looking aghast at their surroundings, their voices soon drowned out by the collective chants of an auditorium full of women, many of them feminists and leaders of women's organizations. After all, this was a gathering of leaders of women's groups, and Moon had just declared himself as a feminist ally. "Later" was the message carried through in the menacing chants of this dominant majority against sexual minorities' rights.

The tension between now and later soon became a key recurring theme in sexual minority politics. What emerged from this tension was a renewed emphasis on the present and a refusal to accept postponement of social change and rights protections. On the heels of the Candlelight Protests, sexual minority activists articulated with urgency their repudiation of a future promised at the expense of the present. It was no surprise that the annual Korea Queer Culture Festival that year in 2017 adopted as its slogan, "Right now! Not later!" Several other political campaigns followed this emphasis on the urgency of the now – labor rights now, anti-discrimination laws now, minimum wage now. While many celebrated the successful end of the Candlelight Protests, sexual minority activists experienced the political moment as a somber and disheartening reminder of the ongoing political challenges to advancing and developing their rights. They had anticipated the possibility that political concessions – especially during elections – would be made at the expense of minorities whose rights were considered dispensable or at least deferrable. Many left-progressives had already predicted that Moon would shift to the right to court centrist and conservative voters. Whatever euphoria of collective action and hopes for radical social change might have been in the air for the millions of participants throughout the Candlelight Protests, human rights for sexual minorities appeared to be indefinitely excluded from the imagined future of collective action for social change, relegated to the territory of "later."

11.7 CONCLUSION

Rather than simply cast doubt on whether *any* progress on LGBTI rights has taken place or to suggest that the future is entirely hopeless, this chapter has focused on the premature death of LGBTI activists and the dismissal of LGBTI rights claims as untimely and premature in order to complicate and destabilize a linear narrative of liberal progress that often emerges in studies of rights-based mobilization. I tried to contextualize the gains and significant resonance that sexual minority politics has had on emergent minority rights discourses in Korea since the 2000s, by focusing on the history of intersectional and coalitional strategies among rights claimants. I sought to show that gender and sexual minority activists on the left have fought for decades and participated in mass mobilizations like the General Strike of 1997, anti-war protests, and the Candlelight Protests in 2016–17 because they arose out of a shared commitment to a broader project of social change. Their coalitional activism countered the tendency for rights discourses to exclude or deprioritize some groups over others, as discussed in the Conclusion chapter.

One might argue that liberals' postponing of LGBTI rights is simply an expression of pragmatism. In the case of Gwak and others' protest in February 2017, Moon's defenders might suggest that he and the audience were simply asking Gwak to wait her turn to speak at the end of the event and that the chants of "Later! Later!" were not meant to be menacing or silencing. But such deferment imposes a normative order and hierarchy. In this volume, Eunkyung Kim (Chapter 3) and Erin Chung (Chapter 13) similarly uncover hierarchies of rights. To accept the terms of "later" – to simply accept the conditions of postponement and waiting – would be for sexual minorities to accept the majority's timeline and prioritization of rights claims and social change that might never actualize.

Postponement in fact is one of the most common liberal reactions to demands for sexual minority rights. In a hegemonic liberal logic of incremental social change that posits there is a *right time* at which legitimate rights claims could be achieved, social consensus is imagined as materializing somehow without disruption or controversy. Gender and sexual minorities discussed in this chapter have resisted this logic. Despite the undeniable gains in visibility and recognition in some regards (see Chapter 12), today we see a more clearly articulated backlash against sexual minority rights, especially from Christian conservatives and others who have intensified their opposition, whether by staging disruptions against the Seoul QCF or by blocking the passage of key human rights legislation. As in the case of the liberal politics of postponement seen in the wake of the Candlelight Protests, we also see continued efforts to forestall LGBTI rights, playing out with remarkable consistency as self-proclaimed liberal politicians and public figures regress or reverse their positions on gender and sexual minority rights. LGBTI activists' most contentious confrontation may in fact occur with liberals rather than with conservatives, who do not even promise postponement.

The postponement of certain rights operates in conjunction with the granting of certain other rights. It thus imposes what Lauren Berlant (2011) would call "cruel optimism." Postponement, perhaps even more so than outright opposition, constitutes an effort to convince us that the present is a better version of the past, even when it is not, insisting that we ought to simply expect the future to be better than the present, even when there is little basis for such hope. If, as Stephen Dillon (2013, 40) writes, "progress, patience, and reform are the temporalities used by the state to justify and erase the violence that continues under the names of justice, equality, and democracy," how are these present conditions of violence rendered invisible even as LGBTI politics become increasingly visible in other ways? Dillon argues that the future is described by the state as "a space of safety and security in order to maintain the violence of the present, and to temper the rage of those who refuse to wait for the future's warm embrace to arrive" (Dillon 2013, 40). The claim that LGBTI rights are premature in Korea, that they do not yet belong in the present, is a dismissal of social movements that have persisted and refused to succumb to power. It negates the fact that sexual minority activism has already been part of numerous human rights and minority coalitions since the 1990s, already constituting an integral part of an interwoven network of progressive politics for nearly thirty years. The brief history of LGBTI rights activism recounted in this chapter demonstrates that a postponement of human rights at heart means a deadly deferment of livable lives.

REFERENCES

Berlant, Lauren. 2011. *Cruel Optimism.* Durham: Duke University Press.

Chang, Paul Y. 2015. *Protest Dialectics: State Repression and South Korea's Democracy Movement, 1970–1979.* Stanford: Stanford University Press.

Cho, Ara. 2016. "Seongsosuja rideo inteobyu – Sarangbadeul yonggi" [Sexual minority interview – Courage to be loved]. *Daehangnaeil [University Tomorrow],* January 14, 2016.

Cho, Kuk. 1997. "Tension between the National Security Law and Constitutionalism in South Korea: Security for What." *Boston University International Law Journal* 15(1): 125–74.

Chua, Lynette J. 2015. "The Vernacular Mobilization of Human Rights in Myanmar's Sexual Orientation and Gender Identity Movement." *Law & Society Review* 49(2): 299–332.

Chun, Jennifer Jihye. 2009. *Organizing at the Margins: The Symbolic Politics of Labor in South Korea and the United States.* Ithaca: Cornell University Press.

Daehakdongseongaeja ingwonyeonhap (Daedongin) [University Gay and Lesbian Human Rights Alliance], 1998a. *Dyke* 1 (March 15).

Daehakdongseongaeja ingwonyeonhap (Daedongin) [University Gay and Lesbian Human Rights Alliance], 1998b. *Dyke* 2 (May 15).

Dillon, Stephen. 2013. "'It's Here, It's That Time:' Race, Queer Futurity, and the Temporality of Violence in Born in Flames." *Women & Performance: A Journal of Feminist Theory* 23 (1) (March): 38–51.

Gilmore, Ruth Wilson. 2007. *Golden Gulag: Prisons, Surplus, Crisis, and Opposition in Globalizing California.* Berkeley: University of California Press.

Gwak, Sang'a. 2017. "Seonggonghoedae chonghaksaenghoejang huboga malhaneun 'naega keomingautan iyu' (inteobyu)" ['The reason I came out' according to the candidate for President of the student government at Sungkonghoe University (interview)]. *Huffington Post Korea,* March 29, 2017. www.huffingtonpost.kr/2017/03/29/story_n_15673314.html.

Han, Ju Hui Judy. 2015. "Kwieo jeongchiwa kwieo jijeonghak" [Queer Politics and Queer Geopolitics]. *Munhwa gwahak* 83 (September): 62–81.

2018. "Shifting Geographies of Proximity: Korean-Led Evangelical Christian Missions and the U.S. Empire." In *Ethnographies of U.S. Empire,* edited by Carole McGranahan and John Collins, 194–213. Durham: Duke University Press.

Han, Woori. 2018. "Proud of Myself as LGBTQ: The Seoul Pride Parade, Homonationalism, and Queer Developmental Citizenship." *Korea Journal* 58(2) (June): 27–57.

Hankyoreh. 2017. "Much work remains to be done on first anniversary of candlelight revolution." *Hankyoreh*, October 28, 2017. www.hani.co.kr/arti/english_edition/e_editorial/
816448.html.

Hong, Grace Kyungwon. 2015. *Death beyond Disavowal: The Impossible Politics of Difference*.
Minneapolis: University of Minnesota Press.

Im, Kim Oju. 2003. "'Dangsindeuldo da dongseongaejaya? Bukkeureoun jul ara'" [Are you all
homosexuals, too? You should be ashamed of yourselves]. *Cham Sesang*, July 30, 2003.
www.newscham.net/news/view.php?board=news&nid=22462&page=1998&cate
gory2=1.

Kim, Nan. 2017. "Candlelight and the Yellow Ribbon: Catalyzing Re-Democratization in
South Korea." *The Asia-Pacific Journal* 15(4) (July 15, 2017).

———. 2018. "The Color of Dissent and a Vital Politics of Fragility in South Korea." *The Journal of
Asian Studies* 77(4) (November): 971–90.

Kim, Sunhyuk. 2000. *The Politics of Democratization in Korea: The Role of Civil Society*.
Philadelphia: Temple University Press.

Kwon Kim, Hyun-young, and John (Song Pae) Cho. 2011. "The Korean Gay and Lesbian
Movement 1993–2008: From 'Identity' and 'Community' to 'Human Rights'." In *South
Korean Social Movements: From Democracy to Civil Society*, edited by Gi-Wook Shin
and Paul Y. Chang, 206–23. Abingdon, Oxon; New York: Routledge.

Lee, Namhee. 2007. *The Making of Minjung: Democracy and the Politics of Representation in
South Korea*. Ithaca: Cornell University Press.

New York Times. 1996. "Ghosts of dictatorship in South Korea." *The New York Times*,
December 30, 1996.

Siu. 2018. *Kwieo apokallipseu: Saranggwa hyeomoui jeongchihak* [Queer apocalypse: Politics
of love and hate]. Seoul, Korea: Hyeonsil Munhwa.

Yang Jeong, Ji-geon. 2003. "Hangiyeon, hangichonge 'dongseongaeja jugeum' sajoe yogu"
[Hangiyeon demands apology from Hangichong for the death of a homosexual]. *News
N Joy*, May 31, 2003. www.newsnjoy.or.kr/news/articleView.html?idxno=4544.

Yi, Sang-heui. 2013. "Dongseongaejaui gomindo 'eumnanmulideon geuttae'" [When gay
worries used to be considered obscene]. *Hankyoreh 21*, May 10, 2013. http://h21
.hani.co.kr/arti/society/society_general/34481.html.

Yi, Se-a. 2017. "'Peminiseuteu daetongnyeong' doegetdaneun Mun Jae-in, seongsosuja
ingweoneun 'najunge'?" ['Feminist President' Moon Jae-in, are sexual minorities'
human rights for later?]. *Yeoseong Sinmun*, February 17, 2017. www.womennews.co.kr
/news/articleView.html?idxno=111816.

Yi, Yong-pil. 2017. "Moon Jae-in 'Dongseongae jiijihaji anchiman, chabyeolbadaseon
andwe'" ['I don't support homosexuality, but you shouldn't face discrimination' says
Moon Jae-in]. *News N Joy*, February 13, 2017. www.newsnjoy.or.kr/news/articleView
.html?idxno=208845.

Yun, Hyeong-jung. 2017. "Bangimun deoktaege mutge dwaetda ... dongseonggyeolhone
chanseonghasinayo?" [Thanks to Ban Ki-moon, we can ask ... do you support same-
sex marriage?]. *Hankyoreh*, January 31, 2017. www.hani.co.kr/arti/politics/polibar/780780
.html.

12

Discovering Diversity

The Anti-discrimination Legislation Movement in South Korea

Jihye Kim and Sung Soo Hong

12.1 INTRODUCTION

The Republic of Korea (South Korea, hereafter, Korea) has played a vigorous role in the United Nations (UN) and its human rights missions during the past decade. Ban Ki-moon serving as UN Secretary-General from 2007 to 2016 is a prominent example. At the state level, Korea has been a member of the UN Human Rights Council since its inception in 2006, assuming the presidency in 2016. Since becoming a UN member state in 1991, South Korea has ratified seven out of the nine core international human rights treaties.[1] However, Korea has yet to fully comply with treaty norms regarding nondiscrimination rights. Treaty bodies have repeatedly recommended that Korea adopt comprehensive anti-discrimination legislation, as noted in the concluding observations of the UN Committee on the Economic, Social and Cultural Rights (CESCR), the UN Committee on the Rights of the Child (CRC), UN Committee on the Elimination of Discrimination against Women (CEDAW), UN Committee on the Elimination of Racial Discrimination (CERD), and the UN Human Rights Committee (CESCR 2009, 2017; CEDAW 2011, 2018; CRC 2011, 2019; CERD 2012, 2019; CCPR 2015). Yet, the Korean government has not complied with these recommendations to date.

Domestically, the Korean Constitution enshrines the principles of equality and nondiscrimination,[2] and some statutes already include anti-discrimination protections concerning sex, disabilities, age, and employment types.[3] However, Korea has

---

[1] As of May 2020, South Korea has not yet ratified the Convention for the Protection of All Persons from Enforced Disappearance and the International Convention on the Protection of the Rights of All Migrant Workers and Members of Their Families.

[2] Article 11 of the Constitution states:

    (1) All citizens shall be equal before the law, and there shall be no discrimination in political, economic, social or cultural life on account of sex, religion or social status.

    (2) No privileged caste shall be recognized or ever established in any form.

    (3) The awarding of decorations or distinctions of honor in any form shall be effective only for recipients, and no privileges shall ensue therefrom.

[3] Specific anti-discrimination laws include *Namnyeo goyong pyeongdeung beop* (Act on Equal Employment between Men and Women), Act No. 3989 (1987), *Jangaeinchabyeolgeumji min gwolli-guje deunge gwanhan beomnyul* (Act on the Prohibition of Discrimination against Persons with

failed to enact a "comprehensive" anti-discrimination law as a basic law that would prohibit all forms of discrimination based on any grounds. While several bills have been proposed with "anti-discrimination act" (*chabyeolgeumjibeop*) in the title, the phrase "comprehensive anti-discrimination law" (*pogwaljeok chabyeolgeumjibeop*) is more widely used in Korean to avoid confusion with narrower anti-discrimination laws, which cover specific areas of discrimination. Adopting the latter term, this chapter explores the movement for a comprehensive anti-discrimination law. The first attempt to pass comprehensive anti-discrimination legislation in Korea occurred in 2007 and was a governmental action that aimed to comply with international human rights treaties. Yet, this bill and subsequent proposals have never passed due to forceful opposition led mainly by conservative Protestant groups.

The repeated failure to enact comprehensive anti-discrimination legislation in Korea seems to indicate the ineffectiveness of international human rights law. If one assumes the state to be a rational actor, then commitments to human rights treaties are motivated by self-interest, whether in response to coercion from powerful states or to emulate powerful states in the international community (see also Chapter 5). Even repressive states may ratify international human rights treaties because they can gain legitimacy and avoid scrutiny of their domestic human rights situation (Moravcsik 1997; Hafner-Burton and Tsutsui 2005; Hathaway 2007; Hafner-Burton et al. 2008). The rational choice model seems to explain the incongruence between the act of treaty ratification in form and the realization of human rights norms in substance; indeed, South Korea, a frontline member of the international community advocating for human rights, falls short of fulfilling international norms on nondiscrimination rights by which it has agreed to abide.

This, however, does not mean that human rights treaties and norms are useless. Scholars indicate that once states ratify treaties, they are more likely to comply with the treaties' obligations at least in part because the treaties empower domestic rights advocates and "precommit" governments to be responsive (Hafner-Burton and Tsutsui 2005; Simmons 2009, 144–46). Koh (1999, 1397–417) likewise highlights the "vertical" process whereby nonstate actors leverage their government's treaty commitments to lobby for compliance with international human rights law. He talks about "norm-internalization," meaning that international human rights law is enforced not just by external pressure from state actors in the global community but also by nonstate individuals and organizations, both locally and globally, that use the international human rights norm to push for domestic changes. Here, democracy is an important precondition for seeking compliance with human rights norms,

Disabilities, Remedies for Infringement of Their Rights, Etc.), Act No. 8341 (2007), *Goyongsang yeollyeongchabyeolgeumji min goryeongjagoyongchokjine gwanhan beomnyul* (Act on Prohibition of Age Discrimination in Employment and Elderly Employment Promotion), Act No. 8962 (2008), *Giganje min dansigangeulloja boho deunge gwanhan beomnyul* (Act on the Protection, Etc. of Fixed-term and Part-time Employees), Act No. 8074 (2006), and *Pagyeongeulloja boho deunge gwanhan beomnyul* (Act on the Protection, Etc. of Temporary Agency Workers), Act No. 5512 (1998).

as it enables civil society groups to organize and seek to influence domestic outcomes. At the same time, it also allows groups opposed to a norm to mobilize (e.g., Bob 2012).

As a society that achieved democracy by overthrowing a military dictatorship in 1987, South Korea seemed ready to integrate international human rights norms. Korea's pro-democracy movement had already incorporated human rights into its discursive framework as early as the 1970s (Chang 2015, 161). Korea's first opposition president, Kim Dae-jung, established the National Human Rights Commission of Korea (hereafter, NHRCK) in 2001 (see Chapter 5). The government's proposed anti-discrimination bill in 2007 was supposed to be the beginning of the new era that would bring society into alignment with international human rights standards in terms of the nondiscrimination principle. Yet, such legislation has still not been achieved, more than a decade later. Korea's long failure to enact comprehensive anti-discrimination legislation, despite repeated recommendations to do so from international human rights bodies, was enough to lead some activists and observers to wonder whether international human rights laws had any meaning.

This chapter contends that a form of "norm-internalization" nevertheless took place at the domestic level in Korea, despite repeated frustration in legislating comprehensive nondiscrimination rights. The analysis seeks to illuminate the significance of this process for the ongoing anti-discrimination movement and broader Korean society. This chapter argues that the movement for an anti-discrimination law was not just a movement to gain actionable legal rights. Rather, it was also a movement to recognize people's diversity and a struggle to reshape social norms so that being different would be respected. This shows that rights movements and the realization of rights should not be simply recognized in terms of their legal achievements; rather, they should be properly seen in their political and social contexts. Indeed, the anti-discrimination movement is simultaneously a social, political, cultural, and legal movement that recognizes and accepts minorities, who were hitherto oppressed, as equal members of society.

The chapter proceeds to introduce the role of the NHRCK in opening up an institutional channel for rights claims. It then explains the origins of the 2007 anti-discrimination bill and its successors, outlining hurdles to their enactment. This analysis shows how controversies over anti-discrimination legislation proposals paradoxically made minority groups, notably LGBTI people, more politically visible.[4] The subsequent section discusses the emergence of diversity as a new phenomenon in Korea and details various NGOs' activities in the anti-discrimination legislation movement. The chapter concludes by arguing that, despite the on-going failure to pass legislation, the last decade of activism has not been

---

[4] In this chapter, the term "LGBTI people" is used to refer to all people who do not fall into heterosexual or cisgender identities, though in Korean "sexual minorities" (*seong sosuja*) or "queer" (*kwuieo*) are most common.

fruitless but has helped to create a new norm of equality that embraces all forms of diversity.

12.2 THE ESTABLISHMENT OF THE NHRCK AND NEW CLAIMS OF DISCRIMINATION

Awareness of discrimination and concerns about equality rights emerged in the context of Korea's establishment of a National Human Rights Commission in 2001. Under Korea's postliberation authoritarian regimes, human rights violations were a serious problem and included torture, illegal detention, and violations of fundamental freedoms of thought and expression (see, e.g., Chapter 4). In the process of Korea's democratization, however, the focus had been on bringing an end to the military dictatorship and establishing a democratic government, which would protect basic political and civil rights. By 1993, when Kim Young-sam was inaugurated as Korea's first civilian president in decades, Korean human rights activists were beginning to take interest in a wider array of human rights and participated in the World Conference on Human Rights in Vienna. President Kim Dae-jung, who had himself been a victim of serious human rights violations during his time as a dissident and opposition politician, took office in 1998 and made human rights a priority.

Korean civil society groups thus began to press the government to comply with international human rights standards. In the 1990s, NGOs emerged to campaign for various human rights, including freedom of expression and the rights of children, students, sexual minorities, and prisoners. As Hwang (Chapter 5) details, they also called for a national human rights institution to ensure compliance (J. Lim 1999; G. Lee 2000). In 1997, presidential candidate Kim Dae-jung pledged a "human rights law agenda and the establishment of a national human rights commission." After winning the election, he included the establishment of a National Human Rights Commission among his top 100 policy priorities. In May 2001, the National Human Rights Commission Act[5] was passed and, in November, the NHRCK was launched.

At first, the NHRCK focused on protecting civil rights. The main human rights goals for Korean society, which had long suffered under a military dictatorship, were understood to be individual civil rights and protection from state violence. Indeed, human rights protections during police investigations and in prisons, protective facilities, and the military dramatically improved after the NHRCK's founding (see C. Lee 2007). Although the NHRCK has statutory jurisdiction over not just civil liberties but also social rights, most of its early efforts were directed at the protection of civil liberties.

As claims made to the NHRCK increased, issues of discrimination gradually gained more attention. The NHRCK Act defines "discriminatory acts violating

---

5 *Gukga ingwon wiwonhoe beop*, Act No. 17126 (2001).

equal rights" as acts of "favorable treatment, exclusion, distinction, or disadvantageous treatment of a person regarding employment, the supply or use of goods and services, and education and training, without reasonable cause." Going beyond Korea's Constitution, it also specifies discrimination on the basis of the following grounds: sex, religion, disability, age, social status, region of origin, state of origin, ethnic origin, physical appearance, marital status, pregnancy or childbirth, family type or family situation, race, skin color, ideology or political opinion, past record of crime, sexual orientation, academic background, medical history, and so on (Art. 3). Discriminatory acts include sexual harassment but exclude temporary favorable treatment to correct existing discrimination.

Through the new channel of the NHRCK, people made rights claims citing the concept of discrimination for the first time. Although, as stated earlier, specific antidiscrimination laws already contained clauses prohibiting the discrimination of women, persons with disabilities, older people, and part-time/temporary workers, discrimination was a rather new way of thinking about people's experiences of injustice. New rights claims related to discrimination on the basis of age, race, religion, sexual orientation, academic background, and others were brought to the NHRCK and resulted in substantive changes in many cases. As shown in Figure 12.1, the number of petitions regarding discriminatory acts steadily increased after 2002 (NHRCK 2005, 2009, 2014, 2018; see also Hong 2011, 89). In contrast, complaints related to civil liberties infringements by state authorities remained stable and then slightly declined (C. U. Park 2008, 3–4).

However, the NHRCK lacked sufficient capacity and power to address discrimination issues. The NHRCK Act was simply a law regarding the NHRCK's organization. According to the NHRCK Act, human rights are based on the Korean Constitution, Korean laws, and international human rights law, but the NHRCK Act does not stipulate any specific substantive rights to prevent and eliminate

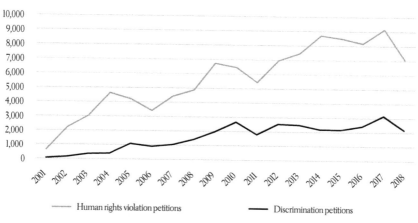

FIGURE 12.1 The number of NHRCK petitions.

discrimination. The Act's only detailed content related to discrimination is the definition of a "discriminatory actions violating equal rights," over which the Act gives the NHRCK jurisdiction to investigate complaints, declare an action a rights violation, and issue nonbinding recommendations. The Act does not elaborate on the concept of discrimination, responsibilities of actors, guiding principles, rules, and standards for determination, or outline specific mechanisms and measures to correct discrimination.

Consequently, activists and experts increasingly considered comprehensive anti-discrimination legislation necessary as a basic law that would provide effective remedies for the increasingly diversified discrimination claims (Han 2011, 91–92). As discussed in detail in the following section, drafting such comprehensive anti-discrimination legislation was initiated by the government at first, but soon became one of the urgent agenda items of many human rights NGOs, human rights lawyers, and progressive political parties. Notably, upon the government's failure to enact an anti-discrimination act in 2007, NGOs began to form an alliance to organize the anti-discrimination movement and started lobbying the National Assembly to enact an anti-discrimination act. Opponents of such legislation also mobilized.

12.3 CONTROVERSIES REGARDING ANTI-DISCRIMINATION LEGISLATION

The first attempt to enact an anti-discrimination law was led by both the NHRCK and the government. In May 2001, the NHRCK held an unofficial "meeting on discrimination research" to determine standards for identifying and remedying discrimination. As a result, in August 2002, the NHRCK issued a report entitled "Guidelines for Judging Discrimination based on the NHRCK Act" (Group to Study Discrimination 2002). In January 2003, a new committee composed of NHRCK staff and outside experts also began studying the question of a general anti-discrimination law, which included examining other countries' laws (S. J. Lee 2009, 430–35).[6] Within a few years, four NHRCK commissioners set up another special committee for this purpose, and it proposed an anti-discrimination bill after gathering opinions from experts, human rights organizations, ordinary citizens, and relevant authorities.

Additionally, the Roh Moo-hyun administration had pledged to enact an anti-discrimination law when it took office in February of 2003 as part of its national agenda. It tasked the NHRCK with designing legislation that would realize an egalitarian society by alleviating five types of discrimination: gender, academic background, temporary worker status, people with disabilities, and foreign workers.

---

[6] Guidelines on the prohibition of discrimination diffused in the European Union (EU), and member states enacted anti-discrimination laws. The 1998 Human Rights Act in the United Kingdom, the 2008 Anti-Discrimination Act in Sweden, and the 2006 General Equal Treatment Act in Germany are representative of this trend.

To further this agenda, the Presidential Committee on Social Inclusion, which was established in June 2004, began addressing discrimination related to the following issues: women, people with disabilities, academic background, temporary worker status, foreigners/migrants, and age. The Committee built on several laws with anti-discrimination clauses, such as the Equal Employment Opportunity Act[7] and the Gender Discrimination Prevention and Relief Act.[8]

In October 2004, the government determined that anti-discrimination institutions should be unified to enhance the efficiency of Korea's extant but fragmented claims-making channels and remedy mechanisms: the NHRCK, the Committee for Gender Equality Promotion, and the Committee on Equal Employment. As a result, the Gender Discrimination Prevention and Relief Act was abolished in June 2005 in order to make the NHRCK the sole body to receive and assess claims regarding gender discrimination. With this, the Korean system took a step closer toward a comprehensive anti-discrimination law and a unified anti-discrimination institution. To complete that process, the NHRCK proposed in July 2006 that the government enact comprehensive anti-discrimination legislation, and the Ministry of Justice announced a draft bill in September 2007, after a yearlong review. This bill detailed the definition of discrimination, the scope and exceptions of discrimination, the obligations of the government and local authorities, remedies, and prohibited conduct in the areas of services, premises, and education.

Strong opposition to the draft bill arose, however, mainly from the business community and conservative Protestant groups. Business groups, such as the Korea Enterprises Federation and the Federation of Korean Industries, argued that the bill would infringe on the freedom of business, which is guaranteed by the Korean Constitution (Art. 15) (K. Y. Kim 2007). Conservative Protestant groups, such as the Christian Council of Korea (*Hanguk gidokgyo chongyeonhapoe*), opposed the inclusion of sexual orientation as a potential basis for discrimination. As a result, when the government presented the bill to the National Assembly in December 2007, it had removed seven grounds and contexts of discrimination that would have been prohibited: medical history, country of birth, language, family type or family situation, criminal and protective disposition history, sexual orientation, and academic background. The excisions were a setback from existing human rights standards, which was unacceptable to proponents of comprehensive anti-discrimination legislation. Adopting the "ragged bill" was likened to "promoting discrimination" because it ran counter to the universality of human rights (S. J. Park 2007, 124–25).

The excised bases of discrimination and the reasons behind the removals paradoxically revealed some of the most entrenched forms of discrimination in Korean society. Conservative Protestant groups' opposition against the inclusion of "sexual

---

[7] *Namnyeo goyong pyeongdeung beop* (Equal Employment Opportunity Act), Act No. 3989 (1987).
[8] *Namnyeo chabyeol geumji beop* (Gender Discrimination Prevention and Relief Act), Act No. 5934 (1999).

orientation" among the prohibited grounds of discrimination spawned an organized movement using protest rallies and advertisements. Instigating the public's negative sentiment with slogans such as "What on earth? Can a man be a daughter-in-law?" they were fiercely opposed to anti-discrimination legislation "that would condone homosexuality" (S. J. Park 2007, 124). The resulting bill from the government seemed to civil society groups as so compromised that it would not legally help realize the principle of nondiscrimination. Rather, the bill, if passed, would give society the opposite message that discrimination against some people for some reasons was permissible (S. J. Park 2007, 125). Civil society groups, therefore, sought an alternative bill, which Rep. Roh Hoe-chan of the small left-wing Democratic Labor Party and nine other lawmakers proposed in January 2008. However, both bills expired without coming to a vote at the end of the 17th National Assembly.

Opposition to anti-discrimination legislation grew even stronger and more organized after successfully scuttling efforts to legislate comprehensive nondiscrimination rights. Conservative Protestant groups emerged as central players in the opposition camp by establishing organizations with specific goals to ban homosexuality and block anti-discrimination legislation, such as the National Union Against Homosexuality Anti-Discrimination Act (*Dongseongae chabyeolguemjibeop bandae gungmin yeonhap*) and the Coalition for Moral Sexuality (*Bareun seongmunhwareul wihan gungmin yeonhap*) (D. W. Lee 2010). Meanwhile, the business community virtually dropped out of the anti-discrimination law debate. Conservative Protestant groups particularly emphasized homosexuality, which became the "black hole" issue that stymied further dialogue on anti-discrimination legislation. Hate speech against LGBTI people – calling them sinners, AIDS transmitters, destroyers of the social order, and even "pro-North Korea sympathizers" – became more common and attracted more people to the anti-LGBTI movement (Go 2008; J. Y. Lee 2013; J. H. Lee 2014).

Five subsequent anti-discrimination bills also failed. In 2011, during the 18th National Assembly, Rep. Park Eun-soo (Democratic Party, Minjudang) proposed the Anti-Discrimination Basic Act bill, using the phrase "sexual equality" to avoid a direct reference to sexual orientation or gender identity. In parallel, Rep. Kwon Young-gil (Democratic Labor Party, Minjunodongdang) submitted the Anti-Discrimination Act bill, which included the core contents of Rep. Roh Hoe-chan's 2008 bill, described earlier. During the 19th National Assembly, three similar bills were proposed. Two of the bills, introduced by Rep. Kim Han-gil and Rep. Choi Won-sik (Democratic Party, Minjudang), respectively, were withdrawn just two months later in April 2013 because conservative Protestant groups bombarded the lawmakers who participated in the bills with protest phone calls and text messages (Lee and Choi 2014).

International human rights treaty bodies expressed concerns over the situation and repeatedly urged the Korean government to take steps to enact comprehensive anti-discrimination legislation that included sexual orientation among the prohibited grounds of discrimination (CESCR 2009, 2017; CEDAW 2011, 2018; CRC 2011, 2019; CCPR 2015). The government's response has been evasive. For example, President Moon Jae-in's administration did not include anti-discrimination legislation among its top 100 policy objectives when it assumed office in 2017, reportedly because it would stoke social controversies (Takeshi 2017). As elaborated in Judy Han (Chapter 11), the government argued that there was a "lack of social consensus" about the need for comprehensive anti-discrimination legislation, even though nondiscrimination principles figure prominently in international human rights law and the Korean Constitution (J. Kim 2018).

This period, however, saw some progress in terms of disability rights, as the Act on the Prohibition of Discrimination against Persons with Disabilities, Remedy against Infringement of Their Rights, Etc.[9] (hereafter Disability Discrimination Act, or DDA) passed unanimously in 2007 (see Chapter 10).[10] The women's movement similarly argued for the need for specific legislation prohibiting gender discrimination and sexual harassment (S. Park 2016), but gender-specific anti-discrimination bills have failed after being lodged multiple times at the National Assembly.[11] A separate bill prohibiting racial discrimination was discussed in 2009 after being proposed by Rep. Jun Byung-hun (Democratic Party), but the public hearing only revealed entrenched racism in Korean society to the point where people expressly denied the basic principle of equal treatment to migrants (K. T. Lee 2009). Although the anti-racism movement consistently called for anti-racial discrimination legislation in compliance with the CERD, it largely participated in the alliance with other minority groups for comprehensive anti-discrimination legislation, rather than a separate law.[12]

12.4 THE EMERGENCE OF MINORITY IDENTITY GROUPS

The backlash against including LGBTI individuals' rights in a comprehensive anti-discrimination law – arguably the most controversial feature of the proposed legislation – has paradoxically rendered sexual minorities more socially visible. For a long time, LGBTI people were largely invisible in Korean society. They were implicitly categorized as "deviant" or "abnormal," but the NHRCK began redefining them as

---

[9] *Jangaein chabyeol geumji beop*, Act No. 15272 (2007).

[10] Disability activists had demanded an independent law on disability discrimination more forcefully than comprehensive anti-discrimination legislation. They insisted on legislation that specified forms of disability-related discrimination and established an independent body in charge of processing disability discrimination claims (Nam 2007). Although an independent DDA was enacted in 2007, it designates the NHRCK as the main claims-making channel for disability discrimination.

[11] Gender-specific anti-discrimination bills, usually titled the Bill on Prohibiting Sex Discrimination and Sexual Harassment and their Remedies, were submitted as follows: by Rep. Kim Sang-hee on November 20, 2013, by Rep. Yu Seung-hui on April 10, 2015, by Rep. Nam In-soon on March 13, 2018, and by Rep. Kim Sang-hee on March 26, 2018.

[12] Interview with Jung Hye-sil, activist of the South Korean Coalition for Anti-Discrimination Legislation (February 12, 2018).

a protected category emblematic of society's diversity. In an early case in 2003, for example, the NHRCK decided that a provision of the Enforcement Decree of the Youth Protection Act, which listed homosexuality as a harmful act from which youths should be barred, was a violation of human rights regarding sexual orientation (NHRCK 2003). The decision and the declaration that "homosexuality is a normal sexual orientation" was an "astonishment" to Protestant churches, "defying the creation order of God" "in the obsession of minority rights," as expressed in a statement released immediately after the decision by the Christian Council of Korea (2003). The CCK thus encouraged Korean churches to stand against homosexuality.

Such backlash targeting LGBTI people, especially gay males, emanated mainly from conservative Protestant groups, which aimed to block comprehensive anti-discrimination legislation. However, it in effect helped LGBTI people become a socially visible identity group. In particular, momentum for the development of identity politics stemmed from two sit-in protests by LGBTI groups in response to aggressive conservative mobilization against the Seoul Student Rights Ordinance of 2012 (hereafter the Seoul Ordinance) and the Charter of Human Rights for Seoul Citizens of 2014 (hereafter the Seoul Charter).[13]

In the case of the proposed Seoul Ordinance, the bill included sexual orientation, gender identity, pregnancy, and birth as prohibited grounds of discrimination. Conservative Protestant groups criticized the bill by claiming that it "would spread homosexuality in schools" and "would create confusion in the value system which keeps our society healthy" (M. K. Kim 2011; Shin 2012). Opponents of the proposed ordinance pressured Seoul Metropolitan Council members with a flood of text messages and emails urging rejection of the bill. About fifty young LGBTI people and activists responded by staging a six-day sit-in in the lobby of the Seoul Metropolitan Council. This was the first time that LGBTI people as a group had ever come out to claim their rights with their faces visible in Korea (Kim and Na 2013, 349–52). They advocated for their rights by demanding "Schools without Discrimination." Despite conservative backlash, the Ordinance eventually passed with the full inclusion of the clauses related to sexual orientation and gender identity, as originally drafted.[14]

The second LGBTI sit-in began in December 2014 when the then Seoul Mayor Park Won-soon rejected the promulgation of the Seoul Charter after facing criticism from Protestant groups. Park, a former human rights lawyer, further shocked civil society organizations on the left by avowing that he "does not support homosexuality" at a meeting with the Council of Presbyterian Churches (S. G. Kang 2014). The resulting sit-in by LGBTI people and advocates in the lobby of the Seoul

---

[13] *Seoulteukbyeolsi haksaengingwon jorye*, Ordinance No. 5247 (2012).

[14] The vote was fifty-four in favor versus twenty-nine against and four abstentions on January 26, 2012; however, the final draft included some revisions to the original draft regarding restrictions on assembly and attire (Chun 2011).

Metropolitan City Hall lasted for seven days. The sit-in gained wide support from both LGBTI and non-LGBTI groups. Four political parties and about 300 NGOs, including the countries' largest, publicly expressed their support for the sit-in (Bae 2014; Jun 2014; S. A. Lee 2014).[15] The Charter, however, was never promulgated, leading the mayor to apologize but also claim that it needed "more time and deeper social discussion" (Eum 2014). Han (Chapter 11) further discusses the idea of deferring rights protections.

Korean society has nonetheless been changing, and various minority identity groups, in addition to LGBTI people, have emerged and asserted their rights as members of Korean society. For example, migrants became more visible as the number of foreigners steadily increased, reaching 2 million in 2016 (Statistics Korea 2019). The historically dominant approach toward people with migrant backgrounds was to exclude and marginalize them, as exemplified by how overseas Chinese (*hwagyo*) were deprived of equal rights (K. T. Park 2008; An and Woo 2015). Also, people with multiracial backgrounds, so-called mixed-blood (*honhyeol*), were historically overrepresented among those put up for overseas adoption. As Timothy Lim put it, "the discourse of Korean homogeneity . . . made/makes possible the near-total exclusion of 'non-Koreans' from membership in Korean society" (T. Lim 2010, 53).

With the growth of the migrant population mainly through marriage and labor, however, the "near-total exclusion" was no longer an option for Korean society (see Chapter 13). Consequently, the concept of multiculturalism emerged (T. Lim 2010). The 2008 Multicultural Families Support Act[16] defines a "multicultural family" as an international marriage that includes at least one Korean national. The intent may have been to reflect the idea of multiculturalism, but the narrow usage of "multicultural" in this context – that is, referring only to marriage migrants and thus their Korea-linked heteronormative families – effectively set Korean culture above the multiplicity of cultures.[17]

This limited view of multiculturalism has failed to deter hate speech toward migrants. Several online communities formed with the aim to oppose multiculturalism and keep Koreans' "purity" (J. G. Kang 2012). Hate speech messages included "Migrants destroy Korean ethnic identity," "Migrants takes away Korean citizens' tax

---

[15] NGOs include People's Solidarity for Participatory Democracy, Minbyeon (Lawyers for a Democratic Society), Korean Confederation of Trade Unions, Korea Women's Associations United, Korea Federation for Environmental Movements, and so on, and political parties include Justice Party, United Progressive Party, Green Party, and Labor Party.

[16] *Damunhwa gajok jiwon beop* (Multicultural Families Support Act), Act No. 8937 (2008), amended as Act No. 15204 (2017).

[17] Article 2(1) of the Multicultural Families Support Act defines "multicultural family" as follows: (a) A family comprised of immigrants by marriage defined in subparagraph 3 of Article 2 of the Framework Act on Treatment of Foreigners Residing in the Republic of Korea and persons who have acquired nationality of the Republic of Korea pursuant to Articles 2 through 4 of the Nationality Act; (b) A family comprised of a person who has acquired nationality of the Republic of Korea pursuant to Articles 3 and 4 of the Nationality Act and a person who has acquired nationality of the Republic of Korea pursuant to Articles 2 through 4 of the aforementioned Act.

money," and "Muslims are rapists" (Kim et al. 2019, 136–48). Societal opposition toward migrants erupted on a large scale when about 500 Yemenis asylum seekers landed on Jeju Island in 2018. Fueled by online hate speech, ordinary citizens mobilized to demand an end to the entry of Yemenis and other asylum seekers. More than 700,000 people signed an online petition to the president asking the government to revise laws and tighten policies on refugees.[18] The government responded by discontinuing visa-free entry for Yemenis traveling to Jeju Island. The anti-migrant backlash, however, also sparked mobilization by migrant rights' advocates, as discussed by Patricia Goedde (Chapter 8).

In recent years, hate speech over women's rights similarly exploded. After the shocking and apparently misogynistic 2016 homicide of a woman in a restroom near Gangnam Subway Station and numerous other instances of gender-based violence, a new wave of feminism sought to combat gender-based violence, gender roles and stereotypes, income disparity, and other gender inequality issues (Choung and Lee 2018). As feminist voices grew, backlash appeared disparaging feminists and asserting that policies for gender equality were reverse discrimination against men, and even developed into employing aggressive methods such as doxing and threatening people who publicly advocated for women's rights (S. J. Park 2017).[19] Anti-feminist groups asserted that Korean society already achieved gender equality and that feminism only causes gender inequality to the disadvantage of men because it favors women (S. H. Kim 2019).[20]

Amid this contestation, the voices of previously oppressed people were emerging and getting stronger, and equality and nondiscrimination rights gradually became salient issues in the political arena. Nevertheless, many politicians opted not to take sides, as if they see that the issues demand an impossible political choice between the interests of the advantaged and the disadvantaged. The silence of the government and the National Assembly exacerbated tensions around inequality, and nonresponse grew increasingly untenable in the face of Korea's growing diversity. Growing social awareness now converged into calls for reforms. For example, a recent survey conducted by KBS in 2019 revealed that 70 percent of respondents supported the regulation of hate speech, and two-thirds of them supported comprehensive anti-discrimination legislation (Ku 2019). Similarly, a survey conducted by the NHRCK showed that 81 percent agreed with strengthening regulations on hate speech and 72.9 percent supported the adoption of an anti-discrimination law (NHRCK 2019, 278, 284). A year later in June 2020, support for anti-discrimination legislation rose to

---

[18] "Petition for Abolition/Constitutional Revision on Refugee Law, No-Visa Entry of Country, and Permission of Refugee Status Application," Office of the President, www1.president.go.kr/petitions/269548 (accessed January 9, 2020). Between June 13 and July 13, 2018, a total of 714,875 people signed the petition.

[19] Doxing describes the tactic of publicizing private or identifying information online.

[20] This backlash was mainly found in some male-dominated internet communities such as ILBE and some books were published (Oserabi 2017; Oserabi et al. 2019).

88.5 percent (Park 2020). The organized backlash against minority rights still seems to hold back the government and politicians from enacting such reforms, but indeed, it is getting harder to avoid the issue of nondiscrimination rights.

12.5 CONTESTING RIGHTS AMID KOREA'S NEWFOUND DIVERSITY

Diversity is rather a new concept to Korean society, but it has fueled increased awareness of equality rights. Historically, Korean culture, as in other East Asian countries, was influenced by Confucianism, which values conformity over diversity (Yum 1988; Yung 2010). The relational emphasis in Confucianism made individuals perceive themselves through the lens of their roles within different groups (Ho 1995, 115–16). This positionality subjugated the self to the group and conflicted with the idea of embracing diversity and recognizing the equal rights of all, regardless of whether they fall outside the range of what is "normal" to most groups. Though harmony is a Confucian ideal, it is usually translated into uniformity "to maintain the status quo or buttress the ruling clique by eliminating opposing views" (Yung 2010, 1921).

The Korean Constitution, which shapes the modern democratic values of society, promotes equality. Indeed, it has enshrined individuals' rights to equality before the law and to nondiscrimination since its establishment in 1948, and the Korean Constitutional Court has interpreted it as protecting the idea of a pluralistic democracy (Constitutional Court of Korea 2003; 2009), as Mosler (Chapter 6) details. However, the Korean Constitution, as last amended in 1987 following democratization, does not expressly refer to the idea of diversity or pluralism. Instead, it reflects ethnic nationalism in its Preamble and Article 9 by requiring the "consolidation of national unity" and "promotion of national culture." While perhaps not intentionally, the Constitution is insufficient for Korea's diversified modern society (S. T. Kim 2010, 18; Choi 2012, 14–17).

Since conservative Korean Protestant groups intervened on issues of discrimination in mid-2005, they have fought to stop changes moving toward diversity. In some respects, Protestant values are congruent with traditional Korean values derived from Confucian teachings. Historically speaking, the similarities were emphasized to make Christianity more acceptable to Korean people (S. Kim 1986; A. Kim 2000). In this regard, teachings on men's superiority and dominance over women, and family values that command wives' subordination to their husbands and children's obedience to their parents, were reinforced by Christian teachings (S. Kim 1986, 128). Christian groups' opposition to gays or migrants was thus not just based on their reading of the Bible, but it also reflected their uneasiness with notions of equality and nondiscrimination, which clashed with Confucian-rooted ideals of social order.

However, anti-gay and anti-Muslim rhetoric from conservative Protestant groups cannot be solely attributed to their theological or Confucian values. Just as transnational human rights advocacy networks and discourses have strengthened NGOs, so has anti-gay and anti-Muslim rhetoric diffused transnationally (e.g., Bob 2012). Homophobic propaganda appealing for the preservation of traditional families or the prevention of HIV/AIDS infections echoes what have been asserted by fundamentalist Christian groups in the United States (Lee and Baek 2017; Cho and Sohn 2018). Portraying Muslims as terrorists is also endemic in the United States and in European countries (J. G. Lee 2011; Kundnani 2015; K. Jung 2018). Conservative Korean Protestant groups search and cite the most current international news and issues, often with distortions for their benefit, to support their arguments (Hankyoreh 2018). They are not just keepers of historical and religious values but also active political actors involved in the creation and dissemination of contemporary hate speech against minorities for their expansion of power (Lee and Baek 2017; K. Jung 2018). As an outcome, a political party, the Christian Liberal Party, was established in 2016 pledging to "Stop Homosexuality, Islam, and the Anti-Discrimination Law," and gained 2.64 percent of the vote in the general election (Song 2016).

Beginning from their stance on LGBTI-related issues, conservative Protestant groups have ended up opposing laws and policies that promote nondiscrimination and human rights in general. For instance, the Human Rights Education Support Bills of 2014 and 2018 failed to pass due to their fierce opposition, which claimed the bill would encourage homosexuality (Y. S. Kim 2014; Hyun 2018). By aggressively arguing that the Ordinance on Promotion of Human Rights for Residents in Chungcheongnamdo Province[21] (hereafter Chungcheongnamdo Ordinance) promoted homosexuality and Islam, conservative Protestant groups also successfully pushed the local council members of the Liberal Korea Party to repeal the Ordinance (J. H. Lee 2018; Woo 2018).[22] Additionally, conservative Protestant groups sought to amend the NHRCK Act to remove "sexual orientation" from the lists of prohibited grounds of discrimination (Ryu 2018; C. Y. Kim 2019), and some of them have even called for the abolition of the NHRCK entirely (H. J. Lim 2018). These efforts led to an Amendment Bill of the National Human Rights Commission Act to remove "sexual orientation" as protected characteristics, which was lodged at the 20th National Assembly in November 2019. This bill was supported by forty-four Representatives, most of whom are from the center-right Liberty Korea Party.

The seeming growth of the movement against human rights was not without counterpart, however. On the other side, many NGOs have actively defended equality and nondiscrimination rights. As an immediate response to countermobilization against comprehensive anti-discrimination legislation in 2007, more than 100 human rights NGOs formed the Anti-Discrimination Collective Action for the

---

[21]   *Chungcheongnamdo domin ingwon jeungjine gwanhan jorye* (Ordinance on Promotion of Human Rights for Residents in Chungcheongnamdo Province), No. 3677 (2012).

[22]   The ordinance, however, was reenacted four months after the repeal, this time entitled *Chungcheongnamdo ingwon gibon jorye* (Chungcheongnamdo Human Rights Basic Ordinance), No. 4387 (2018), when the new local council was elected and the Democratic Party took the majority of the seats.

Enactment of Proper Anti-Discrimination Laws (*Chabyeolgeumjibeobui olbareun jejeonggwa banchabyeol gongdonghaengdong*, hereafter, the Collective Action) (Rainbow Action 2008; Hoon-Chang 2017). The Collective Action criticized the government's removal of seven grounds of discrimination based on conservative or religious opposition, noting that the NHRCK Act already recognized these rights. The Collective Action also opposed the passage of the compromised bill and demanded that the Ministry of Justice, which was in charge of the bill, uphold nondiscrimination rights (Rainbow Action 2008). The Collective Action then began to hold conferences, workshops, and expand discussions about nondiscrimination rights, including through online journals (Hoon-Chang 2017).

In December 2010, the South Korean Coalition for Anti-Discrimination Legislation (hereafter, the Coalition) was launched, succeeding the Collective Action but with clearer goals as a legislative movement (Hoon-Chang 2017). It began devising long-term plans and strategies to enact comprehensive anti-discrimination legislation. The Coalition also turned its attention to raising public awareness about discrimination. Experiences of discrimination were voiced in public "to fight against forces that made them invisible" by many minorities, including homeless people, domestic workers, migrants and their families, people in poverty, sex workers, youth, irregular workers, and LGBTI people.[23] The Coalition organized meetings, conferences, and campaigns with civil society organizations and the general public. They reached out to members of the National Assembly to lobby for anti-discrimination legislation. They aimed to promote discussions of nondiscrimination rights in society generally (Hoon-Chang 2017).

The Coalition, relaunched in March 2017, included 131 NGOs as of December 2019 (Cho 2019, 51). The constituent NGOs exhibit great variety in terms of target issues, religious backgrounds, and regions. They include groups for or of women, children and youth, LGBTI individuals, people with disabilities, workers, homeless people, migrants, people living with HIV, and so on. They also include lawyers, doctors, politicians, educators, artists, professors, researchers, Christians, Buddhists, Catholics, and so on working for democracy and human rights. Political parties, including the Labor Party and Green Party, are part of the Coalition, and groups from different provinces nationwide, as well as some overseas Korean groups, joined the Coalition.[24]

The large number and diversity of NGOs is significant because it demonstrates the expansive scope of nondiscrimination rights that the Coalition seeks to advance. Indeed, the Coalition states that it seeks to "reveal the issue of equality as a universal right for everyone," rather than only as the right of selected minorities (Cho 2019, 53). While acknowledging that a vague and abstract emphasis on universal rights

---

[23] *See* South Korean Coalition for Anti-Discrimination Legislation, "Activity Report" at https://equalityact .kr/action/report/.

[24] *See* South Korean Coalition for Anti-Discrimination Legislation, "Introduction," at https://equalityact .kr/about/.

may risk obscuring some forms of social exclusion, the Coalition finds it crucial for the public to understand nondiscrimination rights as a "living norm and value" for all and an indivisible part of realizing "democracy in which everyone participates on equal footing" (Cho 2019, 54). Thus, the Coalition's activities are not just a political and legislative movement but also a cultural and educational one. The Coalition hopes to establish a new norm of equality where society recognizes and respects the rights of all people in all their diversity.

12.6 CONCLUSION: DISCOVERING DIVERSITY WHILE CONTINUING TO DEMAND "COMPREHENSIVE" ANTI-DISCRIMINATION LEGISLATION

The Coalition primarily seeks "comprehensive" anti-discrimination legislation. "Comprehensive" means that the law should cover all grounds and forms of discrimination extant at the time of legislation. While such legislation would not supersede already existing issue-specific anti-discrimination protections, the Coalition focuses on obtaining a statute that enumerates all possible grounds of prohibited discrimination. Ideally, comprehensive anti-discrimination legislation would also cover all forms of discriminatory acts, including indirect, multiple, and systemic discrimination, as well as harassment and hate speech (Han 2011; Ahn 2018; Hong 2018; J. Kim 2018). As stated earlier, recommendations from international human rights bodies all call for such "comprehensive" anti-discrimination legislation.

It is true that repeated recommendations from international human rights bodies have not compelled the South Korean government to override some of its citizens (conservative Protestant groups) and enact anti-discrimination legislation. The government's noncompliance with such recommendations appears to have had no diplomatic consequences for Korea. It is possible that the Korean government has been unconcerned about any resulting loss of legitimacy or reputation in taking an active role at the UN as an advocate for human rights. After all, the claimed lack of domestic "social consensus" has given the government an ostensible excuse to avoid fulfilling its international treaty obligations.

The case of Korea illustrates that the international human rights regime may paradoxically lack enforcement leverage in contexts where the state presents itself as a democracy. As Hafner-Burton et al. (2008) argue, a state, repressive or not, may have an interest in ratifying human rights treaties to gain symbolic legitimacy, but the enforcement of the rules depends on a different set of interests shaped by domestic political and social conditions. The effectiveness of the international human rights regime lies in a longer-term process of constant reminders to the state as well as to domestic societal actors of the rules such that they internalize the norm (Hafner-Burton et al. 2008, 137). At a minimum, the global, unequivocal consensus on equality and nondiscrimination has set the "normal" international standard to which states should "acculturate" (Goodman and Jinks 2004). South

Korea's culture has long justified treating "abnormal" or "antisocial" people in discriminatory ways. Yet the past decade of struggle to enact comprehensive anti-discrimination legislation has brought issues of equality, discrimination, and social minorities to the fore in Korean society. Few substantive changes have been achieved, as is evident in the repeated failure to enact comprehensive anti-discrimination legislation. However, the political significance of the legislation has changed; it has become a political and social touchstone for equality in Korean society. Recently, the most oft-cited political and social issues are inequality, hatred and discrimination, and hate speech toward minorities, such as women, LGBTIs, and migrants/refugees (NHRCK 2019).

The "discovery of diversity" is palpable in the activism for comprehensive anti-discrimination legislation. With the growing visibility in activism of minorities, such as LGBTIs and migrants (see Chapter 13), the last decade witnessed repeated evidence that hatred, discrimination, and exclusion are still ingrained in Korean society and are threatening human dignity and democracy. The anti-discrimination movement has questioned the norm of assimilation and acculturation, and people have begun to discover diversity that was previously hidden. The discovery is still ongoing. Recently in early 2020, media coverage highlighted gaps in transgender individuals' rights in the context of their university attendance or military service. Some people expressed hostile attitudes toward transgender individuals, but such responses again proved the presence of entrenched discrimination and the need for tolerance and inclusion. Korean society now faces demands to recognize the value of diversity and learn to embrace it. As a Hankyoreh journalist stated in a recent article series on anti-discrimination legislation, the meaning of such legislation lies in "symbolizing the social consensus that we, as human beings with differences, can accept the differences and live together" (H. B. Jung 2020).

The discovery of diversity nevertheless may be just the first step in a long struggle against discrimination and for legal protections of nondiscrimination rights. Building a new culture of respecting diversity will equip Korea to more effectively combat all forms of discrimination, but the National Assembly and the government are crucial for actually drafting and submitting bills, and enacting anti-discrimination legislation. It is still unclear when the government and the National Assembly will take this last step, given the continued reluctance shown in the Moon Jae-in Administration and the ruling Democratic Party, which assumed a historically large majority of seats in the 21st National Assembly starting in May 2020. Some positive signs exist. Rep. Jang Hye-young (Justice Party), together with nine other National Assembly members, submitted an anti-discrimination bill on June 29, 2020. Already, the NHRCK had established the Taskforce for Responding to Hatred and Discrimination in 2019 to enhance social awareness and set out a foundation for anti-discrimination legislation. The NHRCK also released a public statement in June 2020, urging the National Assembly to swiftly move forward for comprehensive anti-discrimination legislation in reference to its model bill entitled "Act on Equality and Nondiscrimination" (NHRCK 2020). Despite the delay of thirteen years, and possibly more, the anti-discrimination legislation movement has not been for naught. Long and winding roads still lie ahead, but the campaign for such legislation has spurred Korean society to imagine a new order wherein everybody enjoys equal respect and rights.

In the end, the law itself is not the goal but rather a means through which to develop and defend equality rights. The movement for an anti-discrimination law is thus more than just legislative activism; it is also a movement for a new social order in which equality is valued. The anti-discrimination legislation movement then cannot be understood as just about achieving some actionable rights in a legal sense. As James Ingram (2008, 413–14) describes, by citing Hannah Arendt's famous phrase, human rights may reside in the democratic political process of right bearers' participation and claiming the "right to have rights."

REFERENCES

Ahn, Jean. 2018. "A Study on Issues of the Legislation of Comprehensive Anti-discrimination Law in South Korea." *Chonnam Law Review* 38(1): 537–89.

An, Mi-Jeong, and Yang-Ho Woo. 2015. "A Reflection on the Multiculturalism of Korea through the Overseas Chinese." *Journal of Koreanology* 56: 383–416.

Bae, Moon-Kyu. 2014. "Seoul simin ingwon heonjang pyegi hupokpung siminsahoero hwaksan iteuljjae sicheong jeomgeo nongseong" [Aftermath of cancellation of Seoul citizens human rights charter spreads . . . second day of sit-in protest at city council]. *Kyunghang Sinmun*, December 7, 2014. http://news.khan.co.kr/kh_news/khan_art_view.html?art_id=201412071647461.

Bob, Clifford. 2012. *The Global Rights Wing and the Clash of World Politics*. Cambridge: Cambridge University Press.

Chang, Paul Y. 2015. *Protest Dialectics: State Repression and South Korea's Democracy Movement, 1970–1979*. Stanford: Stanford University Press.

Cho, Byong-Hee, and Aeree Sohn. 2018. "Why are Korean Protestant Churches Hostile to Homosexuality and AIDS?" *Health and Social Science* 48: 5–28.

Cho, Hye-In. 2019. "Chabyeol geumjibeop jaejeong eotteoke chujinhal geosinga?" [Anti-discrimination legislation: how to make it happen?]. 2019 Conference on Anti-Discrimination Legislation. December 4, 2019.

Choi, Yooncheol. 2012. "Study on the Constitutional Acceptance of Multiculturalism." *Public Law* 41(2): 1–31.

Choung, Yong-Lim, and Na-Young Lee. 2018. "'Post/Gangnam Station': Collective Resistance against Gender Discrimination and Re/Construction of Feminist Subjects." *Issues in Feminism* 18(1): 181–228.

Christian Council of Korea (CCK). 2003. "Gukgagigwani cheongsonyeondeurege 'dongseongae'reul gwonjanghaneunga?" [Does state institution recommend "homosexuality" to youth?]. July 7, 2003. www.cck.or.kr/.

Chun, Yong-Gil. 2011. "Seoulhaksaeng ingwonjorye gagyeol, naenyun 3 wol balhyo yejung" [Seoul student rights ordinance passes, effective march next year]. *News Cham*, December 19, 2011. www.newscham.net/news/view.php?board=news&nid=64368&page=3.

Constitutional Court of Korea. 2003. 10. 30. 2000 Hunba67 et al.

Constitutional Court of Korea. 2009. 10. 29. 2007 Hunma1462.

Eum, Sung-Won. 2014. "Park Won-Soon Sijang, 'ingwonheonjang musan' sagwaneun haettjiman ... " [Mayor Park Won-Soon apologized for the miscarried human rights charter But ...]. *Hankyoreh*, December 10, 2014. www.hani.co.kr/arti/society/rights/668553.html.

Go, Sang-Kyun. 2008. "'Seongjeokjihyang!' Jinjeong mueoseul iyuro sakjeharyeoneunga?" ["Sexual orientation!" What is the true reason behind the attempts to delete?]. *Contemporary and Minjung Theology* 10: 60–84.

Goodman, Ryan, and Derek Jinks. 2004. "How to Influence States: Socialization and International Human Rights Law." *Duke Law Journal* 54(3): 621–703.

Group to Study Discrimination (Chabyeoryeongumoim). 2002. "Gukgaingwonwiwonhoebeopui chabyeol pandaneul wihan jichim" [Guidelines for judging discrimination based on the NHRCK Act].

Hafner-Burton, Emilie M., and Kiyoteru Tsutsui. 2005. "Human Rights in a Globalizing World: The Paradox of Empty Promises." *American Journal of Sociology* 110(5): 1373–411.

Hafner-Burton, Emilie M., Kiyoteru Tsutsui, and John W. Meyer. 2008. "International Human Rights Law and the Politics of Legitimation: Repressive States and Human Rights Treaties." *International Sociology* 23(1): 115–41.

Han, Jee-young. 2011. "Critical Review on Issues over Legislative Debate of the Anti-Discrimination Act: Focusing on the Concept and Relief Measures of Discrimination." *Ewha Journal of Gender and Law* 3(1): 89–122.

Hankyoreh. 2018. "Gajjanyuseuui ppurireul chajaseo" [Series: search for the root of "fake news"]. *Hankyoreh*. www.hani.co.kr/arti/SERIES/1147/.

Hathaway, Oona A. 2007. "Why do Countries Commit to Human Rights Treaties?" *Journal of Conflict Resolution* 51(4): 588–621.

Ho, David Y. F. 1995. "Selfhood and Identity in Confucianism, Taoism, Buddhism, and Hinduism: Contrasts with the West." *Journal for the Theory of Social Behaviour* 25(2): 115–39.

Hong, Sung Soo. 2011. "A Review of Investigation Function of the NHRCK since 2001." *Chonbuk Law Review* 34: 79–120.

2018. "Why Do We Need Comprehensive Anti-Discrimination Act as Equal Basic Law in Korea?" *Ewha Journal of Gender and Law* 10(3): 1–38.

Hoon-Chang. 2017. "Chabyeolgeumjibeob undong 10nyeon, jigeum uriga noin jihyeongeun?" [Ten years of anti-discrimination legislation movement: topography of where we are?]. 2017 First Meeting of the Coalition for Anti-Discrimination Legislation.

Hyun, Hye-Ran. 2018. "Ingwonwiwonjang 'ingwongyoyukjiwonbeoban cheolhoe yugam ... ipbeom noryeok gyesok" [President of NHRCK, "disappointed in withdrawal of human rights education support bill ... will keep making efforts for legislation"]. *Yonhap News*, October 8, 2018. www.yna.co.kr/view/AKR20181008064500004.

Ingram, James D. 2008. "What Is a 'Right to Have Rights'? Three Images of the Politics of Human Rights." *American Political Science Review* 102(4): 401–16.

Jun, Hye-Won. 2014. "Dangsin gyeotedo seongsosujaga itseumnida" [Sexual minorities are living near you too]. *SisaIn*, December 23, 2014. www.sisain.co.kr/news/articleView.html?idxno=21997.

Jung, Hwan-Bong. 2020. "Chabyeolgeumjibeobeun dareum injeonghaneun yeondaeui sonjapgida" [Anti-discrimination law is holding hands of solidarity in recognition of difference]. *Hankyoreh*, April 3 2020, www.hani.co.kr/arti/society/society_general/935473.html.

Jung, Kyeongil. 2018. "Muslimophobia among Christians." *HUFS Law Review* 42(2): 125–40.

Kang, Jin-Gu. 2012. "A Study on the Anti-Multicultural Discourse of Korean Society with a Focus on the Internet Domain Kang." *Studies in Humanities* 32: 5–34.

Kang, Suk-Geun. 2014. "Park Won-Soon sijang tesiminingwonheonjang nollan joesong" [Mayor Park Won-Soon, "Sorry for the controversies over the charter of human rights for Seoul citizens"]. *Kidok-sinmun*, December 2, 2014. www.kidok.com/news/articleView .html?idxno=89130.

Kim, Andrew E. 2000. "Korean Religious Culture and Its Affinity to Christianity: The Rise of Protestant Christianity in South Korea." *Sociology of Religion* 61(2): 117–33.

Kim, Chul-Young. 2019. "Gukgaingwonwiwonhoebeob je2jo 3ho 'seongjeokjihyang'eul sakje gaejeonghara" [Amend article 2 (3) of the NHRCK Act to remove "sexual orientation"]. *Kidok sinmun*, October 14, 2019. www.kidok.com/news/articleView.html?idxno=203709.

Kim, Jihye. 2018. "Modureul wihan pyeongdeung" [Equality for all]. *Minjubeophak* (Democratic Legal Studies) 66: 183–208.

Kim, Jihye, Ji-Rim Kim, Cheol-Hyo Kim, Hyun-Mi Kim, Young-A Park, Wan Lee, and Young-Sook Huoh. 2019. "Hanguksahoeui injongchabyeol siltaewa injongchabyeol-cheolpyereul wihan beopjehwa yeongu" [A study on the status of racial discrimination in Korean society and legislation for elimination of racial discrimination]. National Human Rights Commission of Korea. www.humanrights.go.kr/site/program/board/basic board/view?currentpage=2&menuid=001003001004001&pagesize=10&boardty peid=16&boardid=7605399.

Kim, Kwang-Yi. 2007. "Chuhaejyeo beorin chabyeolgeumjibeoban idaero? Anijyo!" [Ugly anti-discrimination law as it is? No!]. Human Rights Rising (Ingwon oreum).

Kim, Min-Kyeong. 2011. "Seongsosuja chabyeolgeumji johang bandaee … heundeullineun 'seoulhaksaeng-ingwonjorye'" [Oppositions to non-discrimination against sexual minorities shake Seoul student rights ordinance]. *Hankyoreh*, November 21, 2011. www.hani.co.kr/arti/ society/schooling/506508.html.

Kim, Seon-Taek. 2010. "Multicultural Society and the Constitution." *Constitutional Law* 16 (2): 1–41.

Kim, Seyoon. 1986. "Christianity and Culture in Korea: Nationalism, Dialogues, Indigenization and Contextualization." *ACTS Theological Journal* 2: 32–63.

Kim, Sun-Hae. 2019. "Anti peminijeum undongui jeongsangseong hoekdeuk jeollyage gwan-han yeongu" [Studies on strategies to achieve legitimacy of anti-feminism movement]. The Korean Sociological Association Sociology Conference Proceeding, 515–27.

Kim, Yeonju, and Youngjung Na. 2013. "Reconstruction of Citizenship through Enactment Movement for Seoul Student Human Rights Ordinance: Focusing on Age and Sexuality." *Memory & Vision* 28: 312–56.

Kim, Yeon-Sook. 2014. "'Dongseongae jojang' ohaero ingwongyoyukbeop musan" ["Promotion of homosexuality": misunderstanding fails human rights education act]. *Yonhap News*, November 12, 2014. www.yna.co.kr/view/AKR20141112149200004.

Koh, Harold Hongju. 1999. "How Is International Human Rights Law Enforced?" *Indiana Law Journal* 74(4): 1397–417.

Ku, Kyung-Ha. 2019. "Gungmineun chanseonghaneunde 'hyeomo chabyeol daechaekbeop' juljuri cheolhoe, wae?" [Citizens agree but why do "laws tackling hate and discrimination" repeatedly fail?]. *KBS News*, January 17, 2019. news.kbs.co.kr/news/view.do?ncd=4118269.

Kundnani, Arun. 2015. *The Muslims Are Coming: Islamophobia, Extremism, and the Domestic War on Terror*. London: Verso.

Lee, Changsoo et al. 2007. "Special Issue: Five Years of Korean National Human Rights." *Democratic Legal Studies* 33.

Lee, Dae-Woong. 2010. "Dongseongae nollan, chabyeolgeumjibeoban dulleossago dasi bulbutda" [Controversies over homosexuality, reignite with anti-discrimination bill]. *Christian Today*, October 27, 2010. www.christiantoday.co.kr/news/241833.

Lee, Gyesu. 2000. "Gungminingwonwiwonhoee gwanhan yeongu" [A study of he National Human Rights Commission]. *Journal of Social Science* 10(2): 61–76.

Lee, Ji-Hyun. 2014. "Disputes and Perspectives on Sex Orientation in the Legislation of Anti-discrimination Law in Korea." *Chung-Ang Law Review* 16(3): 107–39.

Lee, Jin-Gu. 2011. "Protestant Church's Images of Islam in Multicultural Korea: A Focus on Islamophobia." *The Critical Review of Religion and Culture* 19(19): 163–94.

Lee, Joon-Ho. 2018. "Pyejidoeeotdeon chungnamingwonjorye 4gaewol mane buhwal" [Chungnam human rights ordinance reinstated 4 months after repeal]. *Hankuk Ilbo*, September 14, 2018. www.hankookilbo.com/News/Read/201809141584332643.

Lee, Ju-Yeon. 2013. "'Jongbuk gei' nollane pamuchin chabyeolgeumjibeom gyeolguk" [The end of anti-discrimination law buried in disputes over "pro-North Korea sympathizers"]. *News & Joy*, April 18, 2013. www.newsnjoy.or.kr/news/articleView.html?idxno=193969.

Lee, Kyung-Tae. 2009. "Injongchabyeolgeumjibeom cheon gongcheonghoe … chanban goseong oga" [Racial anti-discrimination act first public hearing … heated with pros and cons]. *Ohmynews*, September 30, 2009. www.ohmynews.com/NWS_Web/View/at_pg.aspx?CNTN_CD=A0001227828.

Lee, Na-Young, and Jo-Yeon Baek. 2017. "'Politics of Disgust': Korean Conservative Protestant Discourses against Homosexuality." *PNU Journals of Women's Studies* 27 (1): 67–108.

Lee, Se-A. 2014. "Jinbojeongdang siminsahoedanche 'seongsosuja sicheong jeomgeononongseong jiji'" [Progressive parties and civil society groups "support of city hall sit-ins of sexual minorities"]. *Women News*, December 7, 2014. www.womennews.co.kr/news/articleView.html?idxno=78519.

Lee, Seo-Young, and Yoo Kyung Choi. 2014. "Political Effects of Interest Groups on the Korean Legislative Process: In the Case of the Withdrawal of Anti-Discrimination Law in 2013." *Journal of Global Politics* 7(2): 89–114.

Lee, Sook-Jin. 2009. "The Legislative Process of the Anti-Discrimination Bill and the Dynamics of Legislation Movement." *Journal of Korean Social Trends and Perspectives* 77: 422–54.

Lim, Hye-Jin. 2018. "Gungmin dasuui ingwon oemyeon … pyeji yogu jingmyeonhan gukgaingwonwi" [Turned away from human rights of majority of citizens … NHRCK faced demand for repeal]. *NewDaily*, November 21, 2018. www.newdaily.co.kr/site/data/html/2018/11/21/2018112100158.html.

Lim, Jaehong. 1999. "Gukgaingwongigu seollibui wonchik" [Principle of establishing a national human rights institution]. *Democratic Legal Studies* 15(1): 44–70.

Lim, Timothy. 2010. "Rethinking Belongingness in Korea: Transnational Migration, 'Migrant Marriages' and the Politics of Multiculturalism." *Pacific Affairs* 83(1): 51–71.

Moravcsik, Andrew. 1997. "Taking Preferences Seriously: A Liberal Theory of International Politics." *International Organization* 51(4): 513–53.

Nam, Chanseob. 2007. "The Making Process and Issues of Prohibition of Discrimination against People with Disabilities Act." *Journal of Disability and Welfare* 6: 5–53.

National Human Rights Commission of Korea (NHRCK). 2003. "Dongseongae saiteuneun cheongsonyeon yuhaemaeche anida" [Website with homosexuality contents is not harmful media for youth]. April 2, 2003.

 2005. Annual Report 2005.

 2009. Annual Report 2009.

2014. Annual Report 2014.

2018. Annual Report 2018.

2019 nyeon hyeomochabyeol gungmin insik josa [2019 Survey on people's perceptions about hatred and discrimination]. Seoul: National Human Rights Commission of Korea.

2020. "'Modureul wihan pyeongdeung' hyanghae damdae han georeum naedidil ttae" [A bold step toward "equality for all"] June 30, 2020, www.humanrights.go.kr/site/program/board/basicboard/view?boardtypeid=24&boardid=7605626&menuid=001004002001.

Oserabi. 2017. *Geu peminijeumeun teullyeotda* [That feminism is not correct]. Goyang: Jopssalhanal.

Oserabi et al. 2019. *Geu peminijeumi dangsineul bulhaenghage haneun iyu* [Why that feminism makes you unhappy]. Seoul: RealNews.

Park, Chan-Un. 2008. "Chabyeolgeumjibeom jejeongui uimiwa chabyeolgeumjibeobanui juyonaeyong" [Meaning of enacting anti-discrimination law in Korea and main contents of its bill]. Public Hearing for Anti-discrimination Law, NHRCK.

Park, Kyung-Tae. 2008. *Sosujawa hankuksahoe* [Minorities and Korean society]. Seoul: Humanitas.

Park, Seonyeong. 2016. Seongchabyeol (seonghuirong) geumji silhyoseong jegoreul wihan beopjedo gaeseonbangan yeongu [Study on the improvement of the legal system for enhancing the effectiveness of gender discrimination (sexual harassment) prohibition]. Korean Women's Development Institute Report.

Park, Soo-Jin. 2017. "Peminijeum bangyeogeul matda" [Feminism, faces backlash]. *Hankyoreh* 21, December 20, 2017. http://h21.hani.co.kr/arti/special/special_general/44633.html.

Park, Suk-Jin. 2007. "Banchabyeorundongeul tonghae modureul wihan haebangui tujaengeuro" [Struggle for liberalization of everybody through anti-discrimination movement]. *The Radical Review* 34: 120–28.

Park, Yoon-kyung. 2020. "Gungmin 10myeongjung 9myeong 'chabyeolgeumjibeop jejeonghaeya'" [Nine out of ten people "agree to anti-discrimination legislation"]. *Hankyoreh*, June 23, 2020. www.hani.co.kr/arti/society/society_general/950570.html#csidxf7c3od0a95539aaaf0d57cb5c6b13df.

Rainbow Action Standing Against Sexual Minorities Discrimination [Rainbow Action]. 2008. *Jigeum urineun miraereul mandeulgo itseumnida* [We are now making the future]. Suwon: Saramsanggak.

Ryu, Inha. 2018. "Seongsosujaga jeongjaengui jaemuringa" [Are sexual minorities offering for political strife?]. *Weekly Kyunghyang*, February 6, 2018. weekly.khan.co.kr/khnm.html?mode=view&artid=201802061355191&code=115.

Shin, Dong-Myung. 2012. "Gyogye, haksaengingwonjorye bandae 20 manmyeong seomyeong dorip" [Churches initiates to gather 200,000 signatures against student rights ordinance]. *Christian Times*, January 11, 2012. www.kmctimes.com/news/articleView.html?idxno=33317.

Simmons, Beth. 2009. *Mobilizing for Human Rights: International Law in Domestic Politics*. Cambridge: Cambridge University Press.

Song, Joo-Yeol. 2016. "4.13. Chongseon, gidokjayudang 2.64% deukpyo wonnae jinchul silpae" [4.13. general election Christian liberal party fails to advance into parliament at 2.64%]. *CBS Nocut News*, April 14, 2016. www.nocutnews.co.kr/news/4578979.

Statistics Korea. 2019. "Status of Foreigner Residents." *E-National Index*, July 26, 2019. www.index.go.kr/potal/main/EachDtlPageDetail.do?idx_cd=2756.

Takeshi, Fujii. 2017. "Chabyeolgeumjibeopgwa chotbulminjujuui" [Anti-discrimination law and candlelight democracy]. *The Hankyoreh*, July 23, 2017. www.hani.co.kr/arti/opinion/column/803946.html.

UN Committee on Economic, Social and Cultural Rights (CESCR). 2009. Concluding observations: Republic of Korea, E/C.12/KOR/CO/3.

2017. Concluding observations: Republic of Korea, E/C.12/KOR/CO/4.

UN Committee on the Elimination of Discrimination against Women (CEDAW). 2011. Concluding observations: Republic of Korea, CEDAW/C/KOR/CO/7.

2018. Concluding observations: Republic of Korea, CEDAW/C/KOR/CO/8.

UN Committee on the Elimination of Racial Discrimination (CERD). 2012. Concluding observations: Republic of Korea, CERD/C/KOR/CO/15–16.

2019. Concluding observations: Republic of Korea, CERD/C/KOR/CO/17–19.

UN Committee on the Rights of the Child (CRC). 2011. Concluding observations: Republic of Korea, E/C.12/KOR/CO/3.

2019. Concluding observations: Republic of Korea, CRC/C/KOR/CO/5–6.

UN Human Rights Committee (CCPR). 2015. Concluding observations: Republic of Korea, CCPR/C/KOR/CO/4.

Woo, Sam-Yeol. 2018. "Jonggyojipdanui chungnam ingwonjorye pyeji undonge natanan injongchabyeol: 'iseullam hyeomo'reul jungsimeuro" [Racial discrimination shown in the religious groups' movement for repeal of Chungnam human rights ordinance: focusing on "Islamophobia"]. *Racial Discrimination Report Meeting: Racial Discrimination in Korean Society*, 139–46.

Yum, June Ock. 1988. "The Impact of Confucianism on Interpersonal Relationships and Communication Patterns in East Asia." *Communication Monographs* 55: 374–88.

Yung, Betty. 2010. "Can Confucianism add Value to Democracy Education?" *Procedia Social and Behavioral Sciences* 22(2): 1919–26.

PART IV

Shaping Rights for New Citizens and Noncitizens

13

The Rights of Noncitizenship

Migrant Rights and Hierarchies in South Korea

Erin Aeran Chung[1]

13.1 INTRODUCTION

Instead of a "sharp distinction between citizen and non-citizen," postwar immigration has contributed to the development of "a continuum of rights attached to membership of a state," as Zig Layton-Henry noted in a seminal essay (1990, 9). While the scholarship on race, migration, and citizenship has yielded important insights into the myriad ways that state and nonstate actors engage in practices that deny the full citizenship of marginalized *citizen* groups, little research has been conducted on hierarchies among *noncitizens*.[2] This area of research is becoming increasingly significant for the study of migration in Asia, Africa, and the Middle East, where borders are, as Smart and Smart's study of Hong Kong illustrates, "only selectively opened" (Smart and Smart 2008). That is, most countries in these regions – including South Korea (hereafter "Korea") – have growing foreign populations but maintain relatively restrictive immigration and citizenship policies.

Given assumptions that Korea is an immigrant-hostile society, we would expect to find highly deprived, politically unincorporated foreign communities with limited rights. Examining national immigration and citizenship policies alone would confirm these expectations. Korea has not opened its borders to immigration at the level necessary to alleviate labor shortages and, despite sweeping reforms, maintains highly restrictive policies that largely prohibit migrant permanent settlement. At the same time, long-term foreign residents have, for the most part, the "rights necessary for individual freedom," as T. H. Marshall (1950, 78) defined civil citizenship, which includes rights to property ownership, freedom from arbitrary imprisonment and deportation, religious freedom, freedom of assembly, and contractual rights.

But migrant rights in Korea are allocated *differentially* to specific categories of migrants based on visa categories that are informed by group-specific attributes such as gender, ethnicity, and country of origin that go well beyond demands in the labor

---

[1] This chapter is a revised version of Chung 2020a. It also draws heavily on Chung 2020b.
[2] For important exceptions, see Kofman 2002; Morris 2002; Cohen 2009; Goldring and Landolt 2013.

market. These visa categories not only determine migrants' length of residency but also their eligibility for specific citizenship rights and citizenship acquisition itself. They have thus led to the development of noncitizen hierarchies, institutionalizing the privileged status of some migrants over others and integrating migrants specifically as wives, co-ethnics, and potential citizens, for example (Chung 2020a).

Noncitizens in Korea range from migrant laborers who are prohibited or discouraged from permanent settlement to migrant spouses who are eligible for dual nationality and facilitated naturalization to native-born permanent residents who are eligible for local voting rights. While Korea has surpassed many liberal democracies in extending rights to foreign residents in some areas, such as local voting rights for permanent residents, the country has remained immune to international pressure in others, such as refugee policies for which Korea holds among the worst records in the industrialized world. Liberal reforms that reflect international norms have, moreover, been applied unevenly to different migrant groups and inconsistently across policy domains (Chung 2020b).

Migrant claims to rights overlap with those made by citizens, especially historically marginalized populations, in their fundamental conceptions of human dignity and their appeals for state protections, as Arrington and Goedde note in the Introduction chapter. To be sure, migrants in Korea have mobilized for human rights; civil rights such as freedom from arbitrary deportation; social welfare benefits; voting rights; women's rights; and constitutional rights using the tried-and-true strategies of protests, candlelight vigils, petitions, public awareness campaigns, litigation, and lobbying. As noncitizens, however, the focus is less on equality with citizens or even citizenship acquisition and more on the terms of migrant incorporation (as potential citizens *or* as foreign residents), the criteria for existing visa statuses, and the rights associated with specific visa categories. Migrant claims-making in Korea adopts the general language of rights (*gwolli*) and human rights (*ingwon*), thereby imbuing their appeals with the moral authority, legibility, and political capital of past and current struggles for democratic inclusion (see Chung 2020b). At the same time, the scope of their claims has tended to be specific to their migrant subcategories or visa statuses: labor protections for migrant workers, equality among co-ethnic migrants, and state protections for marriage migrants. Even within the single context of Korea, the struggle for rights by one migrant group does not necessarily make their claimed rights universal, or even accessible, to others.

This chapter examines the development of noncitizen hierarchies in Korea over the past three decades through the lens of visa categories created to accommodate labor shortages within Korea's restrictive immigration regime. I focus on three visa categories that represent the largest migrant groups in Korea: migrant workers, co-ethnic migrants, and so-called marriage migrants. The following section compares dominant explanations for why and how states extend rights to migrants in the comparative immigration scholarship. The remainder of the chapter analyzes the relationship between visa categories, migrant rights, and migrant hierarchies. For the purposes of this chapter, I define immigrant incorporation as the process by which immigrants and their descendants shift their status from being sojourners to political participants who make claims as permanent members of their receiving societies. Although I use the terms "immigrants" and "migrants" to refer primarily to the first generation, "immigrant incorporation" can refer to policies and practices that pertain to multiple generations of foreign residents (Chung 2010b, 677).

13.2 THE EXPANSION OF MIGRANT RIGHTS

James Hollifield's (2004) influential work on the "migration state" maintains that all industrial democracies face a "liberal paradox": international economic forces push states toward greater openness while security concerns and domestic political forces push them toward closure. Extending institutionalized rights to immigrants is key to addressing the paradox as it allows states to move toward more open immigration policies, maintain their political legitimacy as liberal states, and, at the same time, avoid a political backlash (Hollifield 2004, 905). While most scholars of comparative immigration politics agree that liberal democratic states are converging toward open immigration policies and expanding foreign resident rights, they differ in their claims about whether the source lies in exogenous factors such as international norms (Soysal 1994; Finnemore and Sikkink 1998; Gurowitz 1999; Merry 2006; Tsutsui and Shin 2008; Hosoki 2016) or domestic political elites such as those in left-leaning parties or activist courts (Hammar 1990; Joppke 1999).

Based largely on European and North American case studies, the bulk of the comparative scholarship on immigration politics in the last three decades has taken as a given that the countries in question have relatively open immigration policies and that patterns of immigrant incorporation reflect deliberate decision-making by policymakers. But, because Korea closed its borders to unskilled immigration until the 1990s, migrant workers were populations to be returned or expelled, not incorporated (Chung 2010b). Most reforms to Korea's immigration policies until the early 2000s, moreover, reflect the state's aim to better control immigration, particularly unauthorized immigration, rather than incorporate immigrants. Indeed, Korea's political elites have prioritized social stability over liberal democratic principles in justifying closed immigration policies (Shin 2006). Liberal reforms have been implemented only after considerable pressure has been applied from internal grassroots movements and external actors. Likewise, international norms and pressure have had an uneven and indeterminate impact on Korea's immigration and citizenship policies.

Much of the scholarship in the last few decades asks why liberal convergence has not happened across liberal democracies, especially those outside of North America, Europe, and Australia. Studies of immigration politics in East Asia point us toward an important intervening variable: civil society. The burgeoning English-language scholarship on Korea, Japan, and Taiwan, in particular, prioritizes the role civil society plays in shaping immigrant incorporation (Gurowitz 1999; J. Kim 2003; Lim 2003; Hsia 2008; N. H.-J. Kim 2008; Shipper 2008; Chung 2010a, 2010b; Milly 2014).

The Korea case demonstrates that the presence of civil society alone is insufficient for explaining intranational variations in immigrant incorporation patterns. While civil society actors have been central to securing rights for migrants in Korea, the struggle for rights by some migrants has not generated liberal reforms for all. Chung (2020b) introduces the concept of *civic legacies* to refer to the ideas, networks, and strategies applied in previous struggles for democratic inclusion that shape how civil society actors – including migrants themselves – make claims to the state, negotiate exclusionary policies, and understand democratic inclusion and political empowerment (see also Fishman 2017; Arrington and Moon 2020). Although civic legacies do not *determine* immigrant incorporation patterns, they inform the discourse on citizenship and democracy within civil society and influence the prioritization of issues and agendas among civil society actors. Grassroots movements by immigrants and their supporters, after all, do not transpire in a vacuum; on the contrary, the *residuals* of prior struggles for democratic citizenship shape contemporary rights claiming (see Chapter 3).

The following sections analyze how civic legacies shaped the contested interaction between state officials, migrants, and native civil society groups over the classification, meanings, and rights of noncitizenship. They do so by analyzing rights claiming related to three of the largest categories of noncitizens: migrant workers, co-ethnic migrants, and female migrant spouses of Korean nationals. Specifically, applying insights from my comparative study of Korea, Japan, and Taiwan (Chung 2020b), I focus on how civil society actors – including migrants themselves – drew on the ideas, networks, and strategies of previous struggles for democracy and democratic deepening to make claims to the state. Advocacy for migrant workers that drew on the civic legacies of Korea's democracy movement resulted in structural reforms; litigation by Korean Chinese migrants that contested state-defined classifications of the Korean diaspora expanded access to the most privileged co-ethnic visa category. And publicity campaigns by women's organizations to ensure protections for so-called marriage migrants generated multiple reforms, policies, and social services that also had the unintended consequence of reorienting some women's activist groups to service provision. While each case expanded the rights associated with specific visa categories, each also entrenched noncitizen hierarchies.

13.3 MIGRANT WORKERS: HUMAN RIGHTS AND THE STRUGGLE FOR DEMOCRACY

Until the 1980s, Korea was a major migrant-sending country, with an emigration rate of approximately 30,000 throughout the 1980s (A. E. Kim 2009; Korea Immigration

Service 2011). Even without an official emigration policy, thousands of Koreans migrated to North America, Australia, Germany, and the Middle East from the 1960s to the late 1980s as students and guest workers (Chung and Kim 2012, 207). It was during this same period that Korea began to face significant labor shortages following two decades of rapid growth: between 1965 and 1989, per capita GDP rose from approximately US $100 to over US $5,700. Facing pressure to meet short-term demands for labor, especially in the manufacturing, production, and service industries, authorities turned a blind eye to companies that recruited foreign workers who entered the country with tourist visas and, eventually, overstayed their visas. By 1991, over 45,000 migrant workers from China, South Asia, and Southeast Asia had entered Korea to fill labor shortages in low-skilled jobs and, among them, over 90 percent were unauthorized (Seol 2000, 8; Lim 2006, 244).

In response to the growing undocumented population, Korea instituted the Industrial and Technical Training System (ITTP) in 1991 and the Industrial Trainee Program in 1993, which was intended to provide a government-administered system for overseeing and controlling the migration of unskilled foreign labor (Seol 2000, 6). Yet the two programs left "trainees" vulnerable to exploitation since they were not recognized as workers and, thus, their rights were not protected by labor laws. By posing a one-year limit on the period of sojourn, they further contributed to the growth of undocumented workers in Korea.

13.3.1 *Ideas, Strategies, and Networks: Migrant Workers in Korea's Struggle for Democracy*

As the Roh Tae-woo and Kim Young-sam administrations enacted plans to deport undocumented workers and import additional migrant workers, a few key religious and labor organizations helped migrant workers organize a series of high-profile protests from 1994 to 1995. Their nonviolent protests, especially the 1995 protests by Nepalese workers that were staged in front of the Myeongdong Cathedral in Seoul that Katharine Moon (2000, 155) describes as the "traditional stage and refuge of antigovernment protestors in the era of military rule," won the support of human rights groups throughout Korea. Some advocates came to refer to migrant workers as part of Korea's historically marginalized groups. For example, the Presbyterian Church in the Republic of Korea (PROK) described itself as the advocate for the "poor and the marginalized, the '*Minjung*' (people) such as the disabled, farmers, the elderly, orphans, *undocumented migrant workers*, homeless teenagers, sex workers, and, particularly since the implosion of the national economy, the unemployed and their families" (emphasis added) in its 2006 statement to the World Council of Churches.[3]

---

[3] See the "Presbyterian Church in the Republic of Korea," World Council of Churches website, www .oikoumene.org/en/member-churches/presbyterian-church-in-the-republic-of-korea.

The strength of the migrant worker movement can be attributed to its embeddedness in a powerful civic legacy in Korea: the decades-long democracy movement. Despite their relatively small numbers, advocacy for migrant workers gained momentum quickly because the movement drew on the ideas, strategies, and networks of the larger national struggle for democracy (Chung 2020b). Movement leaders skillfully drew parallels between the mistreatment of migrant workers and police crackdowns of undocumented migrants with the abusive practices and political repression of Korea's past authoritarian regimes; moreover, migrant workers and their advocates applied the language and tactics from Korea's labor movements in their public demonstrations, declarations, and sit-in rallies. Whereas the slogan "We are not machines" represented the Korean workers' movements of the 1970s and 1980s, "We are human, not animals" and "We are not slaves" came to epitomize the migrant workers' movement (see Chapter 9). In their calls for abolishing the industrial trainee system, migrant advocates further used the familiar language of "human rights" (*ingwon*), with demands that the laws on the books for native Korean workers be applied to migrant workers. The migrant workers' movement thus reframed public debate from the dangers that migrant workers posed for Korean society to the threat that an exploitative industrial trainee system posed for the hard-fought rights of workers in Korea (see Lim 2010).

Korea's pro-migrant advocacy organizations were especially effective due to their position within Korea's democratization movement and post-1987 democratic consolidation: They came from moderate and radical labor organizations, Protestant, Catholic, and Buddhist groups, women's organizations, lawyers, and a range of progressive citizen groups as Joon Kim (2003, 253) describes (see also Chapter 8). For example, the Citizens' Coalition for Economic Justice (CCEJ), the NGO that organized the 1994 migrant worker rallies, was established in 1989 by approximately 500 individuals representing various walks of life – "economics professors and other specialists, lawyers, housewives, students, young adults and business people" – as the first civic organization "in pursuit of economic justice" in Korea.[4] Their strong tradition of activism coupled with the reconfiguration of political power from the late 1990s – with the inauguration of the first opposition president, Kim Dae-jung, in 1998 and then a former human rights activist and labor lawyer, Roh Moo-hyun, in 2003 – lent the struggle for migrant labor rights significant potency and magnitude in Korean society.

13.3.2 *Outcome: Structural Reform*

In 1997, the Joint Committee for Migrant Workers in Korea (JCMK), an umbrella organization for migrant advocacy groups, submitted a bill to legalize the status of migrant workers to the National Assembly with the support of the Ministry of Labor

---

4   See CCEJ website, http://ccej.or.kr/eng/who-we-are/about-us/.

and the ruling party. Facing strong opposition from key ministries, opposition parties, and the Korean Federation of Small and Medium Businesses (KFSB), the bill was not passed; nevertheless, the government implemented a modified version of the proposal that permitted trainees to become legal workers with rights protections after a two-year training period (Y. W. Lee and Park 2005). Less than a decade later, Korea established an official guest worker program, the Employment Permit System (EPS), in 2004 and terminated the trainee system in 2007. The new system guarantees foreign workers the same rights as Korean workers, who are protected by labor laws such as the Labor Standards Act, the Minimum Wage Act, and the Industrial Safety and Health Act (SOPEMI 2008). It also replaced the one-year visas for trainees with three-year visas that can be renewed for an additional two years. While the EPS limits eligibility to migrant workers from countries that have signed bilateral agreements with Korea, its institutionalization represented the first time that Korea opened its borders to unskilled immigration.

Two developments altered the trajectory of immigration politics in Korea, shifting the spotlight from migrant workers to marriage migrants (discussed later in this chapter). While pro-migrant activists and government officials worked closely together in designing the EPS, they were uneasy partners when it came to the program's implementation. In particular, the government's announcement that all unauthorized migrant workers in Korea would be deported so that the EPS could be implemented with a "clean slate" generated a contentious movement for legalization that continued even after state officials agreed to grant amnesty and a one-year visa to unauthorized workers who agreed to leave Korea within the designated period. But unlike earlier movements, the push for legalization after the establishment of the EPS lacked both state and public support. With the termination of the despised industrial trainee system, the government could now gain political capital by concentrating on the much less volatile issue of integrating marriage migrants into Korean society.

Second, the heyday of Korea's progressive administrations ended with the inauguration of Lee Myung-bak as president in 2008. Pro-migrant activists who had previously enjoyed access to the highest echelons of the Kim Dae Jung and Roh Moo Hyun administrations had few political allies within the conservative Lee administration. The honeymoon period between the migrant workers' movement and the Korean government had come to an end (Chung 2020b).

13.4 CO-ETHNIC MIGRANTS: DIASPORA, DISCRIMINATION, AND THE COURTS

Of the more than 2 million foreign residents in Korea today, the overwhelming majority are co-ethnic migrants from China (commonly referred to as *Joseonjok*; hereafter "Korean Chinese"). Following the normalization of diplomatic relations between South Korea and mainland China in 1992, Korean Chinese formed the largest foreign resident community in Korea by far, growing more than twentyfold in less than two decades from 32,443 in 2000 to almost 680,000 in 2017 (Korea Immigration Service 2018).

Until the late 1990s, the Korean government had not enacted any formal provisions for defining the Korean diaspora and allocating preferential rights to those thus defined in immigration and citizenship laws. Although co-ethnic migrants were given preferential treatment within the industrial trainee system (and, later, the EPS), with the largest quotas allocated for Korean Chinese, there were no co-ethnic visas that would make them eligible for privileged entry and employment rights along the lines of the long-term residency visa for co-ethnic (*Nikkei*) migrants in Japan. Nor were they automatically conferred South Korean nationality, in contrast to co-ethnic migrants in countries with similar descent-based citizenship policies such as Germany, Italy, and Spain. Only North Korean migrants are recognized as South Korean nationals not on the basis of their co-ethnicity but because the Republic of Korea (ROK) officially regards North Korea as part of its territory (see Chapter 14).

The Overseas Korea Foundation Act, promulgated in March 1997, marks the first such attempt with the stated aim of supporting the "lives of Koreans abroad in their residential countries."[5] This Act initially defined "overseas Koreans" (*jaeoe dongpo*) as those living abroad with ROK nationality or those who lost their ROK nationality when they acquired the nationality of another country. This definition drew strong criticism from politicians and the public alike for its exclusion of pre-1948 emigrants, which prompted the Ministry of Foreign Affairs to add a second definition based on blood (Korean lineage). This blood-based definition, however, was no longer tenable when lawmakers considered a bill the following year that would attach rights to the status of "overseas Koreans."

13.4.1 Ideas, Strategies, and Networks: Litigating Korean Identity

In 1999, the National Assembly passed the Overseas Korean Act (Act on the Immigration and Legal Status of Overseas Koreans, hereafter "OKA") with the stated purpose of creating a "global" Korean community.[6] Defining "overseas Koreans" as "Korean citizens residing abroad" and "Koreans with foreign citizenship" (Article 2–2), the OKA created an "Overseas Korean" (F-4) visa category that gave eligible co-ethnic migrants quasi dual citizenship rights (Park and Chang 2005). It was also part of a broader *segyehwa* (globalization) initiative promoted first by President Kim Young-sam's administration (1993–98) and later by President Kim Dae-jung's administration (1998–2003) to internationalize all sectors of Korea's economy and society (S. Kim 2000). An important component of this initiative was the creation of

---

5   *Jaeoe dongpo jaedanbeop*, Act No. 5313 (1997), amended as Act No. 13348 (2015).
6   *Jaeoe dongpoui churipgukgwa beopjeok jiwie gwanhan beomnyul*, Act No. 6015 (1999), amended as Act No. 14973 (2017).

a "global" Korean community built on networks of Korean diasporic communities throughout the world.

Although all members of the more than 5 million people of Korean descent residing largely in China, the United States, Japan, and the former Soviet Union were targeted in this endeavor, US Korean Americans, especially professionals and adoptees, were the centerpiece of this campaign because they had the potential to make three central contributions to the *segyehwa* campaign's goals: (1) in the United States, they were well positioned to disseminate and consume the cultural products of the *segyehwa* campaign as immigrants and immigrant descendants residing in the most powerful country in the world; (2) as immigrants to Korea (or "return migrants"), they could provide much-needed English language skills to a globalizing Korean economy that demanded English-speaking professionals; and (3) as potential investors from the wealthiest country in the world who had affective ties to Korea, they could provide a significant source of foreign capital in an economy recovering from the 1998 financial crisis (Chung 2020a).

Ethnic Koreans from China and the former Soviet Union were initially excluded from the Overseas Korean status based on the definition of "Koreans with foreign citizenship" as Koreans who had previously held South Korean nationality and their descendants. This definition applied to less than half of all Korean diasporic populations as it limited eligibility to those who left the Korean peninsula after the founding of the ROK in 1948. The largest communities of post-1948 emigrants reside in the United States and Japan; by contrast, the vast majority of ethnic Koreans in China and the former Soviet Union are colonial-era migrants and their descendants.

As the National Assembly prepared to vote on the bill in August 1999, Korean Chinese organizations, including the Korean International Network, plus national and international NGOs, organized a public campaign to rally against the proposed OKA. In contrast to the migrant workers' movement that applied a broad-based approach to securing labor protections for all workers – both Korean and foreign – the campaign against the OKA bill aimed at securing privileges equally for all *co-ethnic* migrants. The issue at hand was thus not human rights, labor protections, Korean nationality, or even access to permanent residency, but, rather, the democratic principle of nondiscrimination applied to members of the Korean diaspora (see Chapter 12). Specifically, the network of Korean Chinese activists and NGOs focused on the question of discrimination against particular categories of co-ethnics based on country of origin. In addition to launching public campaigns, demonstrations, and hunger strikes, this network of activists went to the courts to make their rights claims. The strength of their claims rested on a specific civic legacy of post-authoritarian Korea: constitutional adjudication.

As Mosler (Chapter 6) discusses, thousands of cases have been filed by Korean citizens to redress grievances against the state following the establishment of Korea's Constitutional Court in 1988. Rather than serve as a final arbiter in federal–state relations, the Constitutional Court in Korea's unitary system has allowed individual citizens to file constitutional complaints directly (Hahm 2012). Two weeks after the National Assembly passed the OKA bill, three Korean Chinese residents filed a complaint with the Constitutional Court claiming that the OKA violated the principle of equality in the Constitution. Their constitutional complaint was supported by sixty NGOs (C. Lee 2010).

13.4.2 Outcome: Expansion of the "Overseas Korean" Visa

In 2001, the Constitutional Court ruled that the provision in the OKA that excluded those who emigrated from the Korean peninsula before the establishment of the ROK did not conform to the principle of equality (Article 11) in the Constitution because it discriminated against pre-1948 emigrants (C. Lee 2012).[7] In response to this ruling and continued pressure from civil society groups, the National Assembly passed a 2004 amendment that replaced the prior South Korean nationality requirement with documentary evidence of household registration (*hojeok*) in Korea. Nevertheless, not a single F-4 visa was issued to an ethnic Korean migrant from China or the former Soviet Union for the first three years after the amendment (C. Lee 2012, 94–95). Since then, however, the number of Korean Chinese with Overseas Korean visas has grown by more than sevenfold, from zero to 72 percent of all Overseas Korean visa holders (Lee and Chien 2017, 2201). In 2007, the Ministry of Justice also created the H-2 Working Visit visa exclusively for ethnic Koreans from China and the former Soviet Union (up to the third generation) to work in the labor-starved service and construction industries.

The employment opportunities and rights associated with each visa category institutionalized the privileged status of some migrants over others and, in the case of the Overseas Korean and Working Visit visas, some co-ethnic immigrants over others (see Table 13.1). The H-2 Working Visit visa that was created specifically for ethnic Koreans from China and the former Soviet Union allows for greater labor mobility than its counterpart for general foreign workers, the E-9 Nonprofessional Employment visa. Whereas the latter restricts employment in a single industry – limited to manufacturing, construction, agriculture, or fisheries – and allows for a maximum of three workplace changes in the first three years (and two in the extended two years), which must be approved by their employers, the former has no restrictions in regard to movement between industries – which, for Working Visit visa holders, includes the service industry in addition to manufacturing, construction, agriculture, and fisheries – and workplace changes.[8] Working Visit visa holders

---

7 See the "Act on the Immigration and Legal Status of Overseas Koreans Case" (13-2 KCCR 714, 99Heonma494, November 29, 2001). The proceedings are summarized in the "Decisions of the Korean Constitutional Court (2001)," www.ccourt.go.kr.

8 *Churipguk gwallibeop* (Immigration Act), Act No. 15492 (2018), Articles 8 & 18; *Oegugin geullojaui goyong deunge gwanhan beomnyul* (Act on the Employment, Etc. of Foreign Workers), Act No. 16274 (2019).

TABLE 13.1 *Major Employment and Residential Visa Categories in South Korea*

Visa Category	Year Established	Eligibility	Employment Restrictions	Associated Rights	Duration and Renewals Permitted
F-4 Overseas Korean	1999	"Koreans with foreign citizenship status": those who left the Korean peninsula after ROK founding in 1948 (until 2003)	Prohibited from engaging in manual labor (until 2015)	Property rights, investment rights, health insurance, pensions, and other social welfare benefits + dual citizenship eligibility	Three years + multiple renewals
F-5 Permanent Resident	2002	Five-year continuous residency (exceptions for native-born ethnic Chinese *hwagyo*, F-4 visa holders, F-6 visa holders, and foreign investors)	No restrictions	Property rights, investment rights, health insurance, pensions, and other social welfare benefits + local voting rights	N/A (no renewals necessary) (until 2018)
E-9 Nonprofessional Employment	2004	Nationals of countries that have signed a Memorandum of Understanding (MOU) with the ROK	Employment restricted to a single industry + maximum of three workplace changes in first three years	Labor rights protections under Korean labor laws (including pensions and health insurance)	Three years + single two-year renewal

TABLE 13.1 (continued)

Visa Category	Year Established	Eligibility	Employment Restrictions	Associated Rights	Duration and Renewals Permitted
H-2 Working Visit	2007	Ethnic Koreans from China and the former USSR (up to third generation) aged twenty-five years and above	No restrictions	Labor rights protections under Korean labor laws (including pensions and health insurance)	Three years + single two-year renewal
F-6 Marriage Migrant	2011	F-6-1 Spouse of a Korean national F-6-2 Caregiver of a (Korean citizen) child F-6-3 Divorcee	No restrictions	Property rights, investment rights, health insurance, pensions, and other social welfare benefits + dual citizenship eligibility + simplified naturalization	Three years + multiple renewals

Sources: ROK Ministry of Justice, Office of Immigration; Ministry of Employment and Labor; Chung 2020a.

also have more flexibility in regard to employment contracts (e.g., part time versus full time) and employers, unlike E-9 Nonprofessional Employment visa holders who are required to work full time only for companies that are registered in the EPS (Lee and Chien 2017, 2199). Another central difference between the two labor visas lies in their management: whereas the Ministry of Employment and Labor manages the Nonprofessional Employment visa, both the MOEL and the Ministry of Justice manage the Working Visit visa since it pertains to labor *and* kinship ties. In contrast, the Overseas Korean visa is a residence visa managed solely by the Ministry of Justice. It provides quasi dual citizenship rights for co-ethnic migrants that include access to health insurance, pensions, property rights, investment rights, and broad employment opportunities in Korea.[9] This visa had only one employment restriction: Overseas Korean visa holders were prohibited from engaging in *manual labor* until 2015.[10]

The eligibility criteria for both co-ethnic visas as well their corresponding rights standardized the limits of blood-based membership according to kinship ties and country of origin. That is, the right to work in Korea as a co-ethnic migrant (Working Visit visa) was determined by kinship ties; yet, the right to reside permanently and acquire Korean nationality was determined by occupational status, country of origin, and/or marriage to a Korean national (as discussed in the following section). To be sure, unskilled migrant workers and co-ethnic migrants from China and the former Soviet Union were not *prohibited* from acquiring permanent residency or Korean nationality. At the same time, the visas for which they qualified were valid for three years with a possibility of a single two-year extension for a maximum duration of four years and ten months. This is two months shy of the five-year continuous residency requirement for a permanent resident (F-5) visa and naturalization. Only Overseas Korean, Professional, and Spouse of Korean National/Marriage Migrant visa holders can renew their visas multiple times; all other visas holders can renew their visas once.[11] Since 2002, Overseas Korean visa holders have been permitted to change their status to permanent resident after just two years of residence.[12] In sum, the visa categories created to distinguish co-ethnic migrants from other foreigners and differentiate *between* co-ethnic migrants themselves reinforced asymmetries between migrants from the Global North and Global South even among co-ethnic migrants, correlating their emigration histories and countries of origin with legal status, employment opportunities, rights, and eligibility for permanent settlement and citizenship acquisition. Like the migrant workers' movement, co-ethnic migrant claims to noncitizen rights rested on the civic legacies of Korea's democracy movement.

---

[9]   Employers are required to purchase health insurance for employees in the Employment Permit Service.

[10]   *Churipguk gwallibeop*, Articles 10, 17, & 18.

[11]   *Churipguk gwallibeop*, Articles 10, 17, & 18.

[12]   *Churipguk gwallibeop*, Enforcement Decree, Table 1.

13.5 MARRIAGE MIGRANTS: STATE PROTECTIONS AND GENDERED CITIZENSHIP

While Korea has maintained relatively restrictive immigration policies that discourage the permanent settlement of unskilled immigrants, local governments, especially in depopulated rural areas, have proactively recruited female migrants for one specific national shortage: marriage partners for unmarried men (Chung 2020b). Since 1999, Korea's Ministry of Health and Welfare has issued reports warning of an imminent demographic crisis with plummeting fertility rates and a rapidly aging population. The Korea National Statistical Office projects that the number of working-age Koreans will drop to 54 percent of the total population by 2050, while the population aged sixty-five or older is expected to reach 35 percent. Government officials have attempted to tackle the problem of declining birth rates by providing financial incentives to prospective couples, subsidies for childcare, and tax breaks for families with more than two children. These measures remain insufficient amidst anemic welfare policies and households that continue to rely on the traditional patriarchal family system in which women are expected to stay home to care for their children and aging parents-in-law (Chung 2020b).

The rising numbers of unmarried men in districts with low fertility rates and rapidly aging populations were especially burdensome for local governments in rural districts as they were quickly losing their tax revenue. And their limited social welfare and elder care facilities were unable to keep pace with their rapidly aging resident populations. The push to address the "bride famine" by public and private actors in rural areas flipped international marriage patterns in Korea; international marriages involving native Korean male nationals and foreign women outnumbered those involving female nationals and foreign men by 1995.

Local government officials and agricultural associations in rural areas took it upon themselves to broker arranged marriage meetings between their unmarried male residents and potential spouses. Following the normalization of diplomatic relations between South Korea and mainland China in 1992, they expanded the pool of potential spouses to ethnic Korean women from China. Between 1993 and 2003, the number of marriages between Korean men and migrant women from China increased more than sevenfold from approximately 1,850 to almost 13,350 (Korea Immigration Service 2017). After the Korean government deregulated the marriage industry in 1999, hundreds of private brokers established international marriage agencies that widened the pool of marriage migrants to Southeast Asia and Russia (H. K. Lee 2008, 110–11). In 2009, the number of female migrants entering Korea as spouses of Korean nationals reached over 125,000 and international marriages made up over 10 percent of all marriages in Korea (Korea Immigration Service 2010). What started off with a handful of rural households seeking marriage partners for their unmarried farmers exploded into a profitable, transnational industry by the early 2000s.

13.5.1 *Ideas, Strategies, and Networks: Mobilizing Resistance to Precarity*

In the early 2000s, campaigns by women's organizations, human rights groups, and labor unions brought to light the precarious situation of migrant women who had been recruited to address Korea's "bride shortage" and demographic crisis. Because their legal status and rights were entirely derivative of their spousal status, so-called marriage migrants were in a highly vulnerable position vis-à-vis their principal sponsors – their Korean husbands and in-laws – which led to cases of domestic violence, growing divorce rates, and, subsequently, growing numbers of undocumented female migrants.[13] High-profile cases involving the deaths of marriage migrants galvanized public attention throughout the 2000s. The death of Huan Mai, a 19-year old Vietnamese marriage migrant, at the hands of her forty-one-year old Korean husband in 2007 especially highlighted the need for greater state regulation of the marriage broker industry, on the one hand, and the expansion of support services for marriage migrants, on the other (D. Kim 2015, 130).[14]

In the early 2000s, feminist activists and human rights groups formed the Solidarity Network for the Human Rights of Migrant Women (*Ijuyeoseong ingwon yeondae gongdong*), a coalition to combat domestic and sexual abuse. Drawing on the civic legacies of previous generations of women's movements in Korea, this coalition focused on domestic and sexual violence and prostitution (D. Kim 2017). Daisy Kim (2015, 99–100) notes that the Korean women's movement increasingly integrated the language of human rights following the World Conference on Human Rights held in Vienna in 1993 and the 4th World Conference on Women held in Beijing in 1995. Framing migrant women's issues in the language of human rights – for example, by linking marriage brokers with "human trafficking" (*insinmaemae*) – seasoned women's activists from earlier movements used media campaigns, rallies, and petitions to raise awareness and expand the public narrative of marriage migrants and their children as victims who required state protection.

13.5.2 *Outcome: From Activism to Support Services*

Similar to the migrant workers' movement, advocacy for migrant women that built on the civic legacies of the women's movement converged with the interests of a progressive government under Roh Moo-hyun. This movement succeeded in legalizing alternative pathways for spouses of Korean nationals to remain in Korea without the sponsorship of their husbands; it also led to the expansion of public services and programs for migrant women. The 2004 amendment to the Nationality Act established a pathway for spouses of Korean nationals who are unable to remain

---

[13] For parallels to the position of married women in colonial and postcolonial Korea, respectively, see Lim (Chapter 2) and E. Kim (Chapter 3).

[14] A July 2019 video showing a thirty-six-year old Korean man attacking his thirty-year old Vietnamese wife while she held her two-year old son went viral on social media and reignited calls for instituting greater protections for noncitizen migrant women (Seon and Ahn 2019).

in their marriages due to situations beyond their control to acquire Korean nationality, even in situations when they did not meet the naturalization requirements, with the purpose of "guaranteeing their human rights and protecting their children."[15] In 2005, the Ministry of Gender Equality became the Ministry of Gender Equality and Family and was charged with expanding governmental support and services for migrant women and their "multicultural families" (*damunhwa gajok*).[16] During the following year, the Roh Moo-hyun administration announced the "Grand Plan" for the social integration of migrant women and their "mixed-race" (*honhyeol*) children and the attainment of a "multiracial, multicultural society" (*dainjong damunhwa sahoe*) (Chung and Kim 2012). Also, the establishment of the Korea Immigration Service (KIS) in 2007 came with a social integration (*sahoe tonghap*) division targeted directly at migrant women and their children. The promulgation of the 2007 Basic Act on the Treatment of Foreigners in Korea (*Jaehanoegukin cheou gibonbeop*), which represents the Korean government's first overarching framework for immigrant incorporation, cemented the prioritization of marriage migrants as potential or actual Korean citizens. This far-reaching piece of legislation set distinct guidelines for the targeted incorporation of specific groups of migrants in Korea: social integration for marriage migrants, preferential entry and employment rights for co-ethnic migrants, and human rights protections for migrant workers (Chung 2010b). A separate law specifically targeting marriage migrants and their children, the Act on Support for Multicultural Families (*Damunhwa gajok jiwonbeop*), was then enacted the following year. In 2010, the National Assembly passed a bill to allow for dual nationality, which included marriage migrants among the eligible groups. Finally, the establishment of the marriage migrant visa in 2011 removed the requirement for female migrants to remain married to their Korean spouses with three classifications: (1) spouse of a Korean national (F-6–1); (2) caregiver of a (Korean citizen) child (F-6–2); and (3) divorcee (F-6–3).

This series of policies and programs have put this group of predominantly female migrants at the highest echelon in the hierarchy of noncitizens in Korea, with rights and benefits comparable to the Overseas Korean visa holders and high-skilled professionals. Similar to the Overseas Korean visa, the marriage migrant visa is a residence visa that provides access to health insurance, pensions, property rights, investment rights, unlimited employment rights, and social welfare benefits such as public assistance under the National Basic Livelihood Security Program. Migrant spouses also have access to over 200 so-called multicultural family centers created specifically to facilitate their integration. Not only is this category of visa holders one

---

[15] Revisions of the Nationality Act, Act No. 7075 (2004).

[16] The category of "multicultural family" explicitly excludes the offspring of Korean citizens and undocumented foreign residents, the offspring of unmarried couples, and families of foreign residents, including migrant workers, foreign professionals, and multigenerational Taiwanese residents (*hwagyo*) (H. K. Lee 2008: 116; H. M. Kim 2012).

of the fastest growing immigrant groups in Korea, but marriage to a native citizen now constitutes one of the most widely recognized paths to Korean citizenship.

At the same time, the expansion of state-sponsored support programs for migrant women has changed the organizational structure, leadership positions, and priorities of migrant women's advocacy groups. Women's organizations are now one of many NGOs that compete for government funding to provide services to migrant women in support centers that are overseen by local governments. Moreover, the programs themselves are largely focused on language acquisition and cultural assimilation rather than on political empowerment. For example, the aforementioned multicultural family centers established throughout the country help migrant women prepare for their naturalization proceedings, including the civic integration exam; they also offer Korean language classes that include instruction in honorifics that can be applied in conversations with husbands and in-laws. Likewise, Korean culture classes focus on the household, teaching marriage migrants how to, for example, make *kimchi*, prepare household shrines to honor the husband's family's ancestors, and cook on traditional holidays.

The conservative implementation of seemingly progressive legislation reflects the unintended consequences of this particular state–society partnership. While sustained activism by women's organizations through the early 2000s was central to the adoption of legislation aimed at providing human rights protections for migrant women, negotiations between the state and women's organizations over the terms and conditions of migrant women's incorporation from the mid-2000s led to competitive pressures between groups over government resources, policy implementation, and public debates. Feminist and human rights groups that served as advocates for racially and ethnically distinct migrant women in Korea have become depoliticized in the process of reorganizing themselves as service providers for state-run incorporation programs that aim to assimilate migrant women as wives, mothers, and citizens in the mold of traditional patriarchal ideals of Korean womanhood.

13.6 CONCLUSION

This chapter has analyzed the hierarchies of rights among noncitizens that have developed in Korea over the last few decades as the country grapples with the challenges of falling birth rates, a rapidly aging population, and a shrinking labor force. The proliferation of visa categories that map onto group-specific attributes and range in status from quasi-dual citizens to temporary unskilled workers complicates our understanding of immigrant incorporation and associated rights. Not only is the process of incorporation nonlinear but, depending on the terms of the visa category, it may also be permanently static – in the case of visas that are nonrenewable and/or do not allow for changes in legal statuses – or subject to reversal when migrants no longer "fit" their visa designations (Chung 2020a; 2020b). Consider, for example, marriage migrant visa holders who divorce or female migrant laborers who become pregnant. When visa categories are attached to group-specific identities and/or ascriptive criteria, the process of incorporation may be circumscribed to the visa status itself. Marriage migrant visa holders are "incorporated" when they have become proper Korean wives and mothers; on the other hand, ethnic Koreans from China are "incorporated" when they have met the criteria for the Overseas Korean visa. In some cases, "incorporation" may simply refer to a legal status that is relatively less precarious.

Examining migrant rights and hierarchies through the lens of visa categories has the potential to contribute fresh insights into understanding the intersections of race, migration, and citizenship in East Asia. The concept of nationality in this region is closely related to ethnic, racial, and national identity. If phenotypical difference is the central marker for minority status in North American and European societies, then alienage is increasingly the basis for how minorities relate to the state, mobilize themselves, and voice their collective interests in East Asia (Chung 2017). While national immigration policies establish the parameters for legal entry and employ-ment, the ideas, strategies, and networks of past struggles for democratic inclusion in a given country shape migrant rights claims (Chung 2020b). Further research in this area will contribute to our understanding of how states use migration and citizenship policies as control mechanisms to shape racial, ethnic, and gender politics and how migrants negotiate and contest the terms of their incorporation and rights (Chung 2020a).

REFERENCES

Arrington, Celeste L., and Yong-Il Moon. 2020. "Cause Lawyering and Movement Tactics: Disability Rights Movements in South Korea and Japan." *Law & Policy* 42 (1): 5–30.

Chung, Erin Aeran. 2010a. *Immigration and Citizenship in Japan*. New York: Cambridge University Press.

2010b. "Workers or Residents? Diverging Patterns of Immigrant Incorporation in Korea and Japan." *Pacific Affairs* 83 (4): 675–96.

2017. "Citizenship in Non-Western Contexts." In *Oxford Handbook of Citizenship*, edited by Ayelet Shachar, Rainer Bauböck, Irene Bloemraad, and Maarten P. Vink, 431–52. Oxford: Oxford University Press.

2020a. "Creating Hierarchies of Noncitizens: Race, Gender, and Visa Categories in South Korea." *Journal of Ethnic & Migration Studies* 46 (12): 2497–2514.

2020b. *Immigrant Incorporation in East Asian Democracies*. New York: Cambridge University Press.

Chung, Erin Aeran, and Daisy Kim. 2012. "Citizenship and Marriage in a Globalizing World: Multicultural Families and Monocultural Nationality Laws in Korea and Japan." *Indiana Journal of Global Legal Studies* 19 (1): 195–219.

Cohen, Elizabeth F. 2009. *Semi-Citizenship in Democratic Politics*. New York: Cambridge University Press.

Finnemore, Martha, and Kathryn Sikkink. 1998. "International Norm Dynamics and Political Change." *International Organization* 52 (4): 887–917.

Fishman, Robert M. 2017. "How Civil Society Matters in Democratization: Setting the Boundaries of Post-Transition Political Inclusion." *Comparative Politics* 49 (3): 391–409.

Goldring, Luin, and Patricia Landolt, eds. 2013. *Producing and Negotiating Non-Citizenship: Precarious Legal Status in Canada.* Toronto: University of Toronto Press.

Gurowitz, Amy. 1999. "Mobilizing International Norms: Domestic Actors, Immigrants, and the Japanese State." *World Politics* 51 (3): 413–45.

Hahm, Chaihark. 2012. "Beyond 'Law vs. Politics' in Constitutional Adjudication: Lessons from South Korea." *International Journal of Constitutional Law* 10 (1): 6–34.

Hammar, Tomas. 1990. *Democracy and the Nation State: Aliens, Denizens, and Citizens in a World of International Migration.* Brookfield: Gower Pub. Co.

Hollifield, James F. 2004. "The Emerging Migration State." *International Migration Review* 38 (3): 885–912.

Hosoki, Ralph I. 2016. "The Potential Role of Migrant Rights Advocacy in Mitigating Demographic Crises in Japan." In *Japan's Demographic Revival*, edited by Stephen Nagy, 285–336. Singapore: World Scientific.

Hsia, Hsiao-Chuan. 2008. "The Development of Immigrant Movement in Taiwan: The Case of Alliance of Human Rights Legislation for Immigrants and Migrants." *Development and Society* 37 (2): 187–217.

Joppke, Christian. 1999. *Immigration and the Nation-State: The United States, Germany, and Great Britain.* Oxford: Oxford University Press.

Kim, Andrew Eungi. 2009. "Global Migration and South Korea: Foreign Workers, Foreign Brides and the Making of a Multicultural Society." *Ethnic and Racial Studies* 32 (1): 70–92.

Kim, Daisy. 2015. "Bargaining Citizenship: Women's Organizations, the State, and Marriage Migrants in South Korea." Ph.D. diss., Political Science, Johns Hopkins University.

    2017. "Resisting Migrant Precarity: A Critique of Human Rights Advocacy for Marriage Migrants in South Korea." *Critical Asian Studies* 49 (1): 1–17.

Kim, Hyun Mee. 2012. "The Emergence of the 'Multicultural Family' and Genderized Citizenship in South Korea." In *Contested Citizenship in East Asia: Developmental Politics, National Unity, and Globalization*, edited by Kyung-Sup Chang and Bryan S. Turner, 203–17. London and New York: Routledge.

Kim, Joon. 2003. "Insurgency and Advocacy: Unauthorized Foreign Workers and Civil Society in South Korea." *Asian and Pacific Migration Journal* 12 (3): 237–69.

Kim, Nora Hui-Jung. 2008. "Korean Immigration Policy Changes and the Political Liberals' Dilemma." *International Migration Review* 42 (3): 576–96.

Kim, Samuel, ed. 2000. *Korea's Globalization.* Cambridge: Cambridge University Press.

Kofman, Eleonore. 2002. "Contemporary European Migrations, Civic Stratification and Citizenship." *Political Geography* 21 (8): 1035–54.

Korea Immigration Service, Ministry of Justice. 2010. K.I.S. Statistics 2009 (2009 Chulipguk oegukin tong'gye yonbo).

    2011. K.I.S. Statistics 2010 (2010 Chulipguk oegukin tong'gye yonbo).

    2017. K.I.S. Statistics 2016 (2016 Chulipguk oegukin tong'gye yonbo).

    2018. K.I.S. Statistics 2017 (2017 Chulipguk oegukin tong'gye yonbo).

Layton-Henry, Zig, ed. 1990. *The Political Rights of Migrant Workers in Western Europe.* London: Sage.

Lee, Chulwoo. 2010. "South Korea: The Transformation of Citizenship and the State-Nation Nexus." *Journal of Contemporary Asia* 40 (2): 230–51.

    2012. "How Can You Say You're Korean? Law, Governmentality and National Membership in South Korea." *Citizenship Studies* 16 (1): 85–102.

Lee, Hye-Kyung. 2008. "International Marriage and the State in South Korea: Focusing on Governmental Policy." *Citizenship Studies* 12 (1): 107–23.

Lee, Sohoon, and Yi-Chun Chien. 2017. "The Making of 'Skilled' Overseas Koreans: Transformation of Visa Policies for Co-Ethnic Migrants in South Korea." *Journal of Ethnic and Migration Studies* 43 (13): 2193–210.

Lee, Yong Wook, and Hyemee Park. 2005. "The Politics of Foreign Labor Policy in Korea and Japan." *Journal of Contemporary Asia* 35 (2): 143–65.

Lim, Timothy C. 2003. "Racing from the Bottom in South Korea? The Nexus between Civil Society and Transnational Migrants." *Asian Survey* 43 (3): 423–42.

——— 2006. "NGOs, Transnational Migrants, and the Promotion of Rights in South Korea." In *Local Citizenship in Recent Countries of Immigration: Japan in Comparative Perspective*, edited by Takeyuki Tsuda, 235–69. Lanham: Lexington Books.

——— 2010. "Rethinking Belongingness in Korea: Transnational Migration, 'Migrant Marriages' and the Politics of Multiculturalism." *Pacific Affairs* 83 (1): 22.

Marshall, T. H. 1950. *Class, Citizenship and Social Development*. Cambridge: Cambridge University Press.

Merry, Sally Engle. 2006. "Transnational Human Rights and Local Activism: Mapping the Middle." *American Anthropologist* 108 (1): 38–51.

Milly, Deborah J. 2014. *New Policies for New Residents: Immigrants, Advocacy, and Governance in Japan and Beyond*. Ithaca: Cornell University Press.

Moon, Katharine. 2000. "Strangers in the Midst of Globalization: Migrant Workers and Korean Nationalism." In *Korea's Globalization*, edited by Samuel Kim, 147–69. New York: Cambridge University Press.

Morris, Lydia. 2002. *Managing Migration: Civic Stratification and Migrants' Rights*: London and New York: Routledge.

Park, Jung-Sun, and Paul Y. Chang. 2005. "Contention in the Construction of a Global Korean Community: The Case of the Overseas Korean Act." *Journal of Korean Studies* 10: 1–27.

Seol, Dong-Hoon. 2000. "Past and Present of Foreign Workers in Korea 1987–2000." *Asia Solidarity Quarterly* 2: 1–17.

Seon, Dam-eun, and Kwan-ok Ahn. 2019. "Video of Migrant Woman Being Abused by Husband Incites Public Outrage." *Hankyoreh Sinmun*, July 8, 2019. http://english .hani.co.kr/arti/english_edition/e_national/900962.html. Accessed January 21, 2021.

Shin, Gi-Wook. 2006. *Ethnic Nationalism in Korea : Genealogy, Politics, and Legacy*, Studies of the Walter H. Shorenstein Asia-Pacific Research Center. Stanford: Stanford University Press.

Shipper, Apichai W. 2008. *Fighting for Foreigners: Immigration and Its Impact on Japanese Democracy*. Ithaca: Cornell University Press.

Smart, Alan, and Josephine Smart. 2008. "Time-Space Punctuation: Hong Kong's Border Regime and Limits on Mobility." *Pacific Affairs* 81 (2): 175–93.

SOPEMI. 2008. *International Migration Outlook: Annual Report*. Paris: Organisation for Economic Co-operation and Development.

Soysal, Yasemin Nuhoglu. 1994. *Limits of Citizenship: Migrants and Postnational Membership in Europe*. Chicago: University of Chicago Press.

Tsutsui, Kiyoteru, and Hwa Ji Shin. 2008. "Global Norms, Local Activism, and Social Movement Outcomes: Global Human Rights and Resident Koreans in Japan." *Social Problems* 55 (3): 391–418.

14

Claiming Citizenship

Rights Claiming and Recognition for North Koreans Entering South Korea

Sheena Chestnut Greitens[1]

14.1 INTRODUCTION

When and how does citizenship matter? How are citizenship and its attendant rights reflected, refracted, and challenged when citizens migrate or cross the borders of their country of citizenship? Current conceptions of citizenship focus mostly on membership and rights contestation *within* the political community, but citizens in a globalized world are often reminded of their nationality or citizenship most acutely when they are outside or at the border of their country of citizenship. Korea, with its globally dispersed diasporic population, is no exception to this insight.

This chapter probes what border-crossing tells us about the linkage between citizenship and rights claiming by examining the experiences of North Koreans who seek to resettle in South Korea (the Republic of Korea, ROK).[2] The chapter focuses on these individuals because scholars and journalists often describe them as being granted "automatic citizenship" in the South, with the implication that their struggles for recognition and the rights attendant on citizen status are minimal, particularly in comparison to other groups, such as the Korean-Chinese or non-Koreans examined by Chung (Chapter 13). As I demonstrate, however, "automatic citizenship" is inaccurate. North Koreans must exhibit considerable agency to claim their citizenship status, and when they arrive at the border or the point of entry into the ROK, their rights are heavily circumscribed and contingent on state recognition. The chapter substantiates this argument by drawing on qualitative analysis of narratives of migration and resettlement written and published by North Korean

[1] The author thanks Yujin Julia Jung, Yu Bin Kim, and Myunghee Lee for research assistance; and Wendy Hunter, Aram Hur, Celeste Arrington, and Patricia Goedde for their encouragement and feedback. All errors remain my own.
[2] Different groups use different terms – in English and Korean – to describe North Koreans who leave the DPRK. The most common terms in English are defector, refugee, migrant, or resettler; in Korean, *saeteomin*, *talbukja*, or *bukhanitaljumin*. The choice of terminology in both languages can carry political, causal, even moral connotations. This chapter uses migrant to describe North Koreans during the migration process, and resettler afterward, without intended political or normative connotation.

migrants,[3] as well as evidence from immigration court proceedings, ROK citizenship curricula, interviews with officials and migrants, and participant observation in South Korea and North Korean refugee communities in the United States.[4]

The chapter proceeds in three main sections (Sections 14.2, 14.3, and 14.4). The first outlines the relationship between citizenship and rights claiming, centered on the idea that citizenship confers the "right to have rights." The second uses this linkage to identify a puzzle in the ROK state's treatment of North Koreans: the state that claims North Korean citizens as its own, in legal and communitarian terms, does not automatically and fully recognize claims to that citizenship when they are made by North Koreans seeking to enter South Korea for resettlement. The third section illustrates this argument through a focused examination of the screening that North Korean migrants experience upon entering ROK territory, excavating the ways in which the rights of citizenship, having been claimed, are conditionally and incompletely conferred. The chapter concludes by offering some reflections on the implications of this revised understanding for contemporary theories of citizenship, in Korea and beyond.

14.2 CLAIMING CITIZENSHIP AND CLAIMING RIGHTS

Citizenship is a central concept in the study of political life, but also a contested, multivalent term. It connotes membership in a political community and invokes rights (and obligations) such as welfare provision, participation, or protection (Marshall 1964; Leary 2000). In autocracies, it outlines relational expectations between state and citizens; in democracies, citizenship is a status that, mutually recognized, confers "the right to have rights" (Mann 1987; Benhabib 2001; Tilly 2006; Perry 2008; Pinto 2012; Yashar 2013; Distelhorst and Fu 2019). Scholarly work on democratic citizenship often treats it as either a "formal bundle of rights" secured via "contractual promises" between individual and polity (a liberal contractual concept, grounded in law and policy) or an affective "state of democratic belonging or inclusion" (an identity-based communitarian concept) (Conover et al 1991; Sassen 2003; Yashar 2005, 2013; Bosniak 2006; Sobel 2016).

Debates over citizenship as formal legal status versus affective state of belonging matter greatly in contexts like the Korean peninsula. Patterns of colonialism, state formation, regime transition, and migration have generated ethnic-affinitive communities that span formal international borders, forcing states and individuals to grapple with and revise the meaning of membership, inclusion, and incorporation

---

[3] This chapter focuses specifically on citizenship and rights claiming at the moment of border-crossing. For an overview of the North Korean migrant narratives employed in this chapter, and of the politics of citizenship claiming and recognition/denial across the entire migration and resettlement process, see Greitens 2021.

[4] Project approved by the University of Missouri Institutional Review Board (Projects #2004769, #2002674).

under circumstances where legal state boundaries and identity-based communities are not territorially aligned (Herbst 1989; Soysal 1994; Brubaker 1998; Ekiert and Kubik 1999; Colton 2000; Flynn 2007; S. Kim 2014; Hong Liu & van Dongen 2016; J. Kim 2016; Michalopoulos and Papaioannou 2016; Gamlen et al 2017; Pop-Eleches and Tucker 2017). In these contexts, citizenship is a contestation about not just who is included and how inclusion occurs, but also the "who and how" of exclusion; it is a politics of rights denial alongside rights conferral (Brubaker 1992; Brubaker 2004; Glenn 2004; Isaac 2011). As Erin Chung (Chapter 13) has documented, the outcomes of such contestation create hierarchies of rights among migrants.

For these reasons, much is at stake in the decisions about who gets to make determinations of citizenship. Individuals cannot claim the rights accorded to citizenship unless they can get the state to recognize their standing as citizens in the first place. Although other chapters in this volume reveal that rights claims themselves are not limited to citizens, North Koreans have a much stronger basis upon which to contest and claim rights once they have gotten South Korea's state and society to recognize them as citizens. Moreover, empirical research has found that citizenship is correlated with higher levels of national identification and increased political and civic engagement, as compared to noncitizen permanent residents (Bloemraad 2018, 10). Thus, if an individual's citizenship is unclear or debated, the first claim they must make is to citizen standing; only then can they claim other forms of citizen rights and access the mechanisms and institutional channels of rights claiming discussed elsewhere in this volume.

The sections that follow trace the process that is initiated by North Korean claims to citizenship in the Republic of Korea. It focuses on one particular point in these individuals' journey toward resettlement in South Korea: the period when, upon entering the ROK territory, they are debriefed and questioned by a security team composed of military, police, and National Intelligence Service (NIS) personnel. Before that, North Koreans have typically awaited transfer from a third country, where they have varied forms of contact with ROK personnel and undergo a preliminary investigation.[5] After the screening stage, they are transferred to Hanawon, the resettlement facility south of Seoul that was established in the late 1990s to prepare North Korean resettlers for their new lives in the South. The screening period, which can last several months, provides an in-depth illustration of how citizens experience rights claiming under conditions of what Longo (2018) calls a "deep border," where the processes of border-crossing and state control over citizens' physical movement extend beyond and within the state, both temporally and physically.

---

[5] The ROK's overseas preliminary investigation, outlined in the North Korean Refugees Protection and Settlement Support Act, is usually done by MOFA, but it can involve an interagency Coordinating Council with representatives from the Ministries of Justice and Unification, NIS, and National Police Agency. Yonhap 2014a.

The chapter's analysis focuses specifically on how North Korean migrants make claims to citizenship when they enter South Korea, and how the ROK state and its agents either recognize or deny those claims. This way of approaching citizenship and rights claiming focuses on state practice and citizen experience of that practice (see also Chapter 7), rather than on formal policy or legal status – but the practices examined are, in essence, appeals to obtain formal citizen status, meaning that citizenship as practice and citizenship as status are closely linked (Isin 2009). The framework draws on and extends a literature that defines citizenship not (just) as legal, regulatory, or bureaucratic policy but also explores it as a concept that is "experienced, negotiated, and enacted in everyday life," and constituted through state–citizen interaction (Nyers 2007).

Citizenship as claims-making is a useful and appropriate approach for several key reasons (Bloemraad 2018). As an approach, this method acknowledges the state's distinctive power to "determine borders and terms of membership" (Choo 2016, 4) – including, in this case, the power to physically control the terms and rights of membership at a territorial border – but does not lose sight of citizens' agency to navigate and sometimes challenge that power (on citizen agency vs. state power, see Turner 1990; Conover et al. 1991; Bloemraad 2004; d'Entreves 2006; Korteweg 2006).[6] It unpacks the processes and standards by which the South Korean state evaluates a claimant, revealing the normative dimensions of a state's ideals of (legitimate) citizenship and what factors can trouble or threaten those ideals. It leads readers to examine variations in citizenship acquisition, such as those that exist across individuals and over time, and elucidates how citizenship matters by showing the rights that are available before recognition of citizen status, and afterward. Finally, it provides new avenues of potential inquiry into the constitution of citizenship among migrants, asking us to speculate on how these initial rights claiming interactions shape North Koreans' sense of what it means to be a citizen, and what kind of citizen he/she is, and can become.

To assess the process of claims-making and state response, the chapter employs structured narrative analysis based on memoirs published by North Korean resettlers in English and Korean.[7] This approach allows subjects to tell stories in ways that reveal what aspects of an experience, choice, or interaction are important to them, while identifying recurring themes that illustrate core concepts: in this case, the contingency and incompleteness of rights that accompany contestation over individual's citizen standing. The narratives that I analyze are from the post-1990 period, when famine and social dislocation prompted increased out-migration from North

---

[6]   S. Kim (2014, 9) frames inter-Korean border crossers in terms of "emotional citizenship" precisely to engage "diverse modes of relationship that an individual enters into with a wide range of communities, which may include but are not necessarily equated to the state."

[7]   The chapter does not examine fiction, poetry, or other nonmemoir writing. On narrative analysis, see Patterson and Monroe 1998; Miles and Huberman 1994; Polkinghorne 1995; J. H. Kim 2016; McCormack 2004.

Korea. This means that unlike the Cold War's elite defectors, the escapees whose narratives the chapter examines were not recruited by the South Korean state. Instead, they had to pursue and appeal for resettlement, often against difficult odds and repeated threat of arrest, violation, and repatriation.[8] This context makes claims-making and its "relational process of recognition" an important tool for understanding the interactions between the South Korean state and North Korean migrants who claim citizenship and its attendant rights.

14.3 THE PUZZLE: NORTH KOREANS AS "AUTOMATIC" CITIZENS

North Koreans have strong claims to South Korean citizenship on both constitutional-legal and ethnic-communitarian grounds. In legal terms, the ROK Constitution operates in tandem with the Nationality Act to define North Koreans as ROK citizens. Article 3 of the ROK Constitution defines the territory of the Republic of Korea to include "the Korean peninsula and its adjacent islands," meaning that it explicitly includes not just the current boundaries of South Korea but the entirety of North Korea as well. Article 2 of the 2010 Nationality Act, meanwhile, argues that South Korea extends citizenship at birth to anyone whose parents are ROK nationals, or who were born in the Republic of Korea (if parentage is unknown).[9] As a result, academic and media discourse, as well as interviews with ROK officials, typically describe North Koreans as having "automatic citizenship" based on ROK law.[10]

Legally defining individuals from North Korea as ROK citizens creates several expectations for state practice, including at the border of the national territory. It confers specific rights on individuals, and responsibilities upon the state – among them the right to free entry. Article 12(4) of the International Covenant on Civil and Political Rights, to which South Korea acceded in 1990, specifies the right to enter the country of one's citizenship.[11] Under criminal law, South Korean citizens are also accorded specific rights of due process, including limits on the length of time they can be detained for investigation; the right to remain silent; and the right to counsel.

There is some inherent tension between the rights accorded in the Constitution and provisions in both the Constitution and National Security Law, which specify that rights can be limited when necessary for national security.[12] For example, Article 37(2) of the ROK Constitution stipulates that "[t]he freedoms and rights of citizens may be restricted by law only when necessary for national security, the

[8] Chung (2008) separates North Koreans into six cohorts; this chapter focuses on cohorts 4–6.

[9] *Gukjeokbeop* (Nationality Act), Act No. 16851 (2019).

[10] Author's interviews with three officials at the Ministry of Unification/Institute for Unification Education, July 2013, May 2014, and May 2016.

[11] *International Covenant on Civil and Political Rights* (adopted December 16, 1966, entered into force March 23, 1976) 999 UNTS 171, www.ohchr.org/en/professionalinterest/pages/ccpr.aspx.

[12] *Gukgaboanbeop* (National Security Law), Act No. 13722 (2016).

maintenance of law and order, or for public welfare. Even when such restriction is imposed, no essential aspect of the freedom or right shall be violated." Recognizing individuals from North Korea as ROK citizens, therefore, involves a grey area in which rights and duties are less clear than those specified in the Constitution or elsewhere in South Korean law due to national security concerns vis-à-vis North Korea; it does not, however, call into question the essential claim that North Koreans are ROK citizens.

North Koreans also meet typical communitarian standards for political membership, in which ethnicity plays a central role (Yashar 2005, 44). Ethnic nationalism figures predominantly in studies of Korean history and citizenship: both states on the peninsula, North and South, lay claim to a singular Korean community defined by blood (*minjok*) (Miyoshi-Jager 2003; Grzelczyk 2014). In the South Korean case, the state's sense of ethnic community extends beyond the peninsula and is embodied in the legal frameworks that set out the terms of diasporic citizenship; in Joppke's terms, South Korea "selects by origin" when offering ethnic Koreans preferential basis for citizenship (Joppke 2005; Park and Chang 2005; N. Kim 2013). Even recent scholarship on ROK incorporation of non-Koreans who migrate to and reside in South Korea (including marriage migrants, guest workers, multicultural families, and others) provides an implicit affirmation of ethnicity's long-standing centrality to Korea's sense of political community (G. Shin 2006; Sohn and Lee 2012; Campbell 2016; Choo 2016; N. Kim 2016; Hundt et al 2018).[13]

This does not mean that all ethnic Koreans have equal claim to membership; Chung (Chapter 13) and other scholars have documented and probed the structure of South Korea's "hierarchical nationhood," where incorporation of co-ethnic migrants varies by class, gender, and other dimensions (Moon 2005; Choo 2006; Song 2013; E. Choi 2014). Within this hierarchy, however, North Koreans are often classified as relatively privileged, because they have rights to an "automatic citizenship" not extended to other groups like Soviet Koreans or *Joseonjok* (ethnic Koreans with PRC nationality).[14] Indeed, in 2014, the Ministry of Unification explicitly ruled out applying the multiculturalism (*damunhwa juui*) framework that has been used for other cases of immigrant incorporation, citing North Korean resettlers' special ethnic and constitutional status.[15] North Koreans are therefore not "outside the state, but inside the people" (Shain and Barth 2003, 469). At least in theory, they seem to reside within *both* state and people.

The communitarian conception of rights is especially important to North Koreans, who at the time of their entry into South Korea often have relatively low

---

[13]   This literature treats citizenship in varying ways, from formal rights to informal communal inclusion to affective commitment.

[14]   For various perspectives on this idea, see E. Kim 2010; Lee and Chien 2017; Hur 2018; Denney et al. 2019. For survey data, see Kim et al. 2008; Chung et al. 2011; Kim et al. 2011; Seol and Skrentny 2009.

[15]   The Ministry of Unification argued that although [North Koreans] have lived in a different culture, "it is difficult to regard them as multicultural families" and they "need to be essentially distinguished." Ministry of Unification [MOU] 2014: 6; MOU 2013, 2015, 2018.

familiarity with liberal conceptions of rights and citizenship, and stronger under-standing of and identification with ethnic nationalist conceptions of belonging and political membership (Nasr 2014). In fact, the word that South Korea uses for "democratic citizen," *minju simin*, is not used in North Korea. Both North and South use *minjok* to refer to Koreans as an ethnic people, while DPRK residents use *inmin* (Chinese cognate *renmin*) for public/collective reference, and comrade/friend (*dongmu*, or Sino-Korean *dongji*) interpersonally. The ROK constitution refers to *gungmin* (nationals) and *ingan* (human beings); other rhetoric uses *gong-min* (public/collective "the people"), while Hanawon uses *simin* (originally "city-dweller", as "citizen" is in English).[16] North Koreans tend to emphasize communal membership based on Koreanness – ethnicity, language, and family – in part because the communitarian identification socialized in North Korea remains important to North Koreans after resettlement in the South (Hur 2020).

Both contractual and communitarian theories of citizenship, then, uphold the idea that North Koreans are "automatic" citizens of the Republic of Korea. The phrase "automatic citizenship" may imply relatively little contestation over granting North Koreans either the legal standing or the rights-in-practice that come with national membership. The section that follows, however, challenges that perception by probing the experiences of rights claiming and recognition that occur at the crossing of the border into ROK territory.

14.4 SUSPENDED CITIZENS: NORTH KOREANS AT THE ROK BORDER

Upon arrival on South Korean soil, North Koreans are met by security teams composed of agents from the NIS, military, and police, and are detained for screening at an interrogation and protection center (Yonhap 2014a, 2014b). Information found in the extraterritorial investigation conducted before an individual's arrival in the ROK can lengthen or expedite screening, and the length of the screening process has also varied legally over the past two decades. It is currently a maximum of ninety days, but migrant narratives describe a wide range of experiences: one recounts an intense week plus another six months; another says "about a month"; a third, who entered as a minor, describes just twenty-four hours (Kang 2001, 220–22; D. H. Shin 2012, 159; J. Kim 2015, 295–99).

Time in a group dormitory is typically followed by an individual investigation in solitary confinement. During their investigation, individuals claiming resettlement are asked to draw a map of their hometown in the North and asked detailed questions about their background and journey (often repeatedly, to identify incon-sistencies and to ensure that they are not Korean-Chinese falsely claiming to be

---

[16] Interview with Hanawon instructor, Seoul, July 2014; Cho and Kim 2011. For an examination of the valences of these terms through their Chinese cognates, including a reflection on the term's statist origins, see Guo 2014.

North Koreans). Most describe interrogations as intense, though some taper toward cordiality as investigators gain confidence in interviewees' truthfulness.

Although this stage of resettlement has received relatively little scholarly attention, narrative evidence demonstrates that government recognition of ROK citizenship remains incomplete throughout the screening period. The state typically explains its procedures by reference to the security threat that North Korea poses, particularly in terms of terrorism, espionage, and infiltration of the ROK's territory. Screening is conducted by the NIS, the descendant organization of the Korea Central Intelligence Agency, which managed domestic and foreign intelligence (including counterintelligence and counter-infiltration) throughout the ROK's military-authoritarian period (1961–87) (Greitens 2016). The screening's stated purpose is to identify two groups: spies or infiltrators sent by the DPRK, and ethnically Korean PRC citizens who are not entitled to ROK citizenship (*Joseonjok*; *Chaoxianzu* in Mandarin) (H. Kim 1993).

The government has changed the screening process a number of times, and some of these changes have incrementally expanded the rights available to individuals undergoing the screening process. When the Joint Interrogation Center was opened in 2008, rights provided to full ROK citizens were circumscribed or withheld for North Koreans during interrogation, including freedom of movement, the right to have counsel, and the right to remain silent. Privacy rights were also minimal, with cameras often placed inside rooms to monitor detained individuals and searches relatively unrestricted. Thus, at minimum the ROK's procedures have involved, and still involve today, an absence of rights that are typically accorded to citizens.

Many attempts at improvements in screening procedures and policies have been focused on remedying claims of mistreatment or violations of specific rights that have come to public and policymakers' attention. Following claims of mistreatment and scrutiny from advocacy groups, the center ended the use of closed-door interrogations and announced plans to hire female attorneys – a notable measure given that the defector population has been 70 percent or more female for years (Yonhap 2014a, 2014b). In 2014, the Joint Interrogation Center was renamed the Defector Protection Center and announced other initiatives – such as the naming of a female attorney as a human rights officer (*ingwon bohogwan*) and human rights training for NIS employees (Yonhap 2014b) – with the intent of communicating more benign and rights-conscious objectives on the part of the state.[17] Finally, the length of the screening has been adjusted several times: pre-2010, screening lengths were unspecified; from 2010 to 2018, screenings were supposed to be no longer than 180 days; in 2018, the time allotted was reduced to ninety days, so that screened individuals do not remain in limbo for long periods of time (Yonhap 2014a and 2014b; MOU 2018).

---

[17]   In 2019, two ROK military intelligence personnel were accused of raping a North Korean defector, after the woman had left Hanawon (H. E. Kim 2019).

The screening produces an assessment of each individual's background, and depending on that assessment, the South Korean state can withhold or grant citizenship and its attendant rights of entry and protection. As many North Koreans do not bring documentation proving their identity on the journey to South Korea, especially if they transit through countries known to repatriate defectors, they must prove upon arrival in the ROK that they originated from North Korea, rather than being *Joseonjok*. Theorists note that the need to prove one's identity – in this case, one's identity as a person of DPRK origin rather than an ethnically Korean PRC citizen – raises thorny questions about democratic citizenship. Needing to prove that one is who one claims to be strips citizens of natural rights prior to the state's confirmation of that proof, which "inverts government by consent of the people into a regime of citizens' praying for privileges to be granted by permission of the government" (Sobel 2016, 8). Interestingly, scholars particularly highlight the risk that uncoupling territory from jurisdiction, as has occurred on Korea's divided peninsula where the state claims much more territory than it actually administers, will lead to the disaggregation of rights and the withdrawal of protections to which citizens should be entitled (Benhabib 2005; Glover 2011). This is, indeed, the outcome faced by North Koreans, whose citizenship and rights of entry and protection are held in abeyance until the territorial/jurisdictional discrepancy is resolved and citizen identity is established.

Several narratives written by defectors who have resettled in the ROK articulate their discomfort with this requirement from South Korea. One recalls asking, "[i]f I don't have my identification papers, will I be denied asylum? I'm speaking Korean right now. Is that not proof enough that I'm one of you? If we don't have our papers, do we all have to die like [my friend]?" (Jang 2014, 305). The passage articulates unfairness and outrage that the narrator's protection and safety depend on someone else's determination of his citizen status. In this sense, while they are undergoing screening, North Koreans suffer from what scholars have termed "undocumented citizenship" or "evidentiary statelessness," which Wendy Hunter defines as "nationals who lack the official papers necessary to be recognized as full citizens in their countries" (Hunter 2019; see also Lawrence and Stevens 2017).

As Hunter and others note, proof of nationality is the "beginning of an individual's relationship to the state … [and] the precondition for broader citizenship rights" (Hunter 2019, 3). Undocumented citizenship – the lack of papers to prove citizenship, as opposed to true legal statelessness – often results more from bureaucratic and administrative hurdles than from the state's legal determination, and according to the World Bank may apply to as many as 1.1 billion people worldwide (World Bank 2017). Much as Arrington (Chapter 7) emphasizes the effects of procedural rules on claimants' perceptions of the claims-making process, Bronwen Manby argues:

The systems for proof of nationality are in practice often as important as the provisions of the law on the qualifications in principle. If there are onerous requirements or costs attached to proof of nationality, or discrimination in practice means that proof is not obtainable, then the fact that a person actually fulfills the conditions laid down in law may count for little. (Manby 2015, 32)

The screening process for North Koreans to effectively claim their ROK citizenship is one such example of this phenomenon. Although in the case of North Koreans entering the ROK this condition is intended to be temporary, it nevertheless places a clear burden on the individual to prove identity and leaves them in a condition of undocumented citizenship until such identity can be established. The ROK's reduction of time-in-interrogation suggests that they recognize a problem in the process, but does not fully resolve the onus placed on the individual to prove their identity to the state's satisfaction in order to exit the condition of evidentiary statelessness.

The screening process generates several other departures from standard rights accorded to citizens, even citizens detained for investigation because they are suspected of having committed a crime. Two particularly notable ones involve the right to remain silent and the length of detention. South Korea's criminal procedure law places limits on the length of time allowed for investigation and prosecutorial review before a decision on indictment must be made; typically, that period cannot be longer than thirty days.[18] By contrast, the screening of North Koreans is prescribed to be a maximum of ninety days, even if the individuals in screening are not accused of any crime (MOU 2018). Perhaps more importantly, North Koreans seeking entry and resettlement in South Korea do not – effectively – have the right to remain silent if they wish to pass through the screening. There is no way to prove their North Korean identity and demonstrate that they intend to resettle in South Korea rather than commit espionage without answering investigators' questions.

From the perspective of North Koreans seeking entry and resettlement, the stakes of this stage of the process are high. An individual suspected of being a spy rather than a legitimate resettler could face trial and imprisonment. Potentially even more dangerous, a Korean-Chinese individual who the authorities decide has misrepresented him/herself as North Korean can be deported to China. North Korean migrants are aware that this places them in a twofold jeopardy: if they are sent back to China, PRC authorities may conduct their own investigation, and if they determine that an individual did in fact come originally from North Korea, the PRC authorities could repatriate that individual again, to the DPRK itself.[19]

Moreover, in November 2019, the South Korean government itself chose to repatriate two North Korean fishermen directly back to the DPRK. The men were suspected of killing sixteen of their fellow crew members on a fishing boat, initially returning to port in North Korea, and then fleeing into South Korean waters. The Ministry of Unification said that it could not trust their "intention of defection," and,

---

[18]   *Hyeongsasosongbeop* (Criminal Procedure Act), Act No. 15257 (2019).
[19]   Author's interview, Seoul, May 2014.

calling them "serious criminals," decided not to grant them citizenship and resettlement, and instead repatriate them to North Korea via Panmunjom (BBC, 2019). This case added evidence against the argument that North Koreans who arrive in the South are automatically granted citizenship, entry, and residency.

Prior to November 2019, whether the ROK would actually deny citizenship to a North Korean claimant was unclear. The North Korean Refugees Protection and Settlement Support Act, updated most recently in early 2019, specifies conditions under which North Korean claims to protection/support may be withheld, denied, or revoked by the Republic of Korea.[20] Articles 9 and 27, for example, list offenses including drug trafficking (common along the DPRK-PRC border), murder, terrorism, intentional provision of "false information contrary to the interests of the State," and attempts to return to the DPRK. Article 9 also contains a provision, rarely applied, in which extended third-country residence can render one ineligible; the provision has been infrequently applied, and when it has been, it typically means that an individual would be granted citizenship but not resettlement benefits (Wolman 2014).[21]

In the past, however, the ROK government had provided inconsistent information with respect to its legal position on whether individuals found to be problematic in screening could be denied citizenship status and entry rights altogether. Most of the information we have on this question comes from cases where North Koreans sought asylum in third countries; representatives of the South Korean government submitted information to the foreign courts, and that information was sometimes cited in the foreign court's rulings on asylum. But the answers provided by the ROK have not been entirely clear or consistent. In 2010–11, for example, the ROK stated to Canadian and UK courts that the ROK government could deny nationality on Article 9 grounds.[22] Around the same time, however, it told an Australian court that citizenship was both "automatically and immediately granted" for "genuine North Koreans," but simultaneously that citizenship procedures were "more difficult" in Article 9 cases.[23] In 2015, a UK court found that DPRK spies are prosecuted by the ROK, but not repatriated; the fact that failing the protection procedure did not condemn individuals to repatriation was an important consideration for the court ruling that individuals of North Korean origin were ineligible to claim asylum status in the United Kingdom. During this decade, the (non-Korean) courts that examined this question generally concluded that Article 9 provided grounds for

---

[20] *Bukhanitaljuminui boho mit jeongchakjiwone gwanhan beomnyul*, Act No. 16223 (2019).

[21] Government of the United Kingdom, *KK and Others* (Nationality: North Korea), Korea CG, UKUT 92 (2011), https://tribunalsdecisions.service.gov.uk/utiac/37601, p. 19.

[22] Government of Canada, *Kim v. Canada*, 2010 FC 720, June 30, 2010, para 15; Government of the United Kingdom 2011: para 15.

[23] See esp. para 79, Government of Australia, *RRT Case No. 1001549*, [2010] RRTA 843, 21 September 2010, available at: www.refworld.org/cases,AUS_RRT,4cbf29cc2.html [accessed May 23, 2020].

withholding the resettlement benefits that came with effective activation of one's citizenship, rather than denying or nullifying the claim to citizenship altogether.[24]

Even if an applicant proved North Korean identity, and entry/resettlement was granted, the state did reserve the right to withhold provision of specific protections and support benefits (Choe 2017). This was a fairly common outcome: as of 2019, there were approximately 280 "nonprotected" North Koreans resettled in South Korea (around 1.5 percent), around three-quarters of whom had been denied because they applied after staying in South Korea for more than the year prescribed by law. To address this issue, in 2019, the deadline for application was extended to three years (J. S. Lee 2019). Until early 2017, children born in third countries to a North Korean parent, though usually admitted to the ROK, were also ineligible for financial support; in 2016, this included 1,317 of 2,517 DPRK-heritage refugee youth (52 percent) (UniKorea Blog, 2017). Thus, the courts had evidentiary grounds upon which to conclude that individuals who failed the screening were denied support benefits but not citizen status itself or the right to entry that it invoked.

The 2019 repatriation case makes this distinction much more questionable. Use of the murder provision in Article 9, plus the state's judgment about the "intentions of defection" – over the apparent statements of the claimants themselves – provided justification for the ROK to deny not just resettlement and protection benefits, but also the right to entry altogether. The decision prompted strong criticism from a range of rights groups in South Korea, which claimed that the repatriation violated the UN Convention Against Torture's provision prohibiting refoulement, as well as South Korea's own statutes that guarantee citizens the right to due process and the provision of legal counsel.[25]

The narratives of resettled North Koreans also consistently and clearly interpret the screening as a process in which the state has discretion to grant or withhold citizenship, with the risk that an individual could be refused entry to South Korea. One said, "I was not yet a South Korean citizen; to become one, I had to go through the screening process" (S. Y. Kim 2000, 99). Several describe hearing that their right of entry is conditional on "passing," and that they can be deported if they fail (Park 2015, 209). Guards at the screening center warned one group that "physical fighting was a criminal offense and would hinder progress toward South Korean citizenship" (H. Lee 2015, 199–203). One North Korean migrant describes "the last test, a test to decide my future," adding, "if I passed, I would be eligible for South Korean citizenship" (E. Kim 2015, 173–175).[26] Narratives describe this stage with varied

---

[24] Government of the United Kingdom, *GP and Others* (South Korean citizenship), Korea CG, UKUT 391 (2014), https://tribunalsdecisions.service.gov.uk/utiac/2014-ukut-391, pp. 2, 21–23, 28, 66.

[25] "Joint Statement on Deportation of Two North Korean Fishermen by 20 Human Rights and Civil Society Organizations for North Korean Human Rights," February 13, 2020, https://en.tjwg.org /2020/02/13/joint-statement-on-deportation-of-two-north-korean-fishermen-by-20-human-rights-and -civil-society-organizations-for-north-korean-human-rights/ [Accessed May 20, 2020].

[26] She also recounts her belief that if she and her mother had been Korean Workers' Party members, "the interrogators would have been suspicious that we were spies sent by the north."

emotions: excitement, relief, exhaustion, terror, anxiety, nervousness, confidence (Kang 2001, 222; Y. Kim 2009, 157; J. Kim 2015, 269–99). Interview evidence reveals similar understandings: citizenship is not "automatic" or taken-for-granted, and resettlement in South Korea is likely, not guaranteed.[27] Many North Korean migrants perceive the state's overall security rationale as legitimate, but object to specific procedures; a few women have described the process as dehumanizing.[28] The overwhelming majority, however, perceive it as a test that they can either pass or fail.

Throughout screening, therefore, North Koreans possess formal juridical citizenship, but the state's legal framework and administrative requirements for the entry process render citizenship recognition, in practice, incomplete. At the moment of border-crossing, North Koreans' success in claiming citizen status is fundamentally contingent on resolving the state's concerns, and the state bears limited obligations to confer full citizen rights until these purported citizens have satisfactorily addressed its questions. This leads North Koreans to view their citizenship – understandably – as contingent and insecure, rather than guaranteed and coequal, and to perceive their citizenship status as potentially inferior from the moment they enter ROK society.[29]

14.5 CONCLUSION

How do individuals with claims to citizenship and citizen rights experience the process of claiming those rights in a world increasingly characterized by cross-border movement and globalization? This chapter seeks to shed light on this question by examining the experiences of North Koreans who seek to claim their South Korean citizenship and settle in South Korea. Although these individuals have strong legal and communitarian claims to citizen standing, their purported "automatic citizenship" does not mean that it is easy to effectively claim those rights upon arrival in South Korea. Drawing on a mix of South Korean legal and policy documents and narratives from North Koreans who have come to South Korea, this chapter demonstrates that the rights claims of North Koreans are heavily circumscribed and conditional when they arrive at the border or point of entry into the ROK. The state requires that North Koreans, through the government-administered screening process, both prove their identities and establish a lack of (certain) criminal history

---

[27] Interviews with two North Korean-born individuals, Seoul, May 2016.

[28] On security justification, see E. Kim 2015,166. On dehumanizing procedures, see the comment from Jin-hee Park, quoted in Bell 2013, 241; Park 2015, 208–11; G. Choi 2007, 207–08.

[29] While a full examination of North Korean resettlers' perceptions of citizenship and their rights-claiming activities after they leave screening and enter the ROK is beyond the scope of the chapter, evidence cumulatively suggests that North Korean resettlers continue to perceive their citizenship as contingent on both internal hierarchies and the state's geopolitical interests after reentry. On this point, see Greitens 2021.

in order to effectively claim citizen status – the starting point that they need to claim other rights that citizens normally negotiate and practice.

The chapter, therefore, sheds light on a number of the larger questions engaged in this volume and raises questions that should be considered in future research. First, it provides a window into the ways in which marginalized citizens frame, claim, and negotiate rights, at a moment when the state possesses a high capacity to deny the recognition that would effectively confer those rights. Foreign workers, who depend on the state's recognition of their visa status, are in similarly disadvantaged positions vis-à-vis the state in claims-making (see Chapter 13). Second, the chapter elucidates the gap between formal legal recognition of rights and state practices required to instantiate those rights in the lives of citizens. In doing so, it sheds light on the latent ideals of citizenship as the concept is framed and implemented by the ROK state. It highlights that both criminal and politically threatening behavior can lead the state to not recognize an individual as a full citizen. Finally, the chapter provides new avenues of potential inquiry into the constitution of citizenship and rights claiming among North Korean defectors after resettlement. Given the finding that citizenship acquisition shapes political identification and engagement in other contexts (Bloemraad 2018), future studies should consider whether the rights claiming and recognition interactions that occur during North Koreans' migration and resettlement screening shape their subsequent sense of what it means, as an ROK citizen, to claim the rights that they are legally afforded.

More broadly, for comparative research on citizenship and migration, the chapter sheds light on how citizens navigate rights claiming in the context of "deep" and securitized borders. In Korea, state construction of borders and of border-crossing procedure renders the claiming of citizen status an extended, incremental, and often arduous task even for those who are legally and theoretically privileged with that status – an important observation at a moment when questions of global migration, citizenship, and border security figure prominently in media coverage and policy discussions across the world.

REFERENCES

BBC. 2019. "North Korean Fishermen 'Killed 16 Colleagues' before Fleeing to South." November 7, 2019. www.bbc.com/news/world-asia-50329588.

Bell, Markus. 2013. "Manufacturing Kinship in a Nation Divided." *Asia-Pacific Journal of Anthropology* 14(3): 240–55.

Benhabib, Seyla. 2001. "Transformation of Citizenship: Dilemmas of the Nation-State in the Era of Globalization." Spinoza Lecture.

2005. "Borders, Boundaries, and Citizenship." *Political Science & Politics* 38(4): 673–77.

Bloemraad, Irene. 2004. "Who Claims Dual Citizenship? The Limits of Post-Nationalism, the Possibilities of Transnationalism, and the Persistence of Traditional Citizenship." *International Migration Review* 38: 389–442.

2018. "Theorising the Power of Citizenship as Claims-Making." *Journal of Ethnic and Migration Studies* 44(1): 4–26.

Bosniak, Linda. 2006. *The Citizen and the Alien: Dilemmas of Contemporary Membership.* Princeton: Princeton University Press.

Brubaker, Rogers. 1992. *Citizenship and Nationhood in France and Germany.* Cambridge: Harvard University Press.

1998. "Migrations of Ethnic Unmixing in the 'New Europe'." *International Migration Review* 32(4): 1047–65.

2004. "Reflections on Nationalism and Patriotism." *Citizenship Studies* 8(2): 115–27.

Campbell, Emma. 2016. *South Korea's New Nationalism: the End of "One Korea"?* Boulder: First Forum Press.

Cho, Dong Wun, and Yong Tae Kim. 2011. "Study on Settlement Services for North Korean Defectors." *Journal of Korean Public Police and Security Studies* 8(2): 25–50.

Choe, Sang-hun. 2017. "A North Korean Defector Is Spurned, for Decades, by South Korea." *New York Times*, December 9, 2017. www.nytimes.com/2017/12/09/world/asia/north-korean-defector-south-korea-kim-seok-cheol.html.

Choi, Eun-young. 2014. "North Korean Women's Narratives of Migration." *Annals of Association of American Geographers* 104(2): 271–79.

Choi, Geum Hee. 2007. *Geumhuiui yeohaeng* [Journey of Geum Hee]. Seoul: Mindeulle.

Choo, Hae Yeon. 2006. "Gendered Modernity and Ethnicized Citizenship: North Korean Settlers in Contemporary South Korea." *Gender & Society* 20(5): 576–604.

2016. *Decentering Citizenship: Gender, Labor, and Migrant Rights in South Korea.* Stanford: Stanford University Press.

Chung, Byung-ho. 2008. "Between Defector and Migrant: Identities and Strategies of North Koreans in South Korea." *Korean Studies* 32: 1–27.

Chung, Ki-seon, Seon Mi Lee, Seokho Kim, Sang-lim Lee, and Seong Il Park. 2011. *Hanguginui gungmin jeongcheseonggwa imin gwallyeon taedo yeongu* [Korean national identity and migration-related attitudes]. Goyang: IOM Migration Research/Training Center.

Colton, Timothy. 2000. *Transitional Citizens: Voters and What Influences Them in the New Russia.* Cambridge: Harvard University Press.

Conover, Pamela Johnston, Ivor Crewe, and Donald Searing. 1991. "The Nature of Citizenship in the United States and Great Britain." *Journal of Politics* 53(3): 800–32.

d'Entreves, Maurizio. 2006. "Hannah Arendt." *Stanford Encyclopedia of Philosophy.*

Denney, Steven, Christopher Green, and Peter Ward. 2019. "New Values, Old Orders: Where Do North Koreans Fit in the New South Korea?" *Sino-NK*, May 14, 2019. https://sinonk.com/2019/05/14/new-values-and-old-orders-where-do-north-koreans-fit-in-the-new-south-korea/.

Distelhorst, Greg, and Diana Fu. 2019. "Performing Authoritarian Citizenship: Public Transcripts from China." *Perspectives on Politics* 17(1): 106–21.

Ekiert, Grzegorz, and Jan Kubik. 1999. *Rebellious Civil Society: Popular Protest and Democratic Consolidation in Poland.* Ann Arbor: University of Michigan Press.

Flynn, Moya. 2007. "Reconstructing 'Home/lands' in the Russian Federation: Migrant-Centered Perspectives of Displacement and Resettlement." *Journal of Ethnic and Migration Studies* 33(3): 461–81.

Gamlen, Alan, Michael Cummings, and Paul Vaaler. 2017. "Explaining the Rise of Diaspora Institutions." *Journal of Ethnic and Migration Studies* 45(4): 492–516.

Glenn, Evelyn Nakano. 2004. *Unequal Freedom: How Race and Gender Shaped American Citizenship and Labor.* Cambridge: Harvard University Press.

Glover, Robert. 2011. "Radically Rethinking Citizenship: Disaggregation, Agonistic Pluralism, and the Politics of Immigration in the US." *Political Studies* 59(2): 209–29.

Greitens, Sheena Chestnut. 2016. *Dictators and Their Secret Police*. Cambridge: Cambridge University Press.

2021. "The Geopolitics of Citizenship: Evidence from North Korean Claims to Membership in the South." *Journal of Korean Studies* 26(1).

Grzelczyk, Virginie. 2014. "New Approaches to North Korean Politics after Reunification." *Communist and Post-Communist Studies* 47: 170–90.

Guo, Zhonghua. 2014. "The Emergence of the Citizen Concept in Modern China: 1899–1919." *Journal of Chinese Political Science* 19: 349–64.

Herbst, Jeffrey. 1989. "The Creation and Maintenance of Borders in Africa." *International Organization* 43(4): 673–92.

Hong, Liu, and Els van Dongen. 2016. "China's Diaspora Policies as Transnational Governance." *Journal of Contemporary China* 25: 805–21.

Hundt, David, Jessica Walton, and Soo Jung Elisha Lee. 2018. "Politics of Conditional Citizenship in South Korea." *Journal of Contemporary Asia* 49(3): 434–51.

Hunter, Wendy. 2019. *Undocumented Nationals: Between Statelessness and Citizenship*. Cambridge: Cambridge Elements.

Hur, Aram. 2018. "Adapting to Democracy: Identity and the Political Development of North Korean Defectors." *Journal of East Asian Studies* 18(1): 97–115.

2020. "Refugee Perceptions toward Democratic Citizenship: A Narrative Analysis of North Koreans." *Comparative Politics* 52(3): 473–93.

Isaac, Jeffrey. 2011. "Boundaries." *Perspectives on Politics* 9(4): 779–82.

Isin, Engin. 2009. "Citizenship in Flux: The Figure of the Activist Citizen." *Subjectivity* 29: 367–88.

Jang, Jin-sung. 2014. *Dear Leader: My Escape from North Korea*. New York: Atria Books.

Joppke, Christian. 2005. *Selecting by Origin: Ethnic Migration in the Liberal State*. Cambridge: Harvard University Press.

Kang, Chol Hwan. 2001. *Aquariums of Pyongyang: Ten Years in the North Korean Gulag*. New York: Basic Books.

Kim, Byeong-jo, Boksu Kim, Hocheol Seo, Manseok Oh, Kisu Eun, Miryang Chung, Jegi Chung, and Donggi Cho. 2011. *Hangugui damunhwa sanghwanggwa sahoe tonghap* [Multicultural situation and social integration in Korea]. Seongnam: Academy of Korean Studies.

Kim, Eleana J. 2010. *Adopted Territory: Transnational Korean Adoptees and the Politics of Belonging*. Durham: Duke University Press.

Kim, Eun-sun. 2015. *A Thousand Miles to Freedom: My Escape from North Korea*. New York: St. Martin's Press.

Kim, Hyun Hee. 1993. *The Tears of My Seoul*. New York: William Morrow & Company.

Kim, Hyung Eun. 2019. "South Korean Intelligence Officers Accused of Raping Defector from North." *BBC*, December 5, 2019. www.bbc.com/news/world-50668279.

Kim, Jaeeun. 2016. *Contested Embrace: Transnational Border Politics in Twentieth Century Korea*. Stanford: Stanford University Press.

Kim, Jeong-hee. 2016. *Understanding Narrative Inquiry: Crafting and Analysis of Stories as Research*. Thousand Oaks: Sage.

Kim, Joseph. 2015. *Under the Same Sky: From Starvation in North Korea to Salvation in America*. Boston: Houghton Mifflin Harcourt.

Kim, Nora Hui-Jung. 2013. "Flexible Yet Inflexible: Development of Dual Citizenship in Korea." *Journal of Korean Studies* 18(1): 7–28.

2016. "Naturalizing Korean Ethnicity and Making 'Ethnic' Difference: Comparison of North Korean Settlement and Foreign Bride Incorporation Policies in South Korea." *Asian Ethnicity* 17(2): 185–98.

Kim, Sang-uk [Sang-wook], Dongwoo Ko, Jangyeong Lee, Jonghoe Yang, Jaeon Kim, Woosik Kim, Hoyeong Lee, Jiyeong Ko, Byeongjin Park, Byeongeun Chung, Kyungmi Lee, Jeongjin Lee, Eunyeong Nam, Yujeong Choi, and Seokho Kim. 2008. *Hanguk jonghap sahoe josa 2007* [Korean General Social Survey 2007]. Seoul: Sungkyunkwan University.

Kim, So Yeon. 2000. *Jugeul muni hanamyeon sal muneun aheop* [A Door to Die, Nine Doors to Live]. Seoul: Jeongsinsegyesa.

Kim, Suk-young. 2014. *DMZ Crossing: Performing Emotional Citizenship Along the Korean Border*. New York: Columbia University Press.

Kim, Yong. 2009. *Long Road Home: Testimony of a North Korean Camp Survivor*. New York: Columbia University Press.

Korteweg, Anna. 2006. "Construction of Gendered Citizenship at the Welfare Office." *Social Politics: International Studies in Gender, State, and Society* 13(3): 314–40.

Lawrence, B. N., and J. Stevens, eds. 2017. *Citizenship in Question: Evidentiary Birthright and Statelessness*. Durham and London: Duke University Press.

Leary, Virginia. 2000. "Citizenship, Human Rights, and Diversity," in Alan Cairs et al., eds. *Citizenship, Diversity and Pluralism: Canadian and Comparative Perspectives*. Montreal: McGill-Queens. 247–64.

Lee, Chul-woo. 2012. "How Can You Say You're Korean? Law, Governmentality and National Membership in South Korea." *Citizenship Studies* 16(1): 85–102.

Lee, Hyeon-seo. 2015. *The Girl with Seven Names: A North Korean Defector's Story*. London: William Collins.

Lee, Jin-seo. 2019. "Biboho talbukja, 3nyeonnae jajinsingo haeya" [Unprotected North Koreans must voluntarily report within 3 years]. *Radio Free Asia*, August 26, 2019. www .rfa.org/korean/weekly_program/ad81ae08c99d-d480c5b4c90db2c8b2e4/ne-js -08232019155504.html.

Lee, Sohoon, and Yi-Chun Chien. 2017. "The Making of 'Skilled' Overseas Koreans: Transformation of Visa Policies for Co-ethnic Migrants in South Korea." *Journal of Ethnic and Migration Studies* 43(10): 2193–210.

Longo, Matthew. 2018. *The Politics of Borders: Sovereignty, Security, and the Citizen After 9–11*. Cambridge: Cambridge University Press.

Manby, Bronwen. 2015. "Nationality, Migration, and Statelessness in West Africa." *A Study for UNHCR and IOM*. www.unhcr.org/ecowas2015/Nationality-Migration-and-Statelessness-in-West-Africa-REPORT-EN.pdf.

Mann, Michael. 1987. "Ruling Class Strategies and Citizenship." *Sociology* 21(3): 339–54.

Marshall, T. H. 1964. *Class, Citizenship, and Social Development*. New York: Doubleday.

McCormack, Coralie. 2004. "Storying Stories: A Narrative Approach to in-depth Interview Conversations." *International Journal of Social Research Methodology* 7 (3): 219–36.

Michalopoulos, Stelios, and Elias Papaioannou. 2016. "The Long-Run Effects of the Scramble for Africa." *American Economic Review* 106(7): 1802–48.

Miles, Matthew, and Michael Huberman. 1994. *Qualitative Data Analysis*. Thousand Oaks: Sage.

Ministry of Unification. 2013. 2015. *Bukhan italjumin jeongchak jiweon silmu pyeollam* [Settlement Support Handbook for North Korean Refugees].

2014. Manual for Resettlement Support of North Korean Refugees.

Ministry of Unification statement, February 13, 2018. https://unikorea.go.kr/unikorea/news/release/?boardId=bbs_0000000000000004&mode=view&cntId=54384&category=&pageIdx.

Miyoshi-Jager, Sheila. 2003. *Narratives of Nation-Building in Korea*. New York: M.E. Sharpe.

Moon, Seung-sook. 2005. *Militarized Modernity and Gendered Citizenship in South Korea*. Durham: Duke University Press.

Nasr, Mary. 2014. *(Ethnic) Nationalism in North Korean Political Ideology and Culture*. Ph.D. dissertation, University of Sydney.

Nyers, Peter. 2007. "Why Citizenship Studies." *Citizenship Studies* 11(1): 1–11.

Park, Jung-Sun, and Paul Chang. 2005. "Contention in the Construction of a Global Korean Community: The Overseas Korean Act." *Journal of Korean Studies* 10(1): 1–27.

Park, Yeonmi. 2015. *In Order to Live*. New York: Penguin.

Patterson, Molly, and Kristen Renwick Monroe. 1998. "Narrative in Political Science." *Annual Review of Political Science* 1: 315–51.

Perry, Elizabeth J. 2008. "Chinese Conceptions of Rights: From Mencius to Mao–and Now." *Perspectives on Politics* 6(1): 37–50.

Pinto, Pedro Ramos. 2012. "'Everyday Citizenship' under Authoritarianism: Spain and Portugal," in Francesco Cavatorta, ed. *Civil Society Activism under Authoritarian Rule: A Comparative Perspective*. London: Routledge. 13–33.

Polkinghorne, Donald. 1995. "Narrative Configuration in Qualitative Research." *International Journal of Qualitative Studies* 8(1): 5–23.

Pop-Eleches, Grigore, and Joshua Tucker. 2017. *Communism's Shadow: Historical Legacies and Contemporary Political Attitude*. Princeton: Princeton University Press.

Sassen, Saskia. 2003. "Citizenship Destabilized." *Liberal Education* 89(2): 14–21.

Seol, Dong-Hoon, and John D. Skrentny. 2009. "Ethnic Return Migration and Hierarchical Nationhood: Korean Chinese Foreign Workers in South Korea." *Ethnicities* 9(2): 147–74.

Seol, Dong-hoon, and John Skrentny. 2009. "Why Is There So Little Migrant Settlement in East Asia?" *International Migration Review* 43(3): 578–620.

Shain, Yossi, and Aharon Barth. 2003. "Diasporas and International Relations Theory." *International Organization* 57(3): 449–79.

Shin, Dong Hyuk. 2012. *Escape from Camp 14*. New York: Viking: Penguin.

Shin, Gi-Wook. 2006. *Ethnic Nationalism in Korea: Genealogy, Politics, and Legacy*. Stanford: Stanford University Press.

Sobel, Andrew. 2016. *Citizenship as Foundation of Rights*. Cambridge: Cambridge University Press.

Sohn, Ae-Lee, and Nae-Young Lee. 2012. "A Study on the Attitude of South Koreans toward North Korean Defectors: National Identity and Multi-Cultural Acceptability." *Journal of Asia-Pacific Studies* 19(3): 5–34.

Song, Jiyoung. 2013. "'Smuggled Refugees': Social Construction of North Korean Migration," *International Migration* 51(4): 158–73.

Soysal, Yasemin. 1994. *Limits of Citizenship: Migrants and Post-National Membership in Europe*. Chicago: University of Chicago.

Tilly, Charles. 2006. *Regimes and Repertoires*. Chicago: University of Chicago Press.

Turner, Bryan. 1990. "Outline of a Theory of Citizenship." *Sociology*, 24(2): 189–217.

UniKorea Blog. 2017. "Ddo dareun tongileui sijak, jesamguk chulsaeng cheongsonyeon" [Start of another unification, youth born in third countries]. *UniKorea Blog*, March 13, 2017. https://unikoreablog.tistory.com/6913.

Wolman, Andrew. 2014. "South Korean Citizenship of North Korean Escapees in Law and Practice." *KLRI Journal of Law and Legislation* 4(2): 225–53.

World Bank. 2017. "1.1 Billion 'Invisible' People without ID are Priority for New High-Level Advisory Council on Identification for Development." www.worldbank.org/en/news/ press-release/2017/10/12/11-billion-invisible-people-without-id-are-priority-for-new-high -level-advisory-council-on-identification-for-development (accessed May 23, 2020).

Yashar, Deborah. 2005. *Contesting Citizenship in Latin America.* Cambridge: Cambridge University Press.

   2013. "Institutions and Citizenship: Reflections on the Illicit." in Mario Szanajder, Luis Roniger, and Carlos Forment, eds. *Shifting Frontiers of Citizenship: The Latin American Experience.* Leiden: Brill. 431–458.

Yonhap. 2014a. "S. Korea Reforming N. Korean Defector Interrogation System." July 28, 2014. https://en.yna.co.kr/view/AEN20140728007800315.

   2014b. "Gukjeongwon, talbukja josasil gaebanghyeong bakkwo … ingwon bohogwan immyeong" [At the NIS, the North Korean defectors' investigation office will be replaced … Human Rights Protection Officer appointed]. July 28, 2014. www.yna.co.kr /view/AKR20140728134500043.

Conclusion

Findings and Future Directions

Celeste L. Arrington and Patricia Goedde

"Among countries that underwent colonial rule, dictatorship, and war, few countries maintain human rights standards on par with Korea. I believe this is the fruition of the sincere efforts of each human rights activist here."[1] So declared President Moon Jae-in in a speech on Human Rights Day in 2018. Indeed, rights have been defined, mobilized, and contested by diverse groups of people across a range of venues in Korea in the past century and a half. Women in the Joseon and colonial eras sought to defend their interests and remedy injustices by leveraging neo-Confucian principles about a ruler's duty to hear grievances or by exploiting gaps in the Japanese Civil Code. In the post-liberation era, lawmakers, scholars, and citizens debated limiting equal rights in different spheres of human interaction when those rights ideas clashed with traditional family values, anti-communist national security objectives, or capitalist economic development goals. After Korea transitioned to democracy in 1987, the channels for rights claiming expanded dramatically, offering new remedies. Still, rights claims in democratic Korea were colored by and built on previous decades of claims-making under less favorable circumstances. Previously marginalized groups have also seized on political and legal openings to use rights to frame new claims and advance novel policy objectives, sometimes even before the asserted rights were legally codified or protected by courts. Not all claimants managed to redress grievances or inequities and catalyze social and political change, but rights-based mobilization and discourses are increasingly pervasive. Examining the on-the-ground implementation of legal reforms and the actual functioning of institutional mechanisms through the lens of rights, this volume presented a complex picture of rights claiming in South Korea.

Rights claiming has had varying consequences in Korea, both for legislative and judicial outcomes and for societal perceptions. On the one hand, legal mobilization has diversified rights claims, spawned networks that help identify opportunities and resources for rights claiming, and in some cases spurred legislation or court rulings

---

[1] "Congratulatory Remarks by President Moon Jae-in on 2018 Human Rights Day." (December 10, 2018). https://english1.president.go.kr/Briefingspeeches/Speeches/101.

that create or clarify specific rights. On the other hand, responses to rights-based mobilization from state actors and societal groups have resulted in inconsistencies and hierarchies in terms of rights. Countermobilization citing religion, culture, tradition, nationalism, national security, or economics also continues to hamper some rights claiming, as seen with the recent examples of victims of sexual violence, migrants and refugees, and sexual minorities. Obtaining rights protections and sparking social change remains challenging. Claimants must often use numerous mobilization tactics to see results, combining litigation with protests, media campaigns, international reporting and advocacy, and public interest lawyering or NGO coalitions. Hence, we contend that an interactive and dynamic analytical approach like the one used by contributors to this volume best illuminates when and how multi-sited activism and enhanced access to claims-making channels can translate into more durable rights protections.

LESSONS

This conclusion elaborates three lessons that emerge from the preceding chapters. Our findings relate to the study of legal mobilization, the fluid and plural meanings of rights, and the politics and prioritization of different rights. These lessons stem from contributors' answers to a core set of questions: How do different groups interpret and leverage rights? Are there collisions of rights claims? Do some rights discourses implicitly or explicitly privilege some people over others? How do real or perceived changes and continuities in the institutional channels for rights claiming affect the likelihood and efficacy of rights claiming? What sources of support do claimants have in terms of domestic and international advocacy groups, legal assistance, and funding? How do people navigate deficiencies in the system, and what alternative channels exist for dissent or grievance articulation? Similar questions motivated comparable socio-legal studies regarding Japan, China, Hong Kong, Myanmar, and Vietnam over the last few decades (e.g., Upham 1987; Feldman 2000; Stern 2005; O'Brien and Li 2006; Sidel 2010; Tam 2010; Woo and Gallagher 2011; Chua 2018). This section synthesizes three core takeaways from our Korean cases, which contribute new insights to this burgeoning scholarship on rights mobilization and discourses in East Asia.

First, to fully understand rights and rights claiming, scholars cannot just examine formal institutions or law on the books. Instead, they *must also consider law in action*, scrutinizing the socially constructed and contested meanings of rights and perceptions of possible channels for claims-making. This volume's chapters built on the legal mobilization tradition in socio-legal scholarship and its commitment to integrating insights from studies of law and of social movements (for reviews, see McCann 2006; Barclay, Jones, and Marshall 2011; Lehoucq and Taylor 2020). Rather than assume that rights necessarily empower Koreans, the chapters draw on detailed case studies and ethnographies to show how "patterns in legal mobilization derive from a highly contingent and recursive process, involving the interplay between potential claimants, judges, and a variety of actors not typically associated with the formal legal system" (Taylor 2020, 1328). For example, Hwang (Chapter 5) demonstrates that both international norms about national human rights institutions and the Korean government's aim of becoming an advanced country (*seonjinguk*) affected the establishment and functioning of the National Human Rights Commission, which has become a key venue for rights claiming. As Greitens (Chapter 14) shows, North Korean migrants experience and assert rights even in the particularly controlled process of undergoing a security screening when first arriving in South Korea. Additionally, Mosler (Chapter 6) unpacks how inter-actions among shifting societal perceptions of adultery, claims' framing, and judicial interpretations led the Constitutional Court to eventually decide that criminalizing it was unconstitutional. Cooperation and learning across iterative claims-making helps potential claimants and their lawyers to recognize and sometimes even forge legal opportunities, as Arrington (Chapter 7) and Goedde (Chapter 8) reveal. Thus, the chapters elucidate "the *process* of mobilizing the law" (Arrington 2019, 333). In line with recent legal mobilization scholarship (e.g., Taylor 2020), they demonstrate the value of a constructivist or interactionist approach that is attentive to the social construction of grievances as rights and the ways in which claims-making can cultivate societal, political, and judicial receptivity to rights-based mobilization in a "positive feedback loop."

Many of the chapters also moved beyond law itself to shed interesting light on the relationships between rights claiming in legal institutions and other forms of advo-cacy in Korea. Such multi-sited research is needed to unpack how tactics interrelate. Indeed, the importance of legal versus other tactics varies even when rights language and lawyers are involved, as one recent review article noted (Marshall and Hale 2014, 663). Moreover, exposing the public to issues and framing them as rights are critical to the interactive processes our chapters examine. The case studies demonstrate how activists leverage synergies between legal tactics and other forms of activism, such as simultaneously filing a lawsuit and a complaint with the National Human Rights Commission of Korea or by coordinating protests and advocacy for legislative change. For example, JaeWon Kim (Chapter 10) argues that lobbying and sit-ins helped achieve legislation with justiciable rights and alter policymakers' and society's perceptions of people with disabilities. Kim and Hong (Chapter 12) use insights as both scholars and participants in the movement for general anti-discrimination legislation in Korea to show that multi-sited activism has awoken societal awareness of diversity despite repeatedly failing to achieve the said legisla-tion. In both cases, rights claiming has created legal opportunities for more claims-making and incrementally enhanced judicial receptivity, albeit more so in the case of disability rights. Indeed, Han (Chapter 11) exposes counter-narratives in Korea about how the time may not be ripe for certain rights, such as those of sexual minorities. In addition to their extensive fieldwork, the chapters offer future researchers a detailed record of sources in Korean and English, including Joseon era petitions, legislative debates about the ROK's new Civil Code in the 1950s, and the organizational resources coalescing in Korea's emergent public interest law groups. A strength of the volume is its authors' analysis of the *process* of rights claiming from distinct disciplinary perspectives, which encompass political science, law, history, sociology, and geography.

The second finding of this volume is that *rights are plural and fluid in meaning*. By scrutinizing law and rights in action, the chapters in this volume attest to the diversity of ways in which rights are conceptualized and claimed in South Korea. Rights are neither new to Korea nor imposed on Korea from the international community. Instead, Korea has a rich and complex history with regard to rights. As Jisoo Kim (Chapter 1) noted, the term *gwolli* (rights) first appeared in official Joseon documents at the end of the nineteenth century. However, the lawsuits that women filed during the Japanese colonial period rarely used this term or its first character (*gwon*) but instead used language of can/cannot (see Chapter 2). Eunkyung Kim (Chapter 3) traces how lawmakers' debates about protecting patriarchal family traditions and promoting capitalist development spawned a Civil Code that undermined women's full rights as citizens soon after the Republic of Korea was founded in 1948. In examining societal responses to the Jeju 4.3 events, Hun Joon Kim (Chapter 4) also contends that rights claims' framing changed over time as a result of victims' claiming and opponents' counterclaiming. The evidence in many chapters indicates that activists adapted to overcome state and other powerful actors' reluctance to recognize certain rights. Additionally, Hun Joon Kim (Chapter 4) differentiates general versus particularized rights claims. Labor rights also entail different content depending on workers' status, as Lee (Chapter 9) demonstrates. As an example of generalizing claims, Kim and Hong (Chapter 12) detail that sexual minorities in Korea have linked up with opponents of racial discrimination more broadly in their fight for comprehensive anti-discrimination legislation. Indeed, as the United States witnessed burgeoning Black Lives Matter protests in June 2020, Korea's anti-discrimination legislation movement held protests in Seoul in solidarity even amid the coronavirus pandemic (Y. Park 2020). Framing grievances as rights can facilitate such issue linkages and activate the support structures needed for effective rights claiming.

As the research in this volume indicates, rights concepts in Korea exhibit both universal features and distinctly Korean overtones. The plural and fluid meaning of rights can have productive synergies for activists. As Chung (Chapter 13) shows, migrants adopt the language of rights and human rights to tie their claims to past and ongoing struggles for democratic inclusion, which have moral authority and legibility in Korea (see also Chang 2015, 173). In the twenty-first century, policymakers have sought to use international human rights norms and practices to bolster Korea's global reputation as an advanced industrialized country, as Hwang details (Chapter

5). Activists have also leveraged international ideas and entities like the UN to pressure Korean policymakers and society to broaden shared understandings of rights in Korea, such as the rights of sexual minorities (see Chapter 12). There are thus feedback effects (see also Tsutsui 2017); Korean women with disabilities played leading roles in drafting articles on women in the 2006 UN Convention on the Rights of Persons with Disabilities and the domestic Disability Discrimination Act of 2007 (Arrington and Moon 2020, 18). Bridging specific claims to broader rights concepts from Korean history or with international resonance can bolster movements.

Third, this volume advances our understanding of the politics of rights (Scheingold 2004), particularly in *how contestation over rights can produce hierarchies or prioritization of rights claims and claimants*. Political contestation occurs not just over which rights to recognize, but also how to interpret and enforce those rights. There are hierarchies of rights in all societies, but this volume suggests that they are more pronounced in Korea. The very processes of claims-making and societal groups' interactions with the state influence these hierarchies. The volume's historical chapters show how rights attach to preexisting social hierarchies, such as Korea's patriarchal family structures and associated institutions like the household registry system. State entities also play an outsized role in defining what claims can be brought, which institutional channels are available, and which rights are most salient. Leading figures in government as well as in the media and civil society have the upper hand in determining whose rights matter most. Eunkyung Kim (Chapter 3) documents this dynamic regarding women's rights in the context of democratization, and Chung (Chapter 13) details how it plays out among migrants with different visa status and ethnic backgrounds. Statutes and legal institutional structures also create or reinforce hierarchies of rights by shaping perceptions about state institutions' receptivity or accessibility (see Chapter 7). For example, legal status contributes to rights hierarchies, as Lee (Chapter 9) argues regarding the rights claims of regular versus irregular workers after the 1990s. And Greitens (Chapter 14) shows that North Korean migrants' understandings of citizenship rights are shaped by their initial interactions with South Korean officials in the security screening process.

Perceptions of political power also shape rights hierarchies. Pessimism about whether formal institutions will defend their rights led workers, people with disabilities, and sexual minorities to resort to protracted and risky forms of contention. Such skepticism about formal institutional channels for rights claiming stems from widespread perceptions that the judiciary (but not the Constitutional Court) are conservative institutions, trusted by just 3 percent of respondents in one poll in 2014.[2] Activists are well aware of the greater resources that the state and corporations possess, as they increasingly also mobilize the law and rights language, as

---

[2]   August 2014 Realmeter polling.

Yoonkyung Lee (Chapter 9) notes. State actors may play significant roles in delineating rights claiming options and often have more resources but can also sometimes assist claimants, as has occurred with the National Human Rights Commission of Korea for people with disabilities, sexual minorities, North Korean migrants, and noncitizens. In socio-legal scholarship, the law and legal institutions have long been considered double-edged, for they entail both tools for achieving social change and the prevailing tendency to uphold the status quo (McCann 2006, 19). Our cases elucidate numerous deficiencies or gaps in rights protections and remedy mechanisms available in Korea. These deficiencies lead de-prioritized rights claimants to pursue other and often more contentious tactics, which have legitimacy in Korea due to their role in achieving democratization (S. Kim 2009; Cho, Kim, and Kim 2019).

In addition, societal actors contribute to rights hierarchies. Where there is countermobilization against certain rights claims, such as the conservative Christian movement against sexual minorities, societal actors explicitly delimit which rights deserve protection. As Kim and Hong (Chapter 12) indicate, recent mobilization for and against Yemeni asylum seekers ranked citizens' rights above refugees' rights. Opponents of asylum seekers' claims launched a petition on the presidential Blue House's website, which garnered almost 715,000 signatures in 2018 and spurred the administration to deny most of the Yemeni applicants asylum.[3] The Moon Jae-in administration had established the online platform in 2017 and promised to respond to any petition that received more than 200,000 signatures. Meanwhile, countermobilization against rights claims and discourses about society being unprepared for embracing LGBTI rights, as Judy Han (Chapter 11) details, result in some rights being deferred indefinitely. In some cases, rights hierarchies can result in the costs of claiming rights outweighing the benefits, as Hae Yeon Choo notes (2013).

In other cases, more unconscious selectivity may occur. For example, pro-democracy activists implicitly sidelined women's rights in their focus on obtaining basic civil and political rights (Chapter 3). Women are also overrepresented in the irregular worker category, leading to intersectional disadvantages in contexts when multidimensional rights claims are made (see Chapter 9). Even well-intentioned human rights lawyers from groups like those described by Goedde (Chapter 8) may unconsciously overlook certain rights as they advocate for others. South Korean progressives, for example, have historically paid little attention to North Korean human rights (Goedde 2010). As Hwang (Chapter 5) notes, conservatives had little appetite for the National Human Rights Commission but did double the budget for North Korean human rights. And early mobilization among lawyers for the rights of people with leprosy in Korea was in part catalyzed by a realization that this

---

[3] *Cheongwadae* (Blue House) Petition Website, petition on the Jeju asylum seekers, July 13, 2018, www1 .president.go.kr/petitions/269548 (accessed May 5, 2020).

population of more than 15,000 had been marginalized, even by human rights lawyers who supposedly championed the rights of marginalized people (Arrington 2014). Thus, both state and societal actors, as well as historical contexts, contribute to relatively enduring rights hierarchies in Korea. Rights mobilization, by increasing public exposure to such inequities, can gradually help enhance equality, as Kim and Hong (Chapter 12) argue.

Rather than aim for completeness, this book analyzed heretofore overlooked groups, such as women in the historical case chapters or sexual minorities in Part III. Together the chapters spotlight three lessons about the importance of studying law in action rather than just on the books, recognizing the plural and fluid meanings of rights, and examining rights claims relationally since hierarchies can affect the efficacy of rights-based mobilization. As part of the interactive and relational approach we advocate, the chapters explored changes in the institutional contexts within which rights claims occur – as well as perceptions of those institutions – and in the sources of support available for utilizing different claims-making channels. Our cases are far from exhaustive, as they leave out groups like victims of sexual violence, adoptees, youths, the elderly, homeless persons, and victims of privacy violations. Nonetheless, this volume aims to stimulate further interdisciplinary dialogue about rights-based mobilization in the fields of Korean and comparative studies.

THE FUTURE OF RIGHTS CLAIMING IN KOREA

From our standpoint in mid-2020, many of the rights analyzed in this volume seem quite durable. The judiciary and Korea's Constitutional Court have handed down landmark decisions that define and defend various rights the past three decades since democratization. Rights claiming mechanisms, such as the National Human Rights Commission created in 2001 or the Anti-Corruption and Civil Rights Commission created in 2008, help to protect people's rights, including against public officials. Associated activism for legislative change also resulted in the passage of numerous laws that articulate diverse rights and remedy mechanisms (albeit imperfect), such as for people with disabilities, sexual violence victims, and migrants.

Indeed, human rights discourses continue to proliferate in South Korea. As tracked by Koo and Choi (2019), media references to human rights have numerically risen and widened in scope since 1990 (463). The first wave of the 1990s concentrated on civil and political rights; the second wave coincided with the establishment of the National Human Rights Commission in 2001 and shifted to economic, social, and cultural rights; while minority rights have been more pronounced in the third wave of the past decade (Koo and Choi 2019, 464–65). Media diversifying online and the use of mobile phones gave greater opportunities for citizens' input and expression on a broader range of human rights issues (465). Civil society organizations have also incorporated "human rights" directly into their names.[4] Many government entities from the municipal on up to the national have established human rights units or officers. For example, the national police created a human rights code of conduct, which includes the principle of nondiscrimination toward minorities and disadvantaged members of society (Lee 2020). Many universities have recently created human rights centers, often adjudicating issues of sexual and workplace harassment. Furthermore, users of the internet portal Daum have access to a report function under the heading of "rights violation" (*gwolli chimhae*) for flagging online hate speech. Like Daum, the platform company Kakao has also had explicit rights violation reporting processes (*gwolli chimhae singo*) in place for over a decade for abuses such as defamation and intellectual property infringement. This is in line with the general trend in South Korea of more businesses and public institutions adopting human rights guidelines, under the National Action Plan recommended by the National Human Rights Commission of Korea, which the government adopted in 2018.

What remains fundamentally challenging for groups asserting their rights in South Korea are five factors: obstacles to litigation, partisan polarization, societal backlash, culturally ingrained hierarchies, and national crises. First, for claims-making within legal channels, hurdles remain significant in South Korea: the cost in money and time of litigation is high, the statute of limitations is short, standards of evidence sometimes prove difficult to meet without discovery, and damages remain capped. Legal changes, as Arrington (Chapter 7) detailed, are happening but they are incremental and depend on continued rights claiming, procedural reforms, and legislative changes. Furthermore, litigating remains difficult for disempowered individuals such as the poor, noncitizens, youth, the sick, the uneducated, rural residents, and especially where these identities intersect. Despite the existence of governmental legal aid and public interest law advocates, the respective institutional leaning toward winnable or impact cases and limited public interest law resources may still often prevent the most marginalized and discriminated against from full recourse to the law, as Goedde notes (Chapter 8).

The second challenge for rights claiming is Korea's partisan polarization, leading to different types of rights claims between conservatives and progressives. Print media coverage of human rights over the last three decades reveal that rights discourses have become politically polarized, with human rights references dwindling among conservative newspapers, Chosun and Joongang, from the mid-2000s, but increasing since then among progressive newspapers like Hankyoreh and

---

[4] These include public interest law groups such as Gonggam Human Rights Law Foundation and Korean Lawyers for Public Interest and Human Rights (KLPH) (see Chapter 8) as well as numerous LGBTI groups, including Chingusai – Korean Gay Men's Human Rights Group, Solidarity for LGBT Human Rights of Korea (Dongilyeon), and the larger coalition Korean Homosexuals Human Rights Association (see Chapter 11). Other NGOs include the Sarangbang Group for Human Rights, Women Migrants Human Rights Center of Korea, the Association Migrant Workers Human Rights, and Military Human Rights Center, to name but a few.

Kyunghyang (Koo and Choi 2019, 463). Conservatives are more likely, though, to emphasize North Korean human rights or freedom of speech in South Korea. Still, political parties across the ideological spectrum can elevate overlooked issues onto the public and political agenda with rights framing, thus supporting rights claimants. Additionally, political parties can help mobilize sympathetic groups, as has happened with labor rights activism (see Chapter 9). Yet polarization can also impede compromise and burden some issues with unneeded partisan baggage. One salient example is the issue of North Korean human rights, which is sharply divided between the conservative and progressive parties (see Yeo and Chubb 2018). The Moon Jae-in administration has been largely silent about North Korean human rights for the sake of peace initiatives, and therefore accused of appeasement and hypocrisy by the opposition. As indicators for this division, two high-profile North Korean defectors affiliated with the conservative opposition party became National Assembly members in the April 2020 elections and denounced the administration's apparent hypocrisy on human rights (Yi 2020).

Third, and not entirely separately, societal backlash remains a challenge for some rights claims in South Korea. Since the mid-2000s, conservative forces in Korean society have become more organized and adopted some of the tactics that previously characterized progressive NGOs, including synthesizing legal mobilization and protest, as found with the recent examples of migrants and refugees and LGBTI people. Gender-based violence deserves special mention here for its relevance to rights claiming by women who, spurred by the global #MeToo movement, have protested in the streets against both offline and online misogynistic crimes and the state's feeble legal response. A 2018 survey by Korea Women's Development Institute found that half of men in their twenties and nearly 40 percent of men in their thirties had a hostile attitude toward feminism (Ma et al. 2018). This backlash to feminism, the #MeToo movement, and their cultural representations (e.g., the bestselling book and movie, *Kim Ji-young, Born 1982*) speak to larger insecurities of men's economic status and the online normalizing of the sexual objectification of women and girls, among other factors. Meanwhile, egregious digital sex crime scandals involving blackmailing young women and children (as investigated by two female university students) finally forced the National Assembly in the spring of 2020 to legislate stronger punishments and to raise the age of consent from thirteen to sixteen. These developments briefly illustrate how the law has failed victims of sexual violence, requiring external events such as protests, the arts, and media discoveries in order to update legislation, remedies, and accountability.

Fourth, culturally ingrained hierarchies challenge the key notion of equality in human rights. The long-standing Korean tradition of hierarchy by seniority, whether by age, title, economic status, gender, or some combination thereof, has dominated familial, racial, and institutional dynamics for generations. Increasingly, Koreans are calling out instances of abuse of power by the haves against the have-nots (*gabjil*), contextualizing workplace harassment and bullying as violations of human rights generally and labor rights specifically. Ranking and discrimination persist not just on the basis of race, nationality, and sex but also in terms of where one is situated on the social ladder. For example, prefaced phone messages remind customers that call center representatives are someone's precious child; printed signs on supermarket registers ask that cashiers' human rights be respected; and media exposure of maltreated teaching assistants, bullied apartment guards (often male retirees), and others deemed subordinates continue to surface. Efforts to combat both discriminatory and indiscriminate violence have become more visible but reconciling the fundamental precept of equality in a society based on hierarchy will continue to be a struggle. However, we are likely to witness state, civil society, corporate actors, and workers increasingly engage with international human rights norms to address workplace harassment, especially in light of the recent ILO convention on eliminating workplace violence and harassment and trends in nationalizing best practices in business and human rights.

Finally, not unique to Korea is the difficulty of sustaining human rights protections as other public security issues or crises emerge. The COVID-19 pandemic is one such crisis which gives us a new appreciation for the durability of some rights and also highlights the danger of crises negating reform efforts. The South Korean government was widely hailed as a model of effectively tackling the spread of the novel coronavirus and ramping up extensive testing for COVID-19 without trampling individual rights (S. Kim 2020; M. Park 2020; Tharoor 2020). For example, government guidelines in mid-March 2020 ultimately, if belatedly, barred the release of infected persons' addresses or workplaces to restore privacy rights (Seon 2020), extended a few months later to not publicize age and gender.

However, global examples abound of how the pandemic has exacerbated discrimination or exposed systemic discrimination as in the case of the Black Lives Matter protests. Indeed, the virus especially struck the most vulnerable communities, such as the elderly, homeless, racial and ethnic minorities, essential and irregular workers, people with disabilities, domestic violence victims, and youth. South Korea is no exception as certain minorities have been discriminated against. For example, in May 2020, the LGBTI community suffered backlash when a Christian journalist disclosed the workplace of an infected man who had gone maskless to a popular gay club. Not wanting to be outed themselves, club-goers avoided testing. LGBTI groups began demanding rights protections, leading the government to offer anonymous testing. Foreigners, such as undocumented migrants and refugees, also faced discrimination when masks were first allotted only to those who showed proof of citizenship or foreigner registration. Meanwhile, continued school closures prompted university students to file petitions at the Constitutional Court to recoup tuition for periods when classes were meeting online only (Choi 2020). While some of these rights-related controversies are specific to the pandemic context, they illustrate that claims-making continues through the usual channels such as protest, lobbying, media outreach, and court-petitioning.

In sum, although the types of rights claims are diversifying and opportunities and resources for rights claiming have improved in South Korea, obtaining rights protections and catalyzing social change remain challenging. Claimants must make use of numerous mobilization tactics to see results, combining litigation with protests, media campaigns, international reporting, and elite-led public interest lawyering or NGO advocacy. This volume examined what limits and what enables rights claiming in Korea. On the one hand, there is resistance to rights claiming in terms of public receptivity, judicial outcomes, and satisfactory legislative reform, and opponents of some rights have mobilized to an unprecedented degree. On the other hand, institutional changes have opened up new avenues for rights claiming, and the legal opportunity structure has liberalized. The infrastructure for legal mobilization has also grown more institutionalized, as public interest law firms and foundations have blossomed in Korea, leveraging both domestic and international channels for advocacy. On balance, therefore, the prospects for rights claiming in Korea are bright, in large part due to the creative and sustained efforts of rights claimants.

REFERENCES

Arrington, Celeste L. 2014. "Leprosy, Legal Mobilization, and the Public Sphere in Japan and South Korea." *Law & Society Review* 48 (3): 563–93.
   2019. "Hiding in Plain Sight: Pseudonymity and Participation in Legal Mobilization." *Comparative Political Studies* 52 (2): 310–41.
Arrington, Celeste L., and Yong-il Moon. 2020. "Cause Lawyering and Movement Tactics: Disability Rights Movements in South Korea and Japan." *Law & Policy* 42 (1): 5–30.
Barclay, Scott, Lynn Jones, and Anna-Maria Marshall. 2011. "Two Spinning Wheels: Studying Law and Social Movements." In *Special Issue Social Movements/Legal Possibilities (Studies in Law, Politics, and Society)*, edited by Austin Sarat, 54: 1–16. Bingly: Emerald Publishing Group.
Chang, Paul. 2015. *Protest Dialectics: State Repression and South Korea's Democracy Movement, 1970–1979*. Stanford: Stanford University Press.
Cho, Youngho, Mi-son Kim, and Yong Cheol Kim. 2019. "Cultural Foundations of Contentious Democracy in South Korea: What Type of Democracy Do Korean Citizens Prefer?" *Asian Survey* 59 (2): 272–94.
Choi, Won-hyung. 2020. "University Students Submit Constitutional Court Petition for Tuition Refunds as Online Classes Continue." *Hankyoreh*, April 28, 2020. http://english .hani.co.kr/arti/english_edition/e_national/942390.html.
Choo, Hae Yeon. 2013. "The Cost of Rights: Migrant Women, Feminist Advocacy, and Gendered Morality in South Korea." *Gender & Society* 27 (4): 445–68.
Chua, Lynette J. 2018. *The Politics of Love in Myanmar: LGBT Mobilization and Human Rights as a Way of Life*. Stanford: Stanford University Press.
Feldman, Eric A. 2000. *The Ritual of Rights in Japan: Law, Society, and Health Policy*. Cambridge: Cambridge University Press.

Goedde, Patricia. 2010. "Legal Mobilization for Human Rights Protection in North Korea: Furthering Discourse or Discord?" *Human Rights Quarterly* 32 (3): 530–74.

Kim, Sarah. 2020. "Countries Look to Korea's Approach to Fight Covid-19." *JoongAng Ilbo*, March 16, 2020. http://koreajoongangdaily.joins.com/news/article/article.aspx?aid=3074945.

Kim, Sunhyuk. 2009. "Civic Engagement and Democracy in South Korea." *Korea Observer* 40 (1): 1–26.

Koo, Jeong-Woo and Jaesung Choi. 2019. "Polarized Embrace: South Korean Media Coverage of Human Rights, 1990-2016." *Journal of Human Rights* 18 (4), 455–73.

Lee, Jae-ho. 2020. "S. Korea's National Police Publishes Human Rights Code for Officers on 33rd Anniversary of June Democracy Movement." *Hankyoreh*, June 11, 2020. http://english.hani.co.kr/arti/english_edition/e_national/948933.html.

Lehoucq, Emilio, and Whitney Taylor. 2020. "Conceptualizing Legal Mobilization: How Should We Understand the Deployment of Legal Strategies?" *Law & Social Inquiry* 45 (1), 166–93.

Marshall, Anna-Maria, and Daniel Crocker Hale. 2014. "Cause Lawyering." *Annual Review of Law and Social Science* 10: 301–20.

McCann, Michael. 2006. "Law and Social Movements: Contemporary Perspectives." *Annual Review of Law and Social Science* 2: 17–38.

Ma Gyeong-hui et al. 2018. Seongpyeongdeunggwa namseongui salmui jire gwanhan yeongu (*A study on gender equality and men's quality of life*). Seoul: Korea Women's Development Institute.

O'Brien, Kevin J., and Lianjiang Li. 2006. *Rightful Resistance in Rural China*. Cambridge: Cambridge University Press.

Park, Min-hee. 2020. "S. Korea's Story from Coronavirus Nightmare to Exemplar for Countermeasures and Prevention." *Hankyoreh*, March 23, 2020. http://english.hani.co.kr/arti/english_edition/e_national/933773.html.

Park, Yoon-kyun. 2020. "Civic Groups Call for Swift Anti-Discrimination Legislation in S. Korea." *Hankyoreh*, June 8, 2020. http://english.hani.co.kr/arti/english_edition/e_national/948408.html.

Scheingold, Stuart A. 2004. *The Politics of Rights: Lawyers, Public Policy, and Social Change*. 2nd ed. Ann Arbor: University of Michigan Press.

Seon, Dam-eun. 2020. "Government Decides Not to Disclose Personal Information about Novel Coronavirus Patients." *Hankyoreh*, March 16, 2020. http://english.hani.co.kr/arti/english_edition/e_national/932783.html.

Sidel, Mark. 2010. *Law and Society in Vietnam: The Transition from Socialism in Comparative Perspective*. Cambridge: Cambridge University Press.

Stern, Rachel. 2005. "Unpacking Adaptation: The Female Inheritance Movement in Hong Kong." *Mobilization: An International Quarterly* 10 (3): 421–39.

Tam, Waikeung. 2010. "Political Transition and the Rise of Cause Lawyering: The Case of Hong Kong." *Law & Social Inquiry* 35 (3): 663–87.

Taylor, Whitney K. 2020. "On the Social Construction of Legal Grievances: Evidence from Colombia and South Africa." *Comparative Political Studies* 53 (8): 1326–56.

Tharoor, Ishaan. 2020. "South Korea's Coronavirus Success Story Underscores How the US Initially Failed." *Washington Post*, March 17, 2020. www.washingtonpost.com/world/2020/03/17/south-koreas-coronavirus-success-story-underscores-how-us-initially-failed/.

Tsutsui, Kiyoteru. 2017. "Human Rights and Minority Activism in Japan: Transformation of Movement Actorhood and Local-Global Feedback Loop." *American Journal of Sociology* 122 (4): 1050–103.

Upham, Frank K. 1987. *Law and Social Change in Postwar Japan*. Cambridge: Harvard University Press.

Woo, Margaret Y. K., and Mary E. Gallagher, eds. 2011. *Chinese Justice: Civil Dispute Resolution in Contemporary China*. Cambridge: Cambridge University Press.

Yeo, Andrew, and Danielle Chubb, eds. 2018. *North Korean Human Rights: Activists and Networks*. Cambridge: Cambridge University Press.

Yi, Wonju. 2020. "N. Korean Defector Wins First-Ever Constituency Seat in Parliament." *Yonhap*, April 16, 2020. https://en.yna.co.kr/view/AEN20200416002351325.

Index